professional hairdressing

THE OFFICIAL GUIDE TO LEVEL 3

Habia Series List

HAIRDRESSING

Student textbooks

Begin Hairdressing: The Official Guide to Level 1 1e *Martin Green*
Hairdressing – The Foundations: The Official Guide to Level 2 5e *Leo Palladino and Martin Green*
Professional Hairdressing: The Official Guide to Level 3 4e *Leo Palladino and Martin Green*
The Official Guide to the City & Guilds Certificate in Salon Services 1e *John Armstrong with Anita Crosland, Martin Green and Lorraine Nordmann*
The Colour Book: The Official Guide to Colour for NVQ Levels 2 & 3 1e *Tracey Lloyd with Christine McMillan-Bodell*
eXtensions: The Official Guide to Hair Extensions 1e *Theresa Bullock*
Salon Management *Martin Green*
Men's Hairdressing: Traditional and Modern Barbering 2e *Maurice Lister*
African-Caribbean Hairdressing 2e *Sandra Gittens*
The World of Hair Colour 1e *John Gray*

Professional Hairdressing titles

Trevor Sorbie: The Bridal Hair Book 1e *Trevor Sorbie and Jacki Wadeson*
The Art of Dressing Long Hair 1e *Guy Kremer and Jacki Wadeson*
Patrick Cameron: Dressing Long Hair 1e *Patrick Cameron and Jacki Wadeson*
Patrick Cameron: Dressing Long Hair 2 1e *Patrick Cameron and Jacki Wadeson*
Bridal Hair 1e *Pat Dixon and Jacki Wadeson*
Professional Men's Hairdressing: The art of cutting and styling 1e *Guy Kremer and Jacki Wadeson*
Essensuals, the Next Generation Toni and Guy: Step by Step 1e *Sacha Mascolo, Christian Mascolo and Stuart Wesson*
Mahogany Hairdressing: Steps to Cutting, Colouring and Finishing Hair 1e *Martin Gannon and Richard Thompson*
Mahogany Hairdressing: Advanced Looks 1e *Martin Gannon and Richard Thompson*
The Total Look: The Style Guide for Hair and Make-Up Professionals 1e *Ian Mistlin*
Trevor Sorbie: Visions in Hair 1e *Trevor Sorbie, Kris Sorbie and Jacki Wadeson*
The Art of Hair Colouring 1e *David Adams and Jacki Wadeson*

BEAUTY THERAPY

Beauty Basics: The Official Guide to Level 1 1e *Lorraine Nordmann*
Beauty Therapy – The Foundations: The Official Guide to Level 2 3e *Lorraine Nordmann*
Professional Beauty Therapy – The Official Guide to Level 3 2e *Lorraine Nordmann*
The Official Guide to the City & Guilds Certificate in Salon Services 1e *John Armstrong with Anita Crosland, Martin Green and Lorraine Nordmann*

The Complete Guide to Make-Up 1e *Suzanne Le Quesne*
The Complete Make-Up Artist 2e *Penny Delamar*

The Encyclopedia of Nails 1e *Jacqui Jefford and Anne Swain*
The Art of Nails: A Comprehensive Style Guide to Nail Treatments and Nail Art 1e *Jacqui Jefford*
Nail Artistry 1e *Jacqui Jefford*
The Complete Nail Technician 2e *Marian Newman*
Manicure, Pedicure and Advanced Nail Techniques 1e *Elaine Almond*

The Official Guide to Body Massage 2e *Adele O'Keefe*
An Holistic Guide Massage 1e *Tina Parsons*
Indian Head Massage 2e *Muriel Burnham-Airey and Adele O'Keefe*
Aromatherapy for the Beauty Therapist 1e *Valerie Worwood*
An Holistic Guide to Reflexology 1e *Tina Parsons*
An Holistic Guide to Anatomy and Physiology 1e *Tina Parsons*
The Essential Guide to Holistic and Complementary Therapy 1e *Helen Beckmann and Suzanne Le Quense*
The Spa Book 1e *Jane Cebbin-Bailey, Dr John Harcup, and John Harrington*
Nutrition: A Practical Approach 1e *Suzanne Le Quesne*
Hands on Sports Therapy 1e *Keith Ward*

professional
hairdressing

THE OFFICIAL GUIDE TO S/NVQ LEVEL 3 FIFTH EDITION

MARTIN GREEN AND LEO PALLADINO

with a contribution from Theresa Bullock

City&
Guilds

habia
standards · information · solutions

THOMSON
™

Australia · Canada · Mexico · Singapore · Spain · United Kingdom · United States

THOMSON

Professional Hairdressing, Level 3 – Fifth Edition
Martin Green and Leo Palladino with a contribution from Theresa Bullock

Publishing Director John Yates	**Commissioning Editor** Melody Dawes	**Development Editor** Lizzie Catford
Editorial Assistant Alice Rodgers	**Manufacturing Manager** Helen Mason	**Marketing Manager** Leo Stanley
Typesetter Meridian Colour Repro Pangbourne on Thames	**Production Controller** Maeve Healy	**Production Editor** Emily Gibson
Cover Design Vincent Cusack, CPI London	**Text Design** Design Deluxe, Bath, UK	**Printer** Seng Lee Press, Singapore

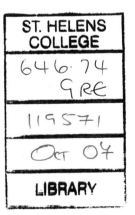

contents

Foreword vii
Preface viii
Acknowledgements ix
Hairdressing S/NVQ Level 3 xi
About this book xviii

part one

1 **Health, safety and security** 2
  G1 Ensure your own actions reduce risks to health & safety 2

  Introduction 3
  Working safely in the salon 5
  General salon hygiene and routine maintenance 6
  Personal hygiene and appearance 8
  Fire safety 11
  Dealing with accidents (first aid) 14
  Salon security 17
  Legal framework (health and safety legislation) 18

2 **Consultation** 31
  G9 Provide hairdressing consultation services 31
  G6 Promote additional products or services to clients 31

  Introduction 32
  Consultation 33
  About you 34
  About the client 42
  Subjective analysis 44
  Objective analysis 51
  The client's influencing features and factors 67
  After the consultation 74
  Promoting the business further 74
  Salon image 77

part two

3 **Cutting hair** 86
  H27 Create a variety of looks using a combination of cutting techniques 86

  Introduction 87
  Cutting and styling 88
  Preparing the client 89
  Consultation aspects 89
  Cutting tools 98
  Shaping and texturising 100
  Before the cut 102
  During the cut 102
  After the cut 102
  Client care 103

4 **Styling and dressing hair** 124
  H25 Style and dress hair to achieve a variety of creative looks 124
  H26 Style and dress long hair 124

  Introduction 125
  General principles of styling hair 126
  Curling and winding techniques 129
  Heated styling equipment 135
  Creative long hair 137

5 **Colouring and colour correction** 161
  H30 Colour hair using a variety of techniques 161
  H28 Provide colour correction services 161

  Introduction 162
  Colour principles 163
  Hair colour types 167
  Colour choice 168
  Bleaching and lightening 183
  Colour variants 188
  Toning 194
  Colour correction 194

6 Perming 221
  H29 Perm hair using a variety of
      techniques 221

  Introduction 222
  Perming principles 223
  Preparing and planning the perm:
      The client 225
  Perming technique 227
  Fashion and alternative winding techniques 236

7 Men's styling and barbering 246
  H7 Cut hair using basic barbering
      techniques 246
  H8 Cut facial hair to shape using basic
      techniques 246

  Introduction 247
  Preparing the client 248
  Consultation 249
  Safe practice for cutting hair and cutting
      equipment 255
  Outline shapes 261
  Clippers 270
  Shaping and trimming facial hair 271
  Advice and home maintenance 275

8 Hair extensions 279
  H23 Add hair extensions to create a
      variety of looks 279

  Introduction 281
  Hair extensions consultation 281
  Hair extension products and equipment 284
  Selecting and blending extensions and
      colours together 288
  Adding hair extensions 290
  Planning and placement 297
  Cutting, styling and finishing 301
  Removing hair extensions 303

9 African Caribbean hairdressing 309
  H33 Style hair using thermal techniques 309
  H35 Create complex styles using African
      Caribbean styling techniques 309
  H31 Provide corrective relaxing services 309

  Introduction 311
  Thermal styling 311
  Equipment 313
  Plaiting and twisting hair 318
  Relaxing hair 327

part three

10 Finance and resources 344
  G10 Support customer service
      improvements 344
  G11 Contribute to the financial effectiveness
      of the business 344

  Introduction 345
  Human resources 347
  Time resources 353
  Other salon resources 355
  Financial resources 361
  Customer service operations 367

11 Creative business promotion 378
  H32 Contribute to the planning and
      implementation of promotional activities 378
  H24 Develop and enhance your creative
      skills 378

  Introduction 379
  Hair creativity 379
  Creative style design 380
  Promoting the salon 386

Self-test answers 406
Useful address and websites 408
Glossary 410
Index 413

foreword

When we developed the first set of standards for Level 3, we had no idea of the incredible impact they would make on the growing professionalism of the hairdressing industry. Yet without the vision of Martin Green and Leo Palladino, and their seminal book *Professional Hairdressing – The Official Guide to Level 3*, that impact would not have been as great.

Both Martin and Leo are incredibly passionate and enthusiastic about their industry. But both also have that rare skill – they are able to communicate that passion and enthusiasm to others and translate it into knowledge based on years of experience working in salons and with clients.

Whatever salon issue it is, from dealing with difficult clients to achieving the perfect cut that will leave your customers glowing, Martin and Leo have been there themselves and have developed solutions that are tried, tested and effective. Add to that the timely contribution from Theresa Bullock on hair extensions, and Professional Hairdressing forms the complete guide for anyone working towards Level 3.

Already an industry standard in its own right, and a must-have for anyone serious about upgrading their skills, this fifth edition of Professional Hairdressing continues the long tradition of the title in helping a generation of hairdressers be the best they absolutely can be.

As I wrote in the foreword for the very first edition; read it, practice it, write on it – but most of all, use it.

Alan Goldsbro
Chief Executive Officer
Habia

preface

If a preface should give a preamble, an insight or a taster of what's to come: this book is about self-improvement. This self-improvement comes about as a result of an increase in expectation. Your customers want more. Not only are they prepared to pay for it, but they will also tell you if they are not totally satisfied.

Customer expectation is far greater than before and this principal factor has fuelled the change culture of business for over a decade. We all hear about changes in systems and practices in everyone's work. We are led to believe that change initiates improved efficiency, minimises costs and streamlines operations. When involved in these processes, change is the only thing that we all see and people 'naturally' resist change. We all gravitate to the norm or 'comfortable' yet boring routines. It needn't be like that though; the big picture is quite different. *These changes are necessary in order to meet customer needs*. Business competes to attract customers and once it has found them, it will survive only if it manages to keep them. Hairdressing is constantly changing and, like many businesses allied to the fashion industry, it responds to the challenges of the '*I want*' and '*I want it now*' culture.

This book fails if the strong message of communication does not come through. It's the one thing that successful and experienced hairdressers do really well. Improve your communication skills and you too will reap the benefits. The technical aspects and procedures of the craft can be learnt; it may be daunting, but it is achievable. However, if you fail to develop the way in which you interact with others your hard efforts will be wasted. The new Level 3 qualification is about building on experiences and combining them with a greater understanding of people. These are the new changes and the new challenges and, what's more, they are here to stay.

acknowledgements

The author and publishers would like to thank the following:

For providing pictures for the book

Alison Stewart
Alistair Hughes
American Dream
Andrew Jose
Angels
Anne McGuigan
Antoinette Beenders
Aveda
BaByliss
Barclays plc
Barrie Stephen
Dr M.H Beck
Best of British
BLM Health
Brendan O'Sullivan, Creative
    Director, Regis International Ltd
Cheynes, Edinburgh
Cheynes Training
    (www.cheynestraining.com)
Chubb Fire Ltd
Clynol
Cream
Cricket Co.
D&J Ambrose
Desmond Murray
James Asafa at Dome Cosmetics Ltd
    (www.domecosmetics.com)
Doreen Domfeh at Doreen Hair
    Fashions
Dylan Bradshaw, Dublin
Echoes Hair & Beauty
Ellisons
Essensuals: Sacha Mascolo-Tarbuck
Farouk Systems, USA
Francesco Group
Gemis

Golden Supreme
Goldwell Professional Haircare
Goody's
Gorgeous PR
Great Lengths
    (www.greatlengths.net)
Guy Kremer
Habia
Hair Direct
Hair Flair
Harringtons
Health and Safety Executive
HMSO
Ishoka, Aberdeen
istockphoto.com
Jacki Wadeson PR
Jackie McShannon and Anders
James Kimber Salon, Birmingham
Jason and India Miller, Charlie Miller
Jean Paton
Dr John Gray
Karly Whitaker, Sarah Hodge
    Hairdressing, Somerset and
    Devon
Kay Wahling
Keith Hall
KPSS (UK) Ltd
Lawrence Anthony
Lee Preston
L'Oréal Professionnel
Mahogany (www.mahogany.co.uk)
Mane Connection
Mark Leeson
Mark Pearson @ Creator
Martine Finnegan
Maurice Medcalf

Michael Balfre

Michele Jorsling

Neil Smith

Namasté Salon System/Splinters
    Academy Ltd

Patrick Cameron

Paul Falltrick for Matrix

Ray Nightingale and Connor Kelly at
    Nightingales

Redken

Robin Callender at McMillan

S. Lewis

Sean Hanna and Fiona Connelly

Sharon Forrester

Sharp

SP Services

Stella Lambrou, The Crib, Lytham

Steven Goldsworthy

Thornton Howdle

Toni & Guy

Umberto Giannini

Wahl (UK) Ltd

Wella UK Ltd

Dr A.L. Wright

John Rawson PR images: pages 235, 381 and 382: Hair by Roberta Kneller at Bobs Hair Company, Grimsby, photography by John Rawson, styling by FiAn, make-up by Chris Atkinson; pages 40 and 384: Hair by Clive Boon at Boons, Retford, photography by John Rawson, styling by FiAn, make-up by Chris Atkinson; page 34: Hair by Lisa Neill at Kaliks, Aberdeen, photography by John Rawson, styling by FiAn, make-up by Chris Atkinson; page 230: Hair by Adrian Allen at Red Hair Couture, Wath-upon-Dearne, photography by John Rawson, styling by FiAn, make-up by Chris Atkinson; page 235: Hair by Zullo and Pack in Nottingham, photography by John Rawson, styling by FiAn, make-up by Chris Atkinson. The publisher would also like to thank J&E Training for their help with the photographs on pages 156–8 and 324–6.

 www.j-etraining.co.uk

For their help with the photoshoot

Photoshoot location:
Cheltenham Film Studios
Arle Court
Cheltenham
Gloucestershire
GL51 6PN

Meredith Gosden
Natasha Wegrzyn
Ollie Ware
Ollivier Koubassi
Serena Reeves
Shelly Edwards

Models:
Chloe Harvey
Francesca Wegrzyn
Georgie Lewis
James Green
Jodi Green
Kim Scudder

Stylists:
HQ Hair Cheltenham
Martin Green
Becci Fincham

Photography:
Fi Deane

hairdressing S/NVQ level 3

National Vocational Qualifications (NVQs) and Scottish Vocational Qualifications (SVQs) have a common structure and design; that is to say, they all follow a particular format for all occupations and vocational sectors. Each vocational qualification is structured the same way and is made up of a number of individual units and main outcomes. Each unit will address a specific task or area of work, and, where a number of tasks are involved within that area of work, the unit is subdivided into a number of smaller components. These components are called main outcomes.

UNITS AND MAIN OUTCOMES

The unit of competence is the smallest component of an S/NVQ that can be credited by certificate: i.e. it is the smallest part of a full S/NVQ that can be awarded to a candidate. An S/NVQ is made up of a number of units each covering specific areas of work. The unit comprises of a unit title and one or more individual main outcomes. An S/NVQ can be made up of mandatory units, or mandatory and optional units. For example, reducing risks to health and safety at work is essential and therefore a mandatory unit. Certain occupations involve technical diversity. Therefore there can be a different emphasis within jobs at the same level. In these situations, optional units provide an alternative. Optional units are often separated into two or more option groups and from these the candidate is able to make selections appropriate to their own needs.

Each unit consists of a number of main outcomes. These are the smallest meaningful activity that has been identified during the process of S/NVQ development.

Unit structure

Unit G6 Promote additional products or services to clients
G6.1 Identify additional products or services that are available
G6.2 Inform clients about additional products or services
G6.3 Gain client commitment to using additional products or services

Main outcome structure

G6.1 Identify additional products or services that are available

Performance criteria
Range
Knowledge and understanding

Main outcome title

This is a brief statement that outlines the task in hand. Main outcome titles are always expressed in '*Do this*' language, e.g. *Identify additional products or services that are available*.

Performance criteria

The performance criteria are a *list* of essential actions (*not necessarily in order*) that must be carried out so that the task can be completed competently, i.e. a definitive list of what needs to be done. During training these performance criteria form the smallest components of method. However, just learning to carry out a procedure in a 'robotic' fashion does not mean that the person understands what they are doing or why they are doing it. The object of S/NVQs is to learn and acquire skills, and skills are derived from the combination of method and understanding.

Performance criteria for G6.1

> G6.1 Identify additional products or services that are available **by**
>
> a) working with others to keep your information regarding your salon's products or services up-to-date.
> b) checking with others when you are unsure of new product or service details.
> c) identifying appropriate products or services which may match individual clients' needs.

Range

The range statements provide a number of conditions or applications in which the main outcomes must be performed; quite simply, under what particular circumstances, on what occasions, or in what special situations the activity must take place.

Range statements

> **Range:** Your performance must cover the following situations
>
> 1 **Additional products and services**
>   a) use of products or services which are new to your client
>   b) more use of the same products or services your client has used before
> 2 **Products or services outside your salon**

Knowledge and understanding

National Vocational Qualifications and Scottish Vocational Qualifications are not only about doing. You will realise that however practical you are about carrying out your work well, you cannot do it well without understanding what you are doing and why you're doing it. The terms 'theory', 'learning' and 'principles' generally refer to essential knowledge and understanding.

Units and main outcomes often share similar components. For example, some of the performance criteria used within the elements: *Style hair using thermal techniques, Style and dress hair to achieve a variety of looks and Style and dress long hair* are the same. Similarly, the knowledge that is essential and underpinning one element will often occur in another. This duplication may at first seem unnecessary, but occurs because of the modular, stand-alone, design of S/NVQs. This can be useful for accelerating the learning process, particularly when knowledge or skills learnt in one activity are applicable to other tasks. Recording these learnt experiences is further made easy by simply cross-referencing the evidence in the candidate's portfolio.

ASSESSMENT REQUIREMENTS

The assessment process is designed to establish at what point the candidate is deemed competent and specific methods of assessment are drafted for each element. At the end of each main outcome there is a specification of the *type* and *how much* evidence is required.

Evidence requirements (example Unit G6)

Simulation is not allowed for any performance evidence within this unit. You must supply all the evidence from work you have carried out with clients in your workplace.

You must prove that you have worked to offer additional products or services to clients over a period of time with different clients on different occasions. The additional products or services offered must include:

- use of products or services which are new to your customer
- more use of the same products or services your customer has used before.

You must prove that you:

- regularly follow agreed salon procedures for offering additional products or services to your clients
- create your own opportunities for encouraging your clients to use additional products or services
- identify what your customer wants by seeking information directly and by collecting information from spontaneous customer comments.

The products or services outside your own area of responsibility may include:

● those offered by other sections of your salon

or

● products or services which you have not supplied before.

The information which you provide to your clients may be given verbally or in written form.

Your evidence must show that you have applied the knowledge and understanding requirements when you are dealing with your clients.

Assessment guidance

The following situations will provide potential sources for the collection of evidence. However, there may be a variety of other appropriate sources.

● Observed performance, for example:
  1 Greeting visitors/clients on arrival at workplace and visitors from within or inside the organisation.
  2 Putting visitors/clients at ease.
  3 Finding out reasons for visit, business, appointment, information.
  4 Referring visitors/clients to other staff when the requirements are beyond their own capability or authority.
● Work products.
● Office records of visitors/clients.
● Authenticated testimonies from relevant witnesses.

Work supervisor and/or trainer:

● Personal accounts of competence.
● Responses to oral and written questions.
● Other sources of evidence to prove knowledge and understanding.

HAIRDRESSING LEVEL 3

National Vocational Qualifications and Scottish Vocational Qualifications have developed considerably in recent years. As occupational sectors develop their own standards for industry a certain amount of duplication occurs. This is particularly noticeable when different occupations carry out similar practices. For instance, many of the day-to-day duties performed by a receptionist in a hairdressing salon are similar to the tasks performed by a receptionist in a leisure centre. Here the common denominator is communication. The communication may be carried out on the telephone, face to face, by e-mail or by other electronic means and this is only one example of how duplication can occur. If we think about the tasks in retail such as stock control, product rotation, restocking of shelves and till operation, you can see that there are many applications for these procedures over a number of different occupations.

So bearing these factors in mind, the modern standards are far more flexible in their approach. It is now common for one industry sector to use another occupational sector's standards. This principle of stand-alone, reusable material is now widely applied. Our revised Hairdressing Level 3 units have been designed in this way. In the next section there is an outline of units and the main outcomes.

As customers' expectations rise, standards must rise too. Therefore the hairdressing industry needs a better trained, far more flexible and highly motivated workforce. Over recent years Level 3 has been the standard of excellence. Originally designed to provide an ongoing route towards specialism and expertise, it was quickly picked up by the manufacturers. These companies have looked at their own training provision and collectively taken on board the increased levels of creativity and craft excellence. Most of these manufacturers now offer diploma or certificated courses to meet Level 3 standards. This has now moved the benchmark and put Level 3 as the preferred qualification of choice and minimum level for occupational competence.

Hairdressing Level 3 mandatory and optional units

Mandatory units (all must be completed)

G1   Ensure your own actions reduce risks to health and safety

G6   Promote additional products or services to clients

G9   Provide hairdressing consultation services

H27   Create a variety of looks using a combination of cutting techniques

Plus 5 optional units, only 1 of which may be chosen from Option 2. (All 5 optional units can be chosen from Group 1, if desired.)

Option Group 1

H23   Add hair extensions to create a variety of looks

H24   Develop and enhance your creative skills

H25   Style and dress hair to achieve a variety of looks

H26   Style and dress long hair

H28   Provide colour correction services

H29   Perm hair using a variety of techniques

H30   Colour hair using a variety of techniques

H31   Provide corrective relaxing services

H33   Style hair using thermal techniques

H35   Create complex styles using African Caribbean styling techniques

H36   Style hair using locksing techniques

BT20 Provide Indian Head Massage treatment

Option Group 2

G10   Support customer service improvements

G11   Contribute to the financial effectiveness of the business

H32   Contribute to the planning and implementation of promotional activities

HOW TO USE THIS BOOK

Each chapter addresses specific units from the S/NVQ Level 3. At the beginning of each chapter a referencing system provides a quick signposting to the information you want, providing a variety of starting and finishing points. There is a variety of features and icons used within the text.

What do I need to learn?

Customised information, telling you about what you need to learn and understand.

What does it mean?

This provides in the simplest terms an overview of the chapter content in relationship to S/NVQ Level 3 expected outcomes.

What do I need to do?

A brief overview of the activities involved in the unit and customised information, telling you what you need to do about practical tasks.

Other info

In order to eliminate unnecessary duplication, these references are linked to other relevant information and can be found from the index in the back of this book.

Key words

Special or technical terms.

 ## Activity

Suggestions for useful learning activities linked with the task.

 ## Remember boxes

Tips or hints on points to remember.

 ## Good practice/Health & safety

Example of good practice or procedure.

 ## Science bit! Did you know

 ## Checkerboard

Self-check system and a means of recording progress towards achievement.

Self-test section

A variety of self-assessment tests including short answer, multiple choice, true or false, etc.

Chapter navigation

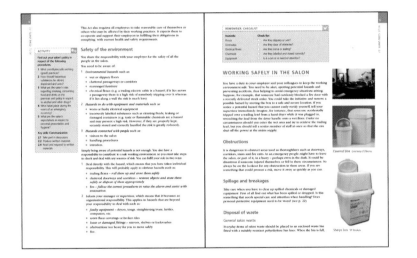

about this book

The common structure and design that exists within NVQ/SVQs is mirrored in many ways within this text. For the first time in the hairdressing NVQ/SVQ official series, revisions and updates have been totally reworked to both 'target' and 'fit' the needs of the learner and the occupational standards. The navigation to standards, access to information, quick referencing and illustration have been redesigned and reorganised in order to help you accelerate through your Level 3 programme. This uniform format or book style incorporates a number of features:

- a common structure and design throughout the text with explanations of the standards and on how to use this book;
- easy referencing systems to include tables, checklists, activities and tips;
- the same format and unit references as S/NVQs, covering both mandatory and the various option groups.

HOW TO USE THIS BOOK

The format will help you to use and read this book more easily. Each chapter addresses specific units from the S/NVQ Level 3. At the beginning of each chapter a referencing system provides a quick signposting to the information you want, providing a variety of starting and finishing points. In this next example, you can see the variety of features and icons used within the text.

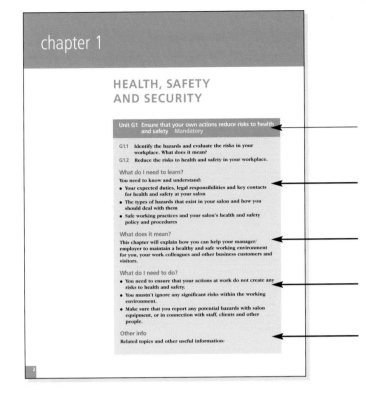

chapter 1

HEALTH, SAFETY AND SECURITY

Unit G1 Ensure that your own actions reduce risks to health and safety Mandatory

G1.1 Identify the hazards and evaluate the risks in your workplace. What does it mean?

G1.2 Reduce the risks to health and safety in your workplace.

What do I need to learn?

You need to know and understand:
- Your expected duties, legal responsibilities and key contacts for health and safety at your salon
- The types of hazards that exist in your salon and how you should deal with them
- Safe working practices and your salon's health and safety policy and procedures

What does it mean?

This chapter will explain how you can help your manager/employer to maintain a healthy and safe working environment for you, your work colleagues and other business customers and visitors.

What do I need to do?
- You need to ensure that your actions at work do not create any risks to health and safety.
- You mustn't ignore any significant risks within the working environment.
- Make sure that you report any potential hazards with salon equipment, or in connection with staff, clients and other people.

Other info

Related topics and other useful information:

S/NVQ reference, unit title and main outcome
An at-a-glance diagrammatic overview of the unit and main outcomes covered in the chapter.

What do I need to learn?
Customised information on what you need to learn and understand in order to complete a task satisfactorily.

What does it mean?
This provides in the simplest terms an overview of the chapter content in relationship to S/NVQ Level 3 expected outcomes.

What do I need to do?
A brief overview of the activities involved in the unit and customised information, telling you what you need to do about practical task.

Other info
In order to eliminate unnecessary duplication, these references are linked to other relevant information and can be found from the index in the back of this book.

Key words Special or technical terms.

Activity A range of task linked activities threaded throughout each chapter

---

- COSHH
- Risk assessment
- Personal health, hygiene and safety at work
- Safe use of salon equipment
- Emergency procedures (fire, first aid, etc.)
- Maintaining salon security
- Display screen equipment (DSE regs)
- Manual handling
- RIDDOR
- Employers liability compulsory insurance

KEY WORDS

Hazard something with potential to cause harm
Risk the likelihood of a hazard occurring

CHECKERBOARD

At the end of this chapter the checkerboard will help to jog your memory on what you have learned and what still remains to be done. Cross them off with a pencil as you cover each of its topics. (See p. 29.)

INTRODUCTION

This mandatory unit comprises of two elements:

G1.1 Identify the hazards and evaluate the risks in your workplace.

G1.2 Reduce the risks to health and safety in your workplace.

The chapter covers the essential information in supporting these tasks and extends to a wide range covering other related information. This includes aspects of legislation and general security of the working environment.

You will need to show that you understand the health and safety requirements in the workplace. This includes monitoring your own work routines and workspace so that hazards are quickly identified and potential risk to others being harmed is minimised.

The Health and Safety at Work Act 1974 is the main piece of 'umbrella' legislation under which all other regulations are made. Employers have a legal duty under this Act to ensure, so far as reasonably practicable, the health, safety and welfare at work of all the people for whom they are responsible and the people who may be affected by the work they do.

Your posture while sitting should be restful. Your back should be supported all the way down. This does not mean that chairs must have a continuous back or contoured, moulded panels, but that your sitting position should provide your body with support so that the pelvis and not the base of the spine takes the body's weight. Avoid sitting with crossed legs as this will restrict blood circulation. It will result in numbness and a sensation of 'pins and needles'.

FIRE SAFETY

Under the Fire Precautions Act 1971, a fire certificate is required for business premises if:
- more than 20 people are employed on one floor at any one time
- more than 10 people are employed on different floors at any one time.

Where premises are shared with other businesses, the employers must include everyone collectively.

All premises must be provided with an adequate means of escape in case of fire and a means of fighting fire, whether or not a fire certificate is required. All fire exits need to be clearly marked with the appropriate signs and all doors must be capable of being opened easily and immediately from the inside.

Every employer must carry out a fire risk assessment covering the premises. This should address the following key aspects:
- Assessment of fire risks within the premises as required under the Management of Health and Safety Regulations 1999.
- The installation of suitable fire detection equipment, e.g. smoke alarms.
- The installation of a suitable warning system (this could be an automatic fire alarm system).
- Checks that everyone can get back safely from the premises in the event of fire and that all means of escape including passageways, stairwells, etc. are kept clear of obstructions at all times. Where necessary adequate emergency lighting should be installed.
- The provision of adequate firefighting equipment.
- The provision of adequate training for employees so that everyone knows what to do in the event of fire.
- Regular checks and maintenance of all fire safety equipment.
- Regular reviews of the fire safety arrangements.

Fire

Fires occurring in salons would be more likely to arise from either an electrical fault, a gas escape, or smoking. Faulty or badly maintained *electrical equipment*, such as hand dryers or hood dryers, may malfunction, overheat, and even ignite. *Gas appliances*, such as ovens or hobs, present a possible risk if left unattended. Staff cooking facilities need to be closely

ACTIVITY

Your workplace will have its own fire safety procedures. Find out what and where the information is displayed and what action should be taken.

Key skills: Communication
2.4 Read and respond to written materials

REMEMBER

Classes of fire
There are four classifications of fire:

Class A Fires involving solid material, i.e. paper, wood, hair, etc.

Class B Fires involving liquids such as petrol, paraffin, etc.

Class C Fires involving gases, i.e. propane, butane

Class D Fires involving metals

Remember Tips or hints on points to remember

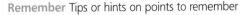

Good practice/Health & safety Example of good practice or procedure

Science bit! Did you know Other technical information relevant to the chapter

increase friction between the cutting surfaces and reduce the amount of movement of the upper, cutting edge. This will need routine checking and lubricating. Accurate resetting, alignment, lubrication and retightening of the blades is essential, so make sure that only trained individuals carry out this regular, routine maintenance.

Preventing infection

A warm, humid salon can offer a perfect home for disease-carrying bacteria. If they can find food in the form of dust and dirt, they may reproduce rapidly. Good ventilation, however, provides a circulating air current that will help to prevent their growth. This is why it is important to keep the salon clean, dry and well aired at all times. This includes clothing, work areas, tools and all equipment.

Some salons use sterilising devices as a means of providing hygienically safe work implements. *Sterilisation* means the complete eradication of living organisms. Different devices use different sterilisation methods, which may be based on the use of heat, radiation or chemicals.

Ultraviolet radiation

Ultraviolet (UV) radiation provides an alternative sterilising option. The items for sterilisation are placed in wall- or worktop-mounted cabinets fitted with UV-emitting lightbulbs and exposed to the radiation for at least 15 minutes. Penetration of UV radiation is low, so sterilisation by this method is not guaranteed.

Chemical sterilisation

Chemical sterilisers should be handled only with suitable personal protective equipment, as many of the solutions used are hazardous to health and should not come into contact with the skin. The most effective form of sterilisation is achieved by total immersion of the contaminated implements into a bath of fluid. This principle is widely used in the sterilisation of babies' feeding utensils.

Disinfectants reduce the probability of infection and are widely used in general day-to-day hygienic salon maintenance. *Antiseptics* are used specifically for treating wounds. Many prepackaged first-aid dressings are impregnated with antiseptic fluids.

PERSONAL HYGIENE AND APPEARANCE

Hairdressing is a personal service industry and your clients will judge your personal and professional standards by the way in which you present yourself. Remember, hairdressing is an image-conscious industry. We strive to provide a high-quality service that gives clients well-cut, well-styled and well-groomed hair, so that they feel pleased and confident and have greater self-esteem. Would you give clients confidence if you turned up for appointments with stained overalls, unkempt hair and dirty hands and nails?

GOOD PRACTICE/ HEALTH & SAFETY

All salons carry out a risk assessment of the substances they use. Any substances that have been identified as potentially hazardous to health will have special handling instructions. These instructions, along with any necessary personal protective equipment (PPE), must be 'publicly' available within the salon.

REMEMBER

Always wear gloves

When? On any occasion where you come into contact with chemicals

Why? Because gloves are a protective barrier against infection

Always wash hands

When? Before work, after eating, using the toilet, coughing, sneezing or blowing your nose

Why? Because your hands are one of the main sources of spreading infection

Always wear protective clothing

When? Always wear a plastic apron for any salon procedure involving chemicals

Why? This will prevent spillages onto your clothes, particularly when colouring and perming

Hands and nails

Your hands should always be perfectly clean. Dirt on your hands and under your nails will harbour bacteria. By spreading germs you could infect other people. Your hands need washing not only before work but also several times throughout the day. Where hands regularly come into contact with water or detergents, the skin may lose its moisture, become dry and crack. Cracked, broken skin allows germs to enter and infection may follow. To prevent this from happening, you should regularly moisturise your skin after washing. If your hands are often in water (for example, in shampooing or conditioning), you may find it helpful to use a *barrier cream*. Barrier creams cover the skin with an invisible barrier which greatly reduces the penetration of hairdressing cleansing and conditioning agents. (Many trainees have given up hairdressing after developing the skin condition called *dermatitis*, in which the hands become sore, cracked, itchy and red. At this stage work becomes painful and medical advice should be sought.)

Long nails not only trap dirt but can also cause discomfort to clients. In certain hairdressing procedures it is quite possible that longer nails could even scratch or damage the skin. The risk of spreading infection and disease can be prevented by keeping nails short and neat. Clean, well-manicured nails without splits or tears are hygienic and safe.

Body

Taking a daily shower/bath is necessary to remove the build-up of sweat, dead skin cells and surface bacteria. Skin in areas such as the armpits, feet and genitals have more sweat glands than elsewhere and the warm, moist conditions provide an ideal breeding ground for bacteria. Regular washing is therefore essential if body odour (BO) is to be prevented.

Mouth

Unpleasant breath is offensive to clients. Bad breath (halitosis) is the result of leaving particles to decay within the spaces between the teeth. You need to brush your teeth after every meal. Bad breath can also result from digestive troubles, stomach upsets, smoking and strong foods such as onions, garlic and some cheeses.

Personal appearance

In addition to personal cleanliness, your personal appearance is an important factor too. The effort you put into getting ready for work reflects your pride in the job. It is alright for you to have your own individual look, provided that you appreciate and accept that there are professional standards of dress and appearance that must be followed – a sort of personal code of practice.

Courtesy of Ellisons

SCIENCE BIT! DID YOU KNOW

Antiperspirants reduce underarm sweating. These products contain astringents, which narrow the pores that emit the sweat and cool down the skin. Alternatively, deodorants can be used. These products will not reduce the amount of sweating but can mask any odour by killing the surface bacteria with antiseptic ingredients.

Step by step Photo sequences to illustrate procedures

Checkerboard A self-check system and means of recording progress towards achievement

STEP BY STEP: RESTYLE LONG HAIR – GRADUATED LAYERS

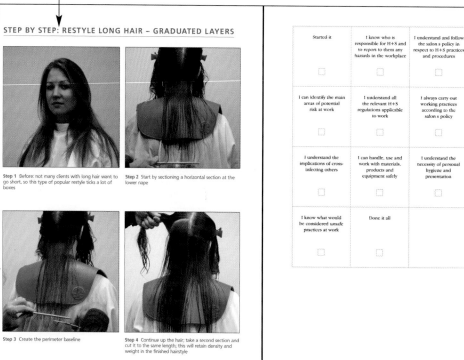

Step 1 Before: not many clients with long hair want to go short, so this type of popular restyle ticks a lot of boxes

Step 2 Start by sectioning a horizontal section at the lower nape

Step 3 Create the perimeter baseline

Step 4 Continue up the hair; take a second section and cut it to the same length; this will retain density and weight in the finished hairstyle

Started it	I know who is responsible for H+S and to report to them any hazards in the workplace	I understand and follow the salon's policy in respect to H+S practices and procedures	I always recognise hazards and potential risks at work and take appropriate action
☐	☐	☐	☐
I can identify the main areas of potential risk at work	I understand all the relevant H+S regulations applicable to work	I always carry out working practices according to the salon's policy	I've covered most of it!
☐	☐	☐	☐
I understand the implications of cross-infecting others	I can handle, use and work with materials, products and equipment safely	I understand the necessity of personal hygiene and presentation	I know the salon's policy and procedures in the event of fire or accidents
☐	☐	☐	☐
I know what would be considered unsafe practices at work	Done it all		CHECKER BOARD ✓
☐	☐		

Tests A variety of self-assessment tests including short answer, multiple choice, true or false etc.

30

NVQ2 & RE UNITS G1

Self-test section

Quick quiz: a selection of different types of questions to check your knowledge

Q1	A is something with potential to cause harm.	Fill in the blank
Q2	Risk assessment is a process of evaluation to ensure safe working practices.	True or False
Q3	Select all that apply. Which of the following are environmental hazards:	Multi-selection

Boxes of stock left in the reception area	☐	1
Stock items upon the shelves	☐	2
Wet or slippery floors	☐	3
Shampoo backwash positions	☐	4
Salon work stations	☐	5
Trailing flexes from electrical equipment	☐	6

Q4	First-aid boxes should contain paracetamol tablets.	True or False
Q5	Which of the following regulations relate to the safe handling of chemicals?	Multi-choice

PPE	☐	a
RIDDOR	☐	b
COSHH	☐	c
OSRPA	☐	d

Q6	All salons must have a written health and safety policy.	True or False
Q7	Which of the following records must a salon keep up to date by law:	Multi-selection

Telephone book	☐	1
Accident book	☐	2
Appointment book	☐	3
Electrical equipment annual test records	☐	4
Health and safety at work checklist	☐	5
Fire drill records	☐	6

Q8	The regulations require employers to provide adequate equipment and facilities in case of an accident occurring.	Fill in the blank
Q9	What colour is the label on a dry powder filled fire extinguisher?	Multi-choice

Red	☐	a
Cream	☐	b
Black	☐	c
Blue	☐	d

Q10	A dry powder filled fire extinguisher can be used on all classes of fire.	True or False

TONI & GUY AT THE 50TH ANNIVERSARY
L'ORÉAL COLOUR TROPHY, LONDON, MAY 2006.

ANTOINETTE BEENDERS AT THE 50TH ANNIVERSARY
L'ORÉAL COLOUR TROPHY, LONDON, MAY 2005.

TREVOR SORBIE AT THE 50TH ANNIVERSARY
L'ORÉAL COLOUR TROPHY, LONDON, MAY 2005.

CHARLES WORTHINGTON AT THE 50TH ANNIVERSARY
L'ORÉAL COLOUR TROPHY, LONDON, MAY 2005.

M. BALFRE AT THE ALTERNATIVE HAIR SHOW, 2005.

part one

HEALTH, SAFETY AND SECURITY

Unit G1 Ensure that your own actions reduce risks to health and safety   Mandatory

G1.1   Identify the hazards and evaluate the risks in your workplace. What does it mean?

G1.2   Reduce the risks to health and safety in your workplace.

What do I need to learn?

You need to know and understand:

- Your expected duties, legal responsibilities and key contacts for health and safety at your salon
- The types of hazards that exist in your salon and how you should deal with them
- Safe working practices and your salon's health and safety policy and procedures

What does it mean?

This chapter will explain how you can help your manager/employer to maintain a healthy and safe working environment for you, your work colleagues and other business customers and visitors.

What do I need to do?

- You need to ensure that your actions at work do not create any risks to health and safety.
- You mustn't ignore any significant risks within the working environment.
- Make sure that you report any potential hazards with salon equipment, or in connection with staff, clients and other people.

Other info

Related topics and other useful information:

- **COSHH**
- **Risk assessment**
- **Personal health, hygiene and safety at work**
- **Safe use of salon equipment**
- **Emergency procedures (fire, first aid, etc.)**
- **Maintaining salon security**
- **Display screen equipment (DSE regs)**
- **Manual handling**
- **RIDDOR**
- **Employers liability compulsory insurance**

KEY WORDS

Hazard something with potential to cause harm

Risk the likelihood of a hazard occurring

CHECKERBOARD

At the end of this chapter the checkerboard will help to jog your memory on what you have learned and what still remains to be done. Cross them off with a pencil as you cover each of its topics. (See p. 29.)

INTRODUCTION

This mandatory unit comprises of two elements:

G1.1   Identify the hazards and evaluate the risks in your workplace.

G1.2   Reduce the risks to health and safety in your workplace.

The chapter covers the essential information in supporting these tasks and extends to a wide range covering other related information. This includes aspects of legislation and general security of the working environment.

You will need to show that you understand the health and safety requirements in the workplace. This includes monitoring your own work routines and workspace so that hazards are quickly identified and potential risk to others being harmed is minimised.

The Health and Safety at Work Act 1974 is the main piece of 'umbrella' legislation under which all other regulations are made. Employers have a legal duty under this Act to ensure, so far as reasonably practicable, the health, safety and welfare at work of all the people for whom they are responsible and the people who may be affected by the work they do.

This Act also requires all employees to take reasonable care of themselves or others who may be affected by their working practices. It expects them to co-operate and support their employers in fulfilling their obligations in complying with current health and safety requirements.

Safety of the environment

You share the responsibility with your employer for the safety of all the people in the salon.

You need to be aware of:

1 *Environmental hazards* such as:

- wet or slippery floors
- cluttered passageways or corridors
- rearranged furniture
- electrical flexes (e.g. a trailing electric cable is a hazard if it lies across a passageway as there is a high risk of somebody tripping over it whereas if it lies along a wall the risk is much less).

2 *Hazards to do with equipment and materials* such as:

- worn or faulty electrical equipment
- incorrectly labelled substances such as cleaning fluids; leaking or damaged containers (e.g. toxic or flammable chemicals are a hazard and may present a high risk. However, if they are properly kept, securely stored and correctly handled the risk is greatly reduced).

3 *Hazards connected with people* such as:

- visitors to the salon
- handling procedures
- intruders.

Simply being aware of potential hazards is not enough. You also have a responsibility to contribute to a safe working environment, so you must take steps to check and deal with any sources of risk. You can fulfil your role in two ways:

1 Deal directly with the hazard, which means that you have taken individual responsibility. This will probably apply to obvious hazards such as:

- trailing flexes – *roll them up and store them safely*
- cluttered doorways and corridors – *remove objects and store them safely or dispose of them appropriately*
- fire – *follow the correct procedures to raise the alarm and assist with evacuation*.

2 Inform your manager or supervisor, which means that it becomes an organisational responsibility. This applies to hazards that are beyond your responsibility to deal with such as:

- *faulty equipment* – dryers, tongs, straightening irons, kettles, computers, etc.
- *worn* floor coverings or broken tiles
- *loose or damaged fittings* – mirrors, shelves or backwashes
- *obstructions* too heavy for you to move safely
- *fire*.

ACTIVITY

Find out your salon's policy in respect of the following procedures.

1 What constitutes safe working (good) practices?
2 How should hazardous substances be stored, dispensed and used?
3 What are the salon's rules regarding smoking and consuming food and drink on the premises, and policy in respect to alcohol and other drugs?
4 What takes place during the event of an emergency occurring?
5 What are the salon's expectations in respect to personal presentation and hygiene?

Key skills: Communication

2.1 Take part in discussions
2.2 Produce written materials
2.4 Read and respond to written materials

WORKING SAFELY IN THE SALON

You have a duty to your employer and your colleagues to keep the working environment safe. You need to be alert, spotting potential hazards and preventing accidents, thus helping to avoid emergency situations arising. Suppose, for example, that someone had carelessly blocked a fire door with a recently delivered stock order. You could take the initiative and remove a possible hazard by moving the box to a safe and secure location. If you notice a potential hazard that you cannot easily rectify yourself, tell your supervisor immediately. Imagine, for instance, that someone accidentally tripped over a trailing lead from a hand dryer while it was plugged in, wrenching the lead from the dryer handle onto a wet floor. Under no circumstances should you enter the wet area and try to retrieve the trailing lead, but you should tell a senior member of staff at once so that she can shut off the power at the mains supply.

Obstructions

It is dangerous to obstruct areas used as thoroughfares such as doorways, corridors, stairs and fire exits. In an emergency people might have to leave the salon, or part of it, in a hurry – perhaps even in the dark. It could be disastrous if someone injured themselves or fell in these circumstances. So always be on the lookout for any obstruction in these areas. If you see something that could present a risk, move it away as quickly as you can.

Covered bins   Courtesy of Ellisons

Spillage and breakages

Take care when you have to clear up spilled chemicals or damaged equipment. First of all find out what has been spilled or dropped. Is this something that needs special care and attention when handling? Does personal protective equipment need to be worn? (See p. 21.)

Disposal of waste

General salon waste

Everyday items of salon waste should be placed in an enclosed waste bin fitted with a suitably resistant polyethylene bin liner. When the bin is full,

Sharps box   SP Services

the liner can be sealed using a wire tie and placed ready for refuse collection. If for any reason the bin liner punctures, put the damaged liner and waste inside a second bin liner. Wash out the inside of the bin itself with hot water and detergent.

Disposing of sharps

Used razor blades and similar items should be placed into a safe screw-topped container. When the container is full it can be discarded. This type of salon waste should be kept away from general salon waste as special disposal arrangements may be provided by your local authority. Contact your local council offices for more information.

General health and safety checklist	Yes	No	Go to page
Has your salon got a written health and safety policy?			12–20
Who is in charge of health and safety in your salon?			19
Has your salon done a risk assessment?			12–22
Do you know what COSHH means?			20–23
Do you know where the first-aid kit is?			15–18
Do you know where the accident book is?			16
Do you know the emergency procedures?			12–18
Do you carry out routine checks/inspections?			19–29

GENERAL SALON HYGIENE AND ROUTINE MAINTENANCE

The salon

REMEMBER ✔

Take all precautions to avoid dermatitis. Use barrier creams and protective gloves where possible.

It is important that you develop an awareness of health and safety risks and that you are always aware of any risks in any situation. Quite simply, a tidy salon is easier to clean so get into the habit of clearing up your work as you go.

Floors and seating

Floors should be kept clean at all times. This means that they will need regular mopping, sweeping or vacuuming. When working areas are damp-mopped during normal working hours, make sure that adequate warning signs are provided close to the wet areas.

The salon's seating will be made of material that is easily cleaned. It should be washed regularly with hot water and detergent. After drying, the seats can be wiped over with disinfectant or an antiseptic lotion.

Working surfaces

All surfaces within the salon, including the reception, staff and stock preparation areas, should be washed down at least once each day. Most salons now use easily maintained wipe-clean surfaces, usually some form of plastic laminate. They can be cleaned with hot water and detergent, and after the surfaces are dry they can be wiped over with a spirit-based antiseptic which will not smear. Don't use scourers or abrasives as these will scratch plastic surfaces. Scratched surfaces look dull and unattractive as well as containing minute crevices in which bacteria will develop.

Saks: Covent Garden

Mirrors

Glass mirrors should be cleaned every morning before clients arrive. Never try to style a client's hair while he or she sits in front of a murky, dusty or smeary mirror. Glass surfaces should be cleaned and polished using either hot water and detergent or a spirit-based lotion that evaporates quickly without smearing.

Salon equipment

Towels and gowns

Each client must have a fresh, clean towel and gown. These should be washed in hot soapy water to remove any soiling or staining and to prevent the spread of infection by killing any bacteria. Fabric conditioners may be used to provide a luxurious softness and freshness.

Photo courtesy Goldwell UK

Styling tools

Most pieces of salon equipment, such as combs, brushes and curlers, are made from plastics. These materials are relatively easy to keep hygienically safe if they are used and cleaned properly.

Combs should be washed daily. When not in use they should be immersed in an antibacterial solution. When needed they can be rinsed and dried and are then ready for use.

If any styling tools are accidentally dropped onto the floor, do not use them until they have been adequately cleaned. Don't put contaminated items onto work surfaces as they could spread infection and disease.

Handle non-plastic items, such as scissors and clipper blades, with care. If they need cleaning use surgical spirit, carefully wiping it over the flat edges of the blades. Although most of these items are made of special steels, don't immerse them in sterilising fluids. Many of them contain chemicals that will corrode the precision-made surfaces of the blades.

Regularly used clippers in the hairdressing salon will require frequent routine checks for both safety and efficiency. Hair will get trapped between the blades, which reduces cutting performance, and constant vibration may loosen the cutting edges. The macerated hair between the blades will

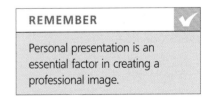

REMEMBER

Personal presentation is an essential factor in creating a professional image.

REMEMBER

On every occasion, before using clippers, make sure you check the alignment and positioning of the blades. Not only will frequent use impair their effectiveness, but the constant vibration may loosen the blades.

increase friction between the cutting surfaces and reduce the amount of **movement** of the upper, cutting edge. This will need routine checking and lubricating. Accurate resetting, alignment, lubrication and retightening of the blades is essential, so make sure that only trained individuals carry out this regular, routine maintenance.

Preventing infection

A warm, humid salon can offer a perfect home for disease-carrying bacteria. If they can find food in the form of dust and dirt, they may reproduce rapidly. Good ventilation, however, provides a circulating air current that will help to prevent their growth. This is why it is important to keep the salon clean, dry and well aired at all times. This includes clothing, work areas, tools and all equipment.

Some salons use sterilising devices as a means of providing hygienically safe work implements. *Sterilisation* means the complete eradication of living organisms. Different devices use different sterilisation methods, which may be based on the use of heat, radiation or chemicals.

Ultraviolet radiation

Ultraviolet (UV) radiation provides an alternative sterilising option. The items for sterilisation are placed in wall- or worktop-mounted cabinets fitted with UV-emitting lightbulbs and exposed to the radiation for at least 15 minutes. Penetration of UV radiation is low, so sterilisation by this method is not guaranteed.

Chemical sterilisation

Chemical sterilisers should be handled only with suitable personal protective equipment, as many of the solutions used are hazardous to health and should not come into contact with the skin. The most effective form of sterilisation is achieved by total immersion of the contaminated implements into a bath of fluid. This principle is widely used in the sterilisation of babies' feeding utensils.

Disinfectants reduce the probability of infection and are widely used in general day-to-day hygienic salon maintenance. *Antiseptics* are used specifically for treating wounds. Many prepackaged first-aid dressings are impregnated with antiseptic fluids.

PERSONAL HYGIENE AND APPEARANCE

Hairdressing is a personal service industry and your clients will judge your personal and professional standards by the way in which you present yourself. Remember, hairdressing is an image-conscious industry. We strive to provide a high-quality service that gives clients well-cut, well-styled and well-groomed hair, so that they feel pleased and confident and have greater self-esteem. Would you give clients confidence if you turned up for appointments with stained overalls, unkempt hair and dirty hands and nails?

GOOD PRACTICE/ HEALTH & SAFETY ✚

All salons carry out a risk assessment of the substances they use. Any substances that have been identified as potentially hazardous to health will have special handling instructions. These instructions, along with any necessary personal protective equipment (PPE), must be 'publicly' available within the salon.

REMEMBER ✓

Always wear gloves

When? On any occasion where you come into contact with chemicals

Why? Because gloves are a protective barrier against infection

Always wash hands

When? Before work, after eating, using the toilet, coughing, sneezing or blowing your nose

Why? Because your hands are one of the main sources of spreading infection

Always wear protective clothing

When? Always wear a plastic apron for any salon procedure involving chemicals

Why? This will prevent spillages onto your clothes, particularly when colouring and perming

Hands and nails

Your hands should always be perfectly clean. Dirt on your hands and under your nails will harbour bacteria. By spreading germs you could infect other people. Your hands need washing not only before work but also several times throughout the day. Where hands regularly come into contact with water or detergents, the skin may lose its moisture, become dry and crack. Cracked, broken skin allows germs to enter and infection may follow. To prevent this from happening, you should regularly moisturise your skin after washing. If your hands are often in water (for example, in shampooing or conditioning), you may find it helpful to use a *barrier cream*. Barrier creams cover the skin with an invisible barrier which greatly reduces the penetration of hairdressing cleansing and conditioning agents. (Many trainees have given up hairdressing after developing the skin condition called *dermatitis*, in which the hands become sore, cracked, itchy and red. At this stage work becomes painful and medical advice should be sought.)

Long nails not only trap dirt but can also cause discomfort to clients. In certain hairdressing procedures it is quite possible that longer nails could even scratch or damage the skin. The risk of spreading infection and disease can be prevented by keeping nails short and neat. Clean, well-manicured nails without splits or tears are hygienic and safe.

Courtesy of Ellisons

**SCIENCE BIT!
DID YOU KNOW ?**

Antiperspirants reduce underarm sweating. These products contain astringents, which narrow the pores that emit the sweat and cool down the skin. Alternatively, deodorants can be used. These products will not reduce the amount of sweating but can mask any odour by killing the surface bacteria with antiseptic ingredients.

Body

Taking a daily shower/bath is necessary to remove the build-up of sweat, dead skin cells and surface bacteria. Skin in areas such as the armpits, feet and genitals have more sweat glands than elsewhere and the warm, moist conditions provide an ideal breeding ground for bacteria. Regular washing is therefore essential if body odour (BO) is to be prevented.

Mouth

Unpleasant breath is offensive to clients. Bad breath (halitosis) is the result of leaving particles to decay within the spaces between the teeth. You need to brush your teeth after every meal. Bad breath can also result from digestive troubles, stomach upsets, smoking and strong foods such as onions, garlic and some cheeses.

Personal appearance

In addition to personal cleanliness, your personal appearance is an important factor too. The effort you put into getting ready for work reflects your pride in the job. It is alright for you to have your own individual look, provided that you appreciate and accept that there are professional standards of dress and appearance that must be followed – a sort of personal code of practice.

We all carry large numbers of micro-organisms inside us, on our skin and in our hair. These organisms, such as bacteria, fungi and viruses, are too small to be seen with the naked eye. Bacteria and fungi can be seen through a microscope, but viruses are too small even for that.

Many micro-organisms are quite harmless, but some can cause disease. Those that are harmful to people are called pathogens. Flu, for example, is caused by a virus, thrush by a fungus and bronchitis often by bacteria. Conditions like these, which can be transmitted from one person to another, are said to be infectious.

The body is naturally resistant to infection; it can fight most pathogens using its inbuilt immunity system, so it is possible to be infected with pathogenic organisms without contracting the disease. When you have a disease, the symptoms are the visible signs that something is wrong. They are the results of the infection and of the reactions of the body to that infection. Symptoms help you to recognise the disease.

Infectious diseases should always be treated by a doctor. Non-infectious conditions and defects can often be treated in the salon or with products available from the chemist.

Clothes

Clothes or overalls should be clean and well ironed. It is sensible to wear clothes made from fabrics that are suitable not only for your intended work but also for the time of year. Clothes that are restrictive or tight will not allow air to circulate around your body and will prevent you from keeping cool and fresh; they could lead to uncomfortable perspiration or possibly BO. Apart from the clothes that other people see, remember that a daily change of underwear is essential.

Shoes

Wear shoes that have low heels. They should be smart, comfortable and made of materials suitable for wearing over long periods of time. Remember that hairdressing involves a lot of standing and your feet can therefore get tired, hot, sweaty and even sore. It is worth wearing shoes that allow your feet to 'breathe', as ventilated feet remain cool and comfortable throughout the working day.

Hair

Your hair reflects the image and expected standards of the salon in which you work. It should be clean, healthy and manageable. Don't let long hair fall over your face, as this will obstruct good communication with the clients and your poor **body language** may give them the wrong message.

Jewellery

Only the minimum of jewellery should be worn in the salon. Rings, bracelets and dangling necklaces will get in the way of normal day-to-day duties and will make the client uncomfortable. In many hairdressing operations, such as shampooing and conditioning, jewellery can catch and pull at the client's hair as well as provide unhygienic crevices for dirt and germs to lurk in.

Posture

Bad posture will lead to fatigue or even longer-term injury. Adopting the correct posture is essential for trainees and competent hairdressers alike. An incorrect standing position will put undue strain on both muscles and ligaments, as well as giving your clients an impression of an uncaring, unprofessional attitude towards work.

Posture fatigue will occur when a part of the body is out of **line** with another part immediately below. Hairdressers have to be on their feet a great deal. Therefore adopting a good posture is a requirement of the job. You will achieve correct posture when your head, shoulders, upper torso, abdomen, thighs and legs distribute your body's weight in a balanced, equally proportioned way, over feet that are positioned forward and slightly apart. Dropping a shoulder will shift your body's weight over one foot. This will cause curvature of the spine, applying strains on muscles and ligaments, as well as exerting pressures on the intervertebral discs in your spine. This will at least be uncomfortable and at worst dangerous, possibly starting a longer-term back problem or injury.

Your posture while sitting should be restful. Your back should be supported all the way down. This does not mean that chairs must have a continuous back or contoured, moulded panels, but that your sitting position should provide your body with support so that the pelvis and not the base of the spine takes the body's weight. Avoid sitting with crossed legs as this will restrict blood circulation. It will result in numbness and a sensation of 'pins and needles'.

FIRE SAFETY

Under the Fire Precautions Act 1971, a fire certificate is required for business premises if:

- more than 20 people are employed on one floor at any one time
- more than 10 people are employed on different floors at any one time.

Where premises are shared with other businesses, the employers must include everyone collectively.

All premises must be provided with an adequate means of escape in case of fire and a means of fighting fire, whether or not a fire certificate is required. All fire exits need to be clearly marked with the appropriate signs and all doors must be capable of being opened easily and immediately from the inside.

Every employer must carry out a fire risk **assessment** covering the premises. This should address the following key aspects:

- Assessment of fire risks within the premises as required under the Management of Health and Safety Regulations 1999.
- The installation of suitable fire detection equipment, e.g. smoke alarms.
- The installation of a suitable warning system (this could be an automatic fire alarm system).
- Checks that everyone can get back safely from the premises in the event of fire and that all means of escape including passageways, stairwells, etc. are kept clear of obstructions at all times. Where necessary adequate emergency lighting should be installed.
- The provision of adequate firefighting equipment.
- The provision of adequate training for employees so that everyone knows what to do in the event of fire.
- Regular checks and maintenance of all fire safety equipment.
- Regular reviews of the fire safety arrangements.

Fire

Fires occurring in salons would be more likely to arise from either an electrical fault, a gas escape, or smoking. Faulty or badly maintained *electrical equipment*, such as hand dryers or hood dryers, may malfunction, overheat, and even ignite. *Gas appliances*, such as ovens or hobs, present a possible risk if left unattended. Staff cooking facilities need to be closely

REMEMBER: CLASSES OF FIRE

There are four classifications of fire:

Class A Fires involving solid material, i.e. paper, wood, hair, etc.

Class B Fires involving liquids such as petrol, paraffin, etc.

Class C Fires involving gases, i.e. propane, butane

Class D Fires involving metals

Health & Safety for Hairdressers
Copyright © Habia 2005

Fire Risk Assessment Checklist

habia
standards • information • solutions

Salon Name:

No.	Item	Yes/No	If yes, how is this controlled? If no, outline problem areas	Additional control measures required
1	**Are all sources of fuel kept to a minimum and stored safely?** • Do not store next to ignition sources such as hot radiators. Remove rubbish regularly and store safely.	No	Aerosols stored on shelves above radiator.	Store aerosols in well ventilated stock cupboard away from heat and direct sunlight.
2	**Are all electrical hand tools regularly inspected/tested?** • Electrical faults can cause overheating and result in fires.	Yes	Staff inspect before use. Formal inspection every six months. Contractor PAT test annually.	
3	**Is the salon electrical wiring inspected regularly by a competent person?** • See section 8.	No	Only hand tools tested by contractor.	Arrange for contractor to test wiring when carrying out PAT testing of portable appliances.
4	**Is the use of adaptors/extension leads kept to a minimum?** • Adaptors/extension leads can overheat.	Yes	No adaptors in salon. One extension lead which can only be used with permission of manageress.	
5	**Are all cables run so that they cannot be damaged?** • Damaged cables can result in fuel such as hair, paper etc. catching fire.	No	Cable to washing machine run across staff room floor.	Install new power point in kitchen.

monitored to prevent gas being left on, whether lit or not. *Smoking* can cause fires when lit cigarettes are dropped, discarded or left unattended to smoulder in ashtrays. Your salon will have set fire safety procedures, which must always be followed.

Raising the alarm

In the event of fire breaking out, your main priorities are to:

- *Raise the alarm.* Staff and customers must be warned and the premises must be evacuated.
- *Call the fire brigade.* Do this even if you believe that someone else has already phoned. Dial 999, ask the operator for the fire service, and give the telephone number from where you are calling. Wait for the transfer to the fire service, then tell them your name and the address of the premises that are on fire.

Firefighting

If the fire is small, you may tackle it with an extinguisher or fire blanket. Under the Fire Precautions Act 1971, all premises are required to have firefighting equipment, which must be suitably maintained in good working order. Different types of fire require different types of fire extinguisher.

Firefighting equipment Chubb Fire Ltd

Firefighting blanket
Chubb Fire Ltd

Firefighting symbols

Types of fire extinguisher

1 **Water**. These are *red* with a label to indicate its type and can only be used for Class A fires. The standard size is 9 litres (2 gallons). (The main problem with this type of extinguisher is the subsequent damage caused by the water and that it cannot be used on electrical fires.)

2 **Foam**. These used to be *cream/buff*, but are now red with a *cream/buff* label, and used for Class B fires and small Class A fires. The standard capacity is 9 litres (2 gallons). (This type of extinguisher has the same problems as water extinguishers.)

3 **Carbon dioxide (CO_2)**. These used to be *black*, but are now red with a *black label* and can be used on all fires but are particularly suitable for Class B and electrical fires. They are available in a range of sizes depending on the weight of CO_2 contained.

4 **Dry powder**. These used to be *blue*, but are now red with a *blue label* and can be used on all classes of fire, but are particularly suitable for Class B, C and electrical fires. They are available in a range of sizes from 0.75kg to 4 kg. The main disadvantage is that the residual powder has to be cleaned up and the powder can cause damage to electronic equipment.

5 **Vaporising liquids (BCF)**. This type of fire extinguisher is no longer available, but may continue to be used until its expiry date. These used to be *green* and can be used on all classes of fire, but are particularly suitable for Class B, C and electrical fires. The main disadvantage is that the vapour is toxic, particularly in confined spaces.

Fire escape

All premises must have a designated means of escape from fire. This route must be kept clear of obstructions at all times and during working hours the fire doors must remain unlocked. The escape route must be easily identifiable, with clearly visible signs. In buildings with fire certificates, emergency lighting must be installed. These lighting systems automatically illuminate the escape route in the event of a power failure and are operated by an independent battery back-up.

Fire safety training

It is essential for staff to know the following fire procedures:

- fire prevention
- raising the alarm
- evacuation during a fire
- assembly points following evacuation.

Training is given to new members of staff during their **induction** period. This training must be regularly updated for all staff and fire drills must be held at regular intervals.

DEALING WITH ACCIDENTS (FIRST AID)

The *Health and Safety (First Aid) Regulations 1981* require employers to provide equipment and facilities which are adequate and appropriate in the circumstances for administering first aid to their employees. Remember that any first-aid materials used from the kit must be replaced as soon as possible. All accidents and emergency aid given within the salon must be documented in the accident book.

Contents of the first-aid box

No. of employees	1–5	6–10	11–50
Contents			
First-aid guidance notes	1	1	1
Individual sterile adhesive dressings	20	20	40
Sterile eye pads	1	2	4
Sterile triangular bandages	1	2	4
Safety pins	6	6	12
Medium size sterile unmediated dressings	3	6	8
Large size sterile unmediated dressings	1	2	4
Extra-large size sterile unmediated dressings	1	2	4

Recording accidents and illness

All accidents must be recorded in the accident book. The recording system should always be kept readily available for use and inspection. When you are recording accidents, you will need to document the following details:

- date, time and place of incident or treatment
- name, and job of injured or ill person
- details of the injury/ill person and the treatment given

- what happened to the person immediately afterwards (e.g. went home, hospital)
- name and signature of the person providing the treatment and entry.

General guidance on first aid

The following basic information is available in leaflet form from HSE ISBN 0 7176 1070 5 (priced packs of 20).

Basic rules for first aiders

REMEMBER: YOU SHOULD NOT ATTEMPT TO GIVE ANYTHING MORE THAN BASIC FIRST AID!

When giving first aid it is vital that you assess the situation and that you:

- take care not to become a casualty yourself while administering first aid (use protective clothing and equipment where necessary)
- send for help where necessary
- follow this advice from the HSE.

What to do in an emergency

Check whether the casualty is conscious. If the casualty is unconscious or semi-conscious:

- check the mouth for any obstruction
- *open the airway* by tilting the head back and lifting the chin using the tips of two fingers.

If the casualty has stopped breathing and you are competent to give artificial ventilation, do so. Otherwise *send for help* without delay.

Unconsciousness

In most workplaces expert help should be available fairly quickly, but if you have an unconscious casualty it is vital that his or her airway is kept clear. If you cannot keep the airway open as described above, you may need to turn the casualty into the recovery position. *The priority is an open airway.*

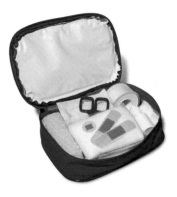

First-aid leaflet HMSO

Wounds and bleeding

Open wounds should be covered – after washing your hands if possible. Apply a dressing from the first-aid box over the wound and press firmly on top of it with your hands or fingers. The pad should be tied firmly in place. If bleeding continues, another dressing should be applied on top. Do not remove the original dressing. Seek appropriate help.

Minor injuries

Minor injuries of the sort which the injured person would treat themselves at home can be treated from the contents of the first-aid box. The casualty should wash his or her hands and apply a dressing to protect the wound and prevent infection. In the workplace special metallic and/or coloured or waterproof dressings may be supplied according to the circumstances. Wounds should be kept dry and clean.

A first-aid kit

Suspected broken bones

If a broken bone is suspected obtain expert help. Do not move casualties unless they are in a position which exposes them to immediate danger.

Burns

Burns can be serious. If in doubt seek medical help. Cool the part of the body affected with cold water until the pain is relieved. Thorough cooling may take ten minutes or more, but this must not delay taking the casualty to hospital.

Certain chemicals may irritate or damage the skin, some seriously. Treat in the same way as for other burns. It is important that irrigation continues, even on the way to the hospital if necessary. Remove any contaminated clothing which is not stuck to the skin. Make sure that you avoid *contaminating yourself* with the chemical.

> **GOOD PRACTICE/ HEALTH & SAFETY: ESSENTIAL BASIC FIRST AID RULE**
>
> Always protect yourself with surgical gloves when administering first aid. Washing hands is not sufficient!

Eye injuries

Eye injuries are potentially serious. The casualty will be experiencing intense pain in the affected eye, with spasm of the eyelids. Before attempting to treat, *always protect yourself with surgical gloves.*

If there is something in the eye, irrigate the eye with clean, cool water or sterile fluid from a sealed container to remove loose material. *Do not attempt to remove anything that is embedded.*

If chemicals are involved, flush the open eye with water or sterile fluid for at least 10 to 15 minutes. Apply an eyepad and send the casualty to hospital.

Special hazards

Electrical and gassing accidents can occur in the workplace. You must assess the danger to yourself and not attempt assistance until you are sure it is safe to do so. If the casualty has stopped breathing and you are competent to give artificial ventilation and cardiac resuscitation, do so. Otherwise *send for help without delay.*

Illness

Many everyday ailments can arise at work. Giving medicines is not within the scope of first aid at work. Application and common sense and reassurance to the casualty are the most valuable help that you can give. If in doubt about the seriousness of the condition, seek expert help.

Record keeping

(See pp. 14–15.)

SALON SECURITY

Effective salon security is essential and your employer is required by law to provide secure business premises. Moreover, insurance companies would either refuse to insure a salon where adequate precautions were not taken, or would demand premiums so high that no salon could afford them. In order for your employer to establish and maintain the security of people and their belongings, money, equipment and premises, set procedures will have been laid down and put into action.

The potential threats to salon security come from either external or internal sources, both in and out of business hours.

External provisions

No salon can make its premises totally burglar proof, but steps may be taken to deter entry by unauthorised people and to minimise any damage they might do. As long as reasonable measures have been taken, insurance will not be withheld. Security devices should be fitted, such as:

- five-lever mortice locks ('deadlocks') to all external doors. These locks are rebated (cut out of both the door and the frame), not surface-mounted like latch locks, and require keys both to lock and unlock them
- locking catches or bolts on all external opening windows
- security bars or grilles on potentially vulnerable points of entry
- burglar alarms that sound in the event of forced intrusion or damage.

During normal hours of business, be very alert to the following risks:

- people in areas without the relevant authority
- unauthorised people asking for private or business information
- security of details relating to customers and staff.

Internal provisions

Unfortunately, outside intruders are not the only threat to the salon's security. Pilfering by staff and clients is also a possibility. Don't let yourself think that taking the occasional product home is a 'perk' of the job. Unless it has been paid for or you have permission, *it is theft*. Your salon may have its own policy in respect to staff purchases. Always ask. Theft at work is defined as an act of *gross misconduct*. A thief faces instant dismissal if your employer exercises her disciplinary rights. Your employer will have taken preventative steps to minimise the risk of theft. Procedures will be set in place to monitor till transactions, stock movements and personal items and valuables.

Money missing from the till will show up during the daily cashing up and book-keeping exercises. Shortfalls will be noticed when the number of clients attended, services and treatments provided and retail items sold do not tally with the available money and cash equivalents, the till rolls and the expected cumulative totals and daily reports and **transaction** breakdowns.

Missing items of stock will be noticed during normal stock control procedures, in routine situations where stock is not available as expected, and during spot checks and searches.

Personal possessions of both clients and staff also need protecting from theft. Make sure that these are kept safely away from risk situations. Clients' handbags, jewellery and any other valuables should remain with them at all times. Valuable items or money belonging to staff should be securely stored during working hours, or kept with the individual, perhaps in an overall pocket.

LEGAL FRAMEWORK (HEALTH AND SAFETY LEGISLATION)

This section will provide you with an outline of the main health and safety regulations that affect hairdressers and their work. The *Health and Safety at Work Act 1974* is the legislation that covers a variety of safe working practices and associated regulations. You do not need to know the contents of this Act, but you should at least be aware of the existence of relevant regulations made under its provisions:

- Management of Health and Safety at Work Regulations 1999
- Workplace (Health, Safety and Welfare) Regulations 1992
- Personal Protective Equipment at Work Regulations (PPE) 1992
- Control of Substances Hazardous to Health Regulations 1999 (COSHH)
- Electricity at Work Regulations 1989
- Health and Safety (First Aid) Regulations 1981
- Reporting of Injuries, Diseases and Dangerous Occurrences Regulations 1995 (RIDDOR)
- Health and Safety (Information for Employees) Regulations 1989
- Fire Precautions Act 1971
- Fire Precautions (Workplace) (Amendment) Regulations 1999
- Health and Safety (Display Screen Equipment) Regulations 1992
- Manual Handling Operations Regulations 1992
- Provision and Use of Work Equipment Regulations (PUWER) 1998.

REMEMBER: POTENTIAL AREAS OF RISK TO YOUNG PEOPLE ✔

- Manual handling
- Electricity and electrical equipment (clippers, etc.)
- Scissors and razors
- Dermatitis
- Chemicals

Management of Health and Safety at Work Regulations 1999

The main regulation requires the employer to appoint competent personnel to conduct risk assessments for the health and safety of all staff employed or otherwise and other visitors to the business premises. Staff must be adequately trained to take appropriate action, eliminate or minimise any risks. Other regulations cover the necessity to set up procedures for emergency situations, reviewing the risk assessment processes. In salons where five or more people are employed, there is the added obligation to set up a system for monitoring health surveillance, should the risk assessments identify a need. Main requirements for management of health and safety are as follows:

- identification of any potential hazards
- assessing the risks which could arise from these hazards
- identifying who is at risk
- eliminating or minimising the risks
- training staff to identify and control risks
- regular reviewing of the assessment processes.

Young workers at risk

There is also a requirement to carry out a risk assessment for young people. Any staff member who is under school leaving age must have a personalised risk assessment kept on file. This would be applicable for those on work experience or Saturday staff.

Risk assessment

Procedure for conducting risk assessment

1 Take a walk around the salon looking for any hazards, i.e. anything with the potential to cause harm. By using a similar form to the example shown above, it will help to organise the necessary information.

2 Decide what the risk is and which staff members could be harmed by those hazards. Broken tiles at the backwash may only affect the staff, whereas loose carpet in reception would affect all visitors.

3 For each of the listed hazards decide what level of risk exists, e.g. low, medium or high. Then looking at each entry, ask yourself if the risk can be eliminated or reduced. A loose carpet in reception is a hazard to

COSHH Risk Assessment

habia
standards · information · solutions

Staff member responsible: **Natasha Smith**　　　Date: **1st September 2005**　　　Review Dates: **10th January 2006**

Hazard	What is the risk?	Who is at risk?	Degree of risk high/med/low	Action to be taken to reduce/control risk
Aerosols (List aerosols used in your salon)	These can contain flammable gases and irritant chemicals. There is a risk of fire, explosion and intoxication.	Everyone in the salon, but in particular the user of the aerosol and the client.	Low	Look for aerosols with non-flammable gases if possible. Do not expose to temperatures above 50°C. Do not pierce or burn containers. Do not inhale.
Permanent wave neutraliser (List products used in your salon)	Irritant to the skin and eyes. Moderately toxic is swallowed or inhaled.	Stylists, juniors, trainees and clients.	Medium	Store in a cool place. Reseal after use. Do not use on damaged or sensitive skin. Avoid breathing in. Never place in an unlabelled container.

HSIP2a

everyone; if it were replaced the hazard is eliminated. You must inform your staff of the findings of the assessment and give them necessary training to minimise the risks.

4　Write down the findings of your risk assessment (salons with less than five employees do not have to record these findings). However, you may get a visit from Environmental Health and physical records will prove that the assessments have been made.

5　Review your risk assessments at regular intervals. The introduction of new equipment, different product ranges or chemical processes will potentially create new hazards. Setting a review date within the assessment process will ensure that your salon is kept up to date in the future.

Workplace (Health, Safety and Welfare) Regulations 1992

These regulations supersede the Offices, Shops and Railway Premises Act 1963 (OSRPA) and cover the following workplace key points:

- maintenance of the workplace and the equipment in it
- ventilation, temperature and lighting

- cleanliness
- sanitary and washing facilities
- drinking water supply
- rest, eating and changing facilities
- storage of clothing
- glazing
- traffic routes
- work space.

Amendments and additions in this Act provide new requirements for employers with particular attention for glazed areas such as windows and doors, etc. Any transparent and translucent partitions must be made of safe materials and if they could cause injury to anyone they should be appropriately marked. (Note narrow panes of glass up to 250mm are excluded from this Act.)

Other amendments have particular rules for rest rooms and rest areas. These must include a suitable alternative arrangements to protect non-smokers from the effects caused by tobacco smoke and suitable rest facilities to be provided for any person at work who is either pregnant or a nursing mother. OSRPA is slowly being phased out and being replaced by the Workplace (Health, Safety and Welfare) Regulations 1992.

Personal Protective Equipment at Work Regulations (PPE) 1992

The PPE Regulations 1992 require managers to make an assessment of the processes and activities carried out at work and to identify where and when special items of clothing should be worn. In hairdressing environments, the potential hazards and dangers revolve around the task of providing hairdressing services – that is, in general, the application of hairdressing treatments and associated products. (Many requirements under this Act will have been met in complying with COSHH regulations.)

Potentially hazardous substances used by hairdressers include:

- **acidic** solutions of varying strengths
- caustic **alkaline** solutions of varying strengths
- flammable liquids, which are often in pressurised containers
- vapours and dyeing compounds.

There are also potentially hazardous items of equipment and their individual applications, such as:

- electrical appliances
- heated/heating instruments
- sharp cutting tools.

All these items require correct handling and safe usage procedures and for several of them this includes the wearing of suitable items of protective equipment.

Control of Substances Hazardous to Health Regulations 1999 (COSHH)

Hairdressing employers are required by law to make an assessment of the exposure to all the substances used in their salons that could be potentially hazardous to themselves, their employees and other salon visitors, who may be affected by the work activity. The purpose of COSHH regulations is to make sure that people are working in the safest possible environment and conditions. A substance is considered to be hazardous if it can cause harm to the body. It only presents a risk if it is:

- in contact with the skin or eyes
- absorbed through the skin or via the eyes (either directly or from contact with contaminated surfaces or clothing)
- inhaled, i.e. breathing in substances in the atmosphere
- ingested via contaminated food or fingers
- injected
- introduced to the body via cuts and abrasions.

Hair products must comply with stringent UK cosmetics products safety regulations. The regulations detail how ingredients such as hydrogen peroxide, perming solutions and some hair dyes can be used. Under new legislation introduced in the EU manufacturers have to list on the label all the ingredients that are used in their products. Therefore employers must make an assessment to find out:

- what products are used
- what is the potential of a product for causing harm
- what is the chance of exposure
- how much people are exposed to, for how long and how often
- can the exposure be prevented and, if not, how is it adequately controlled.

Wherever safer products are available they should be used; where not, the exposure should be controlled. Exposure can be controlled by:

- providing good ventilation
- using the product only in recommended concentrations
- clearing up spillages or splashes immediately
- resealing containers immediately after use
- providing safe storage
- using personal protective equipment.

This information is taken from COSHH Regulations – A Guide to Health and Safety of Salon Hair Products – www.coshh-essentials.org.uk

Further guidance for COSHH risk assessment

The Hair and Beauty Industry Authority (Habia) produces and continually updates a comprehensive information guide for hairdressers. The *Health and Safety Implementation Pack for Hairdressers* is bought on an annual subscription. This pack comprises of a strong, hard cover, four-ring binder

GOOD PRACTICE/HEALTH & SAFETY

1   Read the instructions on the label of each chemical or product in your salon.

2   Further information for each individual type of product can be found in the *Guide to Health and Safety in the Salon Booklet*, or by using the manufacturer's data sheet.

3   If the product could cause harm, list it on the risk assessment form (see example risk assessment form on p. 20) together with the risk and who is at risk.

4   Using the information provided on the label, decide on the level of risk. (From your previous experience with the routine chemicals that you use at work, such as bleach, tint or perming solutions, you'll be able to decide the degree of risk.)

5   Decide how you are going to minimise and control the risk. Try to replace a high risk product with a lower risk product. If this is not possible, try decide how you go on to control risk, remembering that personal protective equipment (PPE) is only to be used as a last resort.

6   In some cases you may need to replace certain products, obtain further information, or source better personal protective equipment. This can be documented as an ongoing action plan, making sure that all relevant members of staff understand the actions that have been taken.

7   Discuss the completed risk assessment with your staff and make sure that they are fully trained to use all products safely.

8   Remember to review your COSHH assessment on a regular basis and don't forget to add in any new products that have been introduced to the salon and keep all data sheets filed safely for future reference.

Information courtesy of (Habia) *The Official Health & Safety Implementation Pack for Hairdressers*

with clearly defined sections. These cover all the necessary aspects of health and safety legislation, combined with ready to use checklists, policy documents and tailor-made systems. Also included within the pack are a number of official documents, advisory leaflets and essential emergency signs. Habia's recommended method for undertaking risk assessments is particularly useful and easy to follow, with pullout, ready-to-complete forms. The Good Practice information for undertaking COSHH risk assessment is based on their recommended system.

Electricity at Work Regulations 1989

The Electricity at Work Regulations 1989 cover the installation, maintenance and use of electrical equipment and systems in the workplace. Equipment must be adequately checked by a qualified electrician on a yearly basis. An electrical testing record should be kept for each piece of equipment, which should clearly show:

- electrician's/contractor's name, address, contact details
- itemised list of salon electrical equipment along with serial number (for individual identification)
- date of inspection
- date of purchase/disposal.

COSHH Action Plan

habia
standards · information · solutions

Staff member responsible: **Mary Murphy**   Date: **1st September 2005**   Review dates: **1st December 2005**

Problem requiring attention	Priority high/med/low	Action to be taken	Staff member responsible	Completion date		Result
				Target	Actual	
Staff complaining that Xedos Perm is making clients and staff feel nauseous and faint.	High	Contact manufacturer for advice. Look for alternative product. Do not use this product.	Mary Murphy	30/09/05	01/09/05	Manufacturer can only suggest using product in well ventilated area.
						Product will not be used in salon again. Newline Perm has been ordered and
						the manufacturer has not experienced any bad reactions with this. Staff to be
						trained to monitor its use carefully and report any problems to Mary Murphy.

HSIP2c

RIDDOR form HMSO

Health and Safety (First Aid) Regulations 1981

(See p. 14.)

Reporting of Injuries, Diseases and Dangerous Occurrences Regulations 1995 (RIDDOR)

Under these regulations there are certain diseases and groups of infections that if sustained at work are notifiable by law. So if any employees suffer a personal injury at work which results in either:

- death
- major injury
- more than 24 hours in hospital
- an incapacity to work for more than three calendar days

you must report them to the incident contact centre. In addition to this, if a member of the public or salon visitor is injured within the salon and taken to hospital, this is also reportable.

Certain industrial diseases are reportable using form F5208A and these include occupational asthma or dermatitis (but only if supported and notified by the employee's doctor).

Other accidents that occur within the salon must also be recorded. Entries must be kept up to date within the *accident record book* (see p. 14).

Health and Safety (Information for Employees) Regulations 1989

The regulations require the employer to make available to all employees, notices, posters and leaflets in either the approved format or those actually published by the Health & Safety Executive (HSE).

The Health and Safety Law leaflet is available in packs of 50 from HSE Books Box 1999, Sudbury, Suffolk CO16 6FS tel. 01787 881165. Other useful HSE publications are:

- *Essentials of Health and Safety at Work* (ISBN 0 7176 0716)
- *Writing your Health and Safety Policy Statement* (ISBN 0 7176 0425)
- *Successful Health and Safety Management* (ISBN 0 7176 0425)
- *A Guide to RIDDOR* (ISBN 0 7176 0432 2)
- *Step by Step Guide to COSHH Assessment* (ISBN 0 11886379 7) or online information at www.cosh-essentials.org.uk
- *First Aid at Work* (ISBN 0 7176 0426 8)

Fire Precautions Act 1971 and Fire Precautions (Workplace) (Amendment) Regulations 1999

(See pp. 11–14.)

Health and Safety (Display Screen Equipment) Regulations 1992

These regulations cover the use of computers and similar equipment in the workplace. Although not generally a high risk, prolonged use can lead to eye strain, mental stress and possible muscular pain. As more hairdressing salons now use information technology it is becoming a major consideration for employees.

It is the employer's duty to assess display screen equipment and reduce the risks that are discovered. They will need to plan the scheduling of work so that there are regular breaks or changes in activity and provide information training for the equipment users. Computer users will also be entitled to eyesight tests which will be paid for by the employer.

SCIENCE BIT! DID YOU KNOW: ELECTRICAL FUSES ?

Different items of electrical equipment have differing power consumption ratings. This is measured in watts (1000 watts = 1 kilowatt).

A powerful, salon hand dryer would typically be rated at 1300 watts (1.3kW)

The power rating of the washing machine may be more than 2.2kW

What fuse should I use?

Up to 750 watts a 3 amp fuse

750 to 1200 watts a 5 amp fuse

1200 to 3000 watts a 13 amp fuse

Health and Safety Law

What you should know

HSE Health & Safety Executive

Health and Safety Law HMSO

Manual Handling Operations Regulations 1992

These regulations apply in all occupations where manual lifting occurs.
They require employers to carry out a risk assessment of the work processes
and activities that involve lifting. The risk assessment should address
detailed aspects:

● any risk of injury
● the manual movement that is involved in the task
● the physical constraints that the loads incur
● the work environmental constraints that are incurred
● the worker's individual capabilities
● steps and/or remedial action to take in order to minimise the risk.

Provision and Use of Work Equipment Regulations (PUWER) 1998

These regulations refer to the regular maintenance and monitoring
of work equipment. Any equipment, new or secondhand, must be suitable
for the purpose that it is intended. In addition to this they require that
anyone using this equipment must be adequately trained.

Code of Hygiene for Hairdressers and Barbers (Habia)

All hairdressers and **barbers** are subject to various pieces of legislation
paramount among which are the *Health and Safety at Work Act 1974, South
Yorkshire Act 1974, South Yorkshire Act 1980* (registration) and the Byelaws.
This code is intended as a guidance to fulfilling these obligations.

General

1 All premises must be kept in a clean condition.
2 All fixtures and fittings should be of such material as to be easily
  cleanable, e.g. fabric covered chairs not suitable. All surfaces should be
  wiped down with a disinfectant regularly throughout the day.
3 All tools or instruments which come into contact with a customer must
  be sterilised before use on each customer (see below for appropriate
  methods).
4 All towels and other items which come into contact with customers must
  be clean and used only once before being washed on a high
  temperature cycle.
5 All gowns should be washed regularly and should any contamination or
  soiling with blood etc. occur that gown should not be reused until it has
  been washed on a high temperature cycle.
6 Solid soap, powder puffs, alum blocks or sponges should not be used.
7 A shaving brush must only be used for the first lather, once shaving has
  commenced the brush cannot be used.

8 Styptics should only be applied using disposable pads, e.g. cotton wool or swabs.

9 Powder should be applied using a spray.

10 Where clippers are used they must be sterilised between customers and if the skin is cut the clipper blades must be removed immediately, washed carefully and then sterilised.

11 The use of razors should be restricted to either disposable or cut-throat razors with disposable blades (e.g. Magic or Alcoso). The blades must be discarded after each customer and the holder washed and sterilised.

- Electric razors should not be used because of sterilisation difficulties.
- Cut-throat razors with integral blades must not be used.
- The disposable razors and blades must be discarded in an approved 'Sharps Disposal' box clearly marked 'Danger Contaminated Needles'.
- These boxes must be disposed of only to an authorised incinerator.
- Details of a suitable collection service are available from the Environmental Services Directorate.

Barbicide *Courtesy of Ellisons*

Personal hygiene

1 Hands should be washed before every client.

2 Any skin problems, cuts or boils must be covered with a waterproof, impervious dressing. Dermatitis or similar condition on the hands or arms should be covered using disposable seamless gloves changed for each customer.

3 Clean, washable overalls must be worn and must be changed if contaminated or soiled by any blood or other body fluid. Dirty overalls should be washed on a high temperature programme.

Disinfection and sterilisation procedures

1 All equipment once used should be disinfected or sterilised (according to contamination) before reuse and should be divided into plastic items – combs, brushes, etc., and metal items – scissors, razors, etc.

2 The plastic items should be rinsed and all hair removed. Any items contaminated by blood or body fluid must be handled with care to ensure that the contaminated area does not come into contact with any broken skin.

3 These should then be placed in a solution of hypochlorite until required.

4 The metal equipment should be sterilised, ideally in an autoclave.

Autoclaves may be automatic and go through a cycle with appropriate holding times, otherwise the times and temperatures shown in the table must be achieved.

Temperature	Holding times
121°C	15 minutes
126°C	10 minutes
134°C	3 minutes

An alternative to an autoclave is to boil all equipment for 30 minutes in a boiler specially designed for instruments.

The third alternative method for dealing with metal instruments is to rinse away visible contamination. Care must be taken to avoid touching any contamination, especially with areas of broken skin. The instruments must then be placed in a solution of glutaraldehyde for at least 30 minutes. It is advisable to use disposable razors.

Disinfectants

The two most commonly used disinfectants are hypochlorite and glutaraldehyde. These do not sterilise, i.e. kill all known germs, but do reduce the number to the extent that there is very little danger of infection.

- *Hypochlorite* (sold commercially as Milton or bleach) is corrosive to metals and therefore can only be used for wiping down work surfaces, chairs, etc. and for soaking combs, brushes, etc. The solution should be made up freshly each day with a dilution of one part Milton to ten parts water or one part good quality bleach to one hundred parts water.

- *Glutaraldehyde* (sold commercially as Cidex or Totacide) can be used for wiping down all surfaces including metals and for soaking metal implements. The solution can be made up weekly according to manufacturers' instructions.

Started it	I know who is responsible for H+S and to report to them any hazards in the workplace	I understand and follow the salon's policy in respect to H+S practices and procedures	I always recognise hazards and potential risks at work and take appropriate action
☐	☐	☐	☐
I can identify the main areas of potential risk at work	I understand all the relevant H+S regulations applicable to work	I always carry out working practices according to the salon's policy	I've covered most of it!
☐	☐	☐	☐
I understand the implications of cross-infecting others	I can handle, use and work with materials, products and equipment safely	I understand the necessity of personal hygiene and presentation	I know the salon's policy and procedures in the event of fire or accidents
☐	☐	☐	☐
I know what would be considered unsafe practices at work	Done it all		CHECKER BOARD
☐	☐		

Self-test section

Quick quiz: a selection of different types of questions to check your knowledge

Q1 A is something with potential to cause harm.   Fill in the blank

Q2 Risk assessment is a process of evaluation to ensure safe working   True or False
    practices.

Q3 Select all that apply. Which of the following are environmental hazards: Multi-selection

                                Boxes of stock left in the reception area   ☐   1
                                        Stock items upon the shelves   ☐   2
                                          Wet or slippery floors   ☐   3
                                        Shampoo backwash positions   ☐   4
                                           Salon work stations   ☐   5
                                Trailing flexes from electrical equipment   ☐   6

Q4 First-aid boxes should contain paracetamol tablets.   True or False

Q5 Which of the following regulations relate to the safe handling of   Multi-choice
    chemicals?

                                                      PPE   ☐   a
                                                   RIDDOR   ☐   b
                                                    COSHH   ☐   c
                                                    OSRPA   ☐   d

Q6 All salons must have a written health and safety policy.   True or False

Q7 Which of the following records must a salon keep up to date by law: Multi-selection

                                            Telephone book   ☐   1
                                             Accident book   ☐   2
                                          Appointment book   ☐   3
                              Electrical equipment annual test records   ☐   4
                             Health and safety at work checklist   ☐   5
                                           Fire drill records   ☐   6

Q8 The regulations require employers to provide adequate   Fill in the blank
    equipment and facilities in case of an accident occurring.

Q9 What colour is the label on a dry powder filled fire extinguisher?   Multi-choice

                                                      Red   ☐   a
                                                    Cream   ☐   b
                                                    Black   ☐   c
                                                     Blue   ☐   d

Q10 A dry powder filled fire extinguisher can be used on all classes of fire.   True or False

chapter 2

CONSULTATION

Unit G9 Provide hairdressing consultation services
Mandatory

G9.1 **Identify client needs and wishes**

G9.2 **Analyse the hair, skin and scalp**

G9.3 **Make recommendations to clients**

G9.4 **Agree services with your clients**

Unit G6 Promote additional products or services to clients
Mandatory

G6.1 **Identify additional products or services that are available**

G6.2 **Inform clients about additional products or services**

G6.3 **Gain client commitment to using additional products or services**

What do I need to learn?

You need to know and understand:

- **The principles of positive communication, i.e. correct body language, listening skills, attention to detail and good customer care**
- **The technical aspects of hair and skin analysis and how that influences future actions**
- **How to negotiate and gain professional respect, whilst mutually benefiting from the relationship**
- **How to eliminate ambiguity arising from the use of technical language and terms**

What does it mean?

This chapter will explain how to carry out thorough, professional client consultation, combining the skills of effective communication with comprehensive analysis, enabling sound technical advice, routes to further services and treatments and product promotion.

What do I need to do?

- You need to be able quickly to gain sufficient information so that only suitable courses for action are taken.
- You need to gain customer confidence and trust so that a professional bond is created and maintained.
- You need to be able to maximise the relationship by enhancing and stimulating an ongoing business.

Other info

Related topics and other useful information:

- Hair tests
- Image analysis for consultation
- Promotion and selling
- Limiting and influencing factors
- Data protection
- Equal opportunities
- Consumer rights

KEY WORDS

Trichology The scientific study of the hair and scalp

Medical referral Any suspect infectious or contagious hair or skin conditions are a **contra-indication** and therefore no service can be provided. Medical referral to a doctor is essential

Incompatibility Refers to incomptible chemistry. When incompatibles are present within the hair – e.g. colour restorers, 'Just for Men' or compound henna – no organic chemicals can be used

A **critical influencing factor** is something that will affect the way in which a service is or can be carried out; for example, a double crown – this will influence the way in which the hair can be cut in order to camouflage the growth pattern

CHECKERBOARD

At the end of this chapter the checkerboard will help to jog your memory on what you have learned and what still remains to be done. Cross them off with a pencil as you cover each of its topics. (See p. 81.)

INTRODUCTION

This chapter combines two mandatory units and covers the following seven elements:

G9   Provide hairdressing consultation service

    G9.1   Identify client needs and wishes

    G9.2   Analyse the hair skin and scalp

G9.3 Make recommendations to clients

G9.4 Agree services with your client

G6 Promote additional products or services to clients

    G6.1 Identify additional products or services that are available

    G6.2 Inform clients about additional products or services

    G6.3 Gain client commitment to using additional products or services

The content covers the essential information surrounding the aspects of client consultation: communication skills, technical evaluation and analysis and a range of other related information. The hairdressing industry exists by providing the levels of service to customers that they expect and are happy to pay for, but it does not end there. It is a constantly changing environment, with new fashions, techniques, products and services. Unless we continue to provide these new options to clients, then we stop advancing. Therefore it is essential that we build on experience and continue to develop the necessary skills.

> **REMEMBER** ✓
>
> You don't get a second chance to create a good first impression.

CONSULTATION

Consultation is arguably the most important service provided in a hairdressing salon. It may not be the most financially lucrative service, but it certainly underpins all the activities that take place within the salon and without it the business would not survive.

From the client's point of view, consultation is the process of how they develop a professional bond with their stylist. It is through consultation that the client learns so much about the salon and the stylist's professionalism, individual care and attention. Consultation is a service, however, that is often 'squeezed into or bolted on to' other booked services. If it is rushed, the risk of unexpected outcomes or possible disaster is heightened. If too much time is taken, it will often erode into the time given over to providing the technical service. This causes a 'knock-on' effect that will either make the stylist and client run late or not provide enough time to conduct the full service. Drawing the correct balance is essential. Enough time must be provided to:

- gain the client's trust and professional respect
- use visual aids either brought by the client or available from the salon
- conduct an analysis of the starting situation
- discuss the client's expectations in line with the analysis
- negotiate and agree a mutually beneficial course of action.

During consultation a client begins to learn about your 'professional wizardry', the breadth and depth of technical knowledge and subject expertise, whereas the **communication** that develops and takes place during the repeated business of routine services takes on a very different relationship.

'So much to do, yet so little time' – the bond that develops during consultation sets the tone for an ongoing business relationship. A professional distance is created during consultation that does not happen at any other time. From the clients' perspective they are observing something as an outsider; they are able to sample the salon's ability to deliver without any commitment. It is therefore the one chance to maximise this

> **ACTIVITY: PUTTING CONSULTATION INTO PRACTICE**
>
> Client consultation can be practised within the salon with your work colleagues; the service ideally lends itself to role plays. So develop your communication and analytical skills by conducting consultation techniques upon each other.
>
> **Key skills: Communication**
>
> **2.1** Take part in discussions
>
> **2.2** Produce written materials
>
> **2.3** Use images
>
> **2.4** Read and respond to written material

Lisa Neill at Kaliks, Aberdeen.
Photograph by John Rawson

Lisa Neill at Kaliks, Aberdeen.
Photograph by John Rawson

Karly Whitaker, Sarah Hodge
Hairdressing, Somerset & Devon

commercial opportunity by changing the level of commitment and creating a strong mutual respect and a first impression that will last.

Even if your regular customers are totally happy with what you provide, take the opportunity to redress the professional balance by treating them to the occasional consultation review.

ABOUT YOU

So what is it that makes a good hairdresser or, for that matter, what makes a bad one? What special attributes does it take to be an outstanding one? The media seem to have a number of stereotypes for the hairdresser. We have all at one time or another either seen on TV or heard on the radio some overused and very poor examples. At one extreme the hairdresser is portrayed as the female, dizzy-headed bimbo with little conversational content other than an apparent interest in their clients' holidays or where they are going out tonight. Then at the other end of the spectrum, we are all familiar with the squeaky voiced, 'camp' individual who refers to everyone as darling and whose acid tongue is as sharp as biting into a lemon. Needless to say, both of these stereotypes are hopelessly incorrect. Yes, such characters do exist, as in all aspects of life, but they are just an example of how the media parcels and packages, i.e. characterises, personalities into pigeon-holes. A recent government campaign to stamp out benefit fraud depicted a variety of practical tradespeople as criminals – needless to say hairdressing takes a part in this too.

So what are the true attributes of the professional hairdresser? One way of looking at it would be from the employer's point of view, that is, in the profile they draw up in the form of a person specification. When recruiting staff, in the early stages long before selection takes place, employers will create a basic profile for the person they are looking for. Obviously within this specification there will be references to the skills that are deemed essential and those that are preferred. However, technical skills are not the only attributes that employers are looking for. There will also be required personality features.

We could now look from the young, aspiring professionals' point of view. Why do they go into hairdressing? What are their expectations? Do they really know from the outset what is required of them? We know what the 'industry drivers' are in hairdressing and we can accept that they will already have been stimulated by fashions, celebrities and the music industry. They may also have friends or relatives employed within the industry. For the young people joining the craft after leaving school, it is unlikely that they know what is really needed. This key factor is one of the main reasons for why the industry has a high fall-out rate. In other words, many people join the craft with an uninformed, unrealistic view of what it is all about.

People joining the craft later in life, perhaps wanting a career change, probably have more idea. Why would that be? Well for one thing this group of people has experienced something over a long period of time that the others have not. They have all been clients. So what difference does that make? A huge one – these people have spent more time on the outside looking in than on the inside looking out – so their perspective is very different. They have had the opportunity to observe and receive at first hand all that the industry has to offer.

Hairdressing is about relationships – the relationships that are created through communication. Good and outstanding hairdressers have one thing in common: they are good communicators. Good communication skills are far more important than technical ability. We would like to think that hairdressing is very **creative** and artistic, and it is, but only in part. When we get the chance to use these skills it is wonderfully exhilarating. However, much of our work is routine. Hairdressing will always appeal to those with creativity and flair. It won't necessarily appeal to good communicators though, and at this point we see the division occurring.

So if we were to prioritise these essential attributes and put them in order we could create a list of important features, an ideal profile for the outstanding hairdresser, who should be:

- a good communicator
- interested in people
- willing to carry on learning
- able to empathise
- prepared to give service
- confident amongst others
- highly self-motivated
- in possession of a good memory
- not afraid to be an individual
- someone with a variety of interests and personal experience.

Why a good communicator?

Good communicators use a mixture of skills in their daily routines. This mix or 'toolbag' of skills comprises the following essential components.

1 Excellent listening skills. This is the ability to hear and understand what the client is saying. This is particularly useful when the one requiring/initiating a change is not the client in the chair.

2 A good speaker. Long silent pauses can often be uncomfortable. Knowing when it is right to speak or keep quiet is an invaluable interpersonal skill. During normal consultation you, the hairdresser, will be taking the lead. You will be asking questions; i.e. trying to elicit enough information in the time span available to make the right judgements. You will be weighing up what the client wants against the limitations arising from the analysis. You will be getting the client to agree on the various possible options and planning the necessary course of action.

In day-to-day, routine interactions with your client the balance changes. More often than not the client will have plenty to say, particularly when you ask them about what has happened since their last visit.

3 'Reading' skills. The ability to read situations, to understand what has been said or not said, is exceptionally useful. There are times when your client will look a certain way or say something that makes you think. In these situations, your ability to read the situation, i.e. perceptiveness in picking this up and responding appropriately, may have a crucial impact on your long-term relationship.

Ray Nightingale and Connor Kelly at Nightingales, for Schwarzkopf

Mark Pearson at Creator

Mark Pearson at Creator

Body language

We have always relied upon our ability to speak and hear as the natural way of communicating. In fact we use all of our **senses** to communicate. (Marketers are particularly interested in using all the sensory channels as a way of getting the message across.) But do we use all of our senses equally? The way we use our sight is probably at the top of the list. This is the fastest but very often unreliable way of drawing conclusions.

In the animal world the main form of communication and interaction from one creature to another is through body language. The cat that is alarmed at being confronted by a dog on the street turns sideways on and hunches up. This makes him look larger than he actually is. Size means everything. You pull the dog away sharply and when you get home he sulks; he gets right in your view and turns his back to you. The positioning, posturing and mannerisms of animals all mean something, conveying very clear and strong messages.

We too express our interest and attitudes by **non-verbal communication** through eye contact, posture and general body positioning. So it is very important that we send the right message, particularly when dealing with clients and potential customers.

Eye contact

Always maintain eye contact when in conversation with your client. Where possible, maintain the same eye level. For example, when you carry out a consultation with the client and she is seated, sit beside her or opposite her. Standing over or above her and looking down will convey a feeling of authority, and might appear as if you are trying to assert yourself and take control. This is threatening, intimidating and definitely the wrong signal to send to a potential client.

Body zones

People have a comfort zone. This the space around the body with which they feel at ease. Obviously this space or distance from the body of this space is notional and it varies from person to person. Within a close, intimate relationship, shared proximity may be welcome, but an uninvited invasion of this space is at best very uncomfortable and at worst menacing or threatening.

Posture/body position and gestures

Much has been written on the subject of **body language** and the psychological effects that it has on those *reading it*. This is far too complex a subject to address in a few simple paragraphs. It is a skill that develops over time and once learnt is never forgotten. However, there are certain obvious rules that can help to convey the right message and create a right impression:

- Slouching in the salon or at reception looks very unprofessional.
- Folded arms and the crossing of arms on the chest are protective gestures and portray a closed mind or show defensiveness.
- Open palms as a gesture supporting explanation or information, with hands at waist height, with palms upwards, indicate that the person has nothing to hide. This is interpreted as openness or honesty.

By Mahogany www.mahogany.co.uk

- Scratching behind the ear or the back of the neck whilst listening indicate that the listener is uncertain or does not understand. Rubbing the nose whilst listening can indicate that you don't believe what you are hearing.
- Talking with your hand in front your mouth may lead the listener to believe you are not being honest. You're hiding yourself behind your gestures.

These forms of communication are only an indication of feelings and emotions. In isolation they may not mean anything at all. However, collectively they can convey a very clear message. Make sure that you send the appropriate signals and look interested, keen, ready to help and positive. Above all show you can listen.

Why interested in people?

Having an interest in other people is essential. Anyone who enters the industry thinking 'I like hairdressing, I always have, ever since I used to style my doll's hair. I can even cut my family's hair, and they think it's OK too' is unfortunately going to learn a hard lesson very quickly. This may be a great starting point, having the interest and basic practical dexterity is very useful, but it's like a one-way street. Hairdressing is not just a practical service carried out in isolation, it is also about developing an *interactive community*. An employer who creates a business develops a community by default. Consciously or subconsciously the community of clients that he

ACTIVITY: BODY LANGUAGE

During your break ask your fellow staff members to identify a range of body language gestures. Create a table to record this information. Then later collectively deliberate on the meaning of each gesture. *Is everyone getting the same message?*

Key skills: Communication

2.1 Take part in discussions

2.2 Produce written materials

2.3 Use images

2.4 Read and respond to writtten material

Desmond Murray

develops has one shared interest. These clients (many of whom have found the salon from links through other external groupings such as friends, work associates, club memberships, etc.) have *bought into* the salon's overall image, synergy, ambience, range of technical services and the staff employed within the establishment.

However, in order to retain the goodwill and loyalty of the clientele, they need to be stimulated. This can only take place when an interaction occurs. Therefore, the stylist plays the key role in maintaining that bond. Clients do not remain with stylists who do not *continue* to stimulate them. Conversely, a hairdresser cannot be all things to all people so often it is teamwork, the collective application of *customer* care afforded by all the staff members, that strengthens the communal bond. The relationship exists because of shared interests. From this we start to see that good technical skills, i.e. hairdressing practical skills, are not enough; they are only part of the story. A sincere *genuine* interest in other people is essential.

Why willing to keep learning?

The truism that you never stop learning is a little bit overplayed and in an occupation where you constantly meet people it is the general fact. Hairdressing is constantly changing. It changes in many ways. From the fashion point of view it is near the leading edge. The main *drivers* for 'street fashion' are:

- *The music industry* – leading bands and artists are *produced* and *groomed* by professional stylists. It is the job of the *style director* to create a unique image that applies to the artist. Behind that image is a theme or thread, a working brief that the stylist must keep to. Hence, from the many layers of *paint* that are applied to create the overall image, i.e. clothes, make-up and hair, the final media image is produced.

- *Film and media industry* – stars and celebrities are born out of prime-time TV. Some will be presenting the news or forecasting the weather. Others will be from the nation's favourite soaps. The really big 'mega stars' are featured in the best 'blockbuster' films. Again, these personalities and their 'public' images have been professionally manufactured.

- *The fashion industry* – at the highest level are the couture fashion houses, the main *label names* and *big brands*, e.g. Versace, Lagerfeld, Paul Smith, Morgan, etc. These companies design and manufacture fashion itself, taking it round the world for display on stage in New York, Paris, London, Milan and Tokyo. The themes produced within these *high fashion* collections create the basis for the high street shops.

The one thing that they all have in common is media publicity. This is communicated via network broadcasting, video, DVD and popular magazines. This constant exposure to the public creates fashion and, at its basic, diluted level, it is recreated in the hair stylist's chair. It's not that hairdressers cannot achieve the same wonderful images as portrayed by the media, but their work is unfortunately more about the client's own lifestyle, confidence and skills. This is reflected during consultation and is the happy medium between *suitability*, *wearability* and *durability*.

So the ever-changing fashion world is just one thing to contend with, but without changing fashions hairdressing would be extremely boring or might

ACTIVITY ⇄

Hair fashions are derived from current trends:

1 Choose one 'supermodel' and *collect* over two fashion seasons a range of visual images from newspapers, magazines, internet, etc.

2 Create a *case study* of the individual's progress, media coverage and fashion shows. See how, and provide supporting *explanation* of why, the portrayed images change and develop over that time.

Key skills: Communication

2.1 Take part in discussions

2.2 Produce written materials

2.3 Use images

2.4 Read and respond to written material

not exist at all. People may choose to just grow their hair longer, never having it cut, or conversely just shave it off in front of the mirror at home. The more we work with people, our clients, the more we learn about them too.

Desmond Murray

Why an ability to empathise?

Clients don't come to the salon just when there is a celebration. Because hair grows at an even rate, they are likely to arrive when all sorts of things are going on in their lives and in yours too. It's easy to have sympathy. As hairdressers we do it every day. We can all relate to the *stories* told by our fellow staff over lunch or during breaks – the stories about our clients in certain situations and circumstances. That's life. However, having the ability to put yourself in somebody else's shoes is quite difficult. It's easy to say 'how sad', or 'you poor thing', but beware because true sincerity is an emotion that is easily *read* through your body language.

The close bond that forms between client and hairdresser is often tested at times like these. Not all clients can be upbeat all of the time. Due to modern living, people's lives have become more stressful. As a result there is an increase in *ambient negativity*. From the clients' point of view, the visit to the salon is not just about having their hair done, it's a lot to do with the feel-good factor too. As hairdressers we must recognise this. The hairdresser's role seems to involve a number of occupations – a little bit of social worker, a touch of psychologist, a bit of entertainer and a huge companion. In order to be this well-rounded individual, we need to *have and show* empathy. It is an extremely useful personal attribute for supporting and understanding others.

Why prepared to give service?

What is the difference if any between customer care and customer service?

Some people may think there's no difference at all, while others would disagree. The two are inextricably linked. If we think about terms another way and add an extra word before each, they may make a little more sense:

- *provide* customer service
- *maintain* customer care.

So we have to do one in order to achieve the other. I think we can all agree that we need to *keep* our customers. Without the repeated business of clients coming back on a regular basis we would not remain in work for very long. So our aim is to retain our clients and therefore maintain our customer care. Customer care is like being a *good shepherd*. We *farm* our *flock* by initially *going to market* to get them, developing, nurturing and tending to their needs and *fencing out* the predators, i.e. fending off the competition. If we get it right, we develop a long-lasting and fruitful relationship. If we get it wrong, one or two will stray away, setting a path for others to follow. From this simple analogy we can see that in order to keep our clients we constantly have to work at it. If we are to retain any goodwill, loyalty and professional respect we have to commit ourselves to providing customer service.

ACTIVITY: HANDLING CLIENTS

Discuss with your fellow staff members how different client personalities will affect the style and method of consultation. Discuss also how you can vary the consultation delivery to ensure that a mutually beneficial outcome is derived.

Key skills: Communication

2.1 Take part in discussions

2.2 Produce written materials

2.3 Use images

2.4 Read and respond to written material

Clive Boon at Boons. Photograph by John Rawson

Photo courtesy Goldwell

How is this done? Gaining new clients is not easy to start with. How do they find us? One way or another we have to invest in our future. We would have had to have spent a great deal of time, money, or both, trying to attract new people. New customers find us from the salon's image and reputation, its location, advertising campaigns, or personal recommendation – that all important word of mouth from already satisfied existing clients.

When the new potential customers make their first visit, they get to sample what we can offer. However, be warned. The professional standards you employ in the way you conduct that initial meeting set down the *basis* for your ongoing relationship. Maintain that service level and the client stays with you. Reduce that standard and the competition picks off another one.

Why confident amongst others?

Working in the salon is like performing in public. You are on show all the time not only to your own clients, but also to all the other salon visitors. You have to remain confident during consultation, particularly when meeting a new customer, because the pressure is really on. You have to take the lead in these situations because of the feelings that the potential customer is already experiencing. For her it is always quite a daunting challenge because she will have to:

- enter unfamiliar surroundings
- meet new people
- put her trust in your knowledge and understanding
- explain in her own words what she would like.

Therefore you will need to:

- break the ice immediately and put her at ease
- take control of the situation and steer the consultation process
- eliminate ambiguity arising from talking at cross-purposes or using technical jargon
- optimise the process to turn it into a mutually beneficial outcome.

Why highly self-motivated?

Motivation is the key. By being self-motivated we inspire those around us with whom we come into contact. Lack of motivation is a downward spiral: the less we contribute, the less we want to. Others see this and the rot sets in. We hear about demotivated people all the time, people not happy at work, troubled at home. Do other people talk about us and our workplace in the same way? If they do we have a serious problem. Even if they are right, the damage to the business could be irreparable.

The positive outlook is the only way of carrying on. Unfortunately our customers get to know and understand our mood swings only too well. As mentioned earlier, we are like actors on a stage. If we drop our mask for a moment the message will have been received and be a short time away from broadcast.

Why a good memory?

You may have done NVQ Level 2 some time ago. In covering that particular qualification you will have learned many scientific aspects of hairdressing that, if forgotten, will have a potentially disastrous impact on both you and the business. For example, if you forget to conduct the variety of tests such as skin tests, perm tests, incompatibility tests, etc. the consequences could be disastrous. You carry out these procedures as a matter of course. They are linked to practical procedures and are essential. So now you are thinking 'I do this all the time'. Good. That's one example of using your memory, but as far as the clients are concerned this is part and parcel of the job.

The truly great hairdresser will take this further. Because they have a genuine interest in each and every client, they will remember exactly what is going on. Here is an example. A client makes a repeat visit back to the salon following an initial visit and introduction two months previously. During that first consultation the stylist prescribes an initial reshaping and home care regimen to follow up the professional salon treatment, thus allowing the client to grow her hair over the next six months to the target length. She sits in the styling chair only to find that the same stylist says, 'Well what can I do for you today, a restyle cut and blow-dry?' The in-depth consultation and agreed plan for the future have been completely forgotten. The stylist's professional standing is compromised and a loyalty has been broken. It's as sensitive as that.

This is just the beginning. Through repeated visits we begin to learn more about our client's background, place of work, social interests and family, as they too learn more about us. Being able to remember where you left off during the last visit is perceived by the client to be an incredible personal skill. They are impressed that you have taken that much notice of them and their life. This will lift their beliefs in your professionalism and set you aside from the rest. It works!

Why not afraid to be an individual?

In life some lead and others follow. The professional bond that exists between you and your customers is very special. You may work in a shop but you are not just a retailer. Your clients will go into a clothes shop and browse through the rails. When they find something that interests them, they will quickly make up their minds about its suitability, how much wear it will give them and whether they can afford it. Regardless of the person who then comes up to sell the item to them, they have already *bought into* the idea so the handling of the sale is fairly circumstantial.

This is not the same in hairdressing. Clients buy from hairdressers that they identify with and respect. In the majority of situations it is easier to take control of the communication during the salon visit, rather than letting the client take the lead. This occurs quite naturally for those who are more individualistic.

When children are at school age they tell their parents and friends that they want to be an individual, they want to be different. This is seldom the case.

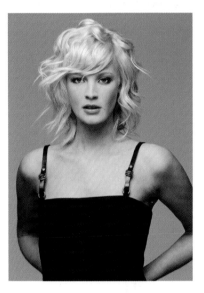

Robin Callender at McMillan Hair

Robin Callender at McMillan Hair

They have to have the same trainers or particular shoes. They need to look a certain way to fit in. Very few children want to stand out in a crowd. So in their search for individuality they find comfort and security by doing exactly the same as everyone else.

Later in life as adults we find that strong characters and individualistic personalities are often alluring. This change of view develops with maturity. It is less important for people to fit in and therefore there is a wider acceptance of people who are different. We may have developed a good rapport with our own customers, but we don't know how others perceive us. What we do know is that our personality has played a big part in maintaining our clients' goodwill and continuing relationship.

Why have a variety of interests and personal experience?

Clients may admire what you do for them in the salon; otherwise they wouldn't return. However, your hairdressing skills are plain to see. You don't need to bang on about technical issues. Very few people are inspired by 'know-it-alls'. They are interested in you as a person. It's difficult for others to see us in any other context than what we do. This is a naturally occurring physiological pattern. Most of us tend to create patterns as a way of remembering things. That's why certain images conjure up linked thoughts, or smells invoke certain situations. Likewise we often compartmentalise people. When we see someone in an unconnected situation we temporarily misplace them saying, 'I didn't recognise you without your work uniform on.'

People are interested in all sorts of social activities, sports and leisure pastimes. It's OK to be into extreme sports, butterfly collecting or wood carving. It stimulates good conversation, genuine interest and the real life experiences that we all like to talk about.

ABOUT THE CLIENT

Introduction

Customer expectation has never been higher. During the latter part of the 1990s and through to the present day there has been a major change in the way that businesses relate and communicate with their customer base. Information technology is now the driver of successful businesses and dominates the core activities of all business operations, giving companies that competitive edge. This advantage has automated many of the traditional business **systems**, enabling companies to react faster to a changing environment. However, this technology still remains to make any significant impact on the majority of hairdressing businesses, save the larger chains and groups which account for less than 10 per cent of the sector.

There are two significant factors that underline this strange anomaly. At present, in this transition away from the traditional ways of doing business and moving towards automated systems, two things seem to be denuding customer confidence in modern company practice:

- accountability
- customer care.

These key issues will be addressed in the not too distant future, but they do give hairdressing a significant boost in its current inability to harness technology.

Large businesses will deny these accusations, but the facts are clear. The utilisation of information technology has so far removed direct contact between people and the distinct benefits of face-to-face business. The swift moves by large corporations to set up call centres (many overseas) to handle business-2-customer services have yet to create a 'truly' satisfied customer base. This modified customer relationship occurs in many other arenas such as automated banking, insurance, household utility companies etc.

What is interesting though is the emerging fact that if customers think they are benefiting in some way, such as getting a good deal, then the *rough handling* becomes acceptable; e.g. internet bookings for travel, holidays, shopping, etc.

The distinct advantage of hairdressing is the one-to-one communication we enjoy with our clients. This relationship ensures that both the key factors – accountability and customer care – are brought into play. From a psychological point of view, we have about ten seconds from the first eye contact to convey the right professional image. The client will consciously or subconsciously analyse what she sees. Therefore, our appearance is as important as our expression. If our body language is welcoming, we are maintaining a professional level of communication.

Who are we dealing with?

The analytical skills used during client consultation will at a higher professional level draw down on the objective and the subjective. These aspects are not examined at Level 2 as we take a more *prescriptive* view of the client before us. At Level 2 the stylist makes a number of observations, looking for influencing factors that control their thinking and arriving at a technically sound course of action. Fine.

At NVQ Level 3, through the very experience of working with people we modify the way that we approach the work in hand. We start to work *intuitively*. In actual fact we subconsciously draw information from the client that shapes the way in which we arrive at a conclusion. It is a natural thought process that makes us look for patterns. In finding those patterns we then sort them into order and compartmentalise them. Obviously, different people will do this to a different extent. The individual who tries to approach things in a logical, systematic way will do this more than someone who does not. Unfortunately, we need to do this, albeit subconsciously, as this gives us the professional edge. The artistic stylist who just visualises the perfect style for their new client without any previous analysis, saying 'leave it to me', is playing Russian roulette. When it works it is fantastic, but the law of percentages is against it. So what information do you need in order to get it right?

Subjective and objective analysis

The objective or technical analysis is covered later and includes all the critical influencing factors that need to be considered along with the variety of tests which may need to be undertaken. The subjective analysis takes on board a variety of *abstract* issues and later in this chapter provides new thinking for creative, professional client consultation.

SUBJECTIVE ANALYSIS

This type of analysis starts at the point when you first meet your new client. Unlike objective analysis, it will seldom change. Some physical aspects relating to the client's hair will change as a result to external influences, e.g. different treatments and services, prescribed drugs, even cutting, but the underlying aesthetic aspects are seldom changed. So what sorts of things are you looking for or going to encounter?

As the stylist you only get one chance to make a good first impression with the client. But what *impressions* should you be noticing that will have an impact on the choice of style and service?

- image/personality types
- colour co-ordination.

Image/personality types

The client's image and **personality** type should be a major influence in consultation, especially for cutting, colouring and perming services. If the style choice is wrong from the outset, then, regardless of technical analysis, you cannot make the best of your client. Our image and personality are what make us individual and are expressed partly through the way we dress and wear colours. They are expressed even more in the physical aspects that cannot easily be changed: natural facial features, body shape, colour of skin and eyes. The main image and personality types for hairdressing purposes fall into four categories: dramatic, classic, natural and romantic. They are all very different so if we do not acknowledge these basic rules how is it possible to get the hairstyle right?

Dramatic

This strong image is self-explanatory and the meeting with the dramatic client is easily recognised.

Dramatic Antea
Essensuals: Sacha Mascolo-Tarbuck

General identification: dramatic image/personality		
Features	*Clothes*	*Hair*
• Often tall and slim • Striking, sometimes sharp and prominent features • Strong, linear or angular bone structure • Attractive, even exotic in appearance • Generally strong, pronounced make-up	• Comfortable in fashion extremes – either straight lines, tailored suits and 'chic' haute couture or full, flowing fabrics • Generally strong colours or elaborate/ exotic prints	• Strong linear shapes. Angles, texture • Head-hugging graduations • Happy with contrastingcolours • Movement and direction without curls • Likes definition from finishing products

Natural

The natural or casual image is often portrayed as a sporty type look.

Natural Gabriella
Essensuals: Sacha Mascolo-Tarbuck

General identification: natural image/personality		
Features	*Clothes*	*Hair*
• Ranges from tall and sturdy to petite and 'boyish' • Ranging from square to extremes – either • Often athletic, swift moving • Pretty, with a perky disposition • Softer make-up looks	• Comfortable in sportswear, jeans and jumpers • Suits casual or chic looks • Tailored suits, skirts, etc. • Natural textured fabrics, linens, raw silks, denims	• Soft ambiguous shapes, textured • Layered hairstyles with feathered outlines • Suits harmonising shades and tones • Movement and direction, including waves and curls • Suits subtle definition from styling and finishing products

Classic

The classic image is 'timeless' – never really in fashion, but never far away either.

Classic Katie
Essensuals: Sacha Mascolo-Tarbuck

General identification: classic image/personality		
Features	*Clothes*	*Hair*
● Any body shape that is balanced and in proportion ● Appears often a little conservative ● Face ranges from linear or angular bone structure to softer wider face shapes ● Not adventurous ● Generally a careful balanced make-up style	● Comfortable in sportswear, ● Not happy in fashion extremes, better suited to tailored, more formal apparel ● Also sporty chic separates ● Not always having to follow the latest fashions ● Generally plain colours not strong, 'busy' printed fabrics	● Strong or defined linear shapes, angles, texture ● One-length styles and bobs, or graduations and layered ● Suits subtle harmonising shades and tones ● Often straighter hair, possibly movement and direction, no curls ● Doesn't like strong finishing products

Romantic

The romantic image shouts femininity with high grooming and high maintenance hair.

Romantic Irene
Essensuals: Sacha Mascolo-Tarbuck

General identification: romantic image/personality		
Features	*Clothes*	*Hair*
● Exudes femininity, often curvaceous or even fuller figures ● Face shapes range from wide and soft to heart and oval shapes ● Often beautiful or alluring special features	● At best in evening wear ● Doesn't suit tailored chic clothes ● Suits satin, silk, brocades, velvets, the more sophisticated fabrics and lacy looks ● Always will accessorise with jewellery, feels undressed without it	● Soft ambiguous shapes, textured ● Highly worked finishes ● Suits harmonising shades and tones ● Movement and direction ● Curls and waves especially ● Suits subtle definition from styling and finishing products

Colour co-ordination

The other aspect of the subjective analysis has already been addressed by the fashion industry. However, very little information is available in text for hairdressing and recently it has been of particular interest to the colour manufacturers, e.g. Wella, L'Oréal, Matrix, etc. Obviously, these companies benefit from hairdressers' practical procedures involving colour. You too can benefit by understanding more about colour co-ordination, colour psychology and their applications with your customers.

So what is colour co-ordination and how is it applied to hairdressing? Understanding your client's needs and being able to make an informed opinion about a suitable course of action is far more challenging at a higher professional level. It is doubtful that your client has any understanding of the number of variables you must take on board in order to make the right decision and come up with the perfect solution.

Lee Preston

People and *art and design* are permanently linked. This is not an 'arty' claim or 'soundbite' but an observation on life. The simplest way that this statement is proven is by the clothes that we wear. We all know that the image we portray is conjured up by the total, visual expression we convey to others. So therefore the *sum total* of our image is made up from a formula of elements or components, each varying in weight and value.

As an art and design aspect, clothes convey colour, shape, form and quality. These are easily changed and a new vision can be created. So outwardly the visual expression is modified for functional or aesthetic reasons. Equally as important is the feeling gained inwardly – the way that clothes can make us feel about ourselves.

Saks Premier Collection

Hair styling is one of the elements that makes up the sum total of our image. It differs from clothing because it is a permanent physical aspect of our bodies. It can be changed, managed, looked after or neglected. But other than shaving it off, it is the basis, the starting point, of that visual formula. In order to get colour right, we need to understand some fundamental principles, technical applications and, at a higher level, have the knowledge about why some colours work while others do not. The fundamental principles and techniques are covered in Chapter 5 on colouring (p. 161).

Colour suitability

Colour can be measured by a number of different variables. The amounts of these variables collectively will give an overall effect. These terms are illustrated overleaf in terms of hairdressing as opposed to the graphic design and print industry.

In the tonal table we see that we have added further dimensions to the fundamental principles of depth and tone. It is illustrated this way to reveal other qualities that we should take on board.

Next we examine the difference between warm tones and cool tones.

Tonal table

Depth	Tone	Density	Contrast	Harmony
Lightness or darkness of colour	Range of colouration	Amount of saturation of colour	The ability of colours to stand apart	The ability of colours to fit together

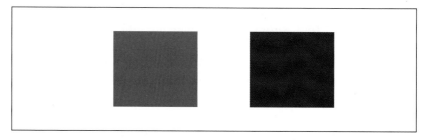

Warm and cool tones

From the warm/cool tones above we see that the *warm shade* contains gold/orange tones whereas the *cool shade* is a red/violet. Where we would normally consider red to be a hot shade, we see that certain reds have cool hues. The reason for this is the colour's basic make-up; i.e. a red with an orange or golden yellow base remains warm, whereas a red with a pink or mauve base is cool.

ACTIVITY: WARM AND COOL TONES

With another stylist, get out your manufacturer's permanent colour shade chart and together work through the ranges and decide collectively whether each shade is cool or warm. Then summarise and record your findings.

Key skills: Communication

2.1 Take part in discussions

2.2 Produce written materials

2.3 Use images

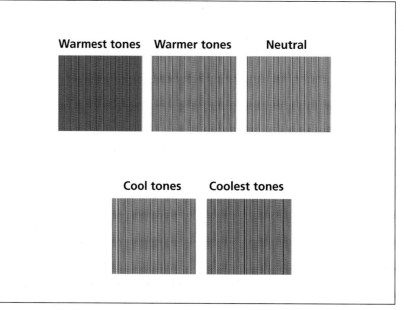

Warmest tones Warmer tones Neutral

Cool tones Coolest tones

Our clients' natural skin tones, eyes and hair make a big difference to what hair colour and colour techniques are suitable for them (colours and techniques, see p. 161). These natural differences of warm and cool tones are divided into four groups or categories: two are warm and two are cool. They are often referred to as Winter, Spring, Summer and Autumn. The reason for applying this seasonal analogy is to express a feeling. Hence a client who has Winter colouration has the coolest of skin tones. Conversely, the Autumn client conjures up the chestnut, golden and red tones associated with that season.

The 'Winter' client

The 'Winter' client has a variety of the cool skin tones, ranging from very pale 'whitish' skin with background undertones of pink or bluish hues. This colouration is typical of many European and North American people. Conversely, at the other end of the tonal spectrum, 'Winters' may also have 'olive' skin, with background undertones of khaki or greenish hues, or blue/black skin, which are both clearly cool. Because many people with these skin tones have very dark hair, this 'Winter' person can also be very dark skinned or of Oriental origin. The natural hair colour is not necessarily just very dark. Clients who have lost their hair colour and now have grey or greying hair may also fit into this category. Others will include dark ash blondes and mahogany hair colours.

'Winter' eye colours range from piercing blue and grey-green to dark brown. This is the only group of people that suits wearing black, white or signal red clothing.

'Winter' client Andrew Jose

'Winter' colour options

Natural hair colour	Full head colour	Highlights/partial colouring
Dark brown (3s + 4s)	Mahogany, burgundy	Violet reds, burgundy, etc.
		Violet browns, beige browns
Mahogany (4s + 5s)	Violet browns	Vibrant reds
Ash brown	Violet browns	Violet browns, beige, champagne
Grey		Beige blonde, champagne

Care should be taken when choosing the correct colour for 'Winters', as they are the 'coolest' of the four categories.

The 'Summer' client

The typical 'Summer' client has rosy pink skin tones with grey or blue eyes. Natural hair colours range through ash blonde, dark ash blonde, hazel and light beige brown. Similar to 'Winters', the 'Summer' client may have very fair skin with the blue undertones. This cool, fresh complexion, sometimes with freckles, is best accompanied by either pastel blues or pinks. Other options for clothes that work well are the naturals – beiges and creams.

'Summer' client Toni & Guy

'Summer' colour options		
Natural hair colour	*Full head colour*	*Highlights/partial colouring*
Hazel blonde (6s + 7s + 8s)	Beige blonde (8s + 9s)	Bleach highlights
	High lift blonde	Blush champagne, lightest beige blonde
Ash blonde (8s + 9s + 10s)	High lift blonde	Bleach highlights
	High lift ash blonde	Blush champagne, lightest beige blonde
Beige blonde (8)	High lift blonde	Bleach highlights, beige, champagne
Grey		High lift blonde highlights, blush champagne

The 'Spring' client

The warmer tones of the typical 'Spring' client are characterised immediately by golden, honey or red undertones within the hair. Often as children their hair colour starts life as very fair or sandy blonde. This changes by the mid-teens to the darker bases of 6 or 7, with hazel and often bronzed tones.

Their skin is always fair and ranges from pale with freckles to the lightest of orange hues such as ivory and peach. Their eyes are typically blue, green, blue/green or hazel.

'Spring' client Andrew Jose

'Spring' colour options		
Natural hair colour	*Full head colour*	*Highlights/partial colouring*
Auburn (5s + 6s + 7s)	Chestnut (5s + 6s)	Copper highlights
	Golden reds (8s)	Bronze highlights, lightest beige blonde
Hazel (7s + 8s)	Beige blondes (7s + 8s)	Fudge/honey highlights golden blonde, lightest beige blonde
Honey blonde (8s + 9s)	Hazel	Pale straw highlights, lightest beige blonde
Beige (8s + 9s)	Caramel (7s)	High lift blonde highlights
	Hazel (8s)	Fudge/honey highlights

The 'Autumn' client

The 'Autumn' client has the warmest of skin and hair colouration. This client often has peach skin tones, accompanied with freckles, and either dark golden or chestnut brown undertones. Also in this group are the strong vivid reds associated with the season. Most 'Autumns' will have green, hazel or brown eyes. They are the only ones who really suit the complementary mixtures of warm brown and orange apparel.

'Autumn' colour options		
Natural hair colour	Full head colour	Highlights/partial colouring
Spicy reds (7s + 8s)		Golden sand highlights, copper/blonde highlights, vivid copper highlights
Auburn (5s + 6s + 7s)		Copper highlights, bronze highlights
Chestnut brown (5s)		Copper/gold highlights
Dark golden brown (4s)		Copper highlights, bronze highlights

'Autumn' client
Antoinette Beenders, for Aveda

OBJECTIVE ANALYSIS

The biggest difference between consultation at Level 3 and Level 2 is that the L3 stylist will need to have a broader understanding of people. Experience enables you to combine improved communication skills with a wider range of technical skills and this is directly proportional to the ability to reach the desired result. So from this we can conclude that the Level 3 stylist (or someone with the same experience) is more likely to be able to handle a far greater range of people, personalities and their styling requirements.

There are two specific attributes that relate to this type of communication at L3 which you must take on board:

- control
- responsibility.

Taking control of the whole situation is essential. This will occur at the moment when the new potential client realises that it is you who is going to conduct the consultation. Everything is summed up (rightly or wrongly) by her and you in a few moments and, contrary to customer service beliefs, you will not be able to satisfy the client fully unless you are in charge of this situation. You have to guide and steer the whole process in order to satisfy the client and maximise the potential commercial benefits.

However, in taking charge and leading the client through this process you have to give something in return. *Every action has an equal and opposite reaction.* The cost for being allowed to lead is responsibility. In assuming control, you have to gain the trust of the client. This can only happen if you are prepared to shoulder the responsibility for the eventual outcome. So this is it, the big chance to get it right and win over another client into your following.

In the previous section we covered the more abstract aspects of client consultation. We now look at the physical features of hair and skin and the range of factors that should influence your judgement in the possible choices for styling and courses of action. These factors are fundamental to any client consultation. Therefore if you have previously covered them at L2 you will already be familiar with the variety of aspects examined. (For general information relating to carrying out the consultation see pp. 54–74.) This section will cover the topics shown in the table.

> **REMEMBER**
>
> Trust is hard earned. Gaining a customer's trust and loyalty takes time. Once you have earned this, the bond remains fragile, so handle with care.

Charlie Miller, Jason and India Miller

Topics pp. 54–74	
Structure of hair and skin	Cortex, cuticle, medulla, physical properties of hair and skin, hair follicle
Growth cycle of hair	Anagen, catagen, telogen
Hair texture	Coarse, medium, fine
Hair tests	Sensitivity test, strand test, colour test, test cutting, test curl, curl check, peroxide test, incompatibility test, elasticity test, porosity test
Infectious skin and scalp	Impetigo, scalp ringworm (tinea conditions capitis), head lice (pediculosis capitis)
Non-infectious skin and scalp	Folliculitis, dandruff (pityriasis conditions capitis), alopecia, seborrhoea, psoriasis, eczema
Hair defects	Split ends (fragilitis crinium), damaged cuticle, trichorrexis nodosa, monilethrix
Head and face shapes	Oval, round, rectangular, square, heart-shaped
Other important physical features	Hair growth patterns, ears, nose, eyes, etc.

Structure of hair and skin

Hair

The cross-section taken through the hair lengthways shown in the diagram provides us with a microscopic view of the three specific layers.

The *cuticle* is the outer layer of colourless cells which forms a protective surface to the hair. It regulates the chemicals entering and damaging the hair and protects the hair from excessive heat and drying. The cells overlap like tiles on a roof with the free edges pointing towards the tips of the hair. The amount of layers is proportional to hair texture. Hair with fewer layers of cuticle is finer than coarser hair types which have several layers. Hair in good condition has a cuticle that is tightly closed, limiting the ingress of moisture and chemicals. Conversely, hair that is in a dry or porous condition has damaged or partially missing cuticle layers. One simple indicator of cuticle condition relates to the time taken to **blow dry** hair. Hair in good condition will dry quickly in proportion to the amount of hair on the head (*density*). The closely packed cuticle allows the drier to chase the water from the hairshaft. Porous hair absorbs moisture and therefore takes far longer to dry and is unfortunately subjected to more heat, which exacerbates the problem.

The *cortex* is the middle and largest layer. It is made up of a long fibrous material which has the appearance of rope. If looked at more closely, each of the fibres is made up of even smaller chains of fibres. The *quality* and condition of these bundles of fibres will determine the hair's strength. The way in which they are *bonded* together has a direct effect upon curl and ability to stretch (*hair elasticity*). It is within this part of the hair that the natural hair colour is distributed. These pigments are diffused throughout the cortex and their colour(s) and rate of distribution determine the colour that we can see. It is also in this layer that both **synthetic** colours and permanent waves make the permanent chemical changes.

The *medulla* is the central, most inner part of the hair. It only exists in medium to coarser hair types and is often intermittent throughout the length. The medulla does not play any useful part in hairdressing processes and treatments.

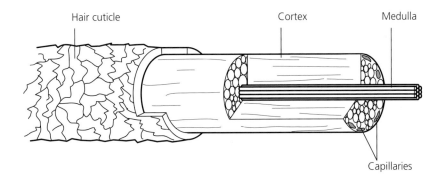

Parts of the hair shaft

Chemical properties of hair

The bundles of fibres found in the cortex are made from molecules of *amino acids*. There are about 22 amino acids in hair and the molecules of each contain atoms of elements in different proportions. Overall, the elements in hair are in approximately these proportions:

Chemical bonds within the hair:
carbon: 50% hydrogen: 7% nitrogen: 18%
oxygen: 21% sulphur: 4%

The amino acids combine to form larger molecules, long chains of amino acids called *polypeptides*, or, if they are long enough, *proteins*. One of the most important of these is keratin. **Keratin** is an important component of nails, skin and hair. It is this protein which makes them flexible and elastic. Because of the keratin it contains, hair can be stretched and compressed, curled and waved.

In hair, keratin forms long chains which coil up like springs. They are held in this shape by cross-links between chains. The three kinds of link are *disulphide bridges* (*sulphur bonds*), *salt bonds* and *hydrogen bonds*. Salt bonds and hydrogen bonds are relatively weak and easily broken, allowing the springs to be stretched out. This is what happens in curling. The normal, coiled form of keratin is called *alpha-keratin*. When it has been stretched, set and dried it is called *beta-keratin*. The change is only temporary. Once the hair has been made wet or has gradually absorbed moisture from the air, it relaxes back to the alpha state. Disulphide bridges are much stronger but these too can be altered, as in perming.

Physical properties of hair

Hair *naturally* contains a certain amount of water that lubricates it, allowing it to stretch and recoil. Hair that is dry and in poor condition is less elastic. Hair is *hygroscopic*; it absorbs water from the surrounding air. How much water is taken up depends on the dryness of the hair and the moistness of the atmosphere. Hair is also *porous*. There are tiny tube-like spaces within the hair structure and the water flows into these by *capillary*

Umberto Giannini

Hair: Lawrence Anthony Team; photography: Pat Mascolo; make-up: Pat Mascolo

action, rather like blotting paper absorbing ink. Drying hair in the ordinary way evaporates only the surface moisture, but drying over long periods or at too high a temperature removes water from within the hair, leaving it brittle and in poor condition. Damaged hair is more porous than healthy hair and easily loses any water, which makes it hard to stretch and mould.

Curled hair returns to its former shape as it takes up water, so the drier the atmosphere, the longer the curl or set lasts. Similarly, curling dry hair is most effective just after the hair has been washed because, although the surface is dry, the hair will have absorbed water internally. Blow-styling and curling with hot irons, heated rollers, hot combs and hot brushes all have similar temporary effects.

The skin

The skin is the largest organ of the body and if laid flat would cover an area of about 21 square feet. It forms the barrier to a multitude of external forces and is made up of many layers.

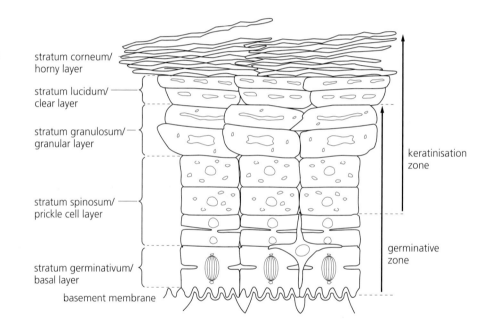

Section through skin

The epidermis

The epidermis is the front line of defence. This outer protective layer of the skin is called the *stratum corneum* and is a hard, cornified layer, consisting of 15 to 40 layers of flattened skin cells or corneocytes, which constantly migrate up from deeper regions and fully replace themselves about once a month. The *corneocytes* are filled with keratin and a fatty *lipid* that make a barrier to prevent loss of water through the skin.

Beneath the stratum corneum lie *keratinocytes* which produce keratin and form the building blocks of the epidermis. In the same area, *langerhans cells* scout for invading pathogens while *melanocytes* produce the pigment **melanin** that protects the skin from UV radiation. *Merkel* or nerve cells send messages via the nerve receptors to the brain to register sensation.

Alison Stewart, Glenrothes, Fife

The dermis

The dermis is the thickest layer of the skin. It is here that the hair follicle is formed. The dermis is made up of elastic and connective tissue and is well supplied with blood and lymph vessels. The skin receives its nutrient supply from this area. The upper part of the dermis, the *papillary layer*, contains the organs of touch, heat and cold, and pain. The lower part of the dermis, the *reticular layer*, forms a looser network of cells.

The subcutaneous fat

The subcutaneous fat lies below the dermis. It is also known as the *subcutis*, or occasionally as the *hypodermis*. It is composed of loose cell tissue and contains stores of fat. The base of the hair follicle is situated just above this area, or sometimes in it. Subcutaneous tissue gives roundness to the body and fills the space between the dermis and muscle tissue that may lie below.

The hair follicle

Hair grows from a thin, tube-like space in the skin called a hair follicle.

- At the bottom of the follicles are areas well supplied with nerves and blood vessels, which nourish the cellular activity. These are called *hair papillae*.
- Immediately surrounding each papilla is the *germinal matrix* which consists of actively forming hair cells.
- As the new hair cells develop, the lowest part of the hair is shaped into the *hair bulb*.
- The cells continue to take shape and form as they push along the follicle until they appear at the skin surface as *hair fibres*.
- The cells gradually harden and die. The hair is formed of dead tissue. It retains its elasticity due to its chemical structure and keratin content.

By Mahogany www.mahogany.co.uk

Oil glands

The oil gland, or *sebaceous gland*, is situated in the skin and opens out into the upper third of the follicle. Oil or *sebum* is secreted into the follicle and onto the hair and skin surface.

Sebum helps to prevent the skin and hair from drying. By retaining moisture it helps the hair and skin to stay pliable. Sebum is slightly acid – about pH 5.6 – and forms a protective antibacterial covering for the skin.

Sweat glands

The sweat gland lies beside each hair follicle. These are appendages of the skin. They secrete sweat which passes out through the sweat ducts. The ends of these ducts can be seen at the surface of the skin as sweat *pores*. There are two types of sweat gland: the larger, associated closely with the hair follicles, are the **apocrine** glands; the smaller, found over most of the skin's surface, are the *eccrine glands*.

Sweat is mainly water with salt and other minerals. In abnormal conditions sweat contains larger amounts of waste material. Evaporation of sweat cools the skin. The function of sweat, and thus the sweat glands, is to protect the body by helping to maintain the normal temperature.

The hair muscle

The hair muscle, or **arrector pili**, is attached at one end to the hair follicle and at the other to the underlying tissue of the epidermis. When it contracts it pulls the hair and follicle upright. Upright hairs trap a warm layer of air around the skin. The hairs also act as a warning system; for example, you soon notice if an insect crawls over your skin.

Hair growth

Robin Callender, at McMillan Hair

Hair is constantly growing. Over a period of between one and six years an individual hair actively grows, then stops, rests, degenerates and finally falls out. Before the hair leaves the follicle, the new hair is normally ready to replace it. If a hair is not replaced then a tiny area of baldness results. The lives of individual hairs vary and are subject to variations in the body. Some are actively growing while others are resting. Hairs on the head are at different stages of growth.

Stages of growth

The life cycle of hair is as follows:

- Anagen is the active growing stage of the hair, a period of activity of the papilla and germinal matrix. This stage may last from a few months to several years. It is at this stage of formation at the base of the follicle that the hair's thickness is determined. Hair colour too is formed in the early part of anagen.
- Catagen is a period when the hair stops growing but cellular activity continues at the papilla. The hair bulb gradually separates from the papilla and moves further up the follicle.
- Telogen is the final stage, when there is no further growth or activity at the papilla. The follicle begins to shrink and completely separates from the papilla area. This resting stage does not last long. Towards the end of the telogen stage, cells begin to activate in preparation for the new anagen stage of regrowth.

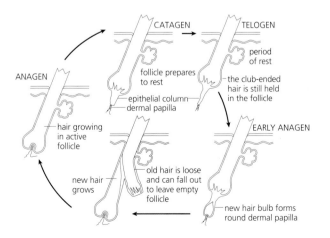

Hair growth stages

The new anagen period involves the hair follicle beginning to grow down again. Vigorous papilla activity generates a new hair at the germinal matrix. At the same time the old hair is slowly making its way up and out of the follicle. Often the old and new hair can be seen at the same time in the follicle.

In some animals most of the hairs follow their life cycle in step, passing through anagen, catagen and telogen together. This results in moulting. Human hair, however, develops at an uneven rate and few follicles shed their hair at the same time. (If all hairs fell at the same time we would have bald periods.)

Hair texture

Individual hair thickness is referred to as hair **texture** and the main types are:

- very fine hair
- fine hair
- medium hair
- coarse hair.

The main differences between the hair textures relate to the number of layers of cuticle.

> **REMEMBER: HAIR TEXTURE** ✔
>
> The more layers of cuticle that the hair has, the greater its resistance to absorbing moisture and chemicals. Therefore coarse hair in good condition can often take longer to perm than finer hair types.

Indicators of hair in good condition

Moisture levels within the hair are essential for maintaining good condition. We can see the evidence of this moisture from the shine that we associate with great-looking hair. 'Bad hair' denotes poor condition and the lack of shine is due to the unevenness of the hair's surface, i.e. the cuticle. A roughened cuticle surface is an indicator of either physical or chemical damage. Each of these states is difficult to correct. In mild cases of dryness, treatments can be applied to improve the hair's manageability and handling. In more serious situations of porous hair, the hair's ability to resist the ingress of chemicals and moisture is severely impaired. There are no long-lasting remedies for this so regular reconditioning treatments must be used.

Properties of good condition hair

- shine and lustre
- smooth outer cuticle surface
- strength and resistance
- good elasticity
- good natural moisture levels

Properties of poor condition hair

- raised or open cuticle
- damaged, torn hair shaft
- split ends

- low strength and resistance
- over-elastic/stretchy
- dry, porous lengths or end

Hair damage

Physical

- harsh or incorrect usage of brushes and/or combs
- excessive heat from styling equipment

Chemical

- hydrogen peroxide levels too strong
- **bleaching** products
- perm products either too strong or over-processing
- chlorine from swimming pools

Weathering

- excesses of sun and sea salts

Hair and skin tests

To minimise the likelihood of problems arising, there are a number of tests that you can carry out to help **diagnose** the condition and likely reaction of your client's skin and hair. These tests will assist you to decide what action to take before, during and after the application of hairdressing processes. You will need to record all these results onto the client's record file.

Strand test

A strand test or **hair strand** colour test is used to assess the resultant colour on a strand or section of hair after colour has been processed and developed. It is carried out as follows:

1 Most colouring products just require the time recommended by the manufacturer – check their instructions.
2 Rub a strand of hair lightly with the back of a comb to remove the surplus colour.
3 Check whether the colour remaining is evenly distributed throughout the hair's length. If it is even, remove the rest of the colour. If it is uneven, allow processing to continue, if necessary applying more colour. If any of the hair on the head is not being treated, you can compare the evenness of colour in the coloured hair with that in the uncoloured hair.

Colour test

This test is used to assess the suitability of a chosen colour, the amount of processing time required and the final colour result. Apply the colour or bleaching products you propose to use to a cutting of the client's hair and process as recommended.

Photo courtesy Goldwell

GOOD PRACTICE/HEALTH & SAFETY: SENSITIVITY TEST

(Also known as patch test or skin test)

The sensitivity test is used to assess the reaction of the skin to chemicals or chemical products. In the salon it is mainly used before colouring. Some people are allergic to external contact of chemicals such as PPD (found in permanent colour). This can cause dermatitis or, in more severe cases, permanent scarring of skin tissue and hair loss. Some are allergic to irritants reacting internally, causing asthma and hay fever. Others may be allergic to both internal and external irritants. To find out whether a client's skin reacts to chemicals in permanent colours, the following test should be carried out at least 24 hours prior to the chemical process.

Note: Skin testing is not just for new clients, it has now been found that clients can develop a sensitivity to chemicals through prolonged use of the same or similar products. Therefore periodic testing for adverse reactions is essential and should be carried out routinely from time to time.

1 Mix a little of the colour to be used with the correct amount of hydrogen peroxide – as recommended by the manufacturer.
2 Clean an area of skin about 8mm square behind the ear or in the fold of the arm. Use a little spirit on cotton wool to remove the grease from the skin.
3 Apply a little of the colour mixture to skin.
4 Cover the colour patch with a simple dressing to protect it. Ask your client to report any discomfort or irritation that occurs over the next 24 hours. Arrange to see your client at the end of this time so that you can check for signs of reaction.
5 If there is a *positive response*, i.e. a skin reaction such as inflammation, soreness, swelling, irritation or discomfort, do not carry out the intended service. Never ignore the result of a skin test. If a skin test showed a reaction and you carried on anyway, there may be a more serious reaction which could affect the whole body.
6 If there is a *negative response*, i.e. no reaction to the chemicals, then carry out the treatment as proposed.

Warning: In recent years there have been a growing number of successful personal injury claims made against salons where the necessary precautions have not been taken.

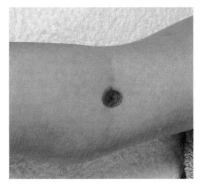

Skin test

REMEMBER: TYPICAL EXAMPLE OF CHEMICAL INCOMPATIBILITY

Henna is still widely used throughout the world as a hair and skin dyeing compound. In the UK people using natural henna will often add other ingredients such as coffee, wine, lemon juice, etc. to intensify the final colour. However, other countries also add compounds to henna; e.g. India and Turkey sometimes add iron ore deposits which are crushed into the powder to increase the 'reddening' effect. If this mix subsequently comes into contact with hydrogen peroxide (either through colouring or perming), a chemical reaction will take place. In the exchange that takes place permanent damage and breakage will occur.

Test cutting

In this test a piece of hair cut from the head is processed to check its suitability, the amount of processing required and the timing, before the process is carried out. The test is used for colouring, **straightening**, **relaxing**, reducing synthetic colouring, i.e. **decolouring**, bleaching and incompatibility.

Courtesy of Ellisons

Test curl

This test is made on the hair to determine the lotion suitability, the strength, the curler size, the timing of processing and the development. It is used before perming.

Curl check or test

This test is used to assess the development of curl in the perming process. The test is used periodically throughout a perm and for final assessment of the result.

Peroxide test

This test is made on hair that has been decoloured or stripped of its synthetic colour. The test is used to assess the effectiveness of the process and to check that no synthetic pigment remains. Any synthetic colour remaining will oxidise later and darken again within two or three days. If the hair darkens after testing, remove all the chemicals from the test section, then reapply the decolourant. It may take several applications to strip all of the unwanted colour.

Incompatibility test

Perm lotions and other chemicals applied to the hair may react with chemicals that have already been used such as home-use products. The incompatibility test is therefore used to detect chemicals/elements which could react with hairdressing processes such as colouring and perming. The test is carried out as follows:

1 Protect your hands by wearing gloves.
2 Place a small cutting of hair in a small dish.
3 Pour into the dish a mixture of 20 parts of 6 per cent hydrogen peroxide and one part ammonium thioglycolate (general purpose perm solution). Make sure that you are not bending over the dish to avoid splashing the chemicals on to your face or inhaling any resultant released fumes.
4 Watch for signs of bubbling, heating or **discolouration**. These indicate that the hair already contains **incompatible** chemicals. The hair should not be permed, coloured or bleached if there are any signs of reaction. Perming treatment might discolour or break the hair and could burn the skin.

Elasticity test

This test is carried out on a dry single hair and used to determine how much the hair will stretch and then return to its original position. It is an indicator of the internal condition of the hair's bonded structure and ability to retain moisture. By taking a hair between the fingers and stretching it you can assess the amount of spring it has. If the hair breaks easily, care needs to be taken before applying any hairdressing process and further tests are indicated – a test curl or a test cutting, for example. Natural healthy hair in good condition will be elastic and more likely to retain the effects of physical curling, setting or blow shaping longer. It will also take chemical processes more readily. Hair with little elasticity will not hold physical shaping or chemical processes satisfactorily.

Porosity test

The **porosity** test is used to assess the ability of the hair to absorb moisture or liquids – another indicator of condition. If the cuticle is torn or broken, it will soon lose its moisture and become dry. It may be able to absorb liquids quicker, but its ability to retain them is reduced. If the cuticle is smooth, unbroken and tightly packed, it may resist the passage of moisture or liquids. By running the fingertips through the hair, from points to roots, you can assess the degree of roughness. The rougher the hair, the more porous it will be and the faster it will absorb chemicals.

Hair and scalp diseases, conditions and defects

Diseases of the hair and scalp may be caused by a variety of infectious organisms. Signs or symptoms are presented which enable us to recognise them. Initial examination during consultation should be carried out before any hairdressing procedure is applied. If this precaution is not taken, there is a danger of cross-infection where both hairdresser and clients may contract and spread disease. Other hair and scalp conditions or defects may be due to abnormal formation or the result of a variety of chemical and physical causes. They are not infectious.

Infectious diseases

> **REMEMBER: HAIR'S NATURAL MOISTURE LEVELS** ✔
>
> The natural moisture levels in hair play a significant part in the way that hair responds to treatments and styling. If the natural levels can be retained following perming, colouring and bleaching the client's hair will remain manageable, easier to detangle and able to hold thermal styling effects for far longer.
> Deplete those natural levels and the hair becomes porous and will tangle easily, is less manageable and not able to hold a set for long. Pre-chemical treatments help to reduce the hair's moisture reduction.

SCIENCE BIT! DID YOU KNOW ?

Bacterial diseases

Condition	Symptoms	Cause	Treatment	Infectious
Folliculitis Inflammation of the hair follicles	Inflamed follicles, a common symptom of certain skin diseases	A contact bacterial infection, or due to chemical or physical action	Medical referral	Yes
Impetigo A bacterial infection of the upper skin layers	At first a burning sensation, followed by spots becoming dry; honey-coloured, crusts form and spread	A staphylococcal or streptococcal infection	Medical referral	Yes
Sycosis A bacterial infection of the hairy parts of the face	Small, yellow spots around the follicle mouth, burning, irritation and general inflammation	Bacteria attack the upper part of the hair follicle, spreading to the lower follicle	Medical referral	Yes
Furunculosis Boils or abscesses	Raised, inflamed, pus-filled spots, irritation, swelling and pain	An infection of the hair follicles by staphylococcal bacteria	Medical referral	Yes

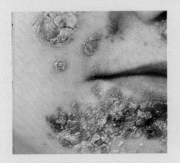

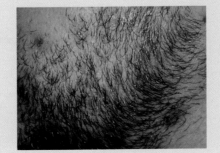

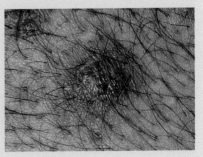

Impetigo Dr M H Beck

Sycosis Dr A L Wright

Furunculosis Dr A L Wright

SCIENCE BIT! DID YOU KNOW ?

Viral diseases

Condition	Symptoms	Cause	Treatment	Infectious
Herpes simplex (cold sore) A viral infection of the skin	Burning, irritation, swelling and inflammation precede the appearance of fluid-filled blisters, usually on the lips and surrounding areas	Possibly exposure to extreme heat or cold, or a reaction to food or drugs; the skin may carry the virus for years without exhibiting any symptoms	Medical referral	Yes
Warts (verrucae) A viral infection of the skin	Raised, roughened skin, often brown or discoloured. There may be irritation and soreness. Warts are common on the hands and face	The lower epidermis is attacked by the virus, which causes the skin to harden and skin cells to multiply	Medical referral	Yes

Herpes simplex Dr M H Beck

Warts Dr M H Beck

SCIENCE BIT! DID YOU KNOW ?

Animal (parasitic) infestations

Condition	Symptoms	Cause	Treatment	Infectious
Head lice (pediculosis capitis) Infestation of the hair and scalp by head lice	An itchy reaction to the biting head louse, 'peppering' on pillowcases and minute egg cases (nits) attached to the upper onto the hair shaft for hair shaft close to the scalp	The head louse bites the scalp feeding on the victim's blood. Breeding produces eggs, which are laid and cemented incubation until the immature louse emerges	Referral to a pharmacist	Yes
Scabies An allergic reaction to the itch mite	A rash in the skin folds around the midriff and on the inside of the thighs, extremely itchy at night	The itch mite burrows under the skin where it lays eggs	Medical referral	Yes

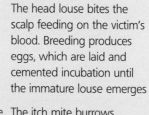

A head louse S Lewis

A louse egg (nit) BLM Health

SCIENCE BIT! DID YOU KNOW

Fungal diseases

Condition	Symptoms	Cause	Treatment	Infectious
Tinea capitis Ringworm of the head	Circular bald patch of grey or whitish skin surrounded by red, active rings; hairs broken close to the skin, which looks dull and rough. The fungus lives off the keratin in the skin and hair. This disease is common in children	Fungal infection of the skin or hair	Medical referral	Yes

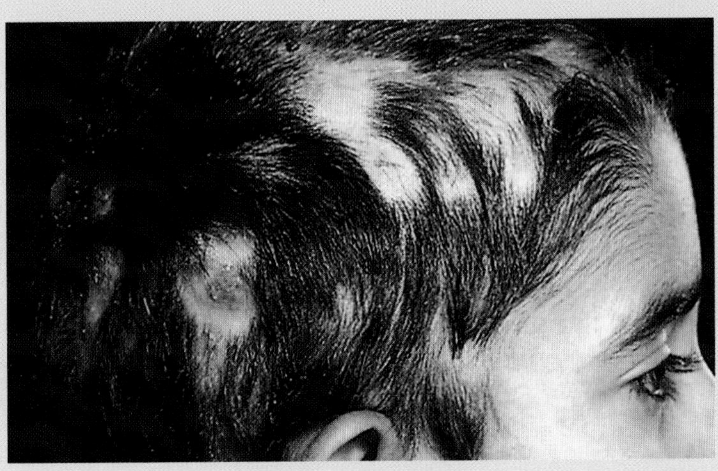

Tinea capitis Dr John Gray

Non-infectious diseases

Conditions of the hair and skin

Condition	Symptoms	Cause	Treatment	Infectious
Acne Disorder affecting the hair follicles and sebaceous glands	Raised spots and bumps within the skin, commonly upon the face in adolescents	Increased sebum and other secretions block the follicle and a skin reaction occurs	Medical treatment required	No
Eczema and dermatitis In its simplest form a reddening of the skin	Ranging from slightly inflamed areas of the skin to severe splitting and weeping areas with irritation and soreness	Many possible causes, eczema often associated with internal factors, i.e. allergies or stress. Dermatitis a reaction or allergy to external factors	Medical treatment required	No
Psoriasis An inflamed, abnormal thickening of the skin	Areas of thickened skin, often raised and patchy. Often on the scalp and also at the joints (arms and legs)	Unknown	Medical treatment required	No

Acne Dr M H Beck

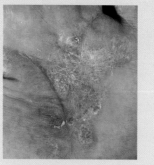

Eczema Dr M H Beck

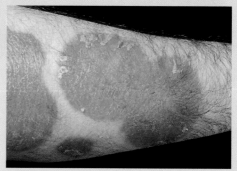

Psoriasis Dr M H Beck

Conditions of the hair and skin

Condition	Symptoms	Cause	Treatment	Infectious
Dandruff (Pityriasis capitis) Dry scaling scalp	Dry, small, irritating flakes of skin. If moist and greasy it sticks to the skin and the condition *scurf* results	Fungal (yeast-like) infection, or physical or chemical irritants	Anti-dandruff treatments	No
Seborrhea Excessive greasiness of the skin exuding on to the hair	Very greasy, lank hair and greasy skin, making styling difficult	Over-production of sebum	Astringent shampoos	No

SCIENCE BIT! DID YOU KNOW

Alopecia (hair loss)

Condition	Description	Treatment
Alopecia areata	The name given to balding patches over the scalp. Often starts around or above the ears, circular in pattern ranging from 1–2.5cm in diameter	Trichological referral
Traction alopecia	Hair loss as a result of excessive pulling at the roots from brushing, curling and straightening. Very often seen with younger girls tying, plaiting or braiding long hair	None
Alopecia totalis	Complete hair loss sometimes as a result of alopecia areata spreading and joining up across the scalp	Trichological referral
Cicatrical alopecia	Baldness due to scarring of the skin arising from chemical or physical injury. The hair follicle is damaged and permanent baldness results	
Male pattern alopecia	Male baldness or thinning of hair occurring in teens or early 20s. Hair recedes at the hairline or loss at the crown area. Condition is hereditary (passed on in families)	Remedies currently being developed

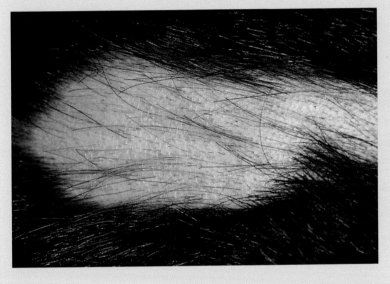

Alopecia areata Dr A L Wright

SCIENCE BIT! DID YOU KNOW   ?

Defects of the hair

Condition	Symptom	Cause	Treatment
Split ends (fragilitas crinium) Fragile, poorly conditioned hair	Dry, splitting hair ends	Harsh physical or chemical treatments	Cutting off or special treatment conditioners
Monilethrix Beaded hair	Beadlike swellings along the hair shaft, hair often breaks at weaker points	Irregular development of the hair forming during cellular production	None
Trichorrhexis nodosa Nodules forming on the hair shaft	Areas of swelling at locations along the hair shaft, splitting and rupturing the cuticle layer	Harsh physical or chemical processing	None, although cutting and conditioning may help
Sebaceous cyst Swelling of the oil gland	Bumps, lumps and swellings on the scalp containing fluid, soft to the touch	Sebaceous gland becomes blocked allowing a build-up of fluid to take place	Medical referral
Damaged cuticle Broken, split, torn hair	Rough, raised, missing areas of cuticle; hair loses its moisture and becomes dry and porous	Harsh physical or chemical processes	None, although cutting and conditioning may help

Fragilitis crinium Wella

Damaged hair Goldwell

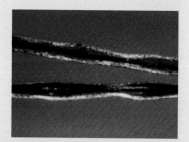

Monilethrix Redken

Trichorrhexis nodosa Dr John Gray

Damaged hair cuticle Dr John Gray

THE CLIENT'S INFLUENCING FEATURES AND FACTORS

The aim of consultation is to arrive at a suitable hairstyle or hair colour which is pleasing to the client. It should be done in a way that gives the client confidence in both the salon and in you. The process should be inspiring.

It is necessary to study the 'complete picture' when you first meet the client. This is to make sure that you have enough information to advise her properly. Your aim is not to alter what the client wears or her self-image, but to harmonise with these to achieve satisfaction. Consider all the aspects of the client's existing image and ask yourself what your impression is. Is there anything that doesn't work? Is the client happy with the existing style? She may point to areas which you feel are wrong or unnecessary, so you need to be able to express your technical appraisal in a clear, simple way without any ambiguity. The use of technical jargon and trade terms will only lead to confusion or misrepresentation.

Consultation is customised for the client. It is personal and individual on each and every occasion. We therefore have to consider technical and personal image aspects:

- cutting and final shape of the hair
- volume or colour which will enhance the style
- finishing options of **blow drying** or **dressing** the hair
- hair type, hair growth, natural colour and face shape
- her personal image, lifestyle and personality
- amount of time she can give to her hair.

Expression

Facial expression is an important part of communication. Even if your client looks disgruntled or is scowling, you will need to use a friendly, pleasant expression to encourage her to relax. Facial expression reflects the client's mood or how she is feeling. You need to pick up on these expressions and react to them appropriately. This will help to understand the client's wants and needs more easily.

Hair and hair growth patterns

Hair is the frame for the face. The length, quantity, quality and texture of the hair all contribute to the total image. Fine hair often lacks body; most clients want fullness and volume which will last. Cutting methods to achieve this include volumising techniques where body can be created by using longer layers levelled in **line** with the client's **baselines** and face shape. You should also consider proportioning the hair weight. By setting hair or using light perms, you can create bulk and volume which give foundation to shape and style.

REMEMBER
- Always make and maintain eye contact with your client.
- Be aware of your client's expressions and react appropriately.

REMEMBER
- Look at the amount and quality of your client's hair.
- Remember that clients with fine hair want volume.
- Look at the proportion, partings and distribution of the hair.
- How much natural movement has the hair got? Will it impede the styling plan?
- Are there any strong growth patterns to contend with?

Hair fashion is constantly changing and the client who wears a hairstyle which is of the moment wants to give the impression of being in touch with trends. Sometimes clients want up-to-the-minute hairstyles to keep a youthful image or to make themselves feel confident. Others will often choose a particular image that complements their career and lifestyle. Television presenters, solicitors and newscasters may go for fashionable but *classic* looks. Models will display the current themes. Those in artistic careers may choose *dramatic* styles.

Growth patterns

The hair's **movement** refers to the amount of curl or wave within the hair lengths. However, its growth pattern denotes the direction from which it protrudes from the scalp. Natural hair fall can be seen on wet and dry hair and strong directional growth will have a major impact on the lie of the hair when it is styled. So it is essential that it is taken into account during consultation.

> **Double crown** – the client with a double crown will benefit from leaving sufficient length in the hair to overfall the whole area. If it is cut too short, the hair will stick up and will not lie flat.
>
> **Nape whorl** – a nape **whorl** can occur at either or both sides of the nape. It can make the hair difficult to cut into a straight neckline or tight 'head-hugging' graduations. Often the hair naturally forms a V-shape. **Tapered** neckline shapes may be more suitable, but sometimes the hair is best left long so that the weight of the hair overfalls the nape whorl directions.
>
> **Cowlick** – a cowlick appears at the hairline at the front of the head. It makes cutting a straight fringe difficult, particularly on fine hair, because the hair often forms a natural parting. The strong movement can often be improved by moving the parting over so that the weight overfalls the growth pattern. Sometimes a fringe can be achieved by leaving the layers longer so that they weigh down the hair.
>
> **Widow's peak** – the widow's peak growth pattern appears at the centre of the front hairline. The hair grows upward and forward, forming a strong peak. It is often better to cut the hair into styles that are dressed back from the face, as any 'light fringes' will be likely to separate and stick up.

Double crown

Cowlick

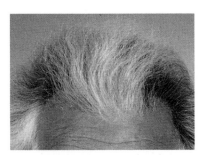

Nape whorls

Widow's peak

Face and head shape

The basic, natural shape of the head, face and features are what form the underlying structure in styling. The proportions of the hair mass and distribution in relation to the face and head are vital in choosing a style. The outer hair shape should fit the face shape to achieve a suitable hair arrangement.

The contours of the head are its focal points. Those on the side of the head are formed by the **parietal** and **temporal** bones. Those on the back of the head and nape are formed by the **occipital** bones, which can be **concave** or **convex**: curving inwards or outwards. The frontal bone forms the forehead shape. It is the beginning of the profile, which follows along the nose to the lips and chin. This can vary in shape and may be concave or convex.

The face shape is made up of straight or curved lines, and sometimes a mixture of the two. Straight, fine shapes appear angular and chiselled or firm and solid. They can be triangular, rectangular, square or diamond shaped. Curved line shapes appear soft and may be round, oval, pear shaped or oblong. Shapes which have some straight and some curved lines are defined as heart shaped or soft square shaped.

To create a pleasant **balance**, the hairstyle and face shape need to be compatible. An angular hair cut will not suit a soft, rounded face. A soft hair shape will not complement a chiselled face. Hair shape outlines can be made to look quite different from the front by simply changing a parting from side to centre. Side partings tend to make the face appear wider, whilst centre partings close down the width of a wide forehead.

An oval face shape suits any hair style. Round faces need height to reduce the width of the face. A centre parting can also help to reduce width. Long facial proportions are improved with short, wider hairstyles. Square-shaped faces need round shapes with texture on to the face to soften them. Longer lengths beyond the jaw line improve the balance and proportion.

Ears, nose and mouth

Often ears are out of balance, which can affect the cut if you use them as a guide. Generally, large ears or even large lobes are accentuated by hair cut short or dressed away from the face. It is often better to leave hair longer over the ears unless it is an essential part of the style's impact.

Your client may wear a hearing aid and this may be a sensitive issue. Some clients wish to have all signs of an aid hidden, but others do not mind and even display it. You should discuss this with your client carefully and with sensitivity; she may feel too embarrassed to bring up the subject herself. The size of the aid will need careful consideration when completing the total image.

The position, shape, size and colour of the nose and mouth are very important in the facial expression. The angles that are created can be softening or harsh and must not be ignored when the image is being planned. Hair shape and make-up can contribute to create the required effect.

> **REMEMBER**
>
> Head shapes can have a major impact on the final profile of the style you are attempting to create. For example, a flatter crown or back of the head is made more noticeable when a contoured, layered cut is selected as the chosen hairstyle.

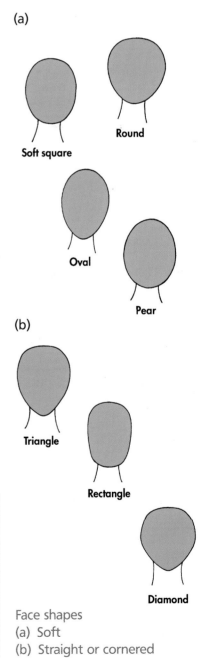

(a)

Soft square
Round
Oval
Pear

(b)

Triangle
Rectangle
Diamond

Face shapes
(a) Soft
(b) Straight or cornered

> **REMEMBER: CHECKLIST** ✔
>
> - What is the shape, position and size of the client's ears?
> - What is the shape and size of the client's nose and mouth?
> - Are these features a major concern to your client?
> - What shape is your client's facial and head shape?
> - Are there any significant features that need to be accounted for?
> - Small faces need 'opening up' while larger faces need narrower framing effects.

REMEMBER: MAKE-UP ✓

- How much make-up is your client wearing?
- What image is she trying to portray: natural, classic and businesslike, dramatic or romantic?

REMEMBER ✓

The eyes are the focal point upon the face. Good images in magazines use this aspect to sell everything from clothes to hairdressing. Your client will be drawn to strong images, but are they wearable in everyday life? The majority of 'hair shots' use hair in ways across the eye line to create artistic impact. These snapshots of 'still lifes' are stimulating but not feasible. You must make a point of this during your consultation.

REMEMBER ✓

- The eyes are the focal point upon the face. Use them within the style's construction.
- What colour and shape are your client's eyes?
- What are the eyebrows like?
- Does your client normally wear spectacles?

REMEMBER ✓

- How long or short is your client's neck?
- How wide or narrow is your client's neck?
- Have you taken these features into consideration?

Make-up

Make-up can enhance features, define eyes and mask or disguise features or blemishes. How the client uses make-up may give a clue to her personality, dress sense and style. In business, a well made-up person is seen to be finished, groomed and in control. Without make-up a person may appear to be 'off duty' or as if she has not made an effort.

Lipstick reflects the **colour depth** of the skin and eyes, creates light on the face and defines the lips. Shiny lipstick is most suitable for someone with a glitzy image. Matt lipstick is more suitable for the quieter person, or when a natural look is required. Lip balm or gloss looks natural and keeps lips soft.

Make-up can create a range of images: soft and kind; bold and extrovert. It can make people feel different about their appearance and so boost confidence if it is properly applied.

Eyes

We already know the importance of maintaining eye contact when communicating with the client, showing that you are listening to each other. But eyes play a major part in the selection of hairstyles too. Heavy fringes can accentuate and frame or they can obstruct vision.

Eye colour is a guide to the natural colouring of the client. This is a useful pointer when choosing hair colour. Eye shape is another element to be considered when choosing which style to create. Ideally, eye, head and face shape should all be complemented by the hairstyle and colour.

The eyebrows frame the eyes. Their shape, size and colour are all significant. A very harsh appearance is created if the eyebrows are removed and various other effects are created by adding shapely lines. Eyelash and brow colouring help to balance facial effects and give the eyes more definition.

Spectacles should be considered when you are deciding on a hairstyle. Frame and lens colour, size and shape have a major impact upon styling and therefore must be taken into account.

Neck and shoulders

The length, fullness and width of the neck will affect the fall of the back and nape hair. Longer necks allow better positioning of long hair. They are complemented by high, neat lines; for example, mandarin collars or polo-neck tops. Short necks need to be uncluttered, with short hair and low collars. Long and thin necks are more noticeable with short styles and will therefore be better suited to longer hair around them. Shorter necks can be counterbalanced with height or upswept hair styles.

Body shape

The body shape also needs to be considered. You need to carefully balance the amount, density and overall shape of the hair to your client's physical body shape. This is particularly important if your client considers her shape or size a particularly important factor. For example, a small, clinging hairstyle would look wrong on a large body shape.

Lifestyle, personality and age

Remember that people are constrained by what they do for a living or what they like to do in their spare time. Usually, people who work in environments where they have face-to-face contact with clients have to be more particular about the image they portray. This is a very important factor in style selection.

From a leisure point of view, you should consider whether the client does a lot of sport or exercise. If so, the hairstyle will have to be versatile and able to withstand a lot of washing. Also, think about how the style could be handled to create a number of different effects when the client is going out. If you are styling for a special occasion, it is worth asking what dress will be worn. A beautiful gown needs to be accompanied by an elegant hairstyle. However, this style will need to be altered for normal wear.

- Many clients want practical and manageable styles for work.
- Nurses, doctors and caterers, among others, may require styles which keep the hair off the face, or they may have to wear face and head coverings at work.
- Dancers, athletes and skaters, among others, need hairstyles which will not get in their eyes and obscure their vision.
- Fashion models may require elaborate styles for special photographic or modelling sessions or displays.

Character and personality can often override physical features when you are choosing a style for your client. A self-confident client will be able to wear looks that a self-conscious client cannot. Make sure you take this into account so that mistakes are not made. Is your client confident and outgoing or shy, timid and retiring, not wishing to stand out in a crowd? Is she professional and businesslike?

And what age group does your client fall in to? There are basic rules that apply to people at certain ages:

children – simple, practical shapes

teenager – something slightly different, especially from older styles, fashionable

young married – something suitable for work, attractive styles

parents – practical and attractive styles, often shorter styles

middle aged – softening shapes to disguise wrinkles

senior age – softening shapes

young businessmen – fashionable cuts

older men – simple, practical styles.

You should note this, but remember we live in a community that is progressive, which can throw off convention and which welcomes visual change.

REMEMBER ✓

- How much time will she have available to style her hair?
- How easy is it for her to replicate the same effect?
- Are products essential for maintaining the look?
- How often does she wash and condition her hair?

Hair: Stella Lambrou, The Crib, Lytham; make-up: Lynsey Alexander; photography: Emma Hughes; styling: Stuart Well

Hair by Anne McGuigan. Photograph by John Rawson

Make me look like this

Manageability

Different styles need different amounts of commitment from the client once she leaves the salon. You need to take these factors on board when consulting with the client to make sure that she will carry on being happy with the style you both choose until it is time for her next visit.

Using visual aids in consultation

Pictures

'A picture paints a thousand words' – the term is a cliché but very true. There are many forms of **communication** and most of them are covered one way or another within the consultation process. We have already stressed the importance of **body language**, the unspoken form of communication that implies much about ourselves and other people.

We know how to speak with clients, we know what to ask and what not to ask. We listen, hear and confirm back to the client. The whole discussion forms a naturally developing contract, an obligation that will be performed, so it is vitally important that we summarise and agree throughout the whole process.

This natural form of check and recheck enables you to move forward. It covers each feature and factor bit by bit. The same feelings are felt by the client. By covering and confirming each aspect, you convey professionalism and competence, which ultimately concludes with you gaining the client's trust.

'Hairdressers don't like clients taking in pictures' – we've all heard that one and it's rubbish too. As hairdressers we needn't develop a complex about it though; it is simply one of those fallacies that clients have. It is a psychological thing; in order for clients to feel more comfortable they say this about hairdressers as it covers a little bit of their embarrassment.

Pictures are an immensely important visual aid and another form of language that hairdressers understand very well. One reason for this is their understanding of visual/spatial imagery. However, there is a vast difference between what the client sees in a photo and what the hairdresser will see.

A client brings in the photo to the left as an example for her own hairstyle. What aspects of this image does she find appealing? What is the client deriving from the image?

- mood
- attitude
- sex appeal
- colour contrasts
- fun 'clubbin' hairstyle
- perimeter shape

What do you, as the hairdresser, see?

- a textured, above the shoulder length bob
- no fringe

- unrealistic hair across the face
- false inference of hair colour produced by photographic lighting
- limited flexibility for work/social wear

From this example you can see that great images convey a lot more than hairstyles. We don't expect the client to understand the technical aspects of the style. She doesn't. She is buying into an ambience. You see something with a trained eye that is quite different. Yes we all find good imagery stimulating, but as hairdressers we are trained to strip off those veneers in order to make sense of what we are seeing.

From a handful of aspects in the client's column, way down the list is the reason for coming to the salon. In identifying this we certainly don't want to devalue our profession. It is simply an example of our client's expectation. She may be wanting to change many things in her life. We can only focus on one, for which we want to benefit commercially. However, this visual aid is very useful. It provides the basis, the fundamental roots, from which constructive conversation will bloom.

Colour charts

Colour charts are extremely useful for hairdressers. We rely on them every day. However, they are not always a very helpful medium for the client. We tend to treat others as we would want to be treated ourselves. This is a good philosophy, but there are times when our expectation of others is a little over-optimistic. Generally speaking, clients have very little ability for self-visualisation. This could be confirmed another way. Think about shopping. How often do women shop in pairs? Other people's comments, assistance and points of view are very important. The reason is obvious. If we need more reassurance about what we are doing we have to involve someone else; ideally someone else who knows us, our likes and dislikes, and most important of all someone who can objectively comment about our decision-making process.

The colour chart is a useful tool for hairdressers and a nice colouring book for clients. Unless you can help the client visualise the amount, intensity, density and saturation of the resultant colour, the visual aid will have little or no impact on the decision-making process of whether to buy colour or not.

Computer-generated images

The internet is a valuable medium for conveying information about hair and hairstyles. Many salons have their own websites. The ease of using computer-generated images and uploading them to salon sites is proving a very cost effective advertising medium. However, there is very little information technology used for graphical purposes within salons. Although many software packages are available for generating makeover effects, very little use is made of this medium at present. The constraints of cost, training and operator time are still barriers to salons that want to harness this technology.

AFTER THE CONSULTATION

Style or service selection

You and the client will select the required style or service together. To avoid disappointment, you must ensure that she knows exactly what is entailed, what it will cost and how long it will take. Remember, the purpose of consultation is to create a commercial opportunity.

REMEMBER: CONSULTATION CHECKLIST

- ☑ Listen carefully to what is requested
- ☑ Use visual aids to assist the consultation process
- ☑ Communicate the possible effects
- ☑ Explain why certain effects are not possible
- ☑ Give good reasons for suggested actions
- ☑ Ensure that the client understands what is being said
- ☑ Agree on a final and suitable course of action
- ☑ Assure and reassure throughout
- ☑ Make it clear if follow-up appointments are necessary
- ☑ Carry out the agreed service or treatment
- ☑ Encourage the client to rebook the next visit before she leaves
- ☑ Maintain the client's goodwill and safety throughout the appointment
- ☑ Record the details for future reference

PROMOTING THE BUSINESS FURTHER

The services and treatments that a salon provides to its clients form the basis of the business functions. This particular business model is built on two specific factors:

- maintaining client satisfaction
- retaining client loyalty.

For the majority of all salons these two factors are directly linked and are therefore essential for a business to succeed. It is possible to make a really good job of satisfying our clients, but unless they return within a reasonable time scale their annual contribution to the salon will be drastically reduced. So we need to stimulate the client's loyalty by encouraging them to:

- return on a regular basis
- buy into other services, products and treatments
- share their experiences with their family, friends and work associates.

We should bear in mind that the bond built between client and stylist is purely a business arrangement. Hairdressing may be a very social occupation but the clients are not your friends. Businesses exist by charging the highest prices that their customers will afford. We leave the marketing to the employer or his agents, as they will have already targeted a specific profile for the types of customer that the business will serve. So how do we serve that target group? We serve them by selling:

- ourselves
- hairdressing services and treatments
- retail
- salon image.

Selling ourselves

Contrary to popular belief, good communication far outweighs technical excellence for a busy, popular stylist. So you don't have to be a brilliant hairdresser to do well. Hairdressing is changing very quickly and not just by fashions and trends. *Customers expect more*. They have a right to anyway. People's opinions in respect to *accountability*, *responsibility* and *recourse* have changed greatly in the last few years. People have learned not to take second best or let corporations push them around. Therefore, competition between companies is fierce. Our customers want us to be able to shoulder these aspects and the quicker they find that these are not only on offer but *actively* **demonstrated**, the faster respect and loyalty will develop.

Good customer service is customer focused. It is centred upon the needs of the client and reflected in all the features involved within routine salon operations: telephone response time, meeting and greeting, refreshments and magazines, visually pleasing interiors and polite and friendly staff. Why do clients come to our salon? To have their hair improved – this part is obvious. Beyond this they want to feel better emotionally, they want to be uplifted. So in order to feel better they need to look good, and that's where you come in. Have you ever considered what the client undergoes before you start the service? Your client's hair is vitally important to her and she is passing on the stewardship to you – a safe pair of hands!

Services and treatments

The clients that are recommended to us form a particularly special group. They have found us through the network of already satisfied customers. The product of our work, the way in which we communicate and our personality have all preceded us. Our satisfied customers feel confident enough in our expertise to promote us to their friends and colleagues.

If recommendation is such a powerful channel of communication, why don't we use it more? Well we can. The perfect time to talk about the variety of services and treatments available to clients is when they are in the chair in front of us. Recommendation is the simplest way of extending the range of services to our clients and enhancing the professional relationship.

Excellent communicators are good listeners, they understand how to ask the right questions and listen effectively to responses, building on the information given to them.

Retail

How well do you sell?

As Britain's largest and oldest trading activity, retailing should be easy. If it were there would be more millionaires around and fewer cracks about pushy salesmen ('so many doors slammed in their faces they've all got flat noses and turned up toes'). But the plain truth is that while more than a million businesses carry out some form of retailing, only about one retail worker in twenty has received adequate training.

In hairdressing, fierce competition and the rise of professional home haircare products have meant that retailing is no longer a neglected area. Innovative stylists, salons and suppliers have led this important turnaround.

REMEMBER: GOOD SELLING ✔

- Listening, asking questions, showing interest
- Using the client's name
- Empathising (putting yourself in the client's place), establishing a bond
- Recognising non-verbal cues (dilated pupils = 'I approve'; ear-rubbing = 'I've heard enough')
- Identifying needs; helping clients reach buying decisions
- Knowing your products/services
- Highlighting the results or user benefits; demonstrating these where possible
- Thinking positively, talking persuasively, projecting confidence and enthusiasm

---

REMEMBER: BAD SELLING ✔

- Doing all the talking
- Not listening, not 'hearing' unspoken thoughts, arguing
- Interrupting – but never letting the clients interrupt you – thus losing an open opportunity for giving extra information
- Hard selling, 'spieling' (working to a script)
- Threatening – 'You won't get it cheaper anywhere else', knocking the opposition
- Manipulating – 'Oh dear, I'll miss my sales target'
- Knowing nothing about the product
- Treating 'no thanks' as personal rejection
- Blinding clients with science
- Staying mainly silent waiting for an order
- Insisting the client should buy the product

Playing your part

What is retailing? Retailing is selling to consumers: in single or bulk quantities, over the counter, off the shelf, on doorsteps and by post; i.e. mail order or 'distance selling' which is particularly successful in own label lines. Done well, retailing enhances the image of both salesperson and salon alike and is enjoyed by clients. People like to shop! It meets needs, fulfils desires and makes them feel good.

So how to shine?

Closing a sale isn't the final notes, it's the whole process from the moment a client walks in: friendly welcome, relaxing ambience, focused attention, pleasant and friendly manner, talking his/her language, heeding their inner concerns, quietly suggesting appropriate solutions ('We should be able to help you', 'Have you thought about').

Retail professionals call it 'creating the right selling atmosphere', one that stimulates people to buy. And it's people – living, breathing individuals – you're dealing with, not logic-driven robots! Our primal needs are shelter, warmth and food; our chief buying emotions are health, security, pride, prestige, status, ego (vanity), greed. This is why simply selling on technicalities doesn't motivate clients. People don't buy formulas – they buy *results*. Yes, you must find the need – but then turn it into a *want*, making it easy for clients to say 'yes'.

How do retailers do that?

Behind the scenes, this sexy approach is backed by thorough market research, finding out client likes/dislikes, sound administration (client list and purchases; costing sales volume per sq. ft, etc.), getting the right packaging and promotional support materials and disciplined use of personal flair. Product presentation is assisted by:

- point-of-sale merchandising – central 'island', open cabinet, shelf displays
- shelftalkers – printed promotional slips/cards fixed to/dangling from shelves; 'mobile' ones that bob or bounce deliver best results
- eye-catching displays are instantly informative – locate them where they'll be seen at reception or centrally in treatment areas
- arrangement of popular lines at eye level with price details; use 'price watch' stickers
- linking displays with money off and other special offers – first visit, loyalty, recommend-a-friend discounts and promotional tie-ins with major local stores.

SALON IMAGE

The salon image is created by the business proprietor. It is communicated to our clients through their senses, sight, hearing, touch, taste and smell. These senses quickly convey an overall impression. If it is positive it will enhance what we try to do as individuals, but if negative it will erode the benefit of the service we aim to provide.

1 **What do they see?** Is the salon in a basement or hidden upstairs? Is it on the main high street or on a housing estate? What colour schemes have been used inside? Is this carried through in printed stationery, e.g. price lists, cards, service information?

2 **What do they hear?** How are they spoken to on the telephone? How are they greeted when they enter the salon? How are they received, directed and consulted afterwards? What background noises can they hear?

3 **What do they feel?** Can they feel the quality of fresh gowns and towels? Can they feel the level of professional contact in the way that services and treatments are carried out?

4 **What can they smell?** What is the salon atmosphere like? What do the products used smell like? Do the staff smell clean and hygienic? Does the fragrance of fresh ground coffee linger in the air?

5 **What can they taste?** What beverages or food are available? What is the quality of these drinks or food? What does it say to our clients?

Handling complaints

When a crisis calls…

In any three-month period around fifty million people visit their hairdresser. It would be a miracle if things did not go wrong – and go wrong they sometimes do. The important thing is knowing how to handle these difficult situations properly and carefully. That way you get to keep your client. In any average salon there tend to be four main types of complaint:

Scenario 1 The client has got what she paid for, but after a few days decides she or her partner hate it. It's all your fault as far as she's concerned.

Scenario 2 A customer who had a body wave perm finds her scalp becomes sore and her hair breaks off at the ends. You forgot to do a strand test. You are at fault.

Scenario 3 A customer who had a body wave perm finds her scalp becomes sore and her hair breaks off at the ends. You provided advice and did a strand test. The day after she left the salon she began taking medication which *caused* the reaction. Nevertheless, she still blames you.

Scenario 4 You've had an off day and your work with the client was not as good as usual.

So what do you do when faced with angry clients? In all these scenarios it is vital that, no matter how abusive the client is being, you receive him/her pleasantly and politely, discuss the nature of the complaint and, when the complaint has been explained, repeat it back and get acknowledgement that you heard it correctly. Analyse it carefully and sympathetically and at all times remain calm and in control. Whatever happens, don't take it personally!

Instead, diagnose the fault and suggest corrective action, making sure the client agrees with what is to be done. Carry out the correction there and then or arrange a convenient time for the client to return. For future reference, *record the complaint* and the *action taken*. Thank the customer for bringing the problem to your attention.

In the case of scenario 2, it might be too late for you to correct the damage. More worrying still, it is one of those cases that these days, with so many law firms offering 'no win no fee', will probably end up in court. In cases such as this there are several important issues you need to address:

- never admit liability
- consult with a senior member of the team immediately, such as the manager or salon owner.

He/she must:

- notify the salon's insurers immediately of the possibility of a claim arising
- pass on all subsequent correspondence unanswered to the insurers.

In the case of scenario 3 you need to establish any changes in the customer's lifestyle since leaving the salon to find out possible causes for these events and also to exonerate the salon. Again, all matters relating to the case should be dealt with by the salon's insurers.

All-important body language

If you follow the rule of thumb that loss of profit and reputation caused by one unhappy customer may require ten new customers to make up for it, you might do better to take a deep breath and put on your most sympathetic face when faced with an angry client.

- Don't fold your arms. It looks defensive.
- Don't lean too far forward. It can look aggressive.
- Don't clench your teeth or tense your muscles. You might be doing so to try and mask your own tension, but it looks as if you are defending your own patch and, at worst, can look as if you're merely trying to control your temper.
- Instead, look interested – and don't interrupt!
- Don't make body contact. Keep a respectful physical distance from your client.

If the worst comes to the worst, gross negligence can result in very large judgments being made in court against the salon. Worse than the fine can be the series of 'Hairdos from Hell' articles in the press and the wailing woman on breakfast television, accompanied by a trichologist, dissecting your bad work. Not only could this damage your reputation, but it can also ruin the salon you are working for, with repercussions for the entire craft.

It is in the salon's interest to resolve the matter there and then. If it means getting the customer to sign to the fact that the matter has been resolved, so much the better. If, however, it is not resolved to the client's satisfaction, the next call could be from their solicitor or from the newsdesk of a popular tabloid. Always pass media calls to the manager or owner.

Never charge for rectification when the mistake is your fault. It could be a goodwill gesture in less serious cases to offer a free haircut or colour the next time the client comes in. *Find out what your salon's policy is on this*. But be careful. Don't make it look like a bribe. This could make a bad situation worse. In a negligence case, the complainant could use this to try to prove that you have admitted liability. If you are convinced that someone is complaining unjustly as a means of exhorting money from the salon, refer the client to the salon manager or owner.

Prevention is better than the cure

This should establish clearly what the client wants. If you think the cut or colour, for example, won't suit them, you should tell them. If they then insist you should go ahead, you should stress your reservations once again. Consult with the manager or salon owner before proceeding if the customer insists this is the service they want.

Ask the client medical and lifestyle questions pertinent to the treatment they want. If the hair style requires a maintenance regime, brief them thoroughly. Make sure they know exactly what they are letting themselves in for. Some salons give clients a questionnaire, which is not only useful to glean information, but can also help defend any subsequent actions by the client.

If in doubt, leave it out

No one likes to turn down business, but if you think a client will leave the salon looking like a 'bad hair day' you could say something like: 'In my professional opinion, I am convinced that this style will not suit you. Another hairdresser may well do it for you, but I want you to be a regular client and I would like you to leave this salon feeling happy. Please be guided by my expertise.' Then suggest alternatives. The client will trust you and respect you for it.

Complaint summary

If the final effects are not what was thought to have been agreed, or not what was expected, the client will have due reasons for complaint. Use the following checklist as a guide.

- Listen carefully to the client's complaint.
- Resolve the problem immediately or as soon as possible.
- Do not allow the disagreement to affect the salon environment and act sensibly and with decorum at all times.
- Record the complaint.
- Refer to senior staff if necessary.
- Refer to the management so that they can inform the insurers if necessary.
- If the client is not happy, she may want to take legal action. This must be dealt with by the management.

ACTIVITY

Discuss with your fellow staff members how different client complaints could be handled. Then as a group activity 'act out' the four different scenarios in a role play.

Key skills: Communication
2.1 Take part in discussions
2.4 Read and respond to written material

Started it	I know and understand the principles of positive communication	I can communicate positively and professionally with the clients	I always recognise the critical influencing factors when I analyse the client's hair
☐	☐	☐	☐
I can identify the range of hair and scalp problems	I know how to negotiate, reaching a mutually beneficial conclusion	I always carry out working practices according to the salon's policy	I've covered most of it!
☐	☐	☐	☐
I always explain technical terms, eliminating ambiguity and false beliefs	I know when and who to refer clients to in situations where external assistance is required	I understand the necessity of personal hygiene and presentation	I know how to advise, promote and sell other services and products to clients
☐	☐	☐	☐
I know and respect the client's rights, equal opportunities, data protection, anti-discrimination and consumer legislation	Done it all		CHECKER BOARD
☐	☐		

Self-test section

Quick quiz: a selection of different types of questions to check your knowledge

Q1 The three stages of hair growth are anagen, ... and telogen.   Fill in the blank

Q2 The cortex is the outermost layer of the hair.   True or False

Q3 Select all that apply. Which of the following are infectious diseases?   Multi-selection

Impetigo	☐	1
Scalp ringworm	☐	2
Alopecia	☐	3
Head lice	☐	4
Psoriasis	☐	5
Eczema	☐	6

Q4 The natural colour of hair depends on the amount of melanin within it.   True or False

Q5 Which of the following is commonly known as split ends?   Multi-choice

Trichorrhexis nodosa	☐	a
Monilethrix	☐	b
Tinea capitis	☐	c
Fragilitas crinium	☐	d

Q6 Dandruff is a condition of the scalp usually caused by fungal infection.   True or False

Q7 Which of the following tests are carried out *during* technical services?   Multi-selection

Skin test	☐	1
Strand test	☐	2
Curl test	☐	3
Incompatibility test	☐	4
Porosity test	☐	5
Test cutting	☐	6

Q8 The lower layers of the skin are called the ....   Fill in the blank

Q9 Which face shape suits most hairstyles and lengths?   Multi-choice

Square	☐	a
Oblong	☐	b
Oval	☐	c
Triangular	☐	d

Q10 During consultation and hair analysis, a contra-indication will not allow the planned service to be carried out.   True or False

TONI & GUY AT THE 50TH ANNIVERSARY
L'ORÉAL COLOUR TROPHY, LONDON, MAY 2006.

ANTOINETTE BEENDERS AT THE 50TH ANNIVERSARY
L'ORÉAL COLOUR TROPHY, LONDON, MAY 2005.

TREVOR SORBIE AT THE 50TH ANNIVERSARY
L'ORÉAL COLOUR TROPHY, LONDON, MAY 2005.

CHARLES WORTHINGTON AT THE 50TH ANNIVERSARY
L'ORÉAL COLOUR TROPHY, LONDON, MAY 2005.

M. BALFRE AT THE ALTERNATIVE HAIR SHOW, 2005.

part two

chapter 3

CUTTING HAIR

Unit H27 Create a variety of looks using a combination of cutting techniques   Mandatory

H27.1   Maintain effective and safe methods of working when cutting hair.

H27.2   Cut hair to achieve a variety of looks for women.

What do I need to learn?

You need to know and understand:

- **Your salon's policy in respect of clients: preparation, services and safety**
- **How you should work safely and hygienically**
- **How to recognise the factors that influence style selection and suitability for different clients**
- **How to use and adapt a variety of cutting techniques that achieve a range of different, creative effects**
- **Ways of communicating ideas, themes and style care routines to clients**

What does it mean?

- **You need to build upon the previously learnt, basic cutting techniques and develop these skills further, extending them into a comprehensive repertoire based upon sound professional knowledge and expertise.**

What do I need to do?

- **You need to develop a variety of skills that become your *personal toolbox*, enabling you to use them independently or collectively in creating a range of different effects for clients, dependant upon individual needs.**
- **You need to work safely at all times.**
- **You need to be able to analyse and recognise any limitations to the client's hairstyling requirements while balancing this with an agreed, suitable course of action.**

Other info

Related topics and other useful information:

Client consultation

Colour and colouring hair

African Caribbean hairdressing

KEY WORDS

Texturising A range of techniques including chipping, pointing, slicing etc., which can create lift, movement, texture or definition within a hairstyle

Point cutting Point cutting uses the point ends of the scissors to reduce bulk and weight to introduce texture and softness and remove layering or **cutting lines**

Brick cutting Similar to point cutting but removes larger amounts or chunks of hair to reduce bulk. Often used nearer the scalp in hairstyles, introducing lift, which is gained from the shorter supporting hair

Slicing Achieved by very sharp scissors or a razor. Slicing will produce a tapering effect in a hair section without reducing the overall length

Slider cutting A scooping action achieved by very sharp scissors as if acting like a razor

CHECKERBOARD

At the end of this chapter the checkerboard will help to jog your memory on what you have learned and what still remains to be done. Cross them off with a pencil as you cover each of the topics. (See p. 122.)

INTRODUCTION

This chapter addresses what is arguably 'the core' activity of hairdressing. The cutting unit comprises of the following elements:

H27   Create a variety of looks using a combination of cutting techniques

    H27.1   Maintain effective and safe methods of working when cutting

    H27.2   Cut hair to create a variety of looks for women

The content in this chapter looks particularly at the aspects of design that will enable you to construct a variety of fashionable styles. It should help you to think more *laterally* about a variety of cutting techniques and give you more freedom in finding new applications for them.

So creative design is deciding what needs to be done, making the right choices and selecting what will suit the client and her requirements. It is

Hair by Ashley/Photography by Jennifer Cheyne @ Cheynes Hairdressing

essential that you and your client understand each other: what people mean by short, long or medium is relative. Hear your client, interpret their needs and be specific, explain what you mean and mutually agree the course of action.

Always make sure you have enough time for the cutting process. Nothing is achieved by rushing work – other than bad habits. Mutual agreement and a well-executed plan are fundamental to a successful finished effect.

CUTTING AND STYLING

As you became more skilled in styling hair, your confidence and willingness to explore new ways of doing things developed into true professionalism. This whole process has a simpler, single word that is unfortunately often overused and something that many new stylists think they already possess. It is *experience*.

Experience is not just time served; it is worked at and achieved by a personal determination and an unfailing quest to be perceived by others as an authority, a loyal and reliable point of contact, the preferred operator within a team of people. True, different stylists have different ways of doing things, but that's what makes it interesting. If there weren't different ways of achieving fabulous effects than the whole industry would fail because everyone would lack the personal motivation to go on. There wouldn't be any need for competitions, shows or exhibitions; hairdressing would cease to be a mode of fashion and people might as well have their hair shaved off.

But it isn't like that at all; hairdressing is attracting more new recruits than ever before. More and more people want to be part of a personal service industry that has flexible work options, provides freedom in allowing its workforce to be individuals and, above all, makes a business out of making other people feel good about themselves.

As you become more skilled in cutting hair, you need to remember that your work still rests on the accurate execution of the fundamental techniques, while continuing to build on the more advanced and creative ones. Level 3 work is a continual process of building on these experiences and good; fashion styling will be the result, providing that you always consider the following points:

- good preparation and planning
- thorough client communication
- identification of individual needs
- identification of any influencing factors and styling limitations
- maintenence of accuracy and standards
- good customer care
- personal hygiene and general health and safety aspects.

Effective communication with the client, as in any service, is an essential prerequisite to cutting hair. So, while the discussion takes place and before any work is carried out, you must determine what the client wants and weigh this against the limiting factors in order to find out what you need to do. You need to understand your client fully and be able to negotiate and seek agreement with her throughout the service.

Be sure to listen to your client's requests. Many mistakes can be avoided if you achieve a clear understanding of what the client is asking for.

The haircutting style that you choose with your client should take into account each of the following points about the client's

- face and head shape
- physical features and body shape, size and proportion
- hair quality, abundance, growth and distribution
- age, lifestyle and suitability
- purpose
- ability or time to recreate the effect herself.

PREPARING THE CLIENT

Your salon has its own policy and codes of practice for preparing clients and you must observe these. Some things are general common sense and courtesy, whereas others are client or salon specific. But at the very least codes of practice will need to cover basic health and safety as well as the other preparations that you need to make the service a successful and enjoyable experience.

You may be an experienced operator but don't forget the basics. Above all you do need to remember the client's personal comfort and safety throughout the salon visit.

This means:

- covering the client and her clothes with a clean, laundered gown
- placing a cutting collar around her shoulders
- making sure that all tools and equipment are safe and hygienic, ready for use.

ACTIVITY

Every salon has their own way of doing things. Write down in your portfolio under the following headings what your salon's code of practice in respect to:

- meeting and greeting clients
- gowning
- maintaining tools and equipment
- disposal of sharps
- hygiene and preventing the spread of infection or infestation.

CONSULTATION ASPECTS

Communication: *understanding, being understanding*

Talk *to* your clients rather than just talking *at* them; it is the start of being a good communicator. Effective communication is fundamental to professional hairdressing; quite simply, being understood is the single biggest barrier to helping clients to achieve what they want. You must eliminate jargon from your consultations; it is confusing and leads the client into expecting something totally different to what you are offering. Keep it simple and, if that's not working, summarise your points by saying things like: 'So you would be happier to have it shorter as long as the tops of the ears still remain covered?'

Keith Hall Hairdressing Creative Team

Classic traditional styling
Hair: Charlotte Cole at Lawrence Anthony (Stratford); photography: Roberto Aguilar; make-up: Amelia Pruen

If the client tries to use technical terms or style names, clarify the points as you go along. A client will often say, 'I would like lots of layers in my hair'. But what does that really mean? It doesn't actually tell you anything. There are some exceptions but, more often than not, the terms that clients use are used in the wrong context.

Always try to find other ways of putting things or use pictures to show what you mean. Visual aids express far more than just a cutting style or technique, they create an overall finished impression too. Choosing a new hairstyle or effect is a big step for anyone, so you need to make sure that you help your client all the way.

Make a habit of summarising the main points as you go through the consultation by saying: 'So, if we do cut the front shorter, into a fringe, you still have a choice where to position the parting.'

Being understood is one thing, but being *understanding* is quite another. The professional stylist not only hears what the client wants, but can also put him- or herself in the client's position. This is a personal quality that sets the true professionals apart; being able to show empathy demonstrates to clients that you see *their* needs from *their* perspective and it is this single factor that that makes the bond between client and stylist so personal.

When looking at communication at this level we begin to see that other people have a huge impact on the styles that we choose. People have their hair done for a number of reasons:

● They want to feel different.
● They want to look different.
● They want to feel good.
● They want to look good.

When people want to look good their personal needs become externalised: *they want other people to notice them*. Now, if they want people to notice them, they won't turn down a compliment either. So thinking this through further, this means that they want other people to comment too. So all of a sudden we are wondering – for what or whom is the hairstyle intended? Could it be work colleagues, friends or a partner?

Remember: it's hard enough to satisfy the client sitting before you in the styling chair. It is almost impossible to satisfy someone who is sitting in a chair at home. You need to know what you are trying to achieve and for *whom* you are trying to achieve it.

Clear communication goes beyond speech too because, as well as using words, we show our interest, attitude and feelings by our bodily

ACTIVITY

Very few people have had professional communication training and when you come across it, it is very plain to see the difference. Professional communicators know how to present themselves; they know what to say and how to make themselves understood. You too can learn from their techniques.

When you watch the news on TV, what do you notice about the way that the presenter provides the news? From this case study, answer the following questions in your portfolio.

What do you notice:

1 About their eye contact?
2 About their posture?
3 About how they present information?
4 About how they switch between other stories and other broadcast personnel

Current fashion styling
Hair: Charlotte Cole at Lawrence Anthony (Stratford); photography: Roberto Aguilar; make-up: Amelia Pruen

expressions. Body language is just as clear to others as speech, so you need to remain professional at all times, regardless how difficult this can be.

The different genres of hairstyling

Hairdressing styles fall into three distinct groupings or genres and knowing which one to use with a client will depend upon your consultation.

Classic or traditional work: could be defined as *timeless* fashion. That is to say that the styles are neither in nor out of fashion. Classic styles were created at a time when the basic rules were first created. Classic styling work tends to be quite different from the other two groups of styles as it has the following distinct qualities:

1 the styles tend to be quite simple in their construction
2 in their simplicity they always looks good
3 they are durable and last well, even between salon visits.

Current fashion trends are changing all the time. These fashions are different to classic styling in that they are of the moment. They often start on the catwalks of fashion shows in Paris, London and New York. Initially, these styles start out as something radical, exaggerated or pushing boundaries. But, like the clothes being displayed, they are modified or *translated* from haute couture into wearable, saleable and commercial fashions that are affordable by the majority and seen in the high street shops.

The **emerging fashions** are the last genre or family of styles. They can be seen on stages, worn by pop stars, in concerts all over the world. The looks are often individualistic and not necessarily durable or wearable in a wider 'street fashion' sense. They cover the fashions that are still on the horizon that are yet to be processed or adapted. As with current fashion styles, we get glimpses of them on the **designer** catwalks, but these are the raw, undiluted or radical and exaggerated fashions that create the next big thing.

Emerging fashions
Hair by Paula; styling by Lorraine Adamczuk; photography by Jennifer Cheyne @ Cheynes Hairdressing

Head and facial shape

The proportions, balance and distribution of the hairstyle will be a frame for the head and face. Therefore you need to examine the head and face carefully, if you look at the outline of your client's face, you will see that it's either round, oval, square, heart shaped, oblong or triangular. Only an oval face suits all hairstyles, so all the others listed present some form of styling limitations; in other words they become a styling choice influencing factor.

General styling limitations

Physical feature	How best to work with it
Square and oblong facial shapes	Are accentuated by hair that is smoothed, scraped back or sleek at the sides and top.
	The lines and angles are made less conspicuous by fullness and softer movement.
Round faces	Are made more conspicuous if the side and front perimeter lengths are short or finish near to the widest part of the face. This is made worse if width is added at these positions too. Generally this facial shape is complemented by length beyond the chin.
Square angular features, jaw, forehead etc.	Is improved with softer perimeter shapes, avoid solid, linear effects around the face. Shattered edges and texturising will help to mask these features.
Flatter heads at the back	Are improved by graduation, creating contour and shape that is missing from having a flatter occipital bone.

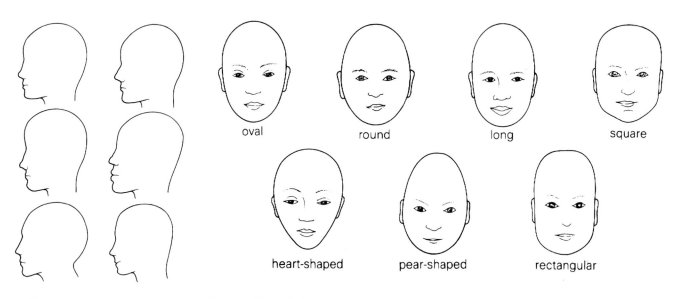

Profiles

oval   round   long   square

heart-shaped   pear-shaped   rectangular

Face and head shapes

Head, face and body physical features

Physical feature	How best to work with it
Prominent nose	Hair taken back away from the face accentuates this feature, while hair around the face and forehead tends to diminish the feature.
Square jaw line	Is softened by longer perimeter lengths either coming around and on to the face or styled with fullness. Conversely, shorter side lengths will have an opposite effect.
Protruding ears	Are better left covered rather than exposed. Sufficient hair should be left to cover and extend beyond their length if at all possible.
Wrinkles around the eyes	Are made more obvious by hair being scraped back at the temples or straighter more angular effects.
Narrow foreheads	Are disguised by softer fringes and side partings, whereas they are made more obvious by hair taken back away form the face.
Larger body shapes	The overall effect is balanced and improved with longer, fuller hairstyles; they are made much worse by short, sleek, layered shapes.
Small faces	Can be swamped if the hair is left long with a centre parting and no fringe.
Large faces	Are accentuated by short cropped or sculpted hair.
Shapes of glasses	There are so many available that they are a fashion accessory. Generally people will have had assistance in the selection and suitability of their frames. Therefore they should not work against the hairstyle that you want to create as they should already suit the shape and size of the face.
The way the head is held	Many people tilt their head to one side or forwards. Sometimes this is because they are tall and want subconsciously to reduce their height; sometimes they *hide* behind their hair because they lack confidence or they think it makes them more alluring. You need to look out for this natural posture but not make any comment other than asking whether they have any preference to finished lengths, fringes and partings.

Reason or purpose for hairstyle

The reason or purpose for the hairstyle is a big factor in deciding what is suitable or otherwise.

- A style suitable for a special occasion will differ from one that is selected for work. The requirements for competition or show work are quite different from those for general daily wear. But versatility needs to be considered for everyone: people want styles that they can dress up or down. Modern hairdressing has parallels with modern lives: both are about flexibility and choice. People like options, so build this into your plans. The majority of clients need hairstyles that are easy to manage and that can be dressed up with styling products or accessories for social events. Versatility is definitely the key: while people like simple, easy to manage effects, they also like the opportunity to look different now and again.

- Some jobs have special conditions about hair lengths and styles; for example, people working in the armed services or police have to wear their hair above the collar while at work. Men have easily accommodated this by using clippers for very short styles. Women they have either had to have short layered styles or hair that is long enough to wear up and out of the way.

The quality, quantity and distribution of hair

- Good hair condition is an essential prerequisite for great hairstyling. It doesn't matter how much work has gone into the thought and design of a hairstyle, *if the hair is in poor condition to start with, it still will be after*. Some aspects cannot be altered by cutting alone; for instance, if the hair is dry, dull and porous when the client enters the slaon, it still will be when she leaves.

- Regular salon clients in the UK – the ones you tend to see more often than the others – tend to have something in common. Difficult hair. It can be difficult for a number of reasons; it can be fine or unmanageable, lank and lacking volume or just not responsive to styling without force. Thin, sparsely distributed hair is always a problem: if there isn't enough hair to get coverage over the scalp, then there is not a lot you can do about it. One thing that you should remember though is not to put too much volume into it; this will only make the problem more noticeable. Fine hair presents many problems too. Very fine hair is affected by dampness and quickly loses its shape. This type of hair always benefits from styling products so get your client used to using them.

- Dry, frizzy hair can also a problem, as the more thermo styling it receives, the more moisture is lost and the less it responds to staying in shape – in other words, the harder it is to style. The problem just keeps going on like a merry-go-around. Dry, thick hair needs to be tamed and most clients with this problem would like their hair to look smoother and shinier. Again this is a conditioning issue and you need to attack the problem before tackling the style. Sometimes this type of hair benefits from finishing products, so put them on as you finish and define the hairstyle.

- Very tight curly hair can be difficult too, particularly if your client wants it to appear straight. It is possible to smoothe and straighten hair, particularly when you use ceramic straighteners or thermal styling. But keeping it straight is another matter, and you may want to consider a chemical relaxer instead.

- Cutting wavy hair presents some problems but not if it is looked at carefully before it's wet. Avoid cutting across the crests of the waves; you can't change the natural movement in the hair so try to work with it.

- Straight hair, particularly if it is fine textured, can be difficult to cut. Cutting marks or lines can easily form if the cutting sections and angles are not right. Make sure that you only take small sections of hair and remember to crosscheck after, at 90° to the angle in which you first cut, to avoid this happening to you.

Hair positioning, type, growth and tendency

The perimeter outline formed by the hair in relation to the shape of the face is the first thing most people see. It is this effect that people make decisions upon and comments about; for example, 'That's a beautiful haircut.' 'I think that really suits you.' The complete hairstyle is based upon the frame that the hair creates for the face. How you 'fill in' the detail – the movement, direction, colour and placement – is down to your interpretation, understanding, technical ability and experience.

Hair growth direction and distribution should be a major consideration for what is achievable within a hairstyle. You need to make allowances for strong movement, high or low hairlines, natural partings, hair **whorls**, cowlicks, widow's peaks and double crowns. Look for these before shampooing. The client cannot compensate for these herself, so when the hair is in need of washing, they will be plain to see. After the hair is washed the degree and strength of the feature can be seen and then you can reconsider how you will tackle it.

Style suitability

Style suitability refers to the effect of the hair shape on the face, and on the features of the head and body. A hairstyle is, quite simply, suitable when it 'looks right'. But this is a difficult or certainly a subjective thing to quantify.

Aesthetically and artistically speaking, the client's 'hair will look right' when the hairstyle does one of two things. It either:

- **harmonises** i.e. fits the shape of the face and head – and is therefore a backdrop to an overall image; or
- **contrasts** i.e. It accentuates features of the face and head – by creating a prominent frame for the overall image.

For example, a line of the face created by the underlying bone structure can be accentuated when the hairlines are continuous with it. Conversely, it can be softened when they are angled away. A young, fashionable hairstyle on an older woman may be totally inappropriate and unattractive. This is because the harder style lines of younger styles accentuate the lines of the face, eyes and forehead. Most fashion styles designed for younger women must be adapted if they are going to be suitable for older women.

Balance

Balance is the effect produced by the amount, fullness and weight distribution of hair throughout the style. The opposite, *imbalance*, is lack of those proportions. *Symmetry* or **symmetrical** *even balance* occurs when the hair is distributed equally as in a mirrored image through a vertical or horizontal plane. *Asymmetry* or *asymmetric effects* occur when the overall shape does not have the same distribution on either side. However, both symmetrical and **asymmetrical** shapes can be balanced – see the illustration 'Aesthetic balance'.

REMEMBER ✔

When you choose a suitable hairstyle always allow for the natural fall of the hair.

Aesthetic balance

Style line

Style line(s) is the direction(s) in which the hair is positioned or appears to flow. This is particularly noticeable on longer hairstyles and long hair up. In these situations the flow and continuity of the movement is an essential part of the overall effect. When a break occurs within this flow the eye is immediately drawn to it. A break can only happen for two reasons: either it's a style feature and accentuates what the observer is meant to see – hair accessories or a colour – or, otherwise, it's a mistake made by the inexperienced.

Partings

Partings have a strong effect. A long, straight centre parting will draw attention to the nose. If the nose is prominent it will exacerbate the feature further. Conversely, a side parting with a sloping fringe will lessen the effect.

Hair: Mark Leeson; photography: Kevin Douglas; make-up: Cheryl Phelps-Gardiner; styling: Charlie Davis

Central partings should also be avoided on rounded, fuller faces as this too will make the features more obvious.

Movement

Movement refers to the variance of direction within a hairstyle. The more variety in direction the more movement there will be. Sometimes this movement is because of natural tendency – i.e. curls and waves – sometimes it is artificially created by perming or hairdressing and placement.

Hard and soft effects

Hard and soft effects result from the balance or imbalance within a hairstyle or from the movement or lack of movement within it. Subtle colouring

Hair: Mark Leeson; photography: Kevin Douglas; make-up: Cheryl Phelps-Gardiner; styling: Charlie Davis

enhances softer harmonising effects, whereas stronger, contrasting effects work better in achieving more dramatic results.

The combinations of the above and the way in which these style variables are used will give you the basic rules for which you can create your own original effects. Creating completely new styles requires a great deal of thought and work, and your clients will want to benefit from your creative abilities.

Finally, when thinking about style, you should consider your client's age.

Age

As much as you would like to demonstrate your creative ability on everyone who walks through the salon door, bear in mind that some styles are inappropriate for certain clients. Beyond the physical aspects of style design, age does create some barriers to suitability.

- Younger children (7–11-year-olds) are better suited to simpler hairstyles that don't require too much maintenance. More often than not, and certainly from a hair health and hygiene point of view, they are better off with shorter hairstyles. The next age banding (12–16-year-olds) want to have fashionable looks and many want colour too! Unfortunately, these are still minors and the paying parent and educational establishments must have the last say.

- Young men and women can get away with anything. Fashion will always dictate, and, more often than not, even if there are reasons for not doing a particular style, they will insist on it. This group can enjoy more extreme and dramatic effects and what's more they can get away with it. There are more styles applicable to this age group (16–25-year-olds) than to any other. This is because of the diversity of music, TV and social cultures; these people are influenced by the music they buy, the celebrities they follow on TV and the people they mix with.

- Professional men and women tend to go for *watered down* versions of young fashion. Thinking this in another way: in the clothing fashion world the designs that are seen on catwalks in Paris, London and New York are always the catalysts and precursors for what the high street shops will sell. Dozens of *haute couture* fashion houses demonstrate their season's offerings at the pre-season shows, but not all designs are picked up by the buyers of commercial high street fashion chains, who usually go for the lesser extreme. People want to appear to be trendy and in touch, but not look ridiculous.

- Older woman require greater consideration. Often the signs of aging in the skin show quite clearly and therefore they must influence the way in which you select only appropriate and suitable effects.

CUTTING TOOLS

The choice of cutting tools is an individual one. It is important to select those that will enable you to achieve the specific effect that you want and to know what is required for the style or design that you are working on.

KMS California

You must be able to control the cutting tool you select. It must be comfortable to hold and not too large to handle skilfully. The cutting edges must be sharp, or the hair will be torn and broken. Loose hair can be used to test the sharpness of scissor edges: if the blades cut cleanly, they are sharp enough; if the hair is bent or dragged during cutting, they are unacceptable.

Scissors

Scissors may be used to produce a variety of effects. Many scissors have serrated (saw-like) edges. If the **serrations** are small and fine, the scissors remove a small amount of hair with each cut; if they are large and coarse, the scissors remove a large amount of hair with each cut. *Thinning scissors* are designed to produce variation in the lengths in a section of hair, giving tapered, thinned or texturised effects.

Cutting techniques reduce the length of some of the hairs in the section. The more hair removed, the more severe the effect of the cutting. The weight of the hair tends to straighten the hair, so the more you remove, especially towards the point ends of the hair section, the more the hair will tend to curl.

When you are **tapering** or thinning hair, remember not to remove hair lower (closer to the head) than the middle third of the hair section – unless you intend to produce a drastic effect. For most style cutting, tapering and texturising is kept to the point third of the hair section (that is, the third furthest from the head). When thinning, it is usually the middle of the hair section where most hair is removed.

Scissors are also used to produce *clubbed effects* – blunted ends of the hair sections. This technique retains the full weight of the hair at the ends. Non-serrated or finely serrated blades may be used to achieve clubbed effects. To ensure accuracy, take only small sections of hair each time you **club cut**, otherwise the cut line produced will be uneven. Although hair may be clubbed when it is either wet or dry, it is easier to control the hair when it is cut wet. Wet cutting is considered to be more hygienic, especially if it is done after cleaning the hair with shampoo.

Keith Hall Hairdressing Creative Team

Razors

Razors have traditionally been used to cut hair. They are mainly used to produce tapered, thinned and **textured** effects. Hair shapers now replace the traditional razor. These have disposable blades, which do away with the honing and stropping needed for open razors – the blade is always sharp and able to produce clean cuts. Although razors and hair shapers are mainly used to produce tapered and thinned effects, they can, with care, be used to produce 'chunky' clubbed effects too.

Clippers

Clippers, which are either hand-operated or electric, are designed to produce clubbed hair effects. The closeness or shortness of the cut they produce is

Keith Hall Hairdressing Creative Team

KMS California

determined by the size of the cutting blades. Some clippers have removeable blades and designed to cut close to or further away from the head. Other clipper models have adjustable blades to determine the fineness of cutting.

A closely graduated effect in the nape may be produced using electric clippers or shapers. Alternatively, finely graduating the hair by cutting with scissors over a comb can be just as effective in achieving the style required.

Cutting baselines

A *baseline* is a cut section of hair, which is used as a cutting guide for the following sections of hair. There may be one or more baselines cut: for example, a graduated nape baseline may be cut; another may be cut into the middle of the hair at the back of the head. Other baselines may be cut at the sides and the front of the head. The baselines will determine the perimeter of the hairstyle, or part of the style, and may take different shapes according to the effects required:

- **Symmetric:** The baseline for evenly balanced hair shapes in which the hair is equally divided on both sides of the head. Examples are hairstyles with central partings or with the hair swept backwards or forwards.
- **Asymmetric:** The baseline to be used where the hair is unevenly balanced, for example where there is a side parting and a larger volume of hair on one side of the head, or where the hair is swept off the face at one side with fullness of volume on the other.
- **Concave:** The baseline may be cut curving inwards or downwards. The nape baseline, for example, may curve downwards.
- **Convex:** The baseline may be cut curving upwards and outwards – the nape baseline, for instance, may be cut curving upwards.
- **Straight:** The baseline may be cut straight across, for example where you wish to produce a hard, square effect.

SHAPING AND TEXTURISING

Removing bulk without affecting the length

You can remove bulk without affecting the length of the style by using conventional scissors, thinning scissors or a razor/shaper in a **texturising** technique. Each of the texturising techniques – *slicing, chipping, chopping*, and so on – removes small amounts of hair bulk without reducing the overall hair length. These techniques should be used with thought and care to achieve the desired individual effects.

To remove bulk from long, thick hair, it is generally necessary to cut the hair at the middle third of the hair section. For more drastic thinning, the hair can be removed from nearer the scalp. This can be achieved by point tapering, by razoring close to the scalp, or by using thinning scissors. On medium-length hair, removal of bulk can be achieved by cutting the hair about the middle section. To achieve bulk removal on short hair, you have to resort to removing hair closer to the scalp area.

Achieving lift and volume

To achieve lift and volume you need to reduce some of the hair lengths from each hair section. You can then use the shorter hairs as support for the longer hair. This applies particularly when you *chip in* or *point cut* into the hair: the shorter hairs are more easily turned back to support the lengths. Thinning, tapering and texturising techniques can be used for these effects, on both short and medium-length hair.

REMEMBER: CUTTING TERMS	✔
Texturising	A way of cutting hair to increase movement and texture
Personalising	Introducing particular features to a style to give unique individuality
Point cutting	A way of shattering clubbed ends by removing slices from the ends of held meshes
Chipping	Removal of hair with in held mesh at root, mid length or ends
Slicing	A technique of removing hair with scissors similar to the action of razoring
Channel cutting	A technique for removing 'laterally' wide but narrow sections of hair from near to the root

Enhancing movement

For this you need to use tapered, thinned and texturised effects. Removing bulk hair, by tapering and thinning, encourages the remaining hair to curl more. This enables you to achieve tight, curly effects on long hair, and curl or waved effects on medium-length and short hair.

Paul Falltrick for Matrix

Producing non-uniform effects

Here you may use a variety or combination of texturising techniques: your choice will depend on the style effect that you want to produce. You must decide how much hair is to be removed, and how much you want to remain. Always remember that the head curves, from above to below and from side to side

Accuracy and checks

To achieve your agreed cut shape and style, you will need to carry out checks before, during and as you finish the cut. Without such care and continuity, unpredictable effects are likely to result.

Freehand cutting using the comb to hold the hair
Paul Falltrick for Matrix

BEFORE THE CUT

- Communicate with your client and discuss the requirements.

- Use visual aids to help interpret the client's wishes or to show ideas and themes.

- Examine the hair – its type, length, quality, quantity and condition. Look for factors that influence the choice of style and **cutting methods**.

- Explain if there are any limitations that will affect the result.

- After your analysis, agree or negotiate with the client the suitable courses of action to take.

- Try to show the hair length to be removed.

- Discuss the time that will be taken and the price that you will charge.

- Proceed only when all checks have been made and the client has agreed to your proposals.

- Ensure that you choose the correct tools and techniques for achieving the variety of effects.

DURING THE CUT

- After shampooing and towel drying, dry off the hair so that any previously masked tendencies can clearly be seen.

- Try to keep the hair damp but not saturated so that any newly added technical features can easily be seen.

- Take care with your precision or accuracy by checking each angle at which the hair is taken and held from the head.

- Create your baselines and guideline cuts first, so that there is a continuity within the section patterning.

- When preparing baselines and guide sections, make sure that you attend to the features of your client's face and head. Use these as guides for accurate directions in the cut lines.

- Remember always that the first cuts you make often determine the finished shape of the style.

AFTER THE CUT

- Crosscheck each of the sections of the side, nape, top and front for accuracy and finish.

- Check the density, texture and features of the haircut.

- Position, place and mould the hair where necessary to see the shape clearly.

- When all the loose hair clippings have been removed and the client is prepared and comfortable, continue to blow dry, set and finish the style.

Paul Falltrick for Matrix

CLIENT CARE

You must take care at all times when you are working on your client. The client should be comfortable. She should never be apprehensive about what is being done: give her your undivided attention.

Bear in mind the following points about client care:

- Check the client's record card if she has attended the salon before. If this is a new client, make out a new record card.

- Protect the client adequately with cutting capes and gowns to prevent hair from spoiling clothes or causing irritation.

- All sharp-edged tools must be carefully used so that they never endanger the client.

- Talk to your client from time to time, explaining what is happening. Don't just ignore her and leave her to wonder.

- Aftercare is necessary if your client is to make the most of the cut style you have achieved. Suggest and show how the hair is best arranged and handled.

- Your client may wish to wash and condition the hair, or use hair sprays or hair cosmetics at home. Be prepared to offer professional guidance.

- Finally, give your client the opportunity to make the next appointment.

Hair: Charlotte Cole at Lawrence Anthony (Stratford); photograph: Roberto Aguilar; make-up: Amelia Pruen

Hair: Charlotte Cole at Lawrence Anthony (Stratford); photograph: Roberto Aguilar; make-up: Amelia Pruen

GOOD PRACTICE/HEALTH & SAFETY +

It is your responsibility to ensure your clients' well-being and safety at all times. First and foremost, cross-infection must be avoided: this requires that you operate hygienically and carefully at all times. All tools and materials must be clean.

- Metal tools should be cleared of all hair and debris. They should be sterilised by being placed in an autoclave for the recommended time, or disinfected by cleaning with 70 per cent alcohol wipes.

- Combs, brushes, plastic section clips and similar implements should be cleared of all hair, then washed and sterilised.

- Towels, gowns, wraps and other coverings must be freshly laundered. Only clean materials should be used on clients; they should then be discarded for washing or cleaning.

- It is important that you follow all the COSHH regulations and meet all other health and safety legislation. See the information on the Health and Safety at Work Act 1974 and the Offices, Shops and Railways Act 1974 in Chapter 2.

Hair: Charlotte Cole at Lawrence Anthony (Stratford); photograph: Roberto Aguilar; make-up: Amelia Pruen

STEP BY STEP: RESTYLE LONG HAIR – GRADUATED LAYERS

Step 1 Before: not many clients with long hair want to go short, so this type of popular restyle ticks a lot of boxes

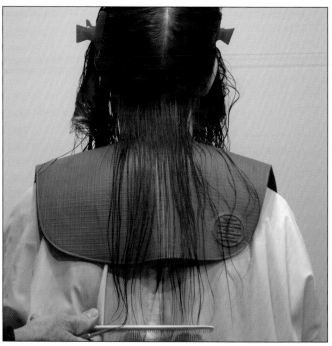

Step 2 Start by sectioning a horizontal section at the lower nape

Step 3 Create the perimeter baseline

Step 4 Continue up the hair; take a second section and cut it to the same length; this will retain density and weight in the finished hairstyle

Step 5 The reverse graduation guideline sets the angle for the general layer patterning

Step 6 After the angle has been created it is continued up through the back towards the crown

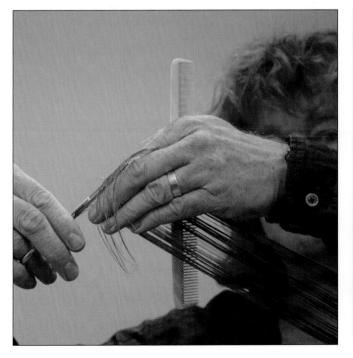

Step 7 Remember to keep the section taut, without slack

Step 8 Create a section at the sides parallel with the hairline

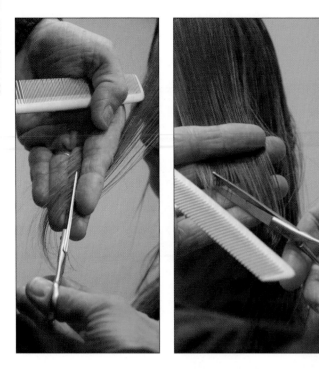

Step 9 Continue the profile shaping up to the half fringe

Step 10 Then work forwards from the crown to the previously cut fringe length to complete

Step 11 Finally, check the profile graduation for accuracy

Step 12 Final effect

STEP BY STEP: CONTEMPORARY ASYMMETRIC

Dylan Bradshaw, Dublin

Step 1 Before

Dylan Bradshaw, Dublin

Step 2 Section the hair down the centre at the back, leaving out a final section 1 inch (3 cm) at the bottom

Dylan Bradshaw, Dublin

Step 3 Begin with a section in this way from the centre to establish a guideline. Cut the hair parallel to the head. Continue to work across the nape section

Dylan Bradshaw, Dublin

Step 4 The length of the cut has now been established. It is important to clean up the hairline at this point, as the shape at the neck will guide the rest of the haircut. The baseline should not be too weighty

Dylan Bradshaw, Dublin

Step 5 Working up the back, take the next section diagonally from the occipital bone to the tip of the ear. Continue to cut sections parallel to the head, following the guideline

Dylan Bradshaw, Dublin

Step 6 Maintain a short length as you work up the back of the head

Dylan Bradshaw, Dublin

Step 7 There should be no weight line at the back

Dylan Bradshaw, Dublin

Step 8 Now begin to join the back sections to the side. Section the hair from the crown to the front temple area. Maintain the short length and establish a soft line around the ear

Dylan Bradshaw, Dublin

Step 9 The perimeter shape has now been established. Repeat the same cutting technique on the left side

Dylan Bradshaw, Dublin

Step 10 Blend to the length of the crown section through to the front by slice cutting at a very steep angle to a top point

Dylan Bradshaw, Dublin

Step 11 Elevate the lengths of the middle section to the centre and cut down towards the crown. Note that the fingers point down parallel to the angle at which the hair will be cut

Dylan Bradshaw, Dublin

Step 12 The internal length of the cut is done. Now create a diagonal part from the centre crown down to the temple area on the far side of the eyebrow for a wide swooping fringe

Dylan Bradshaw, Dublin

Step 13 After creating the part, comb the hair down and blend it to the weightline, maintaining the length at the chin. Make sure you position the head at the correct angle to avoid cutting the lengths too short

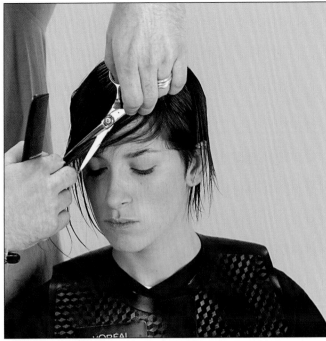

Dylan Bradshaw, Dublin

Step 14 Following the diagonal parting, cut the fringe from the outer corner of the eyebrow down to the point of the chin

Dylan Bradshaw, Dublin

Step 15 The fringe is now complete

Dylan Bradshaw, Dublin

Step 16 Deep point cut the hair to add internal texture

Dylan Bradshaw, Dublin

The final look

STEP BY STEP: CONNEXION CUT

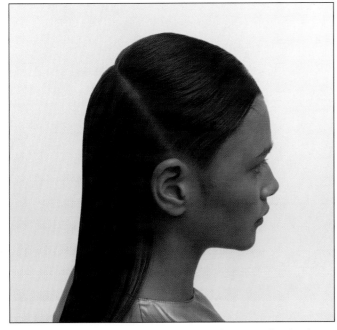

Hair by Sean Hanna; make-up by Pat Mascolo for TIGI; styling by Jiv; photography by Anthony Mascolo for TIGI

Step 1 Divide the hair into a radial dissection (a line from the apex of the ears to a point between the crown and occipital bone). The line should follow the jawline of the face. Check there is a substantial amount of weight at the back as this will be sliced out later

Hair by Sean Hanna; make-up by Pat Mascolo for TIGI; styling by Jiv; photography by Anthony Mascolo for TIGI

Step 2 Starting at the front of the radial dissection, take a central section at the top of the head. This section should sit at a point between the eyes

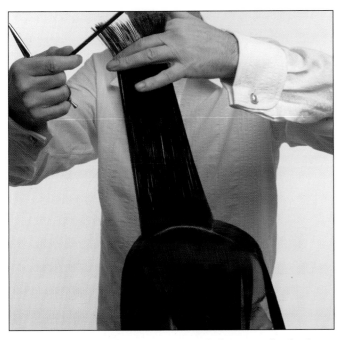

Hair by Sean Hanna; make-up by Pat Mascolo for TIGI; styling by Jiv; photography by Anthony Mascolo for TIGI

Step 3 Cut a line which is shorter in internal shape but longer in the outline. The line should be shorter to longer. To help create the slope of this line, overdirect the hair back towards the crown

Hair by Sean Hanna; make-up by Pat Mascolo for TIGI; styling by Jiv; photography by Anthony Mascolo for TIGI

Step 4 Take the next section from each side of the central section. Overdirect them into the previously cut guideline. This creates a thicker guideline

Hair by Sean Hanna; make-up by Pat Mascolo for TIGI; styling by Jiv; photography by Anthony Mascolo for TIGI

Step 5 From the thick guideline, start to section clockwise, pivoting from the central section. Do each side one after the other to ensure the correct balance; for example, at ten and two of a clock face as shown in this picture

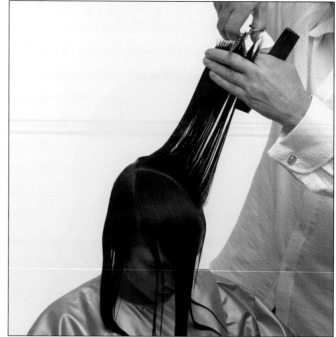

Hair by Sean Hanna; make-up by Pat Mascolo for TIGI; styling by Jiv; photography by Anthony Mascolo for TIGI

Step 6 Continue the shorter to longer layering. Cut each side at the same time to keep the balance correct

Hair by Sean Hanna; make-up by Pat Mascolo for TIGI; styling by Jiv; photography by Anthony Mascolo for TIGI

Step 7 The pivot point should be the shorter point of the haircut. Work round the head from the central section, continuing in pie-shaped sections

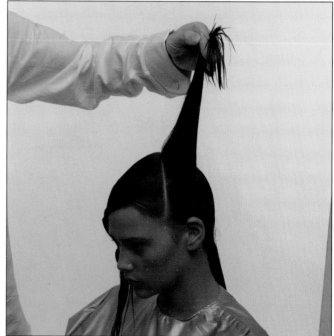

Hair by Sean Hanna; make-up by Pat Mascolo for TIGI; styling by Jiv; photography by Anthony Mascolo for TIGI

Step 8 Keep checking the balance of the outline as it is a very soft outline

Hair by Sean Hanna; make-up by Pat Mascolo for TIGI; styling by Jiv; photography by Anthony Mascolo for TIGI

Step 9 Release the pony tail and point cut a suitable length. Using horizontal sections, cut throught the comb. Always check the balance of the outline

Hair by Sean Hanna; make-up by Pat Mascolo for TIGI; styling by Jiv; photography by Anthony Mascolo for TIGI

Step 10 When the soft outline is complete, create a radial line from the apex of the ears to the top of the head. Using a slicing technique, take a thick vertical section and slice down the hair using previously cut layered lengths as a guide to connect with the outline. This gives the connexion cut its name

Hair by Sean Hanna; make-up by Pat Mascolo for TIGI; styling by Jiv; photography by Anthony Mascolo for TIGI

The final look

STEP BY STEP: CLASSIC INVERTED BOB

Step 1 Before

Step 2 When creating a classic graduated bob, the focus is on precision and the key is the sectioning, which must be perfect. A central parting has been created to give strength to the look

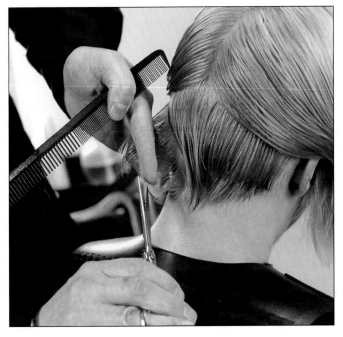

Step 3 Starting at the back, cut the hair from the occipital bone into the nape to establish a very short neat hairline. You can see the length and weight beginning to form

Step 4 Scissor over comb, taper the hair close to the neck. The shape at the nape is now established

Step 5 Now take a diagonal parting from the centre crown down to the top of the ear. Start at the centre and work outwards, cutting fine sections and blending them to the weight line at the nape

Step 6 The shape of the cut is established at the back. The front sections are neatly clipped forward and your sections are clear and precise

Step 7 Continue to work forward. Note that the knuckles are elevated with the fingers pointing down to guide the angle at which the hair should be cut

Step 8 Repeat the same process on the left side, maintaining the angle established towards the chin on the right. Ensure that both sides finish at the same length

Step 9 Next, join the back section to the front area. The sectioning pattern should blend the sides into the back

Step 10 Establish the length for the sides and then work upwards in small sections to the centre parting

Step 11 Cut the final section on the left and then repeat the process on the right side

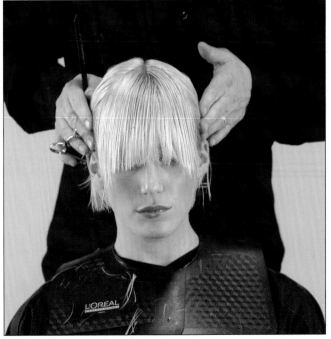

Step 12 After ensuring that both sides are identical, section out the fringe area. Extend it slightly beyond the corner of the eyebrow for a more striking finish

Step 13 To ensure accuracy when cutting the fringe, start by sectioning the top layer of the fringe out very carefully. Focus on cutting a very strong line for the fringe

The final look

CHECKERBOARD

I know and respect the client's rights: data protection, equal opportunities, anti-discrimination and consumer legislation ☐	I know and understand the principles of positive communication ☐	I can communicate positively and professionally with the clients ☐	I always recognise style in limiting factors when I carry out consultation ☐
I can use a variety of cutting techniques and know what their benefits are ☐	I know how to negotiate, reaching a mutually beneficial conclusion ☐	I always carry out working practices according to the salon's policy ☐	I know how to apply a range of creative cutting techniques when cutting hair ☐
I always explain technical terms eliminating ambiguity and false beliefs ☐	I know when and who to refer clients to, in situations where external assistance is required ☐	I understand the necessity of personal hygiene and presentation ☐	I know how to advise, promote and sell other services and products to clients ☐
I know how to adapt cutting techniques to achieve a variety of different creative effects ☐	I can use a variety of cutting tools: scissors, thinning scissors, razors and clippers to achieve differing effects ☐		CHECKER BOARD ✔

Self-test section

Quick quiz: a selection of different types of questions to check your knowledge

Q1 Accuracy is achieved by _ _ _ _ _ _ _ and cutting the hair at the correct angle.   Fill in the blank

Q2 A razor should be used on wet hair.   True or False

Q3 Select from the following list those that are **not** texturising techniques: Multi-selection

Club cutting	☐	1
Graduation	☐	2
Slice cutting	☐	3
Layering	☐	4
Point cutting	☐	5
Chipping	☐	6

Q4 Symmetrical shapes produce equally balanced hairstyles.   True or False

Q5 Which of the following is not a cutting term?   Multi-selection

Crosschecking	☐	1
Thinning	☐	2
Free hand	☐	3
Free style	☐	4

Q6 Precision cutting is dependent upon cutting angles and even tension: True or False

Q7 Which of the following hair growth patterns will affect the way that a fringe lies after it is cut?   Multi-selection

Nape whorl	☐	1
Double crown	☐	2
Widow's peak	☐	3
Low hairline	☐	4
Cow lick	☐	5
High hairline	☐	6

Q8 A _ _ _ _ _ _ _ _ is the perimeter shape produced by cutting?   Fill in the blank

Q9 Which of the following cuts would easily describe a disconnection?   Multi-choice

Graduation in a long hairstyle	☐	1
Reverse graduation in a long hairstyle	☐	2
A fringe in a shoulder-length bob style	☐	3
Texturising in a short cropped style	☐	4

Q10 'Personalising' is the term that refers to any technique that is used to complete a style, tailoring it to the client's specific needs.   True or False

chapter 4

STYLING AND DRESSING HAIR

Unit H25 Style and dress hair to achieve a variety of creative looks		
H25.1	Maintain effective and safe methods of working when styling hair	
H25.2	Style and dress hair creatively	

Unit H26 Style and dress long hair		
H26.1	Maintain effective and safe methods of working when styling hair	
H26.2	Creatively dress long hair	

What do I need to learn?

You need to know and understand:

- **Your salon's policy in respect of clients; preparation, services and safety**
- **How you should work safely and hygienically**
- **How health and safety legislation affects you and your clients**
- **The importance of effective communication**
- **The physical effects on hair from styling and dressing it**
- **The ways in which hair can be dressed to create a variety of effects**
- **The benefits of 'prescribed' aftercare and home maintenance**
- **A range of styling and finishing products, their application, uses and overall benefits to client**
- **A range of styling equipment**

What does it mean?

- **This chapter readdresses the principles of styling and dressing hair that you covered in Level 2 and then extends this, to show how your skill and experience can be applied more creatively to dress different lengths of hair in a variety of ways.**

What do I need to do?

- **You need to create a variety of effects resulting from a range of styling techniques and equipment on different lengths of hair.**

Other info

Related topics and other useful information:

- **Health and safety legislation**
- **Client consultation**

Classic hairstyles Could be defined as *timeless* fashion. That is to say that it is neither in nor out of fashion

1 They tend to be quite simple in its construction

2 In their simplicity they always looks good

3 They are durable and last well, even between salon visits

Current fashions Hair fashions currently in vogue, seen on TV and in hair magazines and other press materials

Emerging hairstyles Hair fashions that are still on the horizon, yet to be processed or adapted. As with current fashion styles, we get glimpses of them on the designer catwalks but these are the raw, undiluted or radical and exaggerated fashions that create the next fashion directions

CHECKERBOARD

At the end of this chapter the checkerboard will help to jog your memory on what you have learned and what still remains to be done. Cross them off with a pencil as you cover each of the topics. (See p. 159.)

INTRODUCTION

This chapter covers two optional units of Level 3. *Styling* and *dressing* are two short words that cover a wide variety of methods, techniques and skills that produce wonderful creative effects. This chapter looks at the basic principles, the methods and the applications beyond everyday requirements.

Dressing involves creating special effects and special styles, some of which may be required for particular occasions only. It may entail adding hair, such as hairpieces, wigs and extensions. Dressing also involves the application of secure, fixing aids, such as grips, clips, combs and slides, as well as imaginative decorative use of hair ornaments. This chapter sets out to provide you with sufficient information to allow you to competently manipulate, fold and style hair with confidence and creativity.

Hair: Mark Leeson; photography: Kevin Douglas; make-up Cheryl Phelps-Gardiner; styling: Charlie Davis

Hair: Mark Leeson; photography: Kevin Douglas; make-up Cheryl Phelps-Gardiner; styling: Charlie Davis

GENERAL PRINCIPLES OF STYLING HAIR

Blow drying and setting are methods of forming wet or damp hair into a dried finished shape. These methods of styling and dressing hair are used to produce the variety of looks that can be either classic or contemporary. You can make hair straighter, curlier, fuller, flatter or wavier.

Blow drying involves drying damp hair into position using brushes, combs and a hand dryer only. In addition to this a variety of other techniques have evolved as finishing techniques:

- *Blow waving:* This involves shaping hair into waves using directed heat from a hand drier using combs and a variety of 'open' vented, flat and round (radial) brushes
- *Scrunch drying:* A technique which uses the hands as the tools for manipulating the roots and ends of the hair to increase lift, body and overall movement.
- *Natural drying:* A variant on leaving hair to dry by itself, achieved by using soft stylers or diffusers as an attachment to hand dryers so that the drying process is speeded up and the overall effect is assisted by some manual manipulation.

Setting involves placing wet hair in to selected positions, and fixing it there while it dries into shape. You may roll the hair round curlers, secure it with clips or pins, or simply use your fingers. Once dry, you complete the process by dressing the hair with brushes and combs. Hair that has been set is called a *pli*. (This term comes from the French *mis-en-pli*, meaning 'put into set'.)

Hair must be controlled effectively, using initiative and a creative interpretation of the client's wishes, taking into account the same factors you consider when you are cutting or styling. Dexterity – skilled, competent hand and finger movements, achieved after much practice – enables you to attain both effective control and shape variety.

As with other techniques, setting produces only a temporary change in hair structure. The pli will be lost as the hair absorbs moisture. Various setting aids are available which slow down this process, holding the shape longer.

Different effects can be produced by different techniques:

- **increasing volume** – adding height, width and fullness, by lifting bases when rollering or curling
- **decreasing volume** – producing a close, smooth, contained or flat style by pincurl stem direction, or by dragged or angled rollering
- **movement or physical changes during setting** – variation of line, waves and curls, produced by using differently sized rollers, pincurls or finger waving.

Relaxed hair effects can be produced by wrapping hair or by using large rollers.

Different techniques are used for hair of different lengths:

- Longer hair (below shoulders) requires large rollers, or alternating large and small rollers, depending on the amount of movement required.

- Shorter hair (above shoulder) requires smaller rollers to achieve movement for full or sleek effects.
- Hair of one length is ideal for smooth bob effects.
- Hair of layered lengths is ideal for full, bouncy, curly effects achieved by, say, barrel or clockspring curls.

Different techniques can also be used to improve the appearance of hair of different textures:

- Fine, lifeless hair can be given increased body and movement. Lank hair can be given increased volume and movement.
- Coarse thick hair requires firmer control.
- Very curly hair can be made smoother and its direction changed.

Hair: Tracey Devine @ Angels; photography: Kevin Douglas; make-up: Sheila Carton; styling: Ferino Daze

SCIENCE BIT! DID YOU KNOW: PHYSICAL CHANGES DURING SETTING ?

Hair is both flexible and elastic. As hair is curled or waved, it is bent under tension into curved shapes. The hair is stretched on the outer side of the curve and compressed on the inner side. If it is dried in this new position, the curl will be retained. This happens because when hair is set the hydrogen bonds and salt bonds between the keratin chains of the hair are broken. The linking system is moved into a new temporary position. (The stronger disulphide links remain unbroken.)

Hair, however, is hygroscopic – it is able to absorb and retain moisture. It does so by capillary action: water spreads through minute spaces in the hair structure, like ink spreading in blotting paper. Wet hair expands and contracts more than dry hair does, because water acts as a lubricant and allows the link structure to be repositioned more easily. So the amount of moisture in hair affects the curl's durability. As the hair picks up moisture the rearranged keratin chains loosen or relax into their previous shape and position. This is why the *humidity* – the moisture content of air – determines how long the curled shape is retained.

The condition and the porosity of hair affect its elasticity. if the cuticle is damaged, or open, the hair will retain little moisture, because of normal evaporation. The hair will therefore have poor elasticity. if too much tension is applied when curling hair of this type it may become limp, overstretched and lacking in spring. Very dry hair is likely to break.

REMEMBER ✓

The keratin bonds of unstretched hair are in alpha state. Keratin bonds of stretched hair are in beta state. (The basis of cohesive setting.)

Preparing the client

Your salon has its own systems and procedures for preparing clients and you must observe these. Some things are general common sense and courtesy, whereas others are client or salon specific. But at the very least they will need to cover basic health and safety as well as the other preparations that you need to make the service a successful and enjoyable experience.

You may be an experienced operator but don't forget the basics. Above all you do need to remember the client's personal comfort and safety throughout the salon visit. Setting and blow drying always follow other services, even if this is only shampooing: there is one thing that is common to all previous services and that is that your client is left with wet hair. You need to make sure that when the towel is taken away that the client's hair doesn't drip. This is not necessarily a safety issue but a measure of your professional care and attention. It's bad enough when saturated short hair drips down on to the gown and soaks the client's clothes, but this becomes even worse and far more uncomfortable if the client has long hair.

If you can, the best way to tackle any service is with the client's hair in a slightly damp i.e. semi-dry state and this goes for several other services too. Working with damp hair is far more comfortable for the client and is the preferred option for busy stylists with little time to spare.

Client positioning

This has a lot to do with your safety too. If a client is slouched in the chair, she is not only a danger to herself, but to you too. Client comfort should extend to the point where it makes the salon visit a welcome and pleasurable experience. But that's where it ends. The salon is not an extension of the client's own front room! Clients should not clutter the floor around the styling chair with bags, magazines and shopping. Anything that can safely be stored away should be; clutter is not only a distraction but a potential security issue and safety hazard too!

Salon chairs are designed with comfort and safety in mind; your client should be seated with her back flat against the back of the chair, her legs uncrossed and the chair at a height at which it is comfortable for you to work. You need to be able to get to all areas around the head, so your working height should be adjusted to suit the particular height of the client. Don't be afraid of asking the client to sit up: it is in her best interest too!

Client protection

Make sure that the gown is on properly and fastened around the neck. It should cover the client's clothes and come up high enough to cover collars and necklines. Don't make the fastening too tight, but close enough at least to stop things going down the back of the neck.

Client consultation

As with any other service your consultation must cover your

- client's expectations
- previous treatment history
- style limitations: hair growth, tendency, amount, texture etc.
- general hair quality/condition.

Hair: Tracey Devine @ Angels; photography: Kevin Douglas; make-up: Sheila Carton; styling: Ferino Daze

Hair: Neil Smith @ Barrie Stephen; photography: Roberto Aguilar; make-up Amelia Pruen; styling: JIV

Where possible use visual aids to put forward ideas; pictures can convey things that the common language finds a barrier. If your client thinks that hairdressers don't like people taking pictures into the salon, it's only because previous hairdressers have not been able to recreate the visuals that they have been offered before.

Long dressed-up hairstyles, say for weddings or balls, should always start with a few visual options, as much of the work is very time consuming and very intricate, so much time would be wasted if you have to start over!

CURLING AND WINDING TECHNIQUES

Curls are series of shapes or movements in the hair. They may occur naturally, or be put there by styling – chemically by perming, or physically by setting. Curls add 'bounce' or lift to the hair, and determine the direction in which the hair lies.

Each curl has a *root*, a *stem*, a *body* and a *point*. The curl base – the foundation shape produced between parted sections of hair – may be oblong, square, triangular and so on. The shape depends on the size of the curl, the stem direction and the curl type. Different curl types produce different movements.

You can choose the shape, size and direction of the individual curls: your choice will affect how satisfying is the finished effect, and how long it lasts. The type of curl you choose depends on the style you're aiming for – a high, lifted movement needs a raised curl stern; a low, smooth shape needs a flat curl. You may need to use a combination of curl types and curling methods to achieve the desired style – for example, you might lift the hair on top of the head using large rollers, but keep the sides flatter using pincurls. Think about this when designing the pli.

Rollering

There are various sizes and shapes of roller. In using rollers you need to decide on the size and shape, how you will curl the hair on to them, and the position in which you will attach them to the base.

- Small rollers produce tight curls, giving hair more movement. Large rollers produce loose curls making hair wavy as opposed to curly.
- Rollers pinned on or above their bases so that the roots are upright, produce more volume than rollers placed below their bases.
- The direction of the hair wound on the roller will affect the final style.

Common rollering problems

- Rollers that are not secured to the base properly, either dragged or flattened, will not produce lift and volume in the final style.
- Too large a hair section will produce reduced movement in the final effect.

Correct winding techniques

REMEMBER ✓

When you do trials for long hair work, say for weddings or balls, remember to take a couple of pictures with the client's mobile. That way they can take them home and review them at their leisure.

It's so easy to forget what the overall effect looks like, particularly from different angles or if the client isn't used to wearing their hair up.

REMEMBER ✓

Evenly tensioned curls produce even movements. Twisted ones produce difficulties.

On- and off-base rollering

- Too small a hair section will produce increased movement or curl in the final effect.
- Longer hair requires larger rollers unless tighter effects are wanted.
- Poorly positioned hair over-falling the sides of the roller will have reduced/impaired movement in the final effect.
- Incorrectly wound hair around the roller will create '**fish hooks**' and/or split ends.
- Twisted hair around the roller will distort the final movement of the style.

Pincurling

Pincurling is the technique of winding hair into a series of curls that are pinned in place while drying. The two most common types of curl produced in this way are the barrel curl and the clockspring.

- The *barrel curl* has an open centre and produces a soft effect. When formed, each loop is the same size as the previous one. It produces an even wave shape and may be used for reverse curling, which forms waves in modern hairstyles. In this, one row of pincurls lies in one direction, the next in the opposite direction. When dry and dressed, this produces a wave shape.
- The *clockspring curl* has a closed centre and produces a tight, springy effect. When formed each loop is slightly smaller than the previous one. It produces an uneven wave shape throughout its length. It can be suitable for hair that is difficult to hold in place.

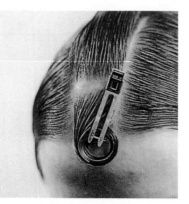

Barrel curl

Clockspring curl

Common pincurl faults

- Tangled hair is difficult to control. Comb well before starting.
- If the base is too large curling will be difficult.
- If you don't turn your hand far enough it will be difficult to form concentric loops.

Finger waving

Finger waving is a technique of moulding wet hair into 'S' shaped movements using the hands, the fingers and a comb. It is sometimes called *water waving* or water setting. The technique is often used as part of an overall finished style.

REMEMBER: FINGER WAVING ✓

You should hold your elbow and arm above your hand when you place it on the head. Only the index finger should touch the head. This gives the required control and pressure. A comb with both widely and closely spaced teeth is the most suitable.

Forming the wave:

1   Use one finger of one hand to control the hair and to determine the position of the wave. Comb the hair into the first part of the crest, and continue along the head.

2   Place the second finger immediately below the crest formed, and comb the hair in the opposite direction.

3   Form the second crest similarly, to complete the final wave shape.

PRODUCTS AND THEIR APPLICATIONS

Application → Product ↓	Short hair	Medium length layered	Medium to long, one length	Long layers
Mousse (Styling product)  Goldwell	Apply a blob the size of a golf ball evenly to the roots and ends on damp hair to give volume and texture	Apply a blob the size of a small orange evenly to the roots and ends on damp hair to give volume and texture	Apply a blob the size of a small orange evenly to the ends for styling hold	Apply a blob the size of an orange evenly to the ends for styling hold
Setting lotion (Styling product) Goldwell	Apply half the contents of the bottle all over evenly for volume and styling hold	Apply the contents of a bottle all over evenly for volume and styling hold		

Hair: Neil Smith @ Barrie Stephen; photography: Roberto Aguilar; make-up Amelia Pruen; styling: Jiv

Hair: Barrie Stephen; Anthony Mascolo; make-up: Pat Mancolo; styling: Ferino Daze

Application → Product ↓	Short hair	Medium length layered	Medium to long, one length	Long layers
Styling gel/glaze (Styling product)	Apply a small amount all over evenly for firmer styling hold	Apply a moderate amount all over evenly for firmer styling hold		
Dressing cream (Finishing product)	Apply a small amount to fingertips, work through before combing out to give control, reduce static and calm down strays	Apply a small amount to fingertips, work through before combing out to give control, reduce static and calm down strays		
Serum (Setting/blow drying finishing product)	Apply a small amount to fingertips; work through to flatten and add shine	Apply a small amount to fingertips, work through to flatten and add shine	Apply a small amount to different areas with the fingertips; work through to flatten and add shine	Apply a small amount to different areas with the fingertips; work through to flatten and add shine

Goldwell

Goldwell

Goldwell

Application → Product ↓	Short hair	Medium length layered	Medium to long, one length	Long layers
Wax (Setting/blow drying finishing product)  Goldwell	Apply a small amount to fingertips; work through to define and hold	Apply a small amount to fingertips, work through to define and hold		Apply a small amount to different areas with the fingertips; work through to define and hold
Hairspray (Setting/blow drying finishing product) Goldwell	Apply mist to hair from about 30–40 cm away from the hair for a 'fixed' hold	Apply mist to hair from about 30–40 cm away from the hair for a 'fixed' hold	Apply mist to hair from about 30–40 cm away from the hair for a 'fixed' hold	Apply mist to hair from about 30–40 cm away from the hair for a 'fixed' hold
Heat protection Goldwell		Apply to lengths after drying to provide protection from intense heat when using straightening irons	Apply to lengths after drying to provide protection from intense heat when using straightening irons	Apply to lengths after drying to provide protection from intense heat when using straightening irons

Hair: Barrie Stephen; photography: Anthony Mascolo; make-up: Pat Mascolo; styling: Ferino Daze

Dressing out

Dressing is the process of applying finish to previously set hair. Setting gives movement to hair in the form of curls or waves. Dressing blends and binds these movements into an overall flowing shape, the style you set out to achieve. It produces an overall form that flows, lightening the head and face and removing dull, flat or odd shapes.

Dressing uses brushing and combing techniques, and dressing aids such as hairspray to keep the hair in place. If you have conducted the pli carefully only the minimum of dressing will be required.

Brushing

Brushing blends the waves or curls, removes the partings left at the curl bases during rollering, and gets rid of any stiffness caused by setting aids.

1   One way of achieving the finished dressing is with a brush and your hand. The thicker the hair, the stiffer the brush bristles need to be. Choose a brush that will flow through the hair comfortably.

2   Apply the brush to the hair ends. Use firm but gentle strokes.

3   Work up the head, starting from the back of the neck.

4   Brush through the waves or curls you have set, gradually moulding the hair into shape.

5   As you brush, pat the hair with your hand to guide the hair into shape. Remember, though, that overdressing and over-handling can ruin the set.

The technique of *double brushing* uses two brushes, applied one after the other in a rolling action.

Backbrushing

Backbrushing is a technique used to give more height and volume to hair. By brushing backwards from the points to the roots, you roughen the cuticle of the hair. Hairs will now tangle slightly and bind together to hold a fuller shape. The amount of hair backbrushed determines the fullness of the finished style.

Tapered hair, with its shorter lengths distributed throughout, is more easily pushed back by brushing. Most textures of hair can be backbrushed; because it adds bulk, the technique is especially useful with fine hair.

Backcombing

This technique is similar to backbrushing, but in this situation a comb rather than a brush is used to turn shorter hairs within a section to provide support and volume. Backcombing is applied deeper toward the scalp than backbrushing and therefore provides a stronger result.

All these styling aspects create the basis for creating a variety of effects the next part of this chapter looks at how this is applied to long hair dressings.

REMEMBER: HEATED STYLING EQUIPMENT ✔

When hairspray or styling products have been used on hair they can cause a build-up on the surface of electric tongs and straighteners. Over time, this will cause tacky or sticky points to develop upon the surface of the equipment when they are hot.

This will make the hair stick to these areas and will cause damage (to the hair and to tongs and straighteners). It stops the equipment from gliding smoothly over the hair.

HEATED STYLING EQUIPMENT

Electric curling tongs, heated brushes and straightening irons are a popular way of applying finish to a hairstyle. They are particularly useful in situations where the hair:

- by blow drying alone will not achieve the desired look
- is not in a suitable condition to be dried into shape.

Sometimes blow drying will not achieve the result that the client is expecting. When extra volume, movement or curl is needed on hair that lacks natural body, or is very fine, additional help is needed to create a lasting effect. Heated tongs and or brushes provide a quick solution to do this. They can be bought in a variety of different sizes (i.e. diameters), which give different levels of movement and are usually pre-heated while the blow dry is in progress.

After the blow dry, the hair is resectioned in a similar way: clipping the large amounts out of the way, until you are ready to work with them. Each section

Desmond Murray

Ceramic straighteners   BaByliss

is then taken and the tongs wound in the direction that you want the hair to move. The same amount of time is given to each section with the hair wound around, then after a few moments the tongs are released and the hair left in position for later combing out and finishing. When the hair is not really in a condition to be blow dried, i.e. is too porous or bleached, you should provide the client with an alternative styling solution. Dry setting, or heated rollers would be a good alternative, but if the client insists that she wanted more of a blow dried effect, you may find that heated tongs or straighteners are the only option left for you.

Straightening irons and particularly, ceramic straightening irons have been a very popular way of calming unruly hair. They work by electrically heating two parallel plates so that the hair can be run between them in one movement from roots to ends, smoothing out the unwanted wave or frizz in the process.

Ceramic straighteners have been particularly successful as they heat up in just a few moments and have a higher operating temperature than metal irons (+170°C). You might think that this alarmingly high temperature would be damaging to hair, but because they have the ability to transfer heat quickly and smoothly to the hair without *grabbing*, they are very effective in creating smoother effects.

When straightening is needed to complement the look on longer hair, it is often better to straighten each section as the blow dry proceeds. This way, by starting at the underneath, each section is completely finished before moving on up the head. The hair stays flatter from the outset and each section is totally dry, stopping the hair from reverting to its previous state (i.e. reverting to alpha keratin).

The use of crimping irons tends to go through phases of popularity every ten years or so. They too have parallel fixed plates but these are wavy and produce flat 'S' waves on longer length hair. They are a great styling accessory for competition and stage work, as crimped effects are visually striking and very unusual. In staged hairdressing shows models with crimped hair will often accompany the look with strong fashion colours too.

Unlike tongs and straightening irons, crimpers are not turned, twisted or drawn through the hair.

1   Each mesh of hair is started near the head and works down to the points of the hair.

2   The meshes should be no wider than the crimping irons and are crimped across the width of the plates.

3   Then after a few moments of heating the crimpers are moved to the last wave crest created and done again.

4   This is repeated down the lengths of the hair until all of the hair is crimped.

5   The final look is not combed out or brushed, but allowed to fall in waved sections.

Crimping irons   BaByliss

Hair: Tracey Devine @ Angels;
photography: Kevin Douglas; make-up:
Sheila Carton; styling: Ferino Daze

Hair: Mark Leeson; photography: Kevin
Douglas; make-up: Cheryl Phelps-
Gardiner; styling: Charlie Davis

CREATIVE LONG HAIR

Long 'hair ups' can be daunting, particularly if you are not used to doing this type of work on a regular basis. They needn't be though, especially if you keep the basics elements firmly in your mind.

Those being:

- having a clear idea of what you are trying to achieve
- building enough structure and support in to the look to ensure that the finished effect is comfortable and durable.

Other than that, the most important things to remember are:

- choosing a style suitable for the occasion
- assessing whether a particular look or effect is going to suit the client
- giving the client enough visual information to help her get an idea of what can be achieved
- agreeing the effect before you start.

It may seem like this list states the obvious, but each one is vital and this is why:

Have clear ideas of what you are trying to achieve

Without clear ideas you could be wasting both your time and the client's. Hair ups can be fun, as they tend to be non-routine work, but overrunning the allotted appointment time is both unproductive and stressful.

If the work is for a forthcoming wedding, the bride will often try to get a package price deal that includes a series of trials too. You need to make sure that from the very first consultation (or before that, if at all possible) you ask the bride-to-be to start collecting images of the sorts of things that she would feel happy with. Remember your creation is part of her total look, so

Hair: Tracey Devine @ Angels;
photography: Kevin Douglas; make-up:
Sheila Carton; styling: Ferino Daze

REMEMBER ✓

Don't put grips in your mouth: it's
unhygienic and could cross-infect
your client.

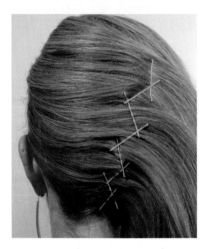

Interlocking grips

ask her to bring in pictures of the dress and also the theme of the wedding
that she is trying to create.

Building enough structure and support in to the look

The simplest mistake that stylists make with hair ups, is not making sure
that there is enough support from the very beginning.

The most common of these mistakes is:

1 Not putting enough backbrushing into the hair initially, because the
   client isn't used to that type of technique.
2 Not creating a comfortable, secure base from which to position and fix
   the hair into style.

The style needs support; it cannot be durable without it. It needs to be
secure as well as creative in its effect. It can only be secure if you use things
like backcombing, grips or bands. Do not be afraid to backcomb the hair. It
may look as if the whole thing is getting too big, but don't forget you can
take out as much as you like within the dressing. **Backcombing/brushing**
provides you with a solid base that you can grip to without the fear of the
grips dropping out. As you become more experienced in handling long hair,
you will find that you won't need to use much spray in the styling stage, but
only later in the finishing off.

The other main tool for giving structure and support is grips. Kirby grips
have one leg with a serrated profile; this helps them to stay in the hair much
better.

Assessing the suitability

This is the first aspect that you should consider. In most cases, hair up is a
special situation. It's not a quick, casual throw up that the client does to get
her hair out of the way. Clients come to the salon for the things that they
can't achieve themselves – that's what hair for special occasions is.

The problem from a suitability point of view is how will the client know if
she is going to like her hair up if she seldom has it styled that way? For
people that don't normally wear their hair up there are always underlying
reasons and these could be:

● their hair is too thick
● they don't like the shape of their ears
● it makes their nose bigger
● they prefer their hair to have volume so they don't like it scraped back
● their hair isn't really long enough in the first place.

Agree the effect before you start

When you have selected a suitable look and you have shown the client
examples of how this would look you will need to help with her self-

Physical features – suitability

Physical features / Hair style	⬭	◯	♡	▽	▢	Protruding ears	Prominent nose	Short neck
			Head shapes					
Vertical roll/pleat	✓	With height to compensate	✓	With height to compensate	With height and width to compensate	Volume at the sides to cover	Volume at the sides	Needs to be sleek
Barrel curls	✓	✓	✓	✓	✓	Volume at the sides to cover (not triangular)	Volume at the sides	Needs to be sleek
Low knot or chignon	✓	With height	✓	✗	With height	Volume at the sides to cover (not triangular)	✗	✗
High knot	✓	✓	✓	✓	✓	Volume at the sides to cover (not triangular)	✗	Needs to be sleek
Plaiting or braiding	✓	With height	✓	✓	✗	Volume at the sides to cover (not triangular)	✓	Needs to be sleek

visualisation. Self-visualisation from the client's point of view is very difficult but you can help very easily. You need to try to rearrange the hair loosely, so that she can get an idea of the balance, proportions and weight distribution. Simple, quick placement can eliminate problems of introduced height or width. If you can convey to your client what it will look like roughly, when her face is exposed, and she likes what she sees, you are halfway there. It will save lots of time later and avoid you having to unpick everything that you have done.

Hair: Phillip Bell, Ishoka; make-up: Karen Lockyer; styling: Peter Breen; photography: Trevor Leighton; products: Wella

REMEMBER: USE THE MIRROR ✔

As you work keep using the mirror to check the shape that you are creating. If you find that the outer contour is misshaped or lacking in volume, don't be afraid to go back to resection and backbrush/comb again.

When you have finished the look hold a back mirror at an angle to maximise what the client can see from her perspective.

French pleat

Vertical roll (French pleat)

The *vertical roll* is a formal classic dressing that suits many special occasions. The hair can be enhanced further by the additions of accessories or fresh flowers. If you review the planning stages for putting hair up you will see, under *building the support* that backcombing is an essential aspect for creating a solid foundation. This should be your starting point for the step by step procedure.

Step by step French pleat

1 Apply a little backbrushing to the back and the sides.
2 Smoothe the hair over to cover any visible tangles.
3 While holding the hair across, interlock a row of grips down from the lower crown to the nape.
4 Take the remaining hair back over smoothly to cover the grips.
5 Fold the ends in and secure into place.
6 Finally, arrange any showing ends into place.

Plaits

Plaiting is a method of intertwining three or more strands of hair to create a variety of woven hairstyles. Plaits can trail away from the head as *singles* or follow the contour of the head as *cane rows* or *French or fishtail plaits*. Whichever plaiting technique you choose, you need to remember to control the hair with an even **tension** while you work. This ensures uniformity and durability in the final effect; it will also save you time as you will not have to dismantle work that you considered already finished. Hair dressed in plaits will last well and it is ideal for specific occasions. It can also be accompanied by **ornamentation**: typical examples would be fresh flowers, coloured ribbons or jewelled accessories. The numerous options for plaited effects are determined by the following factors:

- the number of stems (or plaits) used
- the positioning of the plait or plaits across or around the head
- the way in which the plaits are made (under or over).

Three-stem plait

The three-stem plait is easily achieved and demonstrates the basic principle of plaiting hair.

1 Divide the hair to be plaited into three equal sections.
2 Hold the hair with both hands, using your fingers to separate the sections.
3 Starting from either the left or the right, place the outside section over the centre one. Repeat this from the other side.

REMEMBER

For more information on plaiting or twisting techniques see Chapter 8 on African Caribbean hairdressing as there is a large section covering these effects.

4 Continue placing the outside sections of hair over the centre ones until you reach the ends of the stems.

5 Secure the free ends with ribbon or thread.

Three-stem 'French' plaited style

1 Brush the hair to remove all tangles.

2 With the hair tilted backwards, divide the foremost hair into three equal sections.

3 Starting from either the left or the right, cross an outside stem over the centre stem. Repeat this action with the opposite outer stem.

4 Section a fourth stem (less in thickness than the initial three stems) and incorporate this with an outside stem.

5 Cross this thickened stem over the centre, and repeat this step with the opposite outer stem.

6 Continue this sequence of adding hair to the *outer* stem, before crossing it over the centre.

7 When there is no more hair to be added, continue plaiting down to the ends and secure them.

For information on three-stem braids or scalp plaits, cane rows and twisting techniques, see Chapter 8 pp. 318–23.

For information on working with added hair, see Chapter 7.

Hair: Phillip Bell, Ishoka; make-up: Karen Lockyer; styling: Peter Breen; photography: Trevor Leighton; products: Wella

Desmond Murray

Weaving

Hair weaving is a process of interlacing strands of hair to produce a wide variety of effects. A small area of woven hair can be very effective by itself, or used to highlight a particular part of a style. Hair weaving is also used to place and hold lengths of hair.

At its simplest, hair weaving may be used to hold long hair back from the face. This may be done by taking strands of hair from each side, sweeping them over the hair lengths, and intertwining them at the back.

More intricate is the *basket weave,* which uses a combination of plaiting, twisting and placing to form many shapes and patterns. It is important to wet or gel the hair before starting to weave. Weave tightly or loosely according to the effect you are aiming for.

The hair may be woven as follows:

1 Use six meshes of hair, three in the left hand and three in the right.

2 Start with the furthest right-hand mesh. Pass this *over* the inner two meshes.

3 From the left, pass the outside mesh *under* the next two and *over* one.

4 Continue to the ends of the hair.

5 Tuck in the hair ends and secure them in position.

REMEMBER ✔

Practise on colleagues or models and experiment with different woven shapes before you attempt to weave hair for clients.

STEP BY STEP: HAIR UP – CONTEMPORARY EFFECT WITH A TWIST

Step 1 Before: finding hair ups that are not too formal or too casual can be very difficult. So where do you draw the line? What is the difference between fun and formal?

Step 2 After brushing the hair to remove any tangles, start the style at the front by dividing the hair with a tail-comb

Step 3 Twist the section of hair firmly but not too tightly back towards the crown area

Step 4 Grip the twisted section into place before starting the next channel

Step 5 Continue with the same technique on each of the channels

Step 6 Twist the sections at the back from the nape up to the crown in the same way

Step 7 Leave a section at the front to soften the hairline profile. Lightly backcomb the remaining hair to finish

Final effect

STEP BY STEP: HAIR UP – CLASSIC EFFECT DRESSED IN BARREL CURLS

Step 1 Before: barrel curls are a favourite for weddings or balls. So how do you create a timeless classic in a few easy steps?

Step 2 After brushing the hair to remove any tangles, start the style by fixing the hair into position with a circlet of interlocking pins

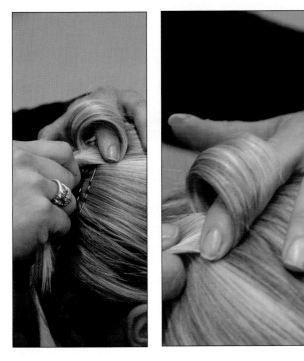

Step 3 Start the barrel curls at the upper centre of the circlet

Step 4 Continue the same technique on adjacent sections of hair

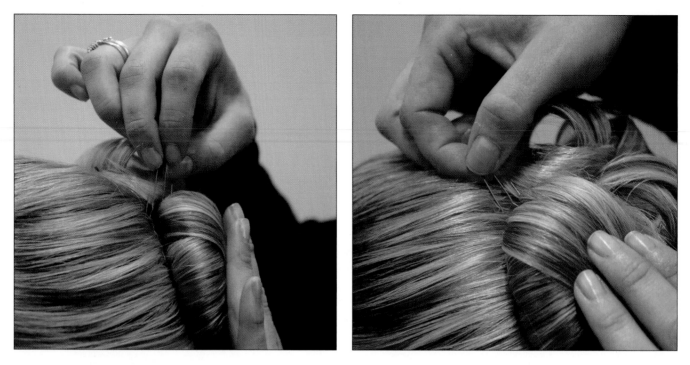

Step 5 Carefully secure each of the barrel curls with pins underneath

Step 6 Then, working downwards, create the curls within the base area of the inner circlet

Step 7 Finished effect

STEP BY STEP: HAIR UP

There are classic, traditional looks and avant garde dramatic effects. This is an example of a romantic effect for special occasions.

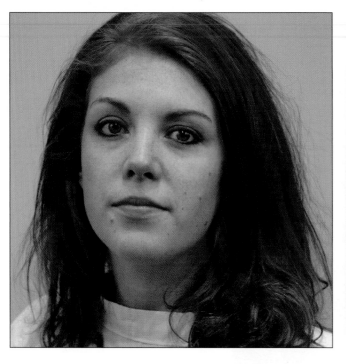

Step 1 Before: clients with this type of look 'shout out' for soft, romantic effects. In this hair up the hair is prepared by curling it first

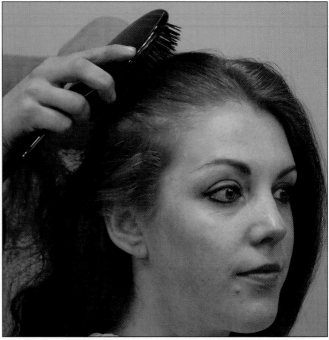

Step 2 Brush the hair to remove tangles

Step 3 Start at the lower nape, so that each curl placed does not disturb those done previously

Step 4 Use ceramic straighteners to produce curls by drawing them quickly down the section of hair in one continuous movement

Step 5 The hair after curling, ready for positioning

Step 6 Lift and grip into place sections of curls

Step 6 *Continued*

Step 7 Work up and around to the final placements at the front

The final effect

STEP BY STEP: HAIR UP – CLASSIC EFFECT PART 1

Step 1 Before: Kim suits classic effects such as chignons, pleats and soft folded hair

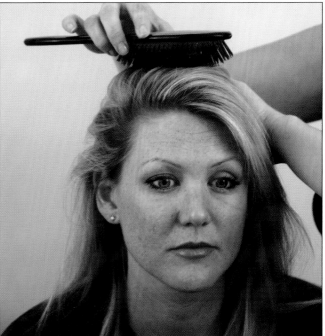

Step 2 Brush the hair to remove tangles

Step 3 Then, starting at the front, take two sections of hair

Step 4 Holding the two sections in one hand, take a third

Step 5 Interlock the sections by weaving them together

Step 6 Introduce another section of hair

Step 7 Continue the technique through the top

Step 8 Now fix these sections into place with grips

A low, asymmetrical chignon finishes the effect to create a simple, classic look suitable for any event

STEP BY STEP: HAIR UP – CLASSIC EFFECT PART 2: CREATING A SIMPLE CHIGNON

Step 1 Brush the hair through to remove any tangles

Step 2 Apply 'doughnut' former around a pony tail at the position where you want the chignon to be

Step 3 Position and grip the former into place

Step 4 Separate the hair and place it around the former. Grip the hair to the base underneath

Step 5 A light mist with spray and the effect is complete

Classic and romantic effects

STEP BY STEP: CONTEMPORARY HAIR INCORPORATING ADDED HAIR

J & E Training

Step 1 Before

J & E Training

Step 2 Start at the crown by dividing the hair horizontally, then again at an angle, to create a triangular section

J & E Training

Step 3 Beginning at the upper part of the section, plait the hair across and fix it into position

J & E Training

Step 4 Divide the lower back hair and affix a contrasting weft by gripping it across near the root

J & E Training

Step 5 The weft can be mixed and blended with the cient's own hair to create a contrast that defines the plaited or twisted technique

J & E Training

Step 6 Take further sections below to create a banding effect

J & E Training

Step 7 Twist the next section throughout the length

J & E Training

Step 8 Grip the twists and plaits into position

J & E Training

Step 9 Take the remaining front hair across and plait it to complete the style

J & E Training

Finished effect

I know and respect the client's rights: data protection, equal opportunities, anti-discrimination and consumer legislation ☐	I know and understand the principles of positive communication ☐	I understand the physical properties of hair in reference to styling and dressing ☐	I always recognise the critical influencing factors when I analyse the clients hair ☐
I can identify the range of hair and scalp problems ☐	I know how to negotiate, reaching a mutually beneficial conclusion ☐	I always carry out working practices according to the salon's policy ☐	I know how to apply a range of styling techniques on short, medium and longer length hair ☐
I know how to create a range of effects on short, medium and longer length hair ☐	I know when and who to refer clients to, in situations where external assistance is required ☐	I can carry out a variety of creative styling effects on different length hair ☐	I know how to advise, promote and sell other services and products to clients ☐
I know how to provide aftercare advice to clients so that they can maintain their own hair between visits ☐			CHECKER BOARD ✔

Self-test section

Quick quiz: a selection of different types of questions to check your knowledge

Q1 Self-cling rollers are commonly known as _ _ _ _ _ _ rollers.   Fill in the blank

Q2 Humidity in the atmosphere will help to retain set hairstyles.   True or False

Q3 Which of the following dressings are traditionally long hair up styles?   Multi-selection

Plaits	☐	1
Knots	☐	2
Weaves	☐	3
Rolls	☐	4
Braids	☐	5
Pleats	☐	6

Q4 The keratin bonds of stretched hair are said to be in the beta state?   True or False

Q5 Which chemical bonds within the hair are not affected during setting?   Multi-selection

Hydrogen bonds	☐	1
Disulphide bonds	☐	2
Salt bonds	☐	3
Oxygen bonds	☐	4

Q6 Heated rollers are a quick way of setting wet or dry hair into style.   True or False

Q7 Hair set on rollers, produces which of the following results and effects?   Multi-selection

Increased body at the roots	☐	1
No body at the roots	☐	2
No movement at the ends	☐	3
Straighter effects	☐	4
Wavy effects	☐	5
Same as blow dried effects	☐	6

Q8 The common name for a centrally positioned, vertically folded effect,   Fill in the blank
worn on the back of the head, on long hair is a _ _ _ _ _ .

Q9 Which item of equipment would smoothe and flatten frizzy, unruly hair best?   Multi-choice

Curling tongs	☐	1
Ceramic straighteners	☐	2
Crimping irons	☐	3
Blow dryer	☐	4

Q10 Hair ups are easier to perform on hair that has just been washed, conditioned   True or False
and dried off.

chapter 5

COLOURING AND COLOUR CORRECTION

Unit H30 Colour hair using a variety of techniques

H30.1   **Maintain effective and safe methods of working when colouring hair**

H30.2   **Prepare for colouring**

H30.3   **Create a variety of colouring techniques**

H30.4   **Resolve basic colouring problems**

Unit H28 Provide colour correction services

H28.1   **Maintain effective and safe methods of working when correcting hair colour**

H28.2   **Determine the problem**

H28.3   **Plan and agree a course of action to correct colour**

H28.4   **Correct colour**

What do I need to learn?

You need to know and understand:

- **How health and safety legislation affects you and your clients**
- **The importance of good communication**
- **Colouring science and a range of colouring processes and products**
- **The range of tests that need to be conducted**
- **The benefits of sound advice followed up by prescribed home maintenance**
- **A range of tools and equipment and their uses**

What does it mean?

- **This chapter covers the fundamental aspects of, colouring and bleaching theory, the variety of techniques used and the advanced principles, skills and methods of colour correction work.**

What do I need to do?

- You need to take adequate precautions in preparing yourself and the client before any colouring procedure.
- You need to undertake the necessary tests prior to any colouring procedure.
- You need to be able to prepare colouring products in readiness.
- You need to be able to apply a variety of colouring products.
- You need to be able to carry out a variety of technical procedures.
- You need to be able to correct a variety of colouring problems.

Other info

Related topics and other useful information:

Health and safety legislation

Client consultation

KEY WORDS

Colour correction   A range of techniques used to counter colouring problems, e.g.

Banding An unwanted effect that appears as distinct bands of uneven colour generally a problem found on longer hair associated with poor colour application/execution or as a result of poor hair condition

Discolouration   An unwanted effect that appears as shadowing or blotches often associated with incompatibles

Tinting back   A process of recolouring previously lightened hair (e.g. highlights) back to the hair's natural hair depth and tone

Prepigmentation   Part of a larger process, tinting back, where missing pheomelanin (yellow/red pigments) are replaced first, so that the final target shade can be achieved without unwanted ashen 'green' tones being present

De-colouring   A process which removes synthetic colour from hair by using a colour reducer (*not* bleach)

CHECKERBOARD

At the end of this chapter the checkerboard will help to jog your memory on what you have learned and what still remains to be done. Cross them off with a pencil as you cover each of the topics. (See p. 219.)

INTRODUCTION

This chapter combines two of the most complex, but exciting, optional units of Level 3. These colouring units comprise of eight elements:

H30 Colour hair using a variety of techniques

H30.1   Maintain effective and safe methods of working when colouring hair

    H30.2   Prepare for colouring

    H30.3   Create a variety of colouring techniques

    H30.4   Resolve basic colouring problems

H28   Provide colour correction services

    H28.1   Maintain effective and safe methods of working when correcting hair colour

    H28.2   Determine the problem

    H28.3   Plan and agree a course of action to correct colour

    H28.4   Correct colour

Colouring is arguably the most exciting and often the most difficult aspect of contemporary hairdressing. The increasing demands and expectations of clients has made colouring and in particular the application of special colour effects the 'must have' of hairdressing … Our clients are getting more informed about hair styling, hair condition and the benefits of product usage. But colouring for them has a compulsory 'magnetic' but *still elusive* draw, techniques and products are developing all the time and the possibilities are boundless, so *dare* to create a little magic!

Goldwell

COLOUR PRINCIPLES

Seeing colour

When you look at an object, what you are actually seeing is light reflected from it. White light is really a mixture of many colours – that is why sunlight *refracted* through falling rain can produce a rainbow. This *splitting* of white light creates what we see as seven different colours. Red, orange, yellow, green, blue, indigo and violet.

A white object *reflects* most of the white light that falls upon it; a black object *absorbs* most of the light falling on it. A red object reflects the red light, and absorbs everything else.

Hair colour depends chiefly on the pigments in the hair, which absorb some of the light and reflect the rest. The colour that we see is also affected by the light in which it is seen, and (to a lesser extent) by the colours of clothes worn with it.

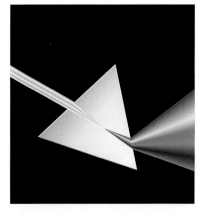

The colour spectrum from visible light   Wella

- White light from halogen bulbs and full daylight will show the hair's natural colour.
- Yellowish light emitted from standard electric light bulbs adds warmth to hair colour, but neutralises blue ash or ashen effects.
- Bluish/green light from fluorescent tubes reduces the warmth of red/gold tones in hair.

Darren Ambrose of D & J Ambrose,
London

Mixing colours

The colours of the pigments in *paints* arise from three primary colours – red, blue and yellow. Pairs of these give the secondary colours – violet, green and orange. The various other colours are made from different proportions of the primary colours: red and blue mixed together creates violet, yellow and blue creates green, and yellow and red create orange.

White and black can be added to vary the tone of the colour.

The primary colours in *light* are different – red, green and blue. (These are the three colours used in video cameras, computer screens and television.) The secondary colours are yellow, cyan and magenta.

Hair colour (pigmentation)

The natural colour of hair is determined by the colour of pigments within the hair's cortex. These are formed when the hair is in its germinating stage of growth.

Hair colour pigments – *melanin* – are deposited into the hair shaft at the region of the papilla and germinal matrix. The pigments responsible for black and brown hair are called **eumelanin**; those responsible for red and yellow hair are called **pheomelanin**. (There are in fact others, but these are the main pigments.) The hair colour you actually see is affected by the amount and proportion of the pigments present, by the light in which the hair is seen, and – to a certain extent – by the colours of the clothes and make-up worn.

With age, or after periods of stress, the production of natural pigments may be reduced. The hairs already on the head will not be affected, but the new ones will. As hairs fall out and are replaced, the proportion that has the original pigmentation diminishes and the hair's overall colour changes. It may become lighter. If no pigment is produced at all, then the new hairs will be white.

The proportion of white hairs among the naturally coloured ones causes the hair to *appear* grey. Greyness is often referred to as a percentage; for example, '50 per cent grey' means that half of the hairs on the head are white and the rest are pigmented.

It is not uncommon for young people to exhibit some grey hairs. This does not necessarily mean that they will go grey, or completely white, at an early age.

Depth and tone

These two key factors help us to describe the hair's colour.

We refer to hair colour in the following terms:

Depth = how light or dark it is

Tone = the colouration or hue i.e. ashen, golden, mahogany, etc.

These terms are easier to understand if we tabulate them in the following way.

Darren and Jackie of D & J Ambrose,
London

REMEMBER: COMPOUND HENNA ✓

Compound henna is not pure vegetable henna; it is mixed with other element oxides and is therefore incompatible with modern colouring and perming materials!

Taking this principle further, the *International Colour Chart* (ICC) offers a way of defining hair colours systematically. (Although charts may vary between manufacturers.) Shades of colour are divided and numbered, with black (1) at one end of the scale and lightest blonde (10) at the other. Tones of other colours (/1 /9 or also stated as .1 .9) are combined with these, producing a huge variety of colours. Charts are usually arranged with shades in rows down the side and tones in columns across the top. To use them, first identify the shade of your client's hair: that row of the chart then shows the colours you could produce with that hair.

For example, if your client has medium blonde hair (depth 7) and you colour with a red tone (.4), the result should be a rich copper blonde (7.4). The possibilities are almost endless, as these examples indicate:

● To produce ash shades, add blue.
● To produce matt shades, add green.
● To produce gold shades, add yellow.
● To produce warm shades, add red.
● To produce purple or violet shades, add mixtures of red and blue.

ACTIVITY: WARM AND COOL TONES ⇄

As a group exercise work through your salon's shade chart and for each shade note down its shade name, number or code, then whether it is a warm tone or a cool tone. Save the tabled information in your portfolio for future reference. How many warm shades were there? How many cool shades were there? How many were neither warm nor cool? Did you find any surprising results?

Key skills: Communication
2.1 Take part in discussions
2.2 Produce written materials
2.3 use images

Darren Ambrose of D & J Ambrose, London

Depth and tone

Depth	Very light				
	Light				
	Medium				
	Dark				
	Very dark				
Tone		Copper	Gold	Natural	Ash

International Colour Chart system

10	Lightest blonde 10						
9	Very light blonde 9	Very light ash blonde 9.1					
8	Light blonde 8			Light golden brown 8.3			
7	Medium blonde 7	Medium ash blonde 7.1			*Paprika* 7.44		
6	Dark blonde 6			Dark golden brown 6.3	*Acapulco* 6.46		Berry 6.62
5	Light brown 5		Truffle 5.2		Russet 5.4	*Burnt Toffee* 7.52	
4	Brown 4			Medium golden brown 4.3			
3	Dark brown 3						
2							
L'Oréal Majirel	Natural .0 or /0	Ash .1 or /1	Soft ash .2 or /2	Gold .3 or /3	Red .4 or /4	Mahogany .5 or /5	Violet .6 or /6

In the table we see how the L'Oréal shades are positioned within the colour table. The three shades Acapulco, Burnt Toffee and Berry are defined in italic as these colours identify additional colour properties. These shades are denoted, as are many others, with a second number after the decimal point: 6.46.

The primary tone denotes the range that the shade is in. Whereas, the secondary tone indicates additional colouration within the shade. This provides lots of extra colouring permutations. Sometimes colour manufacturers want to increase a shade's intensity and vibrancy; this is achieved by adding *double* the tone to the particular shade.

Shade: Acapulco	Depth	Primary tone	Secondary tone
	6	.4	6

Shade: Paprika	Depth	Primary tone	Secondary tone
	7	.4	4

HAIR COLOUR TYPES

Temporary colour

Temporary colourants are available in the form of lotions, creams, mousses, gels, lacquers, sprays, crayons, paints and glitter dust. On hair in good condition these do not penetrate the hair cuticle, nor do they directly affect the natural hair colour, they simply remain on the hair until washed off.

Temporary colourants are ideal for a client who has not had colour before, as they are readily removed if not liked. They have subtle colouring effects, particularly on grey or greying hair. Hair condition, shine and control are enhanced. If used on badly damaged or very porous hair, the temporary colourant may quickly be absorbed into the cortex, producing uneven, patchy results.

Semi-permanent colour

Semi-permanent colourants are made in a variety of forms: some are ready-mixed for immediate use; others need to be mixed and prepared as necessary before use. Always check the manufacturer's instructions to ensure that you know which type of colourant you are going to use.

Semi-permanent colourants contain pigments that are deposited in the hair cuticle and outer cortex. The colour gradually lifts each time the hair is shampooed. Some colourants will last through six washes, others longer.

These colourants are not intended to cover large percentages of white hair – for instance, black used on white hair would not produce a pleasing result. Choose colours carefully.

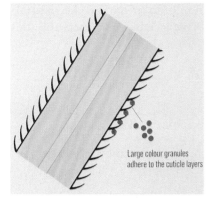
Large colour granules adhere to the cuticle layers

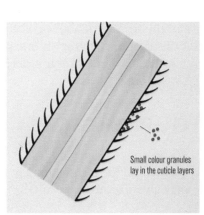
Small colour granules lay in the cuticle layers

During development the granules swell and are trapped in the cuticle layers

Temporary hair colouring Wella

Large/small colour granules
penetrate the cuticle layers

Semi-permanent hair colouring
Wella

Hair: Lindsay Burr at Goody's;
photography: Kevin Douglas;
make-up: Cheryl Phelps-Gardiner;
styling: Ferino Daze

Note that some permanent colourants may be diluted for use as semi-permanents. These products may contain skin sensitisers, however, so skin tests must be performed before they are used in this way.

Longer-lasting colour

Now that 'frequent use' shampoos have become popular, some semi-permanent colourants are soon removed. A new generation of *longer-lasting colourants* has been introduced which are more practical and economical. These colours allow for a greater coverage of white hair and last for up to 12 washes.

Quasi-permanent colours

Quasi-colourants are nearly permanent – they last for a longer period of time than semi-permanent colourants but not as long as the true permanent colourants. When using them, follow the manufacturer's instructions strictly. (Always carry out a skin test.)

REMEMBER: USING COLOURS ✓

If you are in any doubt between to shades, always use the lighter one as it is easier to add more depth to hair, than it is to remove unwanted colour from hair.

Permanent colours

Permanent colours are made in a wide variety of shades and tones. They can cover white and natural-coloured hair to produce a range of natural, fashion and fantasy shades.

Hydrogen peroxide is mixed with permanent colourants. This oxidises the hair's natural pigments and joins the small molecules of synthetic pigment together, a process called *polymerisation*. The hair will then retain the colour permanently in the cortex. Hair in poor condition, however, will not hold the colour and colouring could result in patchy areas and colour fading.

The use of modern permanent colourants can lighten or darken the natural hair colour, or both together in one process. This is achieved by varying the percentage strength of hydrogen peroxide.

COLOUR CHOICE

Your choice of colour is crucial: take time to make it carefully. A hurried choice may give disastrous results!

A number of questions need to be answered before the final choice of colour is made.

What does the client require?

Clients look to colour as a solution for many things:

Many clients requesting a permanent colour are seeking to disguise their greying hair. A client who wants something to tone a few grey hairs may be successfully assisted with temporary, semi-permanent or longer-lasting colourants. However, if the client is really longing simply to be young again it is difficult to help much with any type of colour, though it may well be possible to help her to look a little more youthful.

Most colour work undertaken within the salon has been stimulated by fashion. The majority of this work now falls into the partial colouring techniques. The multi-toning permutations present a 'boundless' choice of options, carried out by an ever-growing range of techniques and applications. With the decline in full-head colouring (probably much to do with the variety and choice of home colouring products) these partial, varietal colouring options remain a 'professionals only' option for the client.

What other factors are relevant?

During your consultation with your client, you will need to consider the following points:

- her age and lifestyle
- her job, if she has one
- her fashion and dress sense, and the colours she prefers to wear
- her natural hair colour and her skin colour
- the hair's texture, condition and porosity
- the colourant you could use
- the techniques you would employ
- the time and cost involved.

When you have taken these points into consideration, you should be able to determine which hair colour shade, colourant and process to recommend to your client.

Remember accuracy: Measuring flasks and mixing bowls

Measurement of hydrogen peroxide at any strength must be accurate; the amount used in relation to colour is a critical factor to a successful outcome. Different types of colour are formulated to be used with particular developers; for example, a Wella *colour perfect* should be mixed with *Welloxon* developer. If you use a different developer the consistency will be wrong and this will make the application difficult. All gel and cream colours, when mixed, will be stiff enough not to run on either the brush or the hair. Using unmatched, alternative developers will do the opposite and could be a potential hazard for the client.

When you measure developer into a measuring flask you must make sure that your eyeline is at the same level as the liquid in the flask. If you do put

Hair by Steven Goldsworthy of Goldsworthy's

a little too much into the flask the pouring edge will allow you to put back what you don't need.

When you mix developer with colour from tubes, you will notice that all tubes have markings on the side showing the $\frac{1}{4}$, $\frac{1}{2}$ and $\frac{3}{4}$ points. These enable you to squeeze from the bottom of the tube up to these points, knowing that your measurement will be accurate.

If you are mixing two or more shades of colour together, always mix these well in the bowl first before adding any developer. This allows the different pigments to be evenly distributed throughout the colour and also throughout the hair when its applied!

GOOD PRACTICE/HEALTH & SAFETY: PREPARING YOURSELF AND THE CLIENT

- Always refer to the results of tests first
- Always gown and prepare your client properly so that she is protected from spillages of chemicals
- Prepare your work area so that you have everything at hand
- Always wear the PPE (i.e. the vinyl gloves and aprons) provided by the salon every time you apply colour
- Apply barrier creams as or where necessary
- Always follow the manufacturer's instructions; never deviate from the tried and tested formulae
- Make sure that your work position is clear and that your posture is correct
- Make sure that the client is comfortable throughout as she will be sitting for some considerable time

---

ACTIVITY: UNDERSTANDING COLOUR CO-ORDINATION

Collect pictures from magazines showing hair colours worn with clothes of various colours. Which ones work well? Why do some hair colours look more suitable with clothes of a particular colour?

Referring back to the section on colour co-ordination in Chapter 2, collect samples of the four different image types and see if any particular patterns emerge. Keep the samples in your portfolio for future reference

Key skills: Communication

2.1 Take part in discussions

2.2 Produce written materials

2.3 Use images

Colour selection principles: 1. Choice, state and condition

Colour selection – the process you go through in choosing the right target shade for your client's hair and the correct mixture of products to achieve that target shade – is based upon:

- The customer's initial choice.

- The existing state of your client's hair (whether it is already processed e.g. highlighted).

- The current condition of your client's hair:

1. If the hair has been regularly coloured before and there is a clear regrowth, with ends that have faded, you may only need to do a straightforward regrowth application with the same colour. Then later in the development process the residual colour can be diluted and taken through to the rest to refresh the total effect. So, in this instance, a regrowth that takes 20 minutes to apply can be left for 30 minutes' development, and then in the last 15 minutes it can be taken through to the ends, until it's all ready to be removed. However, if your client's hair has been coloured before, you also need to remember that it will not be possible to make the hair lighter by colouring. Permanent colour does not reduce permanent (synthetic) pigments from the hair. (If this is required you will have to use a colour remover first.)

2. If you need or want to counteract and neutralise unwanted tones in the hair, you will need to apply the principles of the colour wheel. If the client wants to reduce *calm down* unwanted red tones then you will be choosing a colour slightly darker in *depth* but which has the matt *tones* capable of neutralising that effect. Conversely, if your aim is to eliminate ashen matt tones (the colour often seen on fairer hair colours that are regularly subjected to chlorinated swimming pools) then you will be introducing warmer tones to the hair. So in this situation, a 'greeny'-looking base 6 blonde will be improved by a shade depth 6 but with a tone warmth .03 (for more information see the depth and tone table earlier in this chapter). If you had to reduce a tonal effect that was too yellow, say on a head that had been lightened, then although the principle of **toning** bleached hair is slightly different, you would still be applying the principles of the colour wheel and therefore using a violet-based ash colour to neutralise the unwanted tones.

3. If your client has never had any colour on her hair before (virgin hair) then colour targeting is easy. Your client will be able to choose practically any shade on the permanent shade chart, providing it is at the same depth or darker than her natural colour. (It is possible to lighten a shade or two with colour in certain situations. See the bleaching and lightening section later in this chapter.)

4. If your client has grey or greying (i.e. white) hair then you will have to decide and agree on what reduction of grey is necessary. If the client wants to cover all the grey, then this is only achievable by using or adding base shades to the target colour, i.e. a natural shade or a natural + target shade. The amount of base added to target shade is directly proportional to the amount of grey. Grey hair is referred to as a percentage of the whole head; therefore a client who has about a quarter of their hair that is grey is referred to as 25 per cent grey. Similarly, a client with one tenth of grey hair is 10 per cent grey.

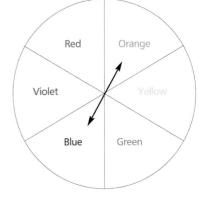

Colour wheel

Pre-softening white hair

Pre-softening is done as a preparation for colouring difficult white/greying hair.

In situations where there is a significant amount of white hair to be coloured, it is advisable that the hair is prepared by prior pre-softening. Resistant white hair often has a shiny or glassy look and this is due to the cuticle layer being packed down tightly in a closed, flat position. If you were to apply a permanent colour to this you will find that the colour will have a shadowed or faded look where you will still see the ashen grey underneath. To stop this from happening you need to pre-soften the hair beforehand.

How to pre-soften white hair:

1. Pour 30 cc of neat 20 volume (6 per cent) liquid hydrogen peroxide into a colouring bowl.

2. Apply the hydrogen peroxide to the resistant, white hair with a colouring brush.

3. Place the client under a pre-heated hood dryer or colour **accelerator** for 15 to 20 minutes.

Or, alternatively, dry in the liquid peroxide with a hand dryer until the hair has dried.

Then, after the drying has finished, the cuticle layer will have lifted sufficiently for you to be able to apply a permanent colour and it will now deposit properly into the cortex as opposed to lying at or around the cuticle's surface.

Current condition

The existing condition also plays a major contributing factor to the way in which the hair will respond when it is coloured. Hair that is too porous will affect the way in which the colour is absorbed. The porosity of hair will never be even along the hair length, let alone throughout the head. This is because the porosity of the hair is directly related to areas of damaged cuticle. Areas of high porosity occur at sites along the hair shaft where cuticle is torn or missing. Here at these points, moisture or chemicals can easily enter the inner hair without cuticle layer resistance. This changes the rate of absorption that ultimately affects the final evenness of the colour and the hair's ability to retain colour in subsequent washing etc. During processing the only other factors that affect the achievement of an even and expected final colour result (providing your selection is correct) are:

- timing
- temperature.

Timing The level of colour saturation is proportional to the length of time that that the hair is exposed to colour. Under-processed hair will not achieve the same saturation as hair that has had full development. In other words, the longer that colour is left on, the more *density* the colour will have.

This can be explained in another way: imagine that you wanted to redecorate a plain, smooth, white wall. First of all, you choose the colour and shade of paint that you want it to be. Then after some preparation, you take a brush and start by applying the first coat. When this is dry you look at the colour, only to find that the effect is uneven and patchy. You can see

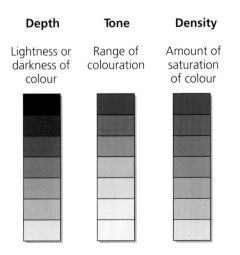

Depth, tone and density

REMEMBER ✔

If you are in doubt about the timing of colouring always follow the manufacturer's instructions. (For more information on faults and correction see the table later in this chapter.)

that the tone you wanted is there but it is often thin and almost transparent in places. So you repaint the wall. When the extra layer of paint dries, the saturation of colour is better and more even but still a little patchy in places. Finally you apply a third coat to the areas that are still patchy and when it dries the colour has an even density throughout. This effect is called *saturation*; it is achieved by the evenness of the density of the colour application throughout the hair.

Temperature is also a contributing factor to colour development. The warmer the colour environment the quicker the hair will take and the term *colour environment* is important here. The colour environment can be localised to the client or relate to the whole salon: the salon temperature may be cool but putting the client under a Climazon or Rollerball accelerates the colour.

This is not the only localised factor though. We know that when colour is introduced to heat it takes more quickly. However, you do need to remember that the human body produces heat too. In fact, up to 30 per cent of body heat is emitted through the top of your head! (This is why wearing a hat in winter keeps you warm.) This heating effect has a dramatic impact on the development of colour and is even more critical when lightening or bleaching!

So, with this extra heat around the scalp area, you can see there are potential problems of controlling the colour and aspects to the client's safety. To help control this process you must make sure that when the colour is applied to the root area, it is lifted away from the scalp and the air is able to circulate and ventilate the scalp evenly. This ensures that there are no 'hot spots' anywhere that would take more quickly or become a safety hazard to the client.

Colour selection principles: 2. Harmonising and contrasting effects

Understanding how colours harmonise or contrast in a hairstyle is fundamental to colour selection. In the illustrations below the same colours have been used in a variety of different ways. Note how the effects convey very different images. In each of the illustrations, the same two colour combinations have been used. But the way in which they have been used differs in each case. (Each of the possible colour variables are denoted in *italic* type.)

1. (Far left) Illustration depicts the balanced *light* and *dark* effect that is created when *vertical*, yet *uniform* sections of *contrasting* colour are *evenly* applied to a plain gold background.

2. (Centre left) This is the predominately *darkened* result when *more vertical* and *varying* sections of *contrasting* colour are *randomly* applied to a plain gold background.

3. (Centre right) This predominantly *lighter* effect is produced when *fewer, vertical* and *varying* sections of *contrasting* colour are *randomly* applied to a plain gold background.

4. (Far right) This *darkened* effect results from *more vertical* yet *uniform* sections of *contrasting* colour being *evenly* applied to a plain gold background.

Before looking at the next illustration we should remember the technique variables having an impact in this scenario. (See table below.)

	Effect	Sections	Direction	Amount	Positioning	Intensity
Technique variables	Light	Uniform	Vertical	Less	Even	?
	Dark	Varying	?	More	Random	Contrasting

In this series of illustrations, new variables have been introduced; they have a major impact on the total effect too. Here a *third*, yet *harmonising* colour is added. This new addition harmonises with its companion colours in two ways:

1. It provides a mid-tone, somewhere halfway between the light gold and the dark brown.

2. It has a natural, tonal 'fit' i.e. it harmonises with the two other colours.

The purpose of the illustration is to show that the same background is totally changed with just the addition of one other shade. Stark contrasts of colour are softened by the addition of a harmonising tone. The reverse happens when the added tone does not harmonise with its background. There are two other aspects to now consider:

1. The dimension of other directions.
2. Uneven background colour.

The next illustration introduces these criteria.

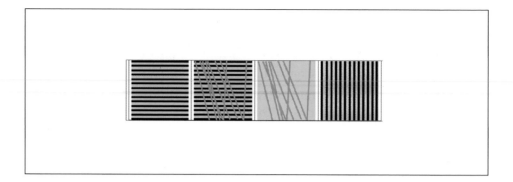

- We can now see that in the first illustration (far left) the image has changed direction. The colours are exactly the same but the resultant effect is very different.
- This is compounded in the next image where the third colour is reintroduced again, but now appears multi-directional.
- The next depicts the removal of contrast colour, just leaving random directional movement.
- Finally, there is the added dimension of uneven colour background.

This is aesthetics – there are no rules here; well, certainly not written ones. However, there are a number of points that have a bearing on taste, good design, artistic appreciation and therefore your colour planning.

1. Taste is subjective; whatever you find appealing may not be acceptable to others. In colour consultation you must get a feel of what the client finds attractive.

2. Good design is again subjective; the images displayed within the text bear no relationship to hair colouring. Or do they? The planning of styles, particularly new fashions, must originate from something. Fashion in clothes starts on the **designer**'s drawing board and the collections you see created for top competitions like the British Hairdressing Awards are also based on a theme. The theme is the inspiration behind the design; therefore, in principle, simple geometry becomes the underlying components of style construction.

3. Hairdressing is not self-indulgent *fine art* – well not for the majority of us. It happens to be a form of commercial art. *Commercial artists* produce work – commission for paying clients. Hairdressers do a very similar thing. The commercial artist finds out what the client wants, produces some visual examples, and then, on agreement, undertakes to complete the task in hand. Therefore, bearing this analogy in mind, we do exactly the same. Our clients use our artistic knowledge and skills to get what they want.

Wherever your inspiration comes from, remember, it has to be applied in a commercial context, unless it is purely for promotional purposes and in that case the sky's the limit.

Bearing this information in mind here are the variables that you need to consider before colouring hair.

Effect	monochrome	duo-toned	multi-toned	light/dark	subtle	strong
Sections	uniform	varied	narrow	wide	blocked	
Direction	vertical	horizontal	angled			
Amount	singles	less than 20%	20–40%	40–60%	over 60%	
Positioning	evenly placed	randomly placed	over other colours	with other colours	below other colours	
Intensity	harmonised	contrasting	vibrant	muted		

Colour-related tests

Don't forget that the following tests are designed to help you and to protect your client:

- *skin test* – to assess the client's sensitivity to the colour
- *porosity test* – to assess the smoothness or roughness of the cuticle
- *elasticity test* – to determine the hair's state or condition
- *incompatibility test* – if metallic chemicals are present
- *strand test* – to check the process of colouring.

> **REMEMBER: USE THE CLIENT'S RECORDS** ✔
>
> Make sure that you refer to the client's record if she has been to the salon before, or make out a new card to note down what you decide and the results of any tests.

Skin or patch test

The sensitivity test is used to assess the reaction of the skin to chemicals or chemical products. In the salon it is mainly used before colouring. Some people are allergic to external contact of chemicals such as PPD (found in permanent colour). This can cause dermatitis or, in even more severe cases, permanent scarring of skin tissue and hair loss. Some people are allergic to irritants reacting internally, and have conditions such as asthma and hay fever. Others may be allergic to both internal and external irritants. To find out whether a client's skin reacts to chemicals in permanent colours, carry out the following test 24 to 48 hours prior to the chemical process.

> **Carrying out a skin test** Remove the client's earrings. Behind the ear and using a cotton-bud , apply a little of the unmixed colourant product sufficient to cover 1cm². Re-apply two or three times allowing it to dry between each application. Leave for 48 hours without washing, covering or touching. If during the 48 hours after the test you or your client notices any abnormal reaction such as intense redness, itching or swelling in or around the test area DO NOT APPLY THE COLOURANT. Recommend that your client seeks medical advice before any colour applications area made.

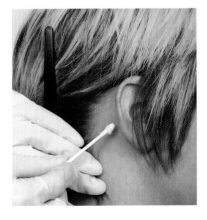

A skin allergy test L'Oréal Professionnel

Porosity test

This test also indicates the hair's current condition by assessing the hair's ability to absorb or resist moisture from liquids. (Hair in good condition has a tightly packed cuticle layer, which will resist the ingress of products.)

Hair that is very porous holds on to moisture; this is particularly evident when you try to blow dry it. The hair takes a long time to dry.

When is it done Before chemical services. If the cuticle is torn or damaged, the absorption of moisture and therefore hydrogen peroxide is quicker therefore the processing time will be shorter. Over-porous hair will quickly take in colour but will not necessarily be able to hold colour as the cuticle is damaged and allows the newly introduced pigments to wash away.

How is it done Rub strands of hair between your fingertips to feel how rough or smooth it is. If it feels roughened, as opposed to coarse, it is likely that the hair is porous.

Elasticity test

This determines the condition of the hair by seeing how much the hair will stretch and return to its original length.

Overstretched hair will not return to the same length and remains permanently damaged.

When is it done Prior to **chemical treatments** and services. (Ideal for hair that has impaired elasticity such as bleached and coloured.)

How is it done Take a couple of strands of hair between your fingers, holding them at the roots and the ends. Gently pull the hair between the two points to see if the hair will stretch and return to its original length. (If the hair breaks easily it may indicate that the cortex is damaged and will be unable to sustain any further chemical treatment.)

Incompatibility test

This will show if there are any chemicals present, such as metallic salts or other mineral compounds, within the hair, which will react against any new proposed services.

When is it done Carried out prior to colouring, highlighting and perming treatments.

How is it done Place a small sample of hair in a mixture of 20 parts hydrogen peroxide (6 per cent) and one part ammonium-based compound from perm solution.

If the mixture bubbles, heats up or discolours do not carry out the service.

Strand test

A strand test or **hair strand** colour test is used to assess the resultant colour on a strand or section of hair after colour has been processed and developed.

A strand test is also useful prior to bleaching natural pigments from hair or prior to removing synthetic pigments (i.e. decolour or colour reducer) to see how the hair will respond.

When is it done

Most colouring products just require the full **development time** recommended by the manufacturer – check their instructions.

(However, some hair conditions take on the colour faster than others and a strand test will check the colour development and see if the product needs to come off earlier.)

How is it done

1. Rub a strand of hair lightly with the back of a comb to remove the surplus colour.
2. Check whether the colour remaining is evenly distributed throughout the hair's length. If it is even, remove the rest of the colour. If it is uneven, allow processing to continue, if necessary applying more colour. If any of the hair on the head is not being treated, you can compare the evenness of colour in the coloured hair with that in the uncoloured hair.

STEP BY STEP: FEATHER AND FLARE HIGHLIGHTING

Step 1 Before: even clients with hair in the best condition can think it's boring. Colour is the key

Step 2 Section off random slices of hair around the hairline for the application of the complementary colour

Step 3 After the complementary colour has been applied, start the highlights at the lower back

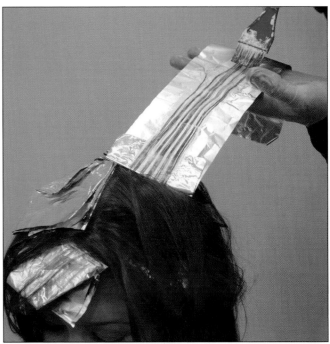

Step 4 Continues the sections around the head, working up to the parting area

Step 5 The woven meshes at the parting are finer and narrower then those beneath – this will graduate the tonal effect

Step 6 With all the foils in place, you can see the angles of the sections taken

Final effect

BLEACHING AND LIGHTENING

Bleaching is a process of making the hair colour lighter. The colour pigment eumelanin is the first to be acted upon; this affects the black and brown colouring. More difficult to alter is pheomelanin, which gives red and yellow colouring. The proportions of the colour pigments present in the hair determine just how light you can bleach hair. As bleaching proceeds, the hair becomes lighter and lighter. The hair changes colour:

Black-brown	red-brown	orange-yellow	light yellow	very light yellow

Pigment range

To check how light you can bleach the hair, take a cutting of the client's hair and apply bleach to it. By careful timing and processing, you should be able to find out exactly how much the hair can take and what colour you can bleach it to. Remember that if the hair contains a lot of red/yellow pigment, it must not be lightened too much – the hair's breaking point will quickly be reached.

The chemistry of bleaching

Powder bleach contains ammonium/potassium persulphate and sodium/magnesium silicate. These chemicals bleach the hair by **oxidation**: i.e. oxygen is added to the chemical pigments. Various types of bleach will do this and the most common is *hydrogen peroxide* (H_2O_2).

Hydrogen peroxide is available in cream, foam and liquid forms. It acts in stages. First the bleaching agent causes the hair to swell: the cuticle begins to lift. The bleach can then penetrate to the hair cortex, where the liberated oxygen acts on the pigment, lightening the hair.

Longer times or stronger bleaches may be required for hair of different colours. Just how long is required, and what strength of bleach must be used, can be determined using a test cutting.

Activating the bleach

Hydrogen peroxide is very reactive – it readily produces oxygen – so it needs to be *stabilised* if its effectiveness is to be maintained. Adding chemicals such as sulphuric or phosphoric acids when the bleach is manufactured does this.

To activate the stabilised hydrogen peroxide, you first need to neutralise the stabilisers. Adding ammonium hydroxide, sodium acetate or ammonium carbonate does this: you mix these bleach products together. Remember to read and follow the manufacturer's instructions carefully when using bleach products.

Hair by Steven Goldsworthy of Goldsworthy's

REMEMBER: DILUTING HYDROGEN PEROXIDE ✔

Strength you have	Strength you want to create	Peroxide	Add	Water
40 vol. (i.e. 12%)	30 vol. (i.e. 9%)	3	+	1
40 vol.	20 vol. (i.e. 6%)	1	+	1
40 vol.	10 vol. (i.e. 3%)	1	+	3
30 vol. (i.e. 9%)	20 vol. (i.e. 6%)	2	+	1
30 vol.	10 vol. (i.e. 3%)	1	+	2
20 vol. (i.e. 6%)	10 vol. (i.e. 3%)	1	+	1

REMEMBER: EFFECTS OF HYDROGEN PEROXIDE ON THE HAIR ✔

Hydrogen peroxide strength	Effect upon the hair
20 vol. or (6%)	✓ Assists the deposit of colour into the hair making it darker
	✓ Enables coverage of white/grey hair
	✓ Will lighten 2 levels above base 6
	✓ Will lighten 1 level below base 4
30 vol. or (9%)	✓ Will lighten hair 3 levels above base 6
	✓ Will lighten hair 2 levels below base 4
40 vol. or (12%)	✓ Will lighten hair 4 levels above base 6 (with high lift colour)

Special note

When hydrogen peroxide lightens hair to any level it will reveal the natural undertone or undercoat hair colour. The undercoat colour is dictated by the amount of warm tones (pheomelanin) within the hair. These pigments are oxidised during the colouring process and can produce difficult to remove unwanted golden or even orange tones within the hair.

Level of depth	Common name	Undertone and visual appearance
10	Lightest blonde	Very pale yellow
9	Very light blonde	Pale yellow
8	Light blonde	Yellow
7	Blonde	Pale straw yellow/orange
6	Dark blonde	Orange
5	Light brown	Red/orange
4	Brown	Red
3	Dark brown	Red
2	Darkest natural brown	Red
1	Black	Red

Levels of depth and their relevant undertones

Over-bleaching

Too much bleaching will destroy the hair's structure. Even if the hair doesn't actually break, it can become spongy, porous or patchy in colour. Further chemical processing – colouring, toning and perming – or general hair management is then very difficult. When wet, over-bleached hair stretches like chewing gum and the effects of blow styling or setting cannot last. If hair ever reaches this state, it needs to be treated very gently and conditioned; all harsh processes must be avoided.

Some causes of over-bleaching

- The hydrogen peroxide solution was too strong.
  The processing time was too long.
  Hair sections overlapped.
- Bleach was repeatedly combed through previously bleached hair.
- The hair was in too poor a condition at the outset, and was very porous.
- The hair had been overexposed to sun, wind, sea or chlorinated water.

Hair by Steven Goldsworthy of Goldsworthy's

The choice of bleach

Explore fully the range of bleach products that are available: make sure that you are confident about their use and effects. For each client, carefully consider which bleaching process and type of bleach would be correct. Determine which techniques will be helpful. Here are some guidelines:

Bleaching service required	What you need to check for	Technique/application	Bleach type
Full head (on virgin hair)	**Test results:** • (Skin tests etc.) **Natural hair depth** • Bleaches will lift five levels quite happily on hair with brown/ash pigments. However, strong red content will be difficult to remove. • Hair beyond base 5 will not lift safely beyond base 9. Suggest other colouring options. **Hair length** • Lengths up to 10 cm lighten evenly, provided the manufacturer's instructions are followed. • Lengths over 15 cm are not recommended, as evenness of colour will be difficult to guarantee.	Bleach mixture must be applied to mid lengths and ends first. A plastic cap should envelope the contents and can be developed with gentle heat until ready. When the bleached hair has lightened, two to three levels of lift the root application can be applied: • Always follow the manufacturer's instructions.	Only emulsion bleach is suggested for application to the scalp. These are used with 6 per cent hydrogen peroxide and sachet controllers to handle levels of lift.

Bleaching service required	What you need to check for	Technique/application	Bleach type
	Hair texture ● Finer hair needs extra care and lower hydrogen peroxide strengths i.e. 6 per cent ● Medium and coarser hair present fewer technical problems **Hair condition** ● Only consider hair in good condition for bleaching. Bleaching removes moisture content during the process, and hair that is porous or containing low moisture levels has insufficient durability for bleaching		
Full head (on previously coloured)	● Not recommended.		

Bleaching service required	What you need to check for	Technique/application	Bleach type
Root application (pre-lightened ends)	**Existing client?** ● **Yes**, check previous records and current hair condition and carry out service. ● **No, new client**, go through all the checks in the full-head application table **and** find out the previous treatment history.	Roots only without overlapping previous lightened ends. ● Always follow manufacturer's instructions.	Only emulsion bleach is suggested for application to the scalp.
Highlights (fine even meshes on virgin hair) **Note:** The success of **highlights on coloured hair** is very poor in comparison. This work is often undertaken in salons, but ends seldom lighten effectively, while the roots lighten very quickly. (Colour should be removed with a synthetic colour remover; see section on colour correction later in this chapter.)	**Test results** ● (Skin tests etc.) **Natural hair depth** ● Bleaches will lift five levels quite happily on hair with brown/ash pigments. However, strong red content will be difficult to remove and require stronger developer and/or additional heat. ● Hair beyond base 5 will not lift safely beyond base 9. Suggest other bleaching technique. **Hair length** ● Hair length will have an impact on evenness of colour. However, a small tolerance is acceptable and visually indistinguishable on longer hair lengths.	● Plastic self-grip meshes (eg Easi-meche™ L'Oréal). ● Foil meshes. ● Colour wraps.	High Lift Powder Bleach with suitable Hydrogen Peroxide developer at 6 per cent, 9 per cent or for highest lift 12 per cent (providing no product is allowed to contact the skin/scalp)

Bleaching service required	What you need to check for	Technique/application	Bleach type
	Hair texture • Finer hair needs extra care and lower hydrogen peroxide strengths i.e. 6 per cent. • Medium and coarser hair present fewer technical problems but generally take longer. **Hair condition** • Only consider hair in good condition for bleaching. Bleaching removes moisture content during the process hair that is porous or containing low moisture levels has insufficient durability for bleaching.		

Bleaching service required	What you need to check for	Technique/application	Bleach type
Slices, blocks and slab, bleaching (on virgin hair)	**Test results** • (skin tests etc.) **Natural hair depth** • Bleaches will lift five levels quite happily on hair with brown/ash pigments. However, strong red content will be difficult to remove. • Hair beyond base 5 will not lift safely beyond base 9. Suggest other colouring options. *Hair length* • Lengths up to 10 cm will lighten evenly, provided manufacturer's instructions are followed. • Lengths over 15 cm are not recommended, as evenness of colour will be difficult to guarantee. However, if the technique used will allow for bleaching of mid lengths and ends first, then the problem may be overcome. **Hair texture** • Finer hair needs extra care and lower hydrogen peroxide strengths i.e. 6 per cent. • Medium and coarser hair present fewer technical problems **Hair condition** • Only consider hair in good condition for bleaching. Bleaching removes moisture content during the process; hair that is porous or containing low moisture levels has insufficient durability for bleaching.	• Plastic self-grip meshes (e.g. Easi-meche™ L'Oréal). • Foil meshes. • Colour wraps.	High lift powder bleach with suitable hydrogen peroxide developer at 6 per cent 9 per cent or, for highest lift, 12 per cent (providing no product is allowed to contact the skin/scalp).

COLOUR VARIANTS

There are many ways of bleaching and toning your client's hair apart from a whole-head bleach process or the usual regrowth application. The hair can be:

- *Highlighted* – colour can be applied or lightened in contrasting streaks or areas.
- *Lowlighted* – colour can be applied or lightened in streaks or areas, matched more closely to the general colour.
- *Tipped, frosted, striped or varicoloured* – names given to various degrees and techniques of lightening or toning parts of the hair.
- *Shaded* without lightening – for instance, adding darker or warmer shades to naturally fair hair, or burgundy/plum shades to brown hair.

There are endless variations – small blocks of lightened or toned hair, a few streaks or stripes, lightly tipped parts to highlight a style line, and so on. Often the more natural, softer, blending tones are the most pleasing, but contrasting tones can be very effective. Check the instructions from your colour manufacturer and take account of their specialist recommendations.

You need to be clear exactly how much and which parts of the hair you are going to lighten. The style worn should help to determine the parts to be bleached. Your proposals should, of course, be fully discussed and agreed with your client.

Methods of bleaching and colouring

To achieve the variety of effects possible, there are several ways in which you can make the bleach or colour application. Always follow manufacturers' instructions on how to use their products. Examples are:

- *Dappling* A popular means of using bleach or colour to produce varied effects.
- *Aluminium foil* This can be ideal for firmly wrapping bleached or coloured parcels of hair. Different coloured foils can be used to identify different areas and colours used.
- *Highlight caps* Basic 'lighting' resources, which can be used to achieve advanced effects such as multi-lighting, spot lighting or vari-toning.
- *Colour wraps* These make it easier to process slices, sections or parcels of bleached or coloured hair safely.

STEP BY STEP: BLONDES AND BEIGES – FULL-HEAD HIGHLIGHTS

Step 1 Before: a graduated restyle may be just what's needed for tired long hair. But doing this often changes the colour balance of what was once a one-length haircut, so now is the ideal time to finish the effect

Step 2 Start by selecting the hair from the graduated profile, which needs to bring contrast and colour next to the face

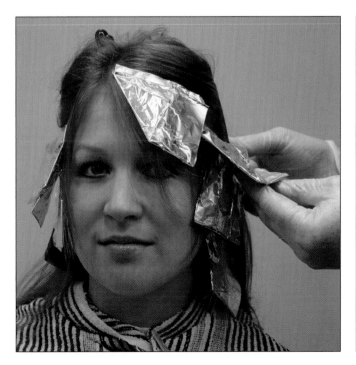

Step 3 Seal off the contrasing colours around the hairline first. This will encapsulate the colours and keep them away from the skin

Step 4 A blonde, lighter mesh will over-lie a broader section of beige beneath it

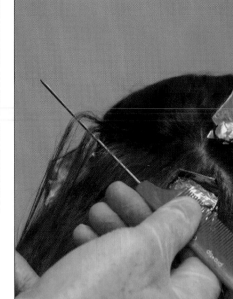

Step 5 Continue the highlights in parallel meshes up through to the parting

Step 6 The completed technique, showing the angles of the foils on either side of the head

Final effect

STEP BY STEP: GENT'S DAPPLED COLOUR TECHNIQUE

Step 1 Before: this colour effect is a simple way to introduce men to permanent colour techniques. Both this dappling technique and a haircut can be performed within a lunch-hour

Step 2 Mix the colour in a bowl and make preparations for colouring

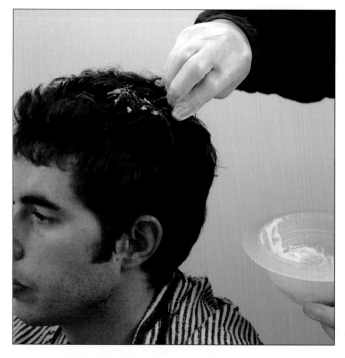

Step 3 Apply the colour by dappling the ends of the hair with your fingertips

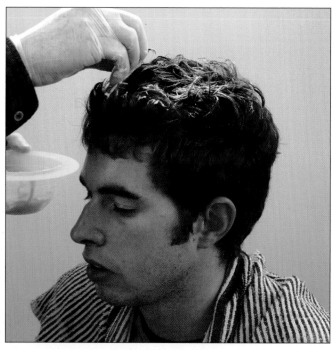

Step 4 Continue this technique throughout the top

After the colour has developed, remove and shampoo in the normal way

Hair: Scott Smurthwaite; photography: Kevin Douglas; make-up: Sheila Carton; styling: Carly Brook

In choosing a process, remember to bear in mind that the bleach must make contact with all of the hair if it is to work properly at all. Often bleaching products are 'thicker' in their consistency when mixed with developer and this makes them a little more difficult to use. The main reason for this is application control: the thicker consistency enables accurate application without running or dripping on to the scalp or towels and gowns.

TONING

Toning is the process of adding colour to previously bleached or lightened hair. A variety of pastel shades, such as silver, beige and rose, are used to produce subtle effects. Different types of toners are available; read the instructions provided by their manufacturers to find out what is possible.

The lightest toners can be used only on the lightest bleached hair: if the hair is too dark, it will absorb the toner colour. Adding colour to colour produces a slightly darker shade of the previous colour.

Bleach toners contain no hydrogen peroxide and rely upon the porosity of the hair to absorb the coloured pigments. They come in the form of liquids or gels and are easy to apply.

COLOUR CORRECTION

Colour correction is proving to be the largest growing market in hair colouring services. This is due to a number of step changes in the overall colouring market:

- More people are having colouring services.
- More people are experimenting with home colouring products.
- Our clients expect more, therefore, pushing the boundaries of safe, guaranteed practice to the limits.

There are far more people having colour now than there was before. This growing market are looking for change and when they arrive in the salon, they want:

1. modification of what they have had before
2. something totally new or
3. their dark roots lightened to match the over-processed, lightened ends, which are the result of set after set of highlighting treatments.

These increasing salon colouring services will inevitably result in colour correction sooner rather than later and is therefore an essential part of Level 3 work.

People experiment at home! Colour after colour is applied with the attitude 'this is easy anyway and it saves a fortune'. We all know what happens in the end. The biggest problem for hairdressers is getting an honest history of what has taken place, when and with what! We can't complain, it's good business. (For those who can sort it out!)

Another reason for the increase in the number of people having colour correction is the unrealistic expectations of many clients. Highlights/lowlights are a very attractive option for professional colouring. However, they do create some serious long-term problems if they are not carried out with the long term in mind, from the outset. That might sound strange, but it's true. It is to do with the success of the service really. Highlights are *addictive*; that is to say that when a new client is introduced to this form of colouring, they are compelled, by the colour technique's benefits to keep coming back.

They are a great way for:

- cleverly and subtly covering grey hair
- introducing clients to colour
- personalising colour to individuals
- advertising your colouring prowess
- expressing the hairstyle's attributes.

However, hair grows and it's the regrowth that creates the problem, at least initially. As the client's hair grows they become more conscious of the demarcation between the coloured hair and the natural roots. At the point where the hair has grown 2.5 cm a natural parting will show 5 cm of regrowth; a further colouring application would now be necessary. But will it be satisfactory to just highlight/lowlight the roots? In most cases not, particularly if several colours have been introduced to the hair. Even if the hair was only lightened, general shampooing, drying and weathering will have modified the colour on the ends, to the extent where newly introduced colour at the root will have little effect. So what do you do? In most situations, faced with the pressure of replicating what you did last time, you redo the service again. This reintroduces colour to hair that has already been processed, even if it is to be taken through to the ends for the last few minutes. And now you have hair that will continue to change in porosity and condition creating a more difficult task for the future; that is, until you and your client agree to sort out the problem with colour correction.

Reintroducing colour into bleached hair: Tinting back

As more clients are willing to experiment with colour at home and want to change the appearance of their hair more frequently, the colour correction service is a growing market within the salon.

When **recolouring** (tinting back) bleached hair back to its original or a darker colour, you need to consider the condition of the hair – how porous it might be, and, in particular, whether there is sufficient colour pigment left in the hair for the hair to retain new pigment. Think back to how permanent colours work within the hair. Synthetic para dyes, for example, work within the cortex of the hair, bonding into the hair's structure where the natural pigments are. Conversely, bleaching products simply remove all natural pigment from the hair and weaken the hair's internal structure.

Hair: Guillaume Vappereau for Guy Kremer International, Winchester; make-up: Pascal Marin; clothes stylist: Darren Knight; photography: Roberto Rubalacava

Hair by Steven Goldsworthy of Goldsworthy's

So, if the hair's internal structure has been impaired then there will be less chance for reintroduced pigments to bond. This fundamental aspect, if ignored, will have a major impact upon the visual effect of the hair.

However, this problem can be resolved by pre-pigmentation. During bleaching all (or most) of the natural pigments are removed. When these pigments are *dissolved* they create colourless, air filled spaces a bit like the inside of a natural sponge. These gaps are not uniform in shape and when synthetic pigments are put back into the hair, not all will fit in the spaces they occupy. Some will come away during washing, leaving a very uneven and unattractive result.

So, to avoid green hair and to ensure that recolouring is successful, it is usual to *pre-pigment* (colour-fill) the hair. This is done by applying red or warm shades to the hair, before the final shade is applied. (If this is not done the hair may fade, become patchy or appear greenish.)

REMEMBER: THE COLOUR WHEEL PRINCIPLES	✔
Green tones are neutralised by the tones of the opposite colour, red; yellow tones by violet, etc.	

Removal of synthetic hair dye: Decolouring

Synthetic (para dyes) permanent hair colour can only be removed with a decolour treatment. All of the main colour manufacturers produce at least one. The decolouring process is also known as *colour stripping* and *colour reducing* and these products are quite different to bleaching products.

If a client's hair has been previously permanently coloured and the client wishes for the colour to be removed or to be changed, in order to go to a lighter shade, then only a colour remover (decolour) may be used. The chemical formulation of a colour reducer is very different from powder and emulsion bleach, hence, the colour reducer is specially developed to seek out and remove (dissolve) only the synthetic pigments within the hair.

Process preparation

Always make sure that you protect your client before undertaking any permanent colouring operation. The removal of hair colour becomes more problematic in proportion to the length of hair: the longer the hair, the more difficult the task and the easier it is for spillages to occur. Clients waiting for chemical processes to take place will often have to wait seated, for long periods of time. Make sure that they are regularly attended to. And not just for checking development, check also for clothing protection placement of towels capes and especially for poorly secured hair and product drips!

Hair: Tracey Devine @ Angels; photography: Keven Douglas; make-up: Sheila Carton; styling: Ferino Daze

Applying depth/tone into previously bleached hair (pale yellow blonde base 10)

Target depth	Amount of bleached lengths	Pre-pigment shade and development	Secondary processing and development
7–9	7.5 cm (approx. 3 inches)	Use a golden/red /04 or /34 shade of same depth (7, 8 or 9) mixed with water. Apply from visible roots to ends. 12–15 mins without heat.	After washing, conditioning and drying, apply target depth 7, 8 or 9 and, if required, tonal ranges /30 or /34 or /03. from visible roots to ends with 3 per cent (10 vol.). Develop without heat for 20 mins
7–9	Over 7.5 cm (3 inches +)	Use a golden/red /04 or /34 shade of same depth (7, 8 or 9) mixed with water Apply to mid lengths and ends for 10 mins then apply to remaining light hair for a further 10–15 mins, without heat	After washing, conditioning and drying, apply target depth 7, 8 or 9, and if required, tonal ranges /30 or /34 or /03 mixed with 3 per cent hydrogen peroxide on mid lengths and ends first. Allow to develop for 10 mins. Then apply to remaining hair for further 10–15 mins
5–6	7.5 cm (approx 3 inches)	Use a red/copper of depth 8.43 or 7.43 mixed with water. Apply from visible roots to ends. Develop for 15 mins without heat	After washing, conditioning and drying, apply target depth 5 or 6, and, if required, tonal ranges /30 or /34 /03 or /4. from visible roots to ends with 3 per cent (10 vol.). Develop without heat for 20 mins
5–6	Over 7.5 cm (3 inches +)	Use a red/copper of depth 8.43 or, 7.43 mixed with water. Apply to mid lengths and ends for 10 mins then apply to remaining hair for a further 10–15 mins without heat	After washing, conditioning and drying, apply target depth 5 or 6, and if required, tonal ranges /3, /34, /03 or /4 mixed with 3 per cent hydrogen peroxide on mid lengths and ends first. Allow to develop for 10 mins. Then apply to remaining hair for further 10–15 mins
4	7.5 cm (approx 3 inches)	Use 7.44 mixed with water. Apply from roots to ends with water for 15 mins. After washing & conditioning dry the hair to check that tone is strong enough to receive secondary colour. If not repeat again.	After washing, conditioning and drying, apply base 4 mixed with 3 per cent roots to ends. Allow to develop for 10–15 mins
4	Over 7.5 cm (3 inches +)	Not recommended	
I.		Note: Colours used within this table refer to L'Oréal Majirel shade chart (see p. 166).	
II.		Ashen tones, violet browns and violet reds should not be applied to pre-pigmented hair.	

Reapplying to natural depth

The removal of synthetic hair colour is usually only a part of a larger technical operation. More likely than not, it will be the client's wishes to return to her natural colour. Clients who merely want to change their hair colour to a different new shade would *not* normally have to go through the process of colour reduction first.

The reapplication of base shade follows the removal of the synthetic tones. However, hair that has undergone the reduction process does now respond to the application of new colour in a different way. This new state of the hair is called *double processed hair*. This degree of treatment will make the hair respond to reintroduced colour more readily. Therefore the porosity levels are increased, which means that the hair becomes more absorbent.

Removal of permanent, synthetic hair dyes

Checklist:	Special attention
● Client expectation/ target colour	What is the purpose for removing the permanent hair dye?
	1. to recolour back to natural depth and tone?
	2. to recolour to a lighter shade?
	3. to remove unwanted/discoloured tonal effects from the hair?
● Treatment history	If you have *no* previous history available for the client and you want to undertake the technical operation you must undertake a skin test and take a test cutting for incompatible chemicals and ability to achieve target shades *before* conducting any chemical process.
● Condition	What are the existing hair condition attributes (elasticity, porosity and strength)? Will these limit the effectiveness of the treatment?
● Hair length	The longer the hair, the more difficulty will be encountered in stabilising the evenness of the lightening.
● Natural hair colour	Do you know what the natural hair colour is?
	1. If the natural hair colour is darker than the resultant, permanent hair colour, can the target colour be achieved without removing previous colour?
	2. If the natural hair colour is lighter than the resultant permanent colour, how many levels of lift are required and is this feasible? (Reducing synthetic hair dye above four levels of lift is not recommended.)
● Uneven, permanent hair colour	Where worn lengths have produced an uneven colour effect the darker bands/areas must be lightened to match the other lighter areas first.
● Work method	Always follow the manufacturer's instructions when mixing and applying the product.
	Start on the darkest areas first, then on to lighter areas.* Often the consistency of colour reducers makes it more difficult to work with on pre-coloured hair, so make sure that the product is applied evenly.
	* It is normally not necessary to apply to mid lengths and ends first, as worn hair colour tends to lighten on the ends anyway
● Development	Slow development is easier to control, so develop without thermal acceleration. Ensure adequate air circulation do not paste hair flat; lift sections and separate the hair to assist an even lifting process.
● Removal of product	Always follow the manufacturer's instructions and remove the product with suitable shampoo and tepid water. After conditioning, dry the hair before further processing.

In these situations there are certain *unwritten* rules that should be observed.

- Do a colour test on the hair first mixed only with water.
- Try using a liquid-based quasi-permanent colour (e.g. Diacolour) as these are easier to apply evenly and more quickly.
- Choose a colour one shade lighter than the expected target shade to avoid *colour grab*.
- Check development every few minutes (scrape colour off the hair and rub between fingers to see the colour development clearly).

Banded hair colour

Sometimes colour correction is undertaken to counteract partial colouring defects. These types of technical problems can seem quite daunting, particularly when we are used to applying colour in either a 'blanket' operation or by sectioning and covering in foil. These problems can be overcome and usually require a change of *mindset* in their execution. There is something particularly different in tackling this type of situation though.

Hair by Steven Goldsworthy of Goldsworthy's

REMEMBER: BANDED HAIR COLOUR AND GRADATION ✔

Normally, when colour is applied to hair people tend to liken the process to painting. This is not a good simile. Imagine painting emulsion on a dining room wall. We paint the wall white and the saturation of the paint covers where we pass the brush. On finishing the wall, say we want to change an area in the middle and we paint a blue horizontal stripe, wherever we apply the brush the saturation of the paint again will provide cover and change it to blue.

Banded hair colour, in contrast, often tends to a type of gradation of colour and this is particularly noticeable at the patchy edges. Part of the effect can be the result of how light reflects off the hair's surface, so when dealing with this situation look at the hair in different lighting backgrounds (ideally, natural daylight, white halogen light and somewhere away from bright lighting in more normally lit interiors).

Gradated colour

Gradated colour or gradation of colour is where the hue changes with the levels of saturation. For example, black and white mixed together create grey and, depending how much white or black is added, the colour either deepens or lightens, moving from shade to shade seamlessly.

This merging of colour occurs in hair naturally after colouring and it is difficult to remedy. It occurs partly by colour fade, i.e. the natural wear and tear and weathering. However, this subtle colour fading is far easier to tackle than the gradated banding that occurs after incorrect colouring. Imagine what happens when a dark colour, say base 5, is applied to natural hair base 7. As the hair grows, the regrowth becomes more obvious. Initially, this appears as a solid line of demarcation. But hair doesn't all grow at the same rate, and this becomes more apparent the further away from the roots the hair grows. The inconsistent growth blurs the edge of demarcation creating a gradated effect. In this scenario the recolouring is simple: just retouch with base 5. However, if the hair were to be colour stripped, then the complexity would be increased because of the uneven edge of colour to be removed.

Hair: Mark Leeson; photography:
Kevin Douglas; Make-up: Cheryl
Phelps-Gardiner; Styling: Charlie Davis

Horizontally banded hair colour will occur from one of the following:

- poor home product application
- poor home product reapplication and subsequent colouring
- poor salon product application
- excessive heat/'hot spots' occurring during development
- uneven porosity of the hair (possibly from *masking* where conditioning treatments have bonded to different sites upon the surface of the hair unevenly).

Horizontally banded hair colour usually appears on long hair at, or near, one length. If the hair is to be restyled or layered it is worth cutting and drying first to see if the problem still exists.

If decolouring is still necessary in these areas, it would be advisable to apply the product by the following methods:

- use a thicker consistency: this will allow you to *spot colour*, applying freehand to the central areas of 'patchiness'.
- apply with the natural fall of the hair so that any natural light shadowing can easily be seen
- later, during development, extend the product to the edges of the gradated patches
- remove occasionally with warm water, then dry smoothly to see when the development is complete
- reapply to those areas requiring further development
- finally remove at the backwash with suitable shampoo and condition the hair with an anti-oxidising treatment.

Discoloured highlights/lowlights and partial applications

Historically, we used the term 'discoloured hair' as a description for hair that has resulted from the presence of incompatible chemicals such as carbon, hydrogen and oxygen, and metallic salts, such as silver nitrate. As cases of this happening are few and far between the term is now more usually applied in a different context. Partial colouring techniques are extremely popular and remain firmly as the 'professional only' route to achieving exciting colour effects. So, therefore, with an ever increasing expectations by clients for partial colouring techniques, it is no surprise to find that much of the colour correction work undertaken within the salon is a result of previous highlighting and/or lowlighting services. Problems will tend to occur in the following instances:

- on longer hair over a period of time following several, subsequent treatments
- on hair that involves two or more newly introduced colours on an uneven background colour
- poorly executed application or removal of product/s
- over-porous hair
- hair subjected to excessive sunlight, UV or chlorinated swimming pools.

Longer highlighted hair

Longer hair that has had several highlighting and/or lowlighting services is the most frequent reason for discoloured hair. Let's look at a typical example: a regular client has shoulder length hair of base 6 (dark blonde). The client has her first colouring service which involves two colours:

1   a bleach with 9 per cent

2   a beige midtone to harmonise the final effect.

After 6–8 weeks with regular washing and blow drying the midtones fade off. Some pigments are washed away and some are absorbed into the more porous lightened hair, discolouring the original highlights. At the 12-week stage the client returns for a *T section* root application (recolouring of the roots at the parting and sides). What do you do? You are unable to do a reapplication of the midtone just at the roots as the ends have faded off and similarly you may not be able to locate the initial bleached highlights! Most stylists will in this situation end up recolouring the hair with both colours again just within the T section but roots to ends.

The client is happy once again. However, a longer-term problem will start to develop. Much of the surface hair is now double processed (it has had two applications of the same chemicals). Double processed hair is more porous and this impaired condition leaves the client's hair in a state less able to retain colour pigments. So again a fade off occurs. This problem is compounded by the fact that the ends will now be predominantly lighter. The new roots will be darker and the hair in between will be lighter than the roots but not as light as the ends.

This colour state has now created an uneven background colour. A gradation from dark at the roots to light at the ends. Before any further partial colouring takes place this must be taken into consideration. At the point where this client wishes to once again have the same colours applied, a colour correction of the discoloured, background hair will have to be undertaken.

This is done at the same time as the highlighting service. When the meshes of coloured hair are secured in their packets/foils, the remainder hair is coloured back to the natural shade. (However, this may exacerbate the problem further. If this newly introduced colour leaches out into the lightened hair all of the hair will be discoloured and the problem will be compounded further.)

Newly introduced colours

A similar problem occurs when newly introduced colours are applied to an uneven background. If the unevenness of the background colour is not corrected during the service the impact of the newly applied colour will be greatly devalued.

REMEMBER: COLOUR STABILITY ✔

The stability of a synthetic colour within the hair is directly affected by the condition of the hair. The better the condition the more able the hair to retain the pigments. Conversely, the poorer the condition the less able the hair to retain the pigments.

The hardest choice to make in this type of colour correction is whether to colour back the uneven background colour first, or to attempt the correction at the same time as the application of the new colours. If the hair needs pre-pigmentation you would be better advised to complete the task in two separate phases:

1. pre-pigment and then tint back the hair to natural base, then

2. carry out the partial colouring technique.

However, remember that hair that has been tinted back will be more porous and less able to sustain further colouring operations. This is particularly problematic if you intend to lighten portions of the hair. (It just won't work satisfactorily!)

If you intend to lighten as well reintroduce colour to the background, you are better off conducting the process in a single phase. In other words, tint back the remaining hair that is not part of the partial colouring effect.

Poorly executed application

As partial colour techniques become more involved the complexity of processes and procedures increases too. This is all too apparent in poorly executed removal of product. When two or more colours are applied in the same operation, particular care must be taken in how they are removed. For example, let's take a client who has lightened highlights with vibrant copper lowlights on a reintroduced background of base 6.

In this example three separate colour combinations exist.

1 the highlight
2 the lowlight
3 the background.

Imagine what would happen in the following scenarios:

- Highlight packets are removed and shampooed at the same time as the lowlight packets!
- Highlight packets are removed and rinsed with the background colour!
- All packets are removed and collectively shampooed at the same time!

Potentially, the effects created by clever techniques and artistic application can be totally wiped out if, during removal, the individual colour combinations aren't removed one by one.

Over-porous hair

The condition of the hair dictates what should and can be done. Never ignore the obvious. As we have already stated, clients want more and this *pressure* by the client should not override common sense. If you believe that a treatment cannot be undertaken or is unachievable, it is your duty to tell the client your assessment of the situation. By all means get another opinion from a colleague, but if the client insists you must make a decision, do you:

- ask her to sign a disclaimer as she refuses to listen to reason or
- recommend another, competing, salon?

Lifestyle

Normal everyday wear and tear is the main reason for colouring problems and colouring problems often lead to colour correction. Lifestyle has the biggest impact upon hair condition and client expectation. Busy work schedules, social lives and the search for the sun all have a major impact. We are all to blame: we want it and we want it now! Very few clients, even armed with the right products and equipment, are capable of the continual analysis and assessment needed to combat the external forces that affect the condition of their hair.

For example: how many time have you recommended a shampoo/conditioner to a client, and the client to have gone away and used it, only to come back and say that it was great for a while, but then it didn't seem to have the same effect? So she went back to using her own particular favourite (probably because it smells nicer or is advertised by a celebrity icon).

The truth of the matter is that what you recommended actually did its job. The client has forgotten the original problem and now focuses on a new one – to her it seems that the product has stopped working because her needs have now changed. This constantly changing situation is difficult to master particularly when the client arrives in the salon and somehow seems to expect you, in the few minutes she is there, to guess what will happen to her hair if:

1 she goes on an exercise binge and swims every day
2 spends two weeks in the Caribbean
3 spills paint on her hair during redecorations at home or
4 gets talked into trying a home colour because a friend found it to be a great winner!

STEP BY STEP: HIGHLIGHT COLOUR CORRECTION

Due to the imbalance of light and dark hair, these highlights have lost all definition. This is a common problem which occurs daily in hairdressing salons.

Step 1 Before: when highlighting fine hair, it is all too easy to overdo it. This technique will correct the light–dark balance problem while redefining the definition with two harmonising colours

Step 2 Several sets of highlights have created over-bleached ends while the roots remain dark

Step 3 Carefully select highlights from the previously lightened areas

Step 4 Position the foil carefully below the individual sections of hair. Only paste the lightener on at the roots as the ends are already light enough

Step 5 Once the foils around the parting are in place, the ends can be coloured back in one easy step

Step 6 When the colour has been applied to the lengths of the hair, a strip of foil can be placed so that it keeps the colour away from the skin while it develops

The final effect

STEP BY STEP: COLOUR CORRECTION (SINGLE STEP 'TINTING BACK')

In this colour correction the hair is taken back to natural depth in one single stage, while vibrant interest is applied at the same time.

Step 1 Before: colour correction of one form or another is becoming the most popular form of colouring in salons. This is because much of the work undertaken is either repair or recolouring of hair that has been coloured many times before

Step 2 Here we see a common problem. Several sets of highlights, and sun, sea and sand, have taken their toll, leaving the hair with excessive regrowth and 100 per cent yellow/gold ends

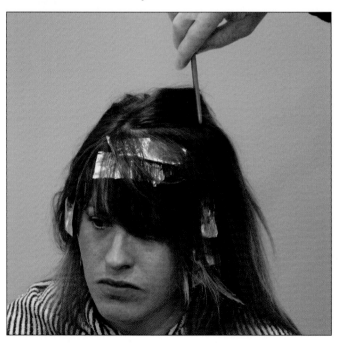

Step 3 Position meshes of dark mahogany lowlights parallel to the hairlines

Step 4 Continue this upwards and through to the parting area

Step 5 With all the lowlights set into position, clip the hair out of the way to introduce a personality colour

Step 6 This can be applied in one single foil angled parallel to the colour slice being applied

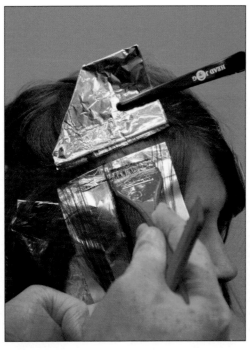

Step 7 The foil can then be folded, creating a barrier away from the skin

Step 8 Now mix and apply an interleave base shade colour of dark brown (base 4) to the remaining hair between the foils

Step 9 The interleave develops

The final effect

STEP BY STEP: COLOUR CORRECTION (TWO-STEP PROCESS – PRE-PIGMENTATION AND TINTING BACK)

This is a common problem with any length of hair. In this scenario the hair has been bleached and the client wants to return to her natural colour. However, the hair no longer has any yellow/gold pigment present. The hair has to be pre-pigmented with red/gold pigment before natural depth can be achieved or the hair will go green!

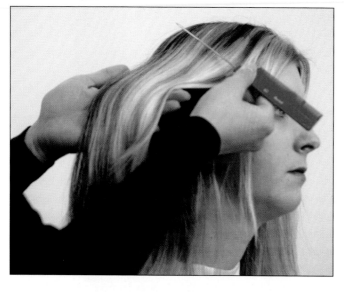

Step 1 Before: although the client wishes to return to her natural depth, experience says that many clients find that type of dramatic change too much to handle. Here is a new, exciting alternative to 'tinting back'. Flat, single dark colours only look good if the hair has lots of shine. Unfortunately, shine doesn't last very long so that best course of action here would be to introduce a variety of tones into the hair. This way the hair 'comes alive' with texture, dimension and a head-turning excitement!

Step 2 The previously bleached hair is too light for single step processing; the lightened hair must be pre-pigmented first

Step 3 Apply a red/gold (Majirel 7.43 + 3 per cent developer) to the dry hair first

Step 4 Start at the lower nape and work up through the back of the head until all of the hair is coloured with the pre-pigmenter

Step 5 Comb through to ensure the application is even

Step 6 After 30 minutes' development, shampoo away the colour and re-dry the hair ready for the next step of the process

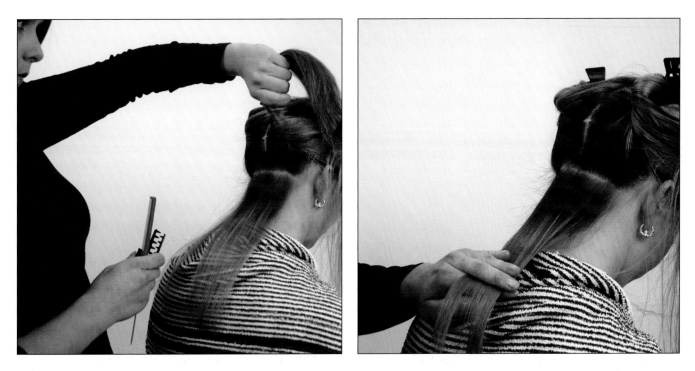

Step 7 A technique of naturalised highlighting is chosen as the preferred way of introducing depth and tone back into the hair. Section the hair ready for woven highlights

Step 8 Introduce the two different highlights to the hair

Step 9 Apply the colour to the foils

Step 10 With all the highlights in place, mix the interleave tone ready for application

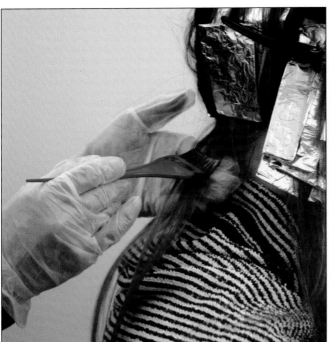

Step 11 Apply a mix of Dark Brown Dia Colour and 3 per cent developer to all the hair between the foils

Step 12 Leave the Dia Colour to develop for maximum saturation, then carefully remove the colours at the basin and dry the hair into style

The final effect

STEP BY STEP: SPONGED TEXTURISING

A simple colour correction on short hair that lacks tonal and style definition.

Step 1 Before: Ollie's hair lacks contrast after a hot holiday in the sun. He wants to retain some brightness but needs the rest to go darker

Step 2 Start by lifting the hair off and away from the head and apply plenty of hairspray

Step 3 Continue to make the hair even spiker by backcoming all over

Step 4 Mix, with 3 per cent developer, a base shade colour the same depth as the darker hair. Then dip a neutralising sponge into the colour and apply just to the discoloured ends

Step 5 Continue to apply through the top section of the hair

Finished effect

And finally…

Colour correction is, as previously mentioned, becoming more frequent within the salon. However, it is still quite some way from becoming a routine service. On the contrary, it is work that is specially tailored to suit the needs of the individual client and therefore it is different every time, in every case.

Your colour confidence will build upon experience; the more that you are involved with the service the better prepared you will be in undertaking this essential work. The main thing is knowing and understanding the situation in hand. You must conduct a thorough consultation to find out exactly what has taken place and over what period of time. Planning a course of corrective action is imperative before you do anything else. Unless you understand what you are seeing, you cannot hope to stumble on the correct course of action. Remember, there will be times when what you see before you, doesn't make sense. In other words, there is a discrepancy between what you see and what your client claims has taken place. Clearly, some vital information is missing. This could happen for a number of reasons but is most likely to be the result of embarrassment on your client's part over things they have done but don't wish to admit.

In order for you to get as much 'honest' information as possible, don't make an issue of the situation. You will get a lot more help if you don't apportion blame or look for someone to be the scapegoat. If this is a new client to you, you have a unique opportunity to forge a professional relationship that is built on respect, which should last and last.

The corrective service doesn't end there either; the condition of the client's hair will always be impaired in some way following double processing. You need the client to help you, in maintaining the colour's fastness and the hair's condition during routine daily handling between salon visits.

Diagnosing a course of action is one thing, but it should be followed by *prescription* too. Selecting and advising on the right products is almost as important as doing the job in the first place. The misuse of products will quickly negate the value of the completed work. You only need to make the client aware of what could go wrong in order for her to take your sound advice in keeping up the regimen.

Colouring problems

Problem	Possible causes	Action
Uneven colour	Poor application Section too large Incorrect mixing	Spot-bleach Recolour Strip colour and recolour if necessary
Dark en ds	Ends under-bleached Toners too dark Toner over processed Dark colour remains	Re-bleach Remove using lighteners After removal, time accurately Remove and tone
Too yellow	Under-bleached Base too dark Wrong toner used Wrong bleach	Re-bleach Try stronger bleach Use violet toner Use other than oil bleach
Too red	Under-bleached Too much alkali Wrong toner used	Re-bleach Use different bleach Use green matt or olive
Problem	Possible causes	Action
Dark roots or patches	Poor application Toner too dark	Re-bleach evenly remove using lightener
Roots not coloured	Under-bleached Under-timed Toner too dilute Unclean or coated	Re-bleach Re-bleach Reapply Clean and reapply
Colour fade	Over-porous Harsh treatment Overexposure	Condition Advise on hair care
Hair breakage	Over-processed Incompatibles present Harsh treatment Sleeping in rollers Tied back long hair	Recondition remaining hair Re-test to make sure Provide hair care advice Provide hair care advice Provide hair care advice
Discolouration	Under-processed Excessive exposure Home treatment	Colour match or develop further Recondition and keep covered Provide hair care advice
Green tones	Incompatibles Blue used on yellow Too-blue ash used	Test hair Use warm or red shades Use violet
Too orange	Under-processed Pigment lacking	Apply blue ash Add blue
Too yellow	Under-processed	Add violet and/or bleach further
Hair tangled	Over-bleached Raised cuticle/over-porous	Use anti-oxidants/treatment reconditioners
Colour not taking	Over-porous Chemicals masking the hair Colour bounce/red pigment grabbing at roots	Recondition and pre-fill hair Use deep cleanser to remove build-up Recolour with brown ash pigments (not deposited into hair correctly)
Colour build up	Over-porous Excessive over-application	Recondition and pre-pigment Consider colour removal

I know and understand the principles of positive communication ☐	I can carry out colour consultation and understand the colour selection process ☐	I always recognise the critical influencing factors when I analyse the client's hair ☐	I always carry out working practices according to the salon's H&S policy ☐
I know and understand the science in respect to colouring and bleaching ☐	I recognise the problems or reasons that necessitate colour correction work ☐	I always carry out tests prior to any new colouring treatment ☐	I know how to carry out a variety of full head and partial colouring techniques on a variety of hair lengths ☐
I know when and to whom refer clients to, in situations where external assistance is required ☐	I know how to recognise and implement colour correction procedures on a variety of hair lengths ☐	I know how to recognise and implement colour correction procedures on a variety of hair colouring problems ☐	I know how to advise, promote and sell other services and products to clients ☐
I know and respect the client's rights: data protection, equal opportunities, anti-discrimination and consumer legislation ☐			CHECKER BOARD ✔

Self-test section

Quick quiz: A selection of different types of questions to check your knowledge

Q1 A _ _ _ _ test will identify a client's sensitivity to colour products.   Fill in the blank

Q2 A quasi-permanent colour lasts longer than a semi-permanent colour.   True or False

Q3 Which of the following products are likely to be an incompatible?   Multi-selection

Permanent colour containing PPD	☐	1
Retail permanent colour containing PPD	☐	2
Vegetable henna	☐	3
Compound henna	☐	4
Single-step applications for covering grey i.e. 'Just for Men'	☐	5
Single-step toners for application to bleached hair	☐	6

Q4 Bleaches and high lift colourants are the same.   True or False

Q5 Which of the following tests do not apply to colouring services?   Multi-choice

Skin test	☐	a
Incompatibility test	☐	b
Porosity test	☐	c
Curl test	☐	d

Q6 Permanent colours alter the pigmentation of hair within the cuticle.   True or False

Q7 Which of the following colour products do not require the addition of hydrogen peroxide as a developer?   Multi selection

Powder bleach	☐	1
Semi-permanent colour	☐	2
Quasi-permanent colour	☐	3
Temporary colour	☐	4
Vegetable henna	☐	5
High lift colour	☐	6

Q8 Green tones within hair are neutralised by adding _ _ _ tones.   Fill in the blank

Q9 Hair lightened from natural base 7 should be capable of maximum lift to: Multi-choice

Base 10	☐	6
Pale yellow	☐	6
Yellow	☐	6
Yellow/orange	☐	6

Q10 Lightened hair that appears too yellow can be neutralised by adding mauve.   True or False

chapter 6

PERMING

H29.1   Maintain effective and safe methods of working when perming hair

H29.2   Prepare for perming

H29.3   Create a variety of permed effects

What do I need to learn?

You need to know and understand:

- How health and safety legislation affects you and your clients
- The importance of good communication
- Perm science and the range of perming processes and products
- The range of tests that need to be conducted
- The benefits of sound advice followed up by prescribed home maintenance
- A range of tools and equipment and their uses

What does it mean?

This chapter covers the fundamental aspects of perming theory and practice. The text later extends to cover more advanced skills and techniques.

What do I need to do?

- You will need to create a range of effects resulting from a variety of winding techniques on different lengths of hair.
- These effects should take account of client requirements, pre- and post-perm tests and physical limiting factors.

Other info

Related topics and other useful information:

- Health and safety legislation
- Client consultation

pH The presence of positive hydrogen ions within a compound which denotes its levels of acidity or alkalinity

contra-indications Any factor or state (of the hair or skin) that will affect the planned service for a client

alpha and beta keratin The two different states of hair that occur during styling

post-damping, pre-damping The introduction of perming lotion to the hair either before or after winding; dependent upon style or hair type requirements

CHECKERBOARD

At the end of this chapter the checkerboard will help to jog your memory on what you have learned and what still remains to be done. Cross them off with a pencil as you cover each of the topics. (See p. 244.)

INTRODUCTION

This chapter covers one of the most difficult optional units of Level 3. This perming unit comprises:

H29 Perm hair using a variety of techniques

    H29.1 Maintain effective and safe methods of working when perming hair

    H29.2 Prepare for perming

    H29.3 Create a variety of permed effects

Perming and colouring are arguably the most complex aspects of contemporary hairdressing. The combination of client's expectations, reality and ability to maintain their hair carefully and competently between salon visits is crucial. These factors have made perming a very problematic technical procedure. As we strive to obtain softer, kinder, longer-lasting results on longer-length hair, a division, based upon technical ability, experience and confidence, now exists between professional hairdressers and it is still growing. These stylists now fall into the following groups: the technicians that *can*, hairdressers that *can but won't*, and others who *cannot*.

Like many other hairdressing services, condition is the main consideration, i.e. the condition before starting and the condition when the job is finished. *Moisture is the key*. If the hair retains its natural *moisture* levels after perming, the signs of healthy hair are obvious: shine, easy 'combability' and great flexibility. Together these features indicate a style that is easily managed. Lose these qualities and the hair will be dull, lifeless, tangled and difficult to manage. So after giving away the big secret, let's see how you get everything else right too.

PERMING PRINCIPLES

Perming is the term given to the physical and chemical processing of hair, changing it into waves or curls. Perming, also known as *permanent waving*, can be achieved by a variety of methods, some using heat, or by cold wave lotions and a variety of winding techniques. Unlike the movement and curl produced by blow drying and setting, the curls produced by perming are permanent. The hair does not straighten out later when dampened. However, hair continues to grow and the new hair retains its natural tendency. So the waves and curls produced by perming gradually get further and further away from the scalp as the hair grows. To keep the same style the hair will at some point need to be permed again.

Because perming really does make a permanent change to the hair, you cannot easily correct mistakes (as you can with blow styling, for example). The process also involves various chemicals. It is therefore important that you make sure you understand what you are doing.

How perming works: Changing the keratin

Before going ahead with this section, refer to 'Chemical properties of hair' in Chapter 2 (p. 53).

Of the cross-links between the polypeptide chains of hair keratin, the strongest are the *disulphide bridges* that give hair its strength. Each disulphide bridge is a chemical bond linking two sulphur atoms, one in each of two polypeptide chains lying alongside each other. Each sulphur atom forms part of an amino acid unit called *cysteine*; the pair of linked units is called *cystine*.

During **cold perming** some of these bridges are chemically broken, converting each cystine into two cysteine units. The breaking of the bridges makes the hair softer and more pliable, allowing it to be moved into a new position of wave or curl. Only about 20 per cent of the disulphide bridges need to be broken during a perm. If too many are broken, the hair will be damaged. You need to keep a check on the progress of the perm and stop it at the right time. You do this by rinsing away the perm lotion and neutralising the hair. During neutralising, pairs of cysteine units join up again to form new cystine groups. The new cross-links thus formed hold the permed hair firmly into its new shape.

Changing the bonds

The hair is first wound onto some kind of former such as a curler or rod. Then you apply perm lotion to the hair, which makes it swell. The lotion flows under the cuticle and into the cortex. Here it reacts with the keratin, breaking some of the cross-links within and between the polypeptide chains. This softens the hair, allowing it to take up the shape of the former. You then rinse away the perm lotion, neutralise the hair and allow it to harden in its new, curlier shape.

This process is often described in chemical terms. The first part – softening the hair by breaking some of the cross-links – is a process of *reduction*. The

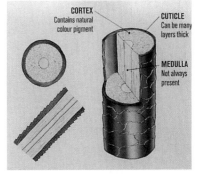
Cross-section of hair Wella

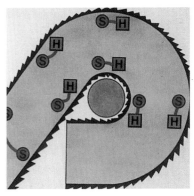
Disulphide bridges Wella

Reduction: breaking existing disuiphide bridges Wella

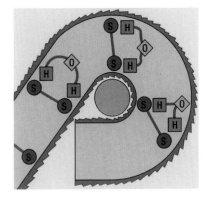
Oxidation: forming new disulphide bridges Wella

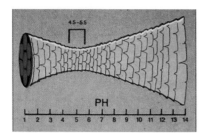

How pH affects the hair   Redken

disulphide bridges are split by the addition of hydrogen from the perm lotion. (The chemical in the perm lotion that supplies the hydrogen is called a *reducing agent*.) The keratin is now stretched: it is beta-keratin.

The last part of the process – hardening the hair by making new cross-links – is an **oxidation** reaction. New disulphide bridges form and the hydrogen that was added is lost again. The hydrogen reacts with the oxygen in the neutraliser, forming water. (The chemical in the **neutraliser** that supplies the oxygen is called an *oxidising agent* or *oxidant*.) The keratin is now in a new unstretched form: it is alpha keratin again.

Reducing agents

In the past, most cold perming lotions were alkaline, but these tend to roughen the cuticle. Newer lotions are acidic instead and these are becoming popular. Some perm lotions contain ammonium thioglycollate. This is environmentally damaging and new perm solutions use other chemicals.

Oxidising agents

Hydrogen peroxide is the most common oxidant. Others include sodium perborate, sodium percarbonate, sodium bromate and potassium bromate.

Acidity and alkalinity: the pH scale

The pH scale measures **acidity** or **alkalinity**. It ranges from pH 1 to pH 14. Acids have pH values from 1–6, whereas alkalis have values ranging from pH 8–14. Substances that are neither acid or alkaline, i.e. neutral, have a pH value of 7. The higher the pH number, the more alkaline is the substance; the lower the pH number, the more acid the substance.

The normal pH of the skin's surface is 5–6, referred to as the skin's acid mantle. This acidity is due in part to the sebum, the natural oil produced by the skin. The pH can be measured using *pH papers, universal indicator papers*. *Litmus papers* will indicate whether something is acid, alkaline or neutral. If hairs are placed in alkaline solution they swell and the cuticle lifts. In slightly acid solutions the hair *clenches* and the cuticle is smooth. However, stronger acidic or alkaline solutions will impair the hair's structure, causing it to break down.

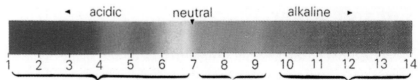

The pH scale

PREPARING AND PLANNING THE PERM: THE CLIENT

For the client a perm is a major step. She will have to live with the result for several months. She may not be familiar with the range of perms available. She will need you to explain what is involved in each and help her decide which is the most suitable.

- There are several cold perms designed to curl straight hair.
- Acid perms are popular because their effects are gentle. Strongly alkaline perms can be too harsh: new forms are being developed.
- Not all perms contain ammonium thioglycollate: 'non-thio' perms tend to be gentler in their action.

Discuss your client's requirements. Find out what she is expecting from a perm and determine whether this is the best solution.

1 Consider the style and cut, together with your client's age and lifestyle.
2 Examine the hair and scalp closely. If there are signs of inflammation, disease or cut or grazed skin, *do not* carry out a perm. If there is excessive grease or a coating of chemicals or lacquer, you will need to remove these by washing first. Previously treated hair will need special consideration.
3 Analyse the hair texture. Carry out the necessary tests to select the correct perm lotion.
4 Always read manufacturers' instructions carefully.
5 Determine the types of curl needed to achieve the chosen style.
6 If this is a regular client, refer to her records for details of previous work done on her hair.
7 Advise your client of the time and costs involved. Summarise what has been decided to be sure there is no misunderstanding.
8 Minimise combing and brushing to avoid scratching the scalp before the perm.

Analysis/examination

It is important to make sure you choose the most suitable perm lotion, the correct processing time and the right type of curl for the chosen style. Consider the following factors:

1 **Hair texture** For hair of medium texture, use perm lotion of normal strength. Fine hair curls more easily and requires weaker lotion; coarser hair can often be more difficult to wave and may require a stronger lotion for resistant hair. (This is not true for Oriental hair types.)
2 **Hair porosity** The porosity of the hair determines how quickly the perm lotion is absorbed. Porous hair in poor condition is likely to process more quickly than hair with a resistant, smooth cuticle (see pre-perming treatments).

3 **Previous treatment history** Virgin hair – hair that has not previously been treated with chemicals – is likely to be more resistant to perming than hair that has been treated. It will require a stronger lotion and possibly a longer processing time.

4 **Length and density of hair** Long, heavy hair requires more perming than short hair because the hair's weight will pull on the curls. Short, fine hair may become too tightly curled if given the normal processing time.

5 **Style** Does the style you have chosen require firm curls or soft, loose waves? Do you simply wish to add body and bounce?

6 **Size of rod, curler or other former** Larger rods produce larger curls or waves; smaller rods produce tighter curls. Longer hair generally requires larger rods. If you use very small rods in fine, easy-to-perm hair, the hair may frizz; if you use rods that are too large you may not add enough curl. To check make a test curl before you start.

7 **Incompatibility** Perm lotions and other chemicals used on the hair may react with chemicals that have already been used, for example, home-use products. Hair that looks dull may have been treated with such chemicals. Ask your client what products she uses at home and test for incompatibility (see below).

Tests

1 **Elasticity** Stretch a hair between your fingers. If it breaks easily the cortex may be damaged and perming could be harmful.

2 **Porosity** Rub the hair between your fingertips to feel how rough or smooth it is. Rougher hair is likely to be more porous and will therefore process more quickly.

3 **Incompatibility** Protect your hands by wearing gloves. Place a small cutting of hair in a mixture of hydrogen peroxide and ammonium hydroxide. Watch for signs of bubbling, heating or discoloration: these indicate that the hair already contains incompatible chemicals. The hair should not be permed, nor should it be coloured or bleached. Perming treatment might discolour or break the hair and might burn the skin.

4 **Test curl** Wind, process and neutralise one or more small sections of hair. The results will be a guide to the optimum rod size, processing time and strength of lotion to be used. Remember though that the hair will not all be of the same porosity.

5 **Processing** Unwind and then rewind rods during processing to see how the curl is developing. If the salon is very hot or cold this will affect the progress of the perm: heat will accelerate it, cold will slow it down. When you have achieved the S shape you want, stop the perm by rinsing and then normalising the hair.

Pre-perming and post-perming treatments

Matching the correct perm lotion to hair type is an essential part of the hair examination. However, many perming solutions come in only a coloured, normal or resistant formula. This alone does not cater for all hair conditions. Dry, porous hair will absorb perming solutions more readily; therefore

REMEMBER

Temperature has a major impact on perming. This could be general salon temperature or added heat. In either case remember that processing times will be reduced considerably.

special attention needs to be given in these situations. Pre-perming treatments are the way to combat these condition defects. Porous hair that is suitable for perming will have an uneven porosity throughout the lengths. Hair that is nearer the root will have a different porosity level to mid-length hair, or that of the ends. Therefore the hair's porosity levels will need to be balanced before the perm lotion is applied. This enables the hair to absorb perm lotion at the same rate, evening out the development process and ensuring that the perm doesn't over-process in certain areas. A pre-perming treatment is applied before winding on damp hair and combed through to the ends. Any excess is removed and the hair is wound as normal.

After perming and neutralising it is also necessary to rebalance the hair's pH value of 5.5. Post-perm treatments do this by removing any traces of residual oxygen from the neutralising process. These treatments are also known as **antioxidants**.

PERMING TECHNIQUE

Perming is a straightforward procedure – the more organised you are, the simpler and more successful it will be. Once you have consulted your client and made the necessary tests, you are ready to start.

General preparation

1 Protect your client and her clothes as necessary with a gown and towels.
2 Shampoo the hair to remove grease or dirt that would otherwise block the action of the perm lotion.
3 Towel-dry the hair. (Excess water would dilute the perm lotion, but if the hair is too dry the perm lotion won't spread thoroughly through the hair.)
4 Some perm lotions contain chemicals to treat porosity. If you are going to use a pre-perm lotion, apply it now. Make sure you have read the instructions carefully. Too much pre-perm lotion may block the action of the perm itself.
5 Prepare your trolley. You will need:

- rods, curlers or formers of the chosen sizes
- end papers, for use while winding
- a tailcomb and clips, for sectioning and dividing
- cotton wool strips to protect your client
- gloves to protect your hands
- perm lotion and a suitable normaliser/neutraliser (read the instructions carefully)
- water spray to keep the hair moist (hence reduces the 'quenching' action of the perming lotion upon the hair)
- a plastic cap to 'envelope' the hair and retain moist heat during processing.

6 Check your client's skin and clothes are adequately protected.

ACTIVITY: CURL EFFECTS

As a group test collect together as many perming rods and formers as you can find within the salon. Then ask each individual to sketch the expected curl size and formation for each one in turn. Keep a record of the findings for your portfolio.

Key skills: Communication
2.1 Take part in discussions
2.2 Produce written materials

REMEMBER

Wear gloves from the beginning. It is inconvenient to have to put them on later.

General sectioning

Standard technique

The first part of the process is to divide the hair into sections that will be easy to manage and wind. Done properly, sectioning makes the rest of the process simpler and quicker. If it's not done well though, you will have to resection the hair during the perm and this may spoil the overall result.

Cold perm sectioning

1 Following shampooing and towel-drying, comb the hair to remove any tangles.

2 Make sure you have the tools you will need, including a curler to check the section size.

3 Now divide the hair into six sections, as follows, using clips to secure the hair as you work:

- divide the hair at or near the crown into a horizontal mesh, no wider than a perm rod, secure the top hair out of the way
- divide the back hair into a vertical, yet parallel section down into the nape, secure in sectioning clip(s)
- divide the front hair approximately above both mid-eyebrows, to create a central parallel section meeting the first division at the crown, secure in sectioning clip(s)
- divide the sides into two equally wide sections, one continuing down into the nape and the other terminating above the ears
- divide the opposite side likewise to give two equal width sections.

Winding techniques

Basic winding

Winding is the process of placing sectioned hair onto rods, curlers or formers. There are various winding techniques, designed to produce different effects, but the method is basically the same in each case. In modern cold perming systems you need to wind the hair firmly and evenly, but without stretching the hair or leaving it in tension (see also 'Fashion and alternative winding techniques' pp. 236–42).

Method

1 Divide off a section of hair of a length and thickness to match the curler being used.

2 Comb the hair firmly, directly away from the head. Keep the hair together, so that it doesn't slip.

3 Place the hair points at the centre of the curler. Make sure the hair isn't bunched at one side and loose at the other, or twisted.

4 Hold the hair directly away from the head. If you let the hair slope downwards, the curler won't sit centrally on the base section: hair will overlap and the curler will rest on the skin.

Winding: taking a hair section

5   Before winding, make sure the curler is at an angle suited to the part of the head against which it will rest when wound.

6   Hold the hair points with the finger and thumb of one hand. The thumb should be uppermost.

7   Direct the hair points round and under the curler. Turn your wrist to achieve this. The aim is to lock the points under the curler and against the main body of hair. If they don't lock, they may become buckled or fish-hooked. Don't turn the thumb too far round or the hair will be pushed away from the curler and won't lock the points.

8   After making the first turn of the curler, pass it to the other hand to make the next turn. The hands need to be in complete control: uncontrolled movement or rocking from side to side may cause the ends to slip, the hair to bunch, or the firmness to slacken.

9   After two or three turns the points will be securely locked. Wind the curler down to the head in a steady and even pressure, keeping the curler horizontal. (If it slips, wobbles or bunches the curl result will be uneven.)

10 At the end the curler should be in the centre of the section. If it isn't it will need to be rewound.

11 Secure the curler. Don't let the rubber band pinch or press the hair as it may cause damage.

Winding the section onto the curler

Winding: securing the curler

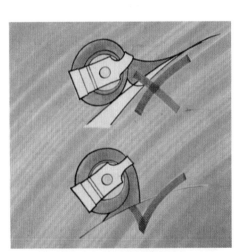

Winding: depth of section Wella

Winding: width of section Wella

Acid and alkaline perming solutions

The systems we currently use to perm hair rely on alkaline or acid based solutions. Their benefits and suitability for use are listed here.

Alkaline

- Effective on strong, coarse, resistant hair which is difficult to wave.
- Alkaline lotion, up to pH 9, is suitable for different hair textures.
- The lotion swells the hair, lifts the cuticle and penetrates to the cortex.

- Less winding tension is required.
- Suitable for all winding techniques.
- The test curl forms a stronger, sharper shape.
- The hair must be normalised or neutralised.
- The higher the pH and the stronger the lotions, the more potential there is for damage.
- No additional heat is required.

Acid

- Suitable for fine, delicate, porous and previously chemically processed hair.
- Shrinks hair and smoothes cuticle.
- Some require additional heat to be applied: climazone, rollerball, **accelerator** or infra-red dryer.
- Make sure that the reagents are activated by mixing the solutions correctly: check with the manufacturer's instructions.
- The test curl forms a softer, looser shape – a crisp, snappy test curl could result in overprocessing.
- Needs a longer processing time than alkaline perms.
- Pre-damp or post-damp – more often post-damp.

John Rawson

Adrian Allen at Red Hair Couture.
Photograph by John Rawson

Desmond Murray

Processing and development

Perm lotion may be applied before winding (pre-damping) or when winding is complete (post-damping). Follow the manufacturer's instructions. Post-damping is perhaps more convenient. You can wind the hair without wearing gloves and the time taken in winding doesn't affect the overall processing time.

Applying the perm lotion

Most perm lotions come in an applicator bottle, ready to use. Others may need to be applied from a bowl, using cotton wool, a sponge or a brush. Read the instructions carefully before applying.

1 Underlying hair is usually more resistant to perming. Apply lotion to these areas first.

2 Keep lotion away from the scalp. Apply it to the section, about 12 mm from the roots.

3 Don't overload the applicator and apply the lotion gently. You will be less likely then to splash your client.

4 If you do splash the skin, quickly rinse the lotion away with water.

Processing time

Processing begins as soon as the perm lotion is in contact with the hair. The time needed for processing is critical. Processing time is affected by the hair texture and condition, the salon temperature and whether heat is applied, the size and number of curlers used and the type of winding used.

- **Hair texture and condition** Fine hair processes more quickly than coarse hair and dry hair than greasy hair. Hair that has been processed previously will perm faster than virgin hair.

- **Temperature** A warm salon cuts down processing time; in a cold salon it will take longer. Even a draught will affect the time required. Usually the heat from the head itself is enough to activate cold perming systems. Wrap your client's head with plastic tissue or a cap to keep in the heat. Don't wrap the hair in towels: these will absorb the lotion and slow down the processing. Some perm lotions require additional heat from lamps or dryers. Don't apply heat unless the manufacturer's instructions tell you to. You might damage both the hair and the scalp. Don't apply heat unless the hair is wrapped; the heat could evaporate the lotion, or speed up the processing too much.
- **Curlers** Processing will be quicker with a lot of small sections on small curlers than with large sections on large curlers. (The large sections will also give looser results.)
- **Winding** The type of winding used and the tension applied also affect processing time. A firmer winding processes faster than a slack winding. Indeed, if the winding is too slack it will not process at all. Hair wound too tightly may break close to the scalp. The optimum is a firm winding without tension.

Testing curls during processing

As processing time is so critical, you need to use a timer. You also need to check the perm at intervals to see how it's progressing. If you used the pre-damping technique, check the first and last curlers that you wound. If you applied the lotion after winding, check curlers from the front, sides, crown and nape.

1 Unwind the hair from a curler. Is the S shape produced correct for the size of curler used?

2 If the curl is too loose, rewind the hair and allow more processing time. (But if the test curl is too loose because the curler was too large, extra processing time will damage the hair and won't make the curl tighter.)

3 If the curl is correct, stop the processing by rinsing.

Rinsing and neutralising

When processing is complete, leave the curlers in place while you rinse away the perm lotion. Use tepid water (not hot). Direct the spray head onto and between the rollers for several minutes to make sure all the lotion is removed. Long hair will require more rinsing than shorter hair.

After rinsing, blot the hair with towels and cotton wool to remove excess water. The hair is now ready for neutralising.

Neutralising

Neutralising is the process of returning hair to its normal condition after perming. The word is a little misleading: chemically speaking, a 'neutral' condition is neither acidic nor alkaline (pH 7.0). In fact, healthy hair is slightly acidic (pH 5.6–5.9).

How neutralising works

As described above, perm lotion acts on the keratin in the hair. The strongest bonds between the polypeptides are the disulphide bridges. Perm lotion breaks some of these, allowing the keratin to take up a new shape. This is how new curls can form.

What neutralising does is to make new disulphide bridges. If you didn't neutralise, the hair would be weak and likely to break and the new curls would soon fall out. Neutralising is an **oxidation** process – a process that uses oxidising agents such as hydrogen peroxide, sodium bromate and sodium perborate.

Preparation

1 Gather together the materials you will need.
2 Make sure there is a washbasin free, preferably one where the client can put his or her head back to use it. (This makes it easier for you to keep chemicals away from the client's eyes.)

First rinsing

1 As soon as the perm is complete, move your client immediately to the washbasin. Make sure she is comfortable. Offer her hand towels or tissues in case any liquid trickles over her face.
2 Carefully remove the cap or other head covering. The hair is soft and weak at this stage, so don't put unnecessary tension on it. Leave the curlers in place.
3 Run the water. You need an even supply of warm water. The water must be neither hot nor cold. Check the pressure and temperature against the back of your hand. Remember that your client's head may be sensitive after the perming process.
4 Rinse the hair thoroughly with the warm water. This may take about five minutes. It is this rinsing that stops the perm process – until you rinse away the lotion, the hair will still be processing. Direct the water away from the eyes and face. Make sure you rinse *all* the hair, including the nape curlers. If a curler slips out, gently wind the hair back onto it immediately.

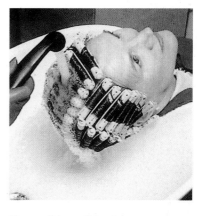

Neutralising: first rinse   L'Oréal

Applying neutraliser

1 Raise your client to a comfortable sitting position.
2 Blot the hair thoroughly using a towel or tissues. It may help if you pack the curlers with cotton wool.
3 When no surplus water remains, apply the **neutraliser**. Follow the manufacturer's instructions. These may tell you to pour the neutraliser through the hair, apply it with a brush or sponge, or use the spiked applicator bottle. Some foam neutralisers need to be pushed briskly into the hair. Make sure that neutraliser comes into contact with all of the hair.
4 When all the hair has been covered, time the process according to the instructions. The usual time is five to ten minutes. You may wrap the hair in a towel or leave it open to the air – follow the instructions.

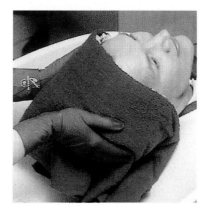

Neutralising: towel-drying the hair   L'Oréal

5 Gently and carefully remove the curlers. Don't pull or stretch the hair. It may still be soft, especially towards the ends.

6 Apply the neutraliser to the hair again, covering all the hair. Arrange the hair so that the neutraliser does not run over the face. Leave for the time recommended, perhaps another five to ten minutes.

Second rinsing

1 Run the water, again checking temperature and pressure.

2 Rinse the hair thoroughly to remove the neutraliser.

3 You can now treat the hair with an after-perm aid or **conditioner**. Use the one recommended by the manufacturer of the perm and neutraliser to be sure that the chemicals are compatible.

Successful neutralising

At the end of the neutralising process, you will have returned the hair to a normal, stable state.

- The reduction and oxidation processes will have been completed

- Finishing aids or conditioners (**antioxidants**) may need to be applied to counteract the oxidants used.

- The hair will now be slightly weaker – fewer bonds will have formed than were broken by the perm. Special conditioners may be needed. If the cuticle is lifting or roughened, this too may be countered with conditioners.

- Record any hair or perm faults on the client's record. Correct faults as appropriate.

- Under-neutralising – not leaving neutraliser on for long enough – results in a slack curl or waves.

- Over-oxidising – leaving the neutraliser on too long or using oxidants that are too strong – results in weak hair and poor curl.

The hair should be ready for shaping, blow-drying or setting.

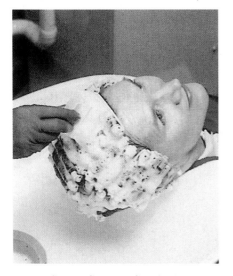

Neutralising: first application   L'Oréal

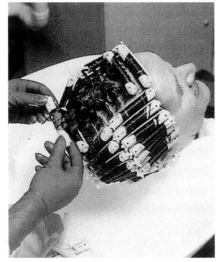

Removing curlers   L'Oréal

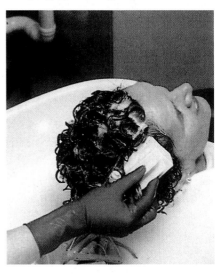

Second application of neutraliser
L'Oréal

After perming

Check the results of perming:

- Has the scalp been irritated by the perm lotion?
- Is the hair in good condition?
- Is the curl even?

Dry the hair into style. Depending on the effect you want, you may now use finger drying, hood drying or blow drying, treat the hair gently. If you handle it too firmly the perm may relax again.

Advise the client on how to manage the perm at home. The hair should not be shampooed for a day or two. The manufacturer's information should be passed on to the client.

Clean all tools thoroughly so they are ready for the next operation. Complete the client record, noting type of perm, strength of the lotion, processing time, curler sizes and winding technique. Record any problems you have had. This information will be useful if the hair is permed again.

Zullo and Pack, Nottingham. Photograph by John Rawson

Roberta Kneller at Bobs Hair Company. Photograph by John Rawson

FASHION AND ALTERNATIVE WINDING TECHNIQUES

Basic sectioning and winding techniques create lateral waves and curl that are in the horizontal plane to the head: this is not the only curl placement option.

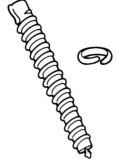

1 Spiral rods

Spiral (vertical) curl movement

Selecting the size and position of the curls

The spiral curl is dependent on the length of the client's hair. If the hair is less than 10 cm long it will be difficult, and perhaps impossible, to form spiral shapes of any size. Hair longer than 10 cm will permit reasonable spiral formations: longer hair will enable fuller, thicker and longer curls to be shaped.

The position that these spiral curls take and the overall effect they produce must be discussed with your clients: you must ensure that they understand what is being done. Because the handling and maintenance of this type of perm is quite different to traditional methods, it is important that they know how to maintain the effects before they leave the salon.

Spiral curls may be formed all over the head, length permitting, or they may be formed and positioned to make a cascade in the nape. Alternatively, bunches of spiral curls may be positioned asymmetrically. The degree of the spiral curl shape and the effect finally produced is for you and your client to determine jointly at the outset.

2 Position on the head

Starting the wind

The spiral wind can be started at the root end of the hair or from the hair points. If you use a curl former that is of the same thickness overall, the curl you produce will be even throughout. If you use a former that tapers or is concave, the results will be uneven.

For the resultant curl to be even, springy and smooth, your winding must be firm without undue tension, wrapped cleanly over the former and secured without indenting or marking the wound hair.

If you apply uneven tension to your winding, the spiral formation will be inconsistent – the loops and turns will not follow on and there may be gaps in the shape.

Securing the wind

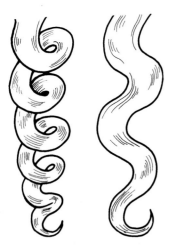

3 The curl expected with a small rod (left) and with a large rod (right)

When you secure the hair formers, be careful not to cut into the wound hair. Breakage could result if you did. Follow the recommendations of the makers of the curl former that you are using. You must also ensure that the formers are secured firmly: if they are loose, the hair may drop or unwind.

Monitoring the perm process

Once you have completed your winding and secured the formers, you must monitor the perm process. If the perm lotion is applied to the hair before winding – a technique called pre-damping – the winding must be carried out without delay. Alternatively, the lotion can be applied after the winding is complete – post-damping. Perm processing is always timed from the moment the lotion is applied.

You will need to check the development of the perm process. You can achieve this by taking a test curl. By gently unwinding the hair part-way you can check the development of the S shape. If the shape is loose then further development may be required. If the shape is well formed, begin normalising straightaway: the perm is said to have 'taken'.

As well as monitoring the timing carefully you must check the following:

- ensure your client's comfort
- keep excess lotion off the skin to avoid skin irritation
- remove damp cotton wool (used to protect the skin) when it has absorbed the lotion or scalp 'burns' will occur
- continually reassure the client so that she never feels she has been forgotten
- use a timer which makes an audible noise when the time has elapsed.

Photo courtesy Goldwell

A completed spiral wind

Normalising

When the perm has taken, you must stop the perming process quickly. This is an important stage. If you are supervising a junior hairdresser, be sure to double-check with her that she is monitoring whether the perm has taken and is ready to normalise the hair. Normalising should include the following stages:

1 Rinse the wound hair thoroughly with warm water to remove the perm lotion. Make sure the water is not too hot or there may be a sudden tightening of the perm.

2 Blot the curlers or formers to remove surplus water, using tissues or towels. (If this is not done the normaliser may become diluted and the perm is likely to drop.) When monitoring others, ensure that this has been done thoroughly.

3 Apply the normaliser as recommended by the manufacturer. Care must be taken that it covers all of the wound hair. Ensure that the curlers in the nape and around the ears are not missed.

4 When you have completed the normaliser application, start the timing. The time the normaliser should remain on the hair varies with the type and make of perm used: make sure that you know the recommended time for the normaliser you are using.

5 When the first application of the normaliser has been on the hair for its allotted time, the curlers may be removed. This must be done with care as the hair may still be soft. Harsh handling could weaken the perm.

6 You may now apply the second stage of normalising. This too must be carefully timed. Again, check that the normaliser has covered all the hair.

7 Now rinse the hair well to remove all traces of normaliser. At this stage the hair may be conditioned and made ready for setting for blow styling.

Philip Bell, Ishoka

GOOD PRACTICE/ HEALTH & SAFETY

Take care not to splash your client's face while rinsing. Even dilute perm lotion can irritate the skin.

Hair: Patrick Cameron; photography: Thornton Howdie; make-up: Alison Chesterton

Hair: American Dream

Problems

Below are some problems that you may encounter when producing permanent spiral curls:

- **The root end is straight** You can avoid this by securing the former firmly at the root end of the hair. The helical loops of hair will be too loose if they are not firmly wound and in close contact with the former.

- **Hair flicks out** Ensure that the hair is not twisted when you form the spiral curl. After each turn, the hair should be repositioned. If you allow the hair to twist, an irregular spiral will be formed: this could cause the hair to stick out from the head. It is difficult to remedy this afterwards.

- **The spiral curl is too loose** Provided that the hair condition permits it, the hair may be reprocessed. You must take special care if you do this as the hair will be far more receptive to the perm lotion and could easily become over-processed.

Perming hair of different lengths

Short lengths of hair (less than 10 cm) are not suitable for permanent spiral curls because it is impossible to form the helical shape on the curl former.

Medium hair lengths (10–15 cm) do allow spiral formations. These are likely to be short and narrow.

Longer lengths of hair (15 cm and longer) are the most suitable. Here there is sufficient hair to produce a variety of full, long, springy shapes. Greater lengths allow the hair to be placed onto the former more easily and a wider variety of curl formers may be used.

Direction and degree of movement

The direction of perm movement is determined by the angle that you wind and position the curlers or rods. If a forward direction of the fringe area is required, the wound curlers must be positioned accordingly.

The degree of perm movement is the 'tightness' or 'looseness' of the wave or curl. This is determined by:

- size of curlers, rods or formers used
- time for which the hair is processed
- amount of tension used
- hair texture and its condition
- perm lotion strength
- type of winding used.

Directional winding

The hair is wound in the direction in which it is to be finally worn. This technique is suitable for enhancing well-cut shapes. The hair can be wound in any direction required and the technique is ideal for shorter hairstyles.

DIRECTIONAL WIND

Pincurl

Double wind

Directional wind

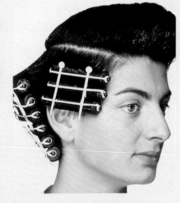

Weave wind

Stack wind

Winding and the finished effects

Staggered winding or brick winding

The wound curlers are placed in a pattern resembling brickwork. By staggering the partings of the curlers, you avoid obvious gaps in the hair. It is suitable for short hairstyles.

Weave winding

The normal size section is divided into two and then the hair is woven. A large curler is used to wind the upper subsection and a smaller one is used for the lower subsection. This produces two different curl sizes, giving volume without tight curls. Alternatively, one subsection is wound and the other left unwound. With short hair this produces spiky effects.

Double winding

This technique consists of winding a section of hair halfway down on a large curler, then placing a smaller curler underneath and winding both curlers down to the head. This produces a varied curl effect.

Piggyback winding

This is winding using a small and a large curler. The normal size section is wound from the middle onto a large curler, down to the head. The ends are then wound from the points onto a smaller curler, which is placed on top of the large curler. This produces softly waved roots and curly points. Alternatively this technique can be used to produce root movement only by not winding the point ends.

Stack winding

This is used where fullness of long hair is required, with little curl movement on top – it is ideal for bobbed hair lengths. The sections are wound close to the head in the lower parts; the upper sections are part wound only at the points. This allows the curlers to stack one upon another.

Other types of perm which give volume support

- **Root perms** – perming the lower root ends of the hair. The hair is wound at the root ends only: the point ends are left out and not processed. This allows the hair to produce fullness and volume. Reperming must be kept strictly to the regrown root ends.
- **Body perms** – the root and middle hair lengths can be processed to give added body to the hair.
- **Pin perms, roller perms, semi- or demi-perms** – these involve the application of a weaker form of perm lotion, which lasts for six to eight weeks. Reprocessing can take place through the hair lengths after this time has elapsed. These are not intended to be permanent, but to produce body fullness.

Other types of perming equipment

Foam rollers and formers

1 Take a small rectangular section of hair.
2 Secure the hair points in an end paper.
3 Wind the hair around the foam roller.
4 Secure the roller in position by bending over the ends.
5 Repeat steps 1–4 to complete the entire head.

1 The formers being wound on
Clynol

2 Winding complete

3 The finished effect

Chopsticks

1 Take a small square section of hair and protect it with one or more end papers.
2 Place the hair section through the loop and hold it securely.
3 Separate the chopstick legs and wind in a figure of eight.
4 Secure the end paper on to the chopsticks using a rubber band.
5 Repeat steps 1–4 to complete the entire head.

1 Chopsticks

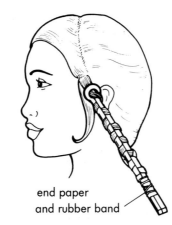

end paper
and rubber band

2 Position on the head

3 The expected curl

U-stick rods

1 Take a small square section and pull it through the middle of the u-stick.
2 Wind the hair in a figure-of-eight movement around the u-stick.
3 Protect the ends with one or more end papers.
4 Secure the end papers on the u-stick with a rubber band.
5 Repeat steps 1–4 to complete the whole head.

1 U-stick rods

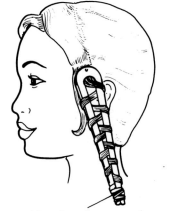

rubber band over end papers

2 Position on the head

3 The expected curl

Perming problems and solutions

	Possible cause	Immediate action	Future action
Hair/scalp damage			
Breakage	Too much tension or bands on curlers too tight. Hair over-processed – chemicals far too strong	Apply restructurant or deep-action conditioner to remainder of hair	Use less tension. Review choice of lotion, timing, etc.
Pull burn	Perm lotion allowed to enter follicle. Tension on hair excessive. Poor rinsing of surplus perm lotion	Apply soothing moisturiser to affected area. If condition serious, refer to doctor	Use less tension. Take smaller meshes
Sore hairline, skin irritation	Chemicals allowed to come into contact with skin. Poor scalp ventilation	Consult regarding allergies, then apply soothing moisturiser to affected area. If condition serious refer to doctor	Curlers to rest on hair not skin. Keep lotion away from scalp. Renew cotton wool after damping
Straight frizz	Lotion too strong for hair. Excessive winding tension. Hair over-processed	Cut ends to reduce frizz. Apply restructurant or penetrating conditioner	Ensure appropriate lotion is used in future. Wind with less tension. Time carefully
Perm result/effect			
Too curly	Curlers too small. Lotion too strong	If hair condition allows, reduce curl amount by relaxing	Ensure appropriate curlers and lotion are used

	Possible cause	Immediate action	Future action
No result	Lotion too weak or not enough used. Curlers too large. Poor neutralising. Hair under-processed	If hair condition allows, reperm hair with suitable lotion	Use appropriate lotion and rods. Process perm and neutraliser in line with manufacturer's instructions
Fish-hooks	Hair points not wrapped properly. No end papers	Remove ends by cutting	Check points of hair are wrapped correctly. Use end papers
	Possible cause	Immediate action	Future action
Perm weakens	Poor neutralising. Hair stretched excessively while drying	If hair condition allows, reperm hair	Check method and timing of neutraliser. Do not overstretch while drying hair
Good result when wet, poor when dry	Hair stretched while drying. Ineffective neutralising. Over-processed	If hair condition good, reperm. Apply conditioning agents to moisturise hair	Check method and timing of neutraliser. Avoid stretching while drying
Uneven curl	Uneven winding technique. Uneven tension. Uneven lotion application. Ineffective neutralising	If hair condition allows, reperm affected areas	Check wound curlers before applying perm lotion or neutraliser
Straight pieces	Lotion not applied evenly. Rods too large	If hair condition allows, reperm affected area	Ensure even lotion application

Perming techniques: quick reference guide

Perm technique	Final effect	Ideal length	Lotion type	Equipment
Root	Lift and body at root area only	Layered hair or graduated hair 100–150 mm long	Acid or alkaline, often used as thick cream or paste	Conventional rods, often used with non-porous end papers
Pincurl	Lift and body with soft end curl	Layered hair of uniform length 50–75 mm long	Acid or alkaline, often used as thick cream or paste	Aluminium or plastic pin clips
Directional	Lift and body with definite forced movement	Layered hair or graduated hair 100–150 mm long	Acid or alkaline	Conventional or oval rods
Weaving	Textured soft and stronger movement at ends	Layered hair or graduated hair over 75 mm long	Acid or alkaline	Conventional or oval rods
Piggyback (double wind)	Textured curl with varying curl diameters	Layered hair or graduated hair over 75 mm long	Acid or alkaline	Conventional rods
Stack wind	No root lift but strong end movement/curl	Graduated hair 150 mm down to 70 mm	Acid or alkaline	Conventional rods
Zigzag	Strong geometric, angular movement	One length or long layered hair 250 mm	Alkaline	Perming chopsticks/u-stick rods
Spiral	Vertical cascade curls with uniform diameter	Long layered hair or one length over 250 mm	Alkaline	Spiral rods or foam covered flexible wavers

Started it	I know and understand the principles of positive communication	I know when and how to conduct tests on the hair for perming	I always recognise contra-indications when I analyse the client's hair
☐	☐	☐	☐
I am familiar with a range of perming equipment and winding techniques and know when to apply them	I know how to negotiate, reaching a mutually beneficial conclusion	I always carry out working practices according to the salon's policy	I've covered most of it!
☐	☐	☐	☐
I understand the science of perming and know the effects of heat and chemicals upon the hair	I know when and to whom to refer clients in situations where external assistance is required	I understand the necessity of personal hygiene and presentation	I know how to advise, promote and sell other services and products to clients
☐	☐	☐	☐
I know and respect the client's rights: data protection, equal opportunities, anti-discrimination and consumer legislation	Done it all!		CHECKER BOARD ✓
☐	☐		

Self-test section

Quick quiz: a selection of different types of questions to check your knowledge

Q1 A test _ _ _ _ _ _ _ will identify when optimum movement is achieved.　　Fill in the blank

Q2 Cold wave perms are usually post-damped.　　True or False

Q3 Which of the following factors are likely to be affected by perming?　　Multi-selection

Elasticity	☐	1
Natural colour	☐	2
Thickness	☐	3
Apparent length	☐	4
Porosity	☐	5
Abundance	☐	6

Q4 Neutralisers contain hydrogen peroxide.　　True or False

Q5 Which of the following chemical bonds are permanently rearranged?　　Multi-selection

Salt bonds	☐	1
Hydrogen bonds	☐	2
Disulphide bonds	☐	3
Oxygen bonds	☐	4

Q6 Time and temperature have a direct impact upon perm development.　　True or False

Q7 Which of the following tests are *not* applicable to perming?　　Multi-selection

Strand test	☐	1
Incompatibility test	☐	2
Peroxide test	☐	3
Porosity test	☐	4
Elasticity test	☐	5
Skin test	☐	6

Q8 The rearrangement of chemical bonds take place within the _ _ _ _ _ _ _ _　　Fill in the blank

Q9 The chemical compound responsible for modifying the hair's structure during perming is?　　Multi-choice

Hydrogen peroxide	☐	1
Ammonium hydroxide	☐	2
Ammonium thioglycolate	☐	3
Sodium perborate	☐	4

Q10 'Smaller perming rods produce tighter curl effects.　　True or False

chapter 7

MEN'S STYLING AND BARBERING

Unit H7 Cut hair using basic barbering techniques

H7.1 **Maintain effective and safe methods of working when cutting hair**

H7.2 **Cut hair to achieve a variety of looks**

Unit H8 Cut facial hair to shape using basic techniques

H8.1 **Maintain effective and safe methods of working when cutting facial hair**

H8.2 **Cut beards and moustaches to maintain their shape**

What do I need to learn?

You need to know and understand:

- **Your salon's policy in respect of clients preparation, services and safety**
- **How you should work safely and hygienically**
- **How to recognise the factors that influence suitable styling/shaping choices**
- **A variety of cutting techniques that will help to achieve a range of different effects**
- **How to provide advice on maintaining the effect and a healthy skin condition**

What does it mean?

- **You need to have the skills necessary to create a range of different looks for men, which could be classic/traditional, the current fashions and those that are at the beginning of being the next big thing.**

What do I need to do?

- **You need to be able to take adequate precautions in preparing yourself and the client before cutting hair.**
- **You need to be able to work safely at all times.**
- **You need to be able to analyse and recognise any limitations to the client's hairstyling requirements whilst balancing this with an agreed, suitable course of action.**
- **You need to be able to cut a range of different hairstyles, beards and moustaches.**

Other info

Related topics and other useful information:

Client consultation

Colour and colouring hair

African Caribbean hairdressing

KEY WORDS

Club cut or clubbing hair or blunt cutting The most basic and most popular way of cutting sections of hair straight across, parallel to the index and middle finger

Scissor over comb A technique of cutting hair with scissors, using the back of the comb as a guide, especially when the hair is at a length that cannot be held between the fingers

Clipper over comb A technique of cutting hair with electric clippers, using the back of the comb as a guide, especially on very short hair and hairline profiles

Texturising/personalising A range of techniques used in addition to the above – chipping, pointing, slicing etc. – which can create, lift, movement, texture or definition within a hairstyle

CHECKERBOARD

At the end of this chapter the checkerboard will help to jog your memory on what you have learned and what still remains to be done. Cross them off with a pencil as you cover each of the topics. (See p. 277.)

INTRODUCTION

Over the past 20 to 30 years contemporary men's hairstyling in Britain has been based around suitability and purpose. This has meant that the decisions that men make about their hair reflect upon what they do in their working lives, how they spend their leisure time and how much hair they have got.

In many other cultures hair and facial hair styling is part of an intricately crafted process that has its roots in tribal history and status.

REMEMBER ✔

Cutting men's hair (as with colouring) uses many of the principles of cutting women's hair. Review other chapters in this book for more information.

KMS California

REMEMBER ✔

A finished hairstyle always looks better if it is cut wet. Try to educate your own clients into booking for a wet cut at least.

- It will be easier for you to create the effect.

- They will be able to see a better, more professional result.

- You will generate a better professional service with your clientele.

- You will break the habits of men expecting a quick, cheap cut.

- It is more hygienic for everyone concerned.

Hair and hairdressing have always been an essential part of the females' appearance and they have now become a major issue for men too.

ACTIVITY: TRADITIONAL, CURRENT AND EMERGING FASHIONS ↔

The hairdressing standards expect you to achieve a variety of different men's looks and effects. These will fall into traditional, current and emerging fashions.

What is meant by these terms?

Find examples of each genre from styling magazines and then give a short account for how each style could be achieved.

PREPARING THE CLIENT

Each salon has its own specific ways for doing things and your salon's code of practice must always be observed. At the very least this should extend to preparing yourself and the client so that you are ready to complete the service, ensuring that he will be comfortable and well protected throughout the cutting process.

This means:

- covering him and his clothes with a clean, laundered gown

- placing a cutting collar around his shoulders (preferably after shampooing and) before the cutting starts to prevent any hairs going down his neck

- making sure that all tools and equipment are safe and hygienic, ready for use.

Cutting short-layered or clippered styles (particularly on dry hair) often involves a lot of small, sharp, spiky hairs that need to be kept constantly cleared with the neck brush for the client's comfort, personal hygiene and safety.

You need to be careful too as flying fragments of hair can easily enter the skin if you wear open toed shoes and sandals. They can penetrate T-shirts or, even worse, enter your eyes and be potentially harmful.

ACTIVITY: SALON CODE OF PRACTICE FOR CLIENT PREPARATION ↔

Every salon has their own way of doing things. Write down in your portfolio under the following headings what is your salon's code of practice in respect to:

- meeting and greeting clients

- gowning

- maintaining tools and equipment

- disposal of sharps

- hygiene and preventing the spread of infection or infestation.

Preparation checklist

✓ Make sure that the styling section and chair is clean, safe and ready to receive clients.

✓ Make sure that the seat is lowered, providing easier access for the clients whether they be young, old or with physical constraints.

✓ Make sure that the client is well protected with a clean fresh gown and a close-fitting cutting collar.

✓ Find out what the client wants. Men can often be more difficult during consultation as they are often reluctant to use a technical term that they are not sure about or express themselves clearly to people they don't know (see the section on communication below).

✓ Style books/files provide lots of male looks to help the diagnostic process.

✓ Make sure you consider the reasons and the purpose for the style. Hairstyles required for professional purposes have more restrictions on freedom and expressions than fashionable, trendy looks or more general wear.

✓ Assess the styling limitations – hair and skin problems or physical features.

✓ Avoid technical jargon or style names; if you do use them, always clarify in simple terms what you mean to avoid confusion; this will help to educate your clients for the future.

✓ Don't just do the style if you think that it's wrong. If there are reasons why you think it will be unsuitable, you will be doing the client a big favour in the longer term if you tackle the issue straight away.

✓ Always give them some advice on how to maintain their hairstyle; men often need products to help them achieve similar effects themselves. Make sure you show them how they can use and apply any new product at home to maintain their own hair/skin condition or styling effect.

✓ Give them an idea of how long it will last and remember to re-book their next appointment before they leave. Alternatively, if they prefer just to pop in on the off chance tell them when they should expect a revisit.

KMS California

CONSULTATION

Communication

Above all clear communication is the key to successful hairdressing. Poor communication is the complete opposite: its biggest barrier. This doesn't just go for men's hairdressing either; many people try to use the names of styles or techniques (technical terms) when they try to describe what they want. Sometimes it works but generally, more often than not, the terms that they (and sometimes the stylists too!) use are incorrect!

This at the very least will lead to an unexpected result and general dissatisfaction. At the worst it could lead to a disaster! In any event this should be avoided at all costs. When you consult the client try not to use jargon or technical terms; it's not clever and definitely won't impress either.

Images courtesy of Wahl (UK) Ltd; hair: Simon Shaw, Artistic Director Wahl (UK); styling: Rebecca Shaw; make-up José Basse; photography: Carl Shaw

Always try to find other ways of putting things or use pictures to show what you mean. Often a pictorial illustration will express far more than just a cutting style or technique. It creates an overall finished impression too. Choosing a new hairstyle or effect is a big step for anyone, so you need to make sure that you help them all the way.

Make a habit of summarising the main points as you go through the consultation by saying:

'So you would like to keep the overall length at the back although you don't mind it shorter around the ears?'

'You want to keep the parting where it is because you find it doesn't lie very well elsewhere?'

It is also worth remembering that other people have a huge impact on the styles that we choose and that goes for your male clients as well. Many men have no *real* opinions about their self-image and this makes it difficult for hairdressers to contend with. This is because it's hard enough to consult and analyse the needs and requirements of the client who is sitting in the styling chair; it is almost impossible to satisfy someone who is sitting in a chair at home. You need to know what you are trying to achieve and *for whom* you are trying to achieve it. Communication on a one-to-one basis is problematic, but *telepathy* is a skill only afforded to a very select few.

Clear communication goes beyond speech too, because as well as using words we show our interest, attitude and feelings by our bodily expressions. Body language is just as clear to others as speech, so you need to remain professional at all times, regardless of how difficult this can be.

We express our innermost feelings via our body posturing, our eyes and mannerisms. Collectively, these can be *saying* something quite different to our mouths. As a senior operative, you will be well aware of the issues addressed here; you will have seen this daily in a busy salon. Normally, the people that you supervise in your work will still be trying to come to terms with it and that goes for many of the clients too.

Very few people have had professional communication training and when you come across it, it is very plain to see the difference. Professional communicators know how to present themselves; they know what to say and how to make themselves understood. You too can learn from their techniques.

> *As a hairdresser you are already capable of learning by observation and not everyone can do this.*

In fact, when you started your training, it was a bit like *'one step forwards and two backwards'*. That didn't last for ever, though, you soon got to the point where you didn't keep making mistakes and you didn't need constant help. Once you had grasped the fundamental skills, you found that you could adapt these in new ways to achieve different effects. When you arrived at this point, you were able to assess what methods and techniques are used in creating any number of given styles.

In summarising the difference between effective communication and professional communication, you can look at it like this: effective communication is making sure that you are understood, whereas professional communication is making sure that everyone understands.

The different genres of hairstyling

Hairdressing styles fall into three distinct groupings or genres and knowing which one to use with a client is key to its success. Choosing a fashion look for a barrister may sound fun, but is unlikely to carry any weight in the High Court. Similarly, choosing a traditional look for someone working in 'street fashion' retail is definitely 'uncool'. Knowing the differences between the genres and when to use what is vitally important.

Classic or traditional work could be defined as *timeless* fashion; that is to say that it is neither in nor out of fashion. It was a fashion created at a time when the basic rules were first exploited by either the celebrity hairdressers of the time (for example Vidal Sassoon and the 'bob') or the necessity of conformity in society (for example, the armed services).

Current fashion tends to change all the time. Some leading salons will constantly push the boundaries of creativity and individuality. There belief is that they can lead by example and this makes them a preferred employer in attracting new and creative personnel. So the business model is self-perpetuating:

Create new fashion – attract creative people – who create new fashion.

The last genre covers the fashions that are still on the horizon. These are fashions that we get glimpses of on the designer catwalks of London, Paris and New York. They are also seen on stages, worn by pop stars, in concerts all over the world. The people creating and producing these effects are almost gambling on the next big thing. Their brief is to create something that helps the wearer to get notice from the media through general PR. The looks are often individualistic and not necessarily durable or wearable in a wider 'street fashion' sense.

Classic traditional styling
Images courtesy of Wahl (UK) Ltd; hair: Simon Shaw, Artistic Director Wahl (UK); styling: Rebecca Shaw; make-up José Basse; photography: Carl Shaw

REMEMBER

As many men have shorter hair, their nape hair growth patterns will have far more impact on what hairstyle you choose.

REMEMBER

Personal hygiene is especially important to hairdressers. You work in close proximity to the client so make sure that you eliminate body odour, bad breath or dirty hands and nails by taking the appropriate action.

Apart from the differing genres there are also cultural differences and sometimes these become the drivers for fashion too. Over time many 'tribal' effects have found their way through to fashion. Admittedly, it takes a celebrity to make the look popular, but there are many lasting images and impressions created by the likes of reggae legend Bob Marley, rock star Jimi Hendrix and soul man Stevie Wonder. These people were not necessarily making a deliberate fashion statement, they were simply people who brought their cultures to the forefront in the way that they looked and led their lives.

Current fashion styling
Hair by Nikki @ Cheynes Hairdressing, Edinburgh

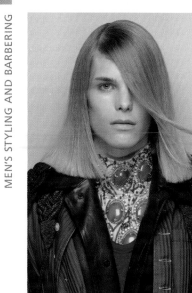

Emerging fashion looks
Hair by Michelle @ Ishoka, Aberdeen

Hair by Michelle @ Ishoka, Aberdeen

REMEMBER ✔

Always look for contra-indications for styling and facial hair shaping; these could relate to infections, infestations, poor hair/skin condition, difficult hair growth patterns, face shape and physical features.

Influencing factors – Contra-indications

Influencing factors: Facial shapes

Facial shapes	How best to work with it
Square and oblong facial shapes (rectangular)	Square and oblong women's faces are not considered ideal; conversely, these face shapes are typically masculine and provide a perfect base for traditional classic well groomed looks.
Round faces (round)	If shorter, more classic styles are required, the round face is improved by the introduction of angular or linear perimeters. Conversely, if the hair is to be worn longer the roundness of the face will be diminished, as more will be covered.
Square angular features, jaw, forehead etc. (square)	Again these are traditionally accepted as a feature of masculinity. They do not really pose any limitations for classic type work. They also work well with longer hair too. Squarer more angular features are softened with beards and moustaches.
Flatter heads at the back	Are improved by tailored graduation. This creates a contour and shape that is missing from having a flatter occipital bone. Sometimes the head is both flat and wide and this can make the problem harder to deal with. Wider flatter heads are made less noticeable by longer hair, if this is not possible than explain what the effect will look like if taken very short.

Influencing factors: Physical features

Physical features	How best to work with it
Prominent nose	Hair taken back away from the face accentuates this feature, whilst hair around the face and forehead tends to diminish the feature.
Protruding ears	Are better left covered rather than exposed. Sufficient hair should be left to cover and extend beyond their length if at all possible.
Narrow foreheads	Are disguised by softer fringes and side partings, whereas they are made more obvious by hair taken back away form the face.
Bushy, thick eyebrows	If the eyebrows are a different colour to the natural hair, the feature will be even more prominent. The hairstyle will be improved with some form of light trimming and grooming.
Large faces	Are augmented by classical, short-cropped or sculpted hair.
Shapes of glasses	Generally people will have had assistance in the selection and suitability of their frames. Therefore they should not work against the hairstyle that you want to create as they should already suit the shape and size of the face.
Long side burns	Are made more prominent with shorter hairstyles, make sure that this is acceptable to your client first as he might be rather attached to his facial hair feature.
Beards	Make sure that the client's beard is still going to be balanced to the amount of hair on top of his head in the finished effect. If an imbalance is going to occur, mention it first and give him the option of taking the beard shorter to compensate.

Influencing factors: Hair growth patterns

Hair growth patterns	*How best to work with it*
 Thinning hair/baldness Dr A L Wright Thinning hair/baldness	Younger men can be quite sensitive about thinning hair. Be tactful and try to find solutions that are realistic and sympathetic to the problem. When dealing with male pattern baldness most men will tend to opt for shorter 'close cropped' or clippered hairstyles rather than long.
 Double crown Double crown	A double crown is particularly problematic when it is cut short. It sticks outwards and will not lie down until it grows longer. This is improved if the hair is left longer to over-fall the opposing growth movement and sometimes benefits for a little thinning if the hair is thick.
 Nape whorls Nape whorls	Nape whorls can occur on either or both sides; the movement caused by this growth pattern forces the hair to flatten and move towards the centre. This growth pattern is not necessarily a problem for short clippered lengths or longer over-falling hair, it affects shorter layered shapes that need to keep a perimeter baseline.
 Cowlick Cowlick	A cowlick appears at the hairline at the front of the head. It makes cutting a straight fringe difficult, particularly on fine hair, because the hair often forms a natural parting. This strong movement can often be improved by moving the parting over so that the weight over-falls the growth pattern. Sometimes a fringe can be achieved by leaving the layers longer so that they weigh down the hair.
 Widow's peak Widow's peak	The widow's peak is a hair growth pattern that appears at the centre of the front hairline. The outline shape protrudes downwards in a 'v' shape and the hair grows upwards and forwards, forming a strong peak. It is often better to cut the hair into styles that are dressed back from the face, as any light fringes will separate around this area.

There are other contra-indications to styling in the section on hair and scalp diseases, conditions and defects, in Chapter 2.

Examination of hair and scalp

While you are looking at the client's hair and scalp, be particularly aware of the texture of the hair. If it is coarse and tightly curled, you will need stronger combs to stretch the hair out from the head before cutting, and firmer movements will need to be applied. The density of the hair is important too: if it is thick, then styles with varied hair lengths are possible. Conversely, sparse hair, particularly if it is fine, requires a great deal of attention and expertise. If finely textured hair has to cover sparse area of the head, it will have to be longer than hair of coarser texture. The amount, type and distribution pattern of hair are all-important too. Younger men may have distinctly higher forehead hairlines than women of similar age. Thinning crowns and decreasing density of hair marks many male patterns, though these are not usually seen in women until much later in life. Take this into consideration when designing and cutting hairstyles specifically for men and women. Hair growth, at a rate of about 12 mm each month, is more noticeable with shorter layered styles. To keep them tidy, regular trimming is essential.

More influencing factors affecting hair styling	
Look out for:	*Why is it a concern?*
Hair density	Scalps with densely populated hair can always be reduced, thinned or controlled in some way, whereas thinner hair or male pattern baldness create a range of limitations that you will need to both express and contend with.
Hair tendency	Curly hair has more styling limitations than straighter hair. Wavy hair is always easier to direct or position than straight hair. Point these factors out before you start.
Hair texture	Fine hair is always difficult to handle, whereas coarser hair when straight will often appear spiky or blunt. Conversely, coarse, wavy hair can often appear dry regardless of natural condition. Each hair texture type creates a different problem.

Finding out what the client wants

Finding out what the client wants is fundamental to achieving a satisfactory result. Factors such as practicality, suitability and the client's ability to cope with his hair are aspects that you should never overlook.

The final effects will be influenced by other considerations too:

- the amount of hair
- the distribution of the hair over the scalp
- the texture of the hair

- the condition of the hair and scalp
- the tendency of the hair, i.e. the amount of wave or curl.

Unless you do take all these factors into consideration, you could have an unhappy, disgruntled client on your hands.

Although men can wear longer hair as well as short a whole range of modern contemporary styling effects has developed since the basic and traditional short back and sides. The application of hair products will often 'dress up' an otherwise professional or classic looking hair turning it into something with a more distinctive 'fashion look' for social and special occasions.

Now and again a men's named style becomes fashionable. Some of these names, such as '**crew cut**', the 'mullet', the wedge or a mohawk, have passed into the general vocabulary. Always make sure that you know what your client means if he uses a name to describe a style, remember, it may be completely different from your idea of that style.

REMEMBER ✔

How often do you find people using the wrong expression or term to explain what they want? Always make a point of correcting misused terms; it will show that you:

- listen to the client and you are hearing what he says
- have a professional knowledge of your craft and its skills and techniques
- have pride and professional interest in your work.

ACTIVITY: CONSULTATION ROLE-PLAY ⇄

Role-play is an important way of finding out how people can react in different situations; so with your colleagues, take it in turns to act out the consultation process.

One can act as a stylist, another as the client.

Your other colleagues can observe the scenario and take it in turns to go through the consultation process.

Notice how different stylists adopt different approaches.

Make a record of the different situations in your portfolio. You may even want to take this further, by tackling a complaint scenario or dealing with angry clients too.

SAFE PRACTICE FOR CUTTING HAIR AND CUTTING EQUIPMENT

Like all other practical services in hairdressing, it is essential that you work safely when cutting hair. In doing this you must take the time to prepare and protect the client adequately.

This means that you have:

- pre-selected all the equipment that you are going to use; gowns, towels, combs, scissors, razor and clippers etc.
- checked that they are prepared for use i.e. new blades for the razor, freshly laundered towels and gowns, washed cutting collars, cleaned and sterilised combs, brushes, clipper blades and scissors
- got them all at hand and ready for use
- ensured that the client is comfortable and in a position where you can work safely.

Hair by Paul @ Cheynes Hairdressing, Edinburgh

Hair by Michelle @ Ishoka, Aberdeen

Protect the client: gowning

Gowning can take place before or after consultation, it really depends upon your salon's policy. However, gowning must always take place before a dry cut is started or, if the service is a wet cut, then before the client is shampooed.

For dry cutting	Use a clean fresh cutting gown and put it on your client while he is sitting at the styling location. Make sure that the back is fastened and that any open, free edges are closed together, keeping any loose clippings away from the client's clothes. Place a cutting collar around his neck to ensure that any bumps or lumps in his clothing don't present any false, physical baselines for the haircut and that the collar edges fit snugly against the neck, so that there are no irritating hair fragments that will leave the client itching until he gets home.
For wet cutting	Do the same as the gowning above but when your client is at the basin, place a clean fresh towel around his shoulders before positioning him back carefully and comfortably. Make sure that the basin supports the client's neck properly and that the flanged edges of the basin nestle comfortably on to the client's shoulders which are protected from any spills or seepage by a clean fresh towel.

Seat positioning

The positioning of the client at the workstation is just as important as at the backwash. Both areas have implications for personal safety, quality of service and good customer care.

From a working point of view any angle of the head other than perpendicular to the mirror, combined with the angle of the head to the client's seated position, will affect the line, quality and balance of the haircut. Salon workstations have built in footrests and there are good reasons for this. The footrest:

1 is there to improve the comfort for the seated client at any cutting height.

2 helps balance the client and encourages him to sit squarely in front of the mirror

3 tries to discourage the client from sitting cross-legged

4 promotes better posture by making the client sit back properly with his back flat against the back of the chair.

All of the above factors are critical for you and the client in ensuring his comfort throughout, and that you are not hindered in doing your task. For example, if your client sits with crossed legs, it will alter the horizontal plane of his shoulders and this will make your job trying to get even and level baselines more difficult.

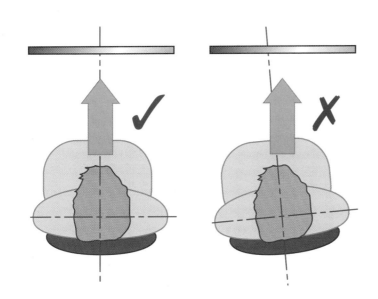

Chair/client angle to mirror

Your work position

The client's cutting position and height from the floor have a direct effect on your posture too. You must be able to work in a position where you do not have to bend 'doubled up' to do your work. Cutting involves a lot of arm and hand movements and you need to be able to get your hands and fingers into positions where you can cut the hair without bad posture.

1 You should adjust the seated client's chair height to a position where you can work upright without having to over-reach on the top sections of his head.

2 You should clear trolleys or equipment out of the way so that you get good all round access (360°) around the client.

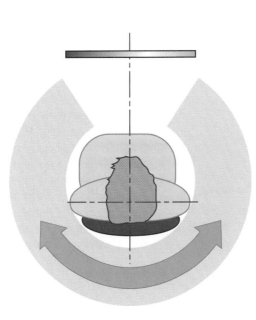

Cutting access

Hair by Kipps @ Cheynes Hairdressing, Edinburgh

GOOD PRACTICE/HEALTH & SAFETY ✚

Health and safety factors to consider whilst cutting	What do I do?
Spillages Take care when moving trolleys around in the salon, or when you place products, drinks etc. on the shelves in front of clients	If you do spill anything onto the floor, mop it up straight away. If the spillage is chemical make sure you know how to handle it. If you don't, tell someone in charge
Slippery floors Other than spillages the hair clippings are also a potential hazard as people could easily slip on them	Sweep clippings up immediately and put them into a lined and covered bin
Tools and equipment Clippers, dryers, tongs and straighteners can also be a hazard to clients and staff alike	Always unplug them and ravel up the trailing leads so that they can be stored safely for next time
Obstructions Trolleys and moveable equipment – Rollerballs, Climazones, hood dryers and steamers – are potential hazards	Equipment should always be removed from the work area as soon as they are finished with and put back into their storage areas

Scissors, clippers, combs and brushes

Good care and regular maintenance of your tools are an essential part of hairdressing and barbering. For more information on looking after these items see Chapter 3 on cutting hair.

Cutting tools and techniques

Cutting tools	Techniques that can be achieved	Explanation of technique
Scissors (straight or flat parallel blades)	**Club cutting** (blunt cutting)	The most basic and most popular way cutting sections of hair straight across, parallel to the index and middle finger
	Freehand cutting	This technique relies upon one hand holding and combing the hair into position, and the other controlling the scissors to make the cut
	Pointing (point cutting)	It is a way of reducing bulk from the ends (2–3 cm) of the hair in order to create softer, more shattered, textured edges. It uses the point ends of the scissors and is more successful on straighter hair than wavy, and does not add any value to curly hairstyles at all

Cutting tools	Techniques that can be achieved	Explanation of technique
	Deep chipping	Reduces fine sections of hair from much deeper, closer to the root (1–3 cm from the scalp). It will add texture but is better for creating and adding lift in medium to thicker hair types
	Brick cutting	A combination of pointing and chipping to gain benefits of both forms of cutting techniques. The cutting action would resemble the position of bricks in a wall
'Japanese style' scissors (Hollow ground edges)	All of the above plus **slicing or slider cutting** (a technique only suitable for extra sharp scissors or a razor)	Slicing is always done with the hair held at an angle slightly downwards; and the scissors or razor is introduced to the hair nearer the root and then in one continuous and angled, downward motion, takes a longer slice out in a scooping movement towards the ends of the held hair
Thinning scissors	Thinning/texturising	Thinning scissors will remove uniform bulk from any point between the root area and ends. However, they have more creative uses when they are used to 'feather' the perimeter edges of hairstyles (which is often more difficult with straight bladed scissors)
Razors	Tapering	Tapering produces a similar effect to that produced by thinning scissors. Razors are often a better choice, as when used correctly they will produce a non-uniform effect
	Slicing/slider cutting	See above under 'Japanese style' scissors
Electric clippers	Clippering with grade attachments	Clipper grades (the attachments that provide uniform cutting lengths) are made in a range of sizes for different purposes, and are numbered accordingly they will provide closely cut uniform layering or if differing grades are used; they can provide graduation on hair that is too short to hold between the fingers
	Clipper over comb	Ideal for clubbing level lengths on short styles

Club cutting Paul Falltrick for Matrix

Freehand cutting Paul Falltrick for Matrix

Pointing Paul Falltrick for Matrix

Deep chipping Paul Falltrick for Matrix

Brick cutting Paul Falltrick for Matrix

Slicing or slider cutting
Paul Falltrick for Matrix

Slicing or slider cutting
Paul Falltrick for Matrix

Thinning/texturising
Paul Falltrick for Matrix

Tapering Paul Falltrick for Matrix

OUTLINE SHAPES

Many short, layered cuts are graduated at the sides and into the nape sometimes by clipper over comb or, when left slightly longer, by scissor over comb techniques. On shorter hairstyles the neck- and hairlines become the main focal perimeters of the hairstyle and in emphasising these, they require careful attention.

Natural necklines lack consistency the growth is often uneven, intermittent or sparse. Therefore the outline shapes for men wearing shorter hair need to be defined. The more natural the nape line, the softer and less severe will be the look. The higher the cuts made into the hairline, the harsher and starker the look becomes.

The nape line can be of a variety of shapes; rounded, tapered, or square. These can be achieved by shaping with the electric clippers, or shaving the outlines. Traditionally shaving was carried out with open-bladed razors; now electric shavers or safety razors can be used. Often outlining is done with the points of the scissors. Softer, graduated lines are to be preferred to blocky, blunt effects. The precise outline is determined by the style required.

The shaping of front hair into a fringe can produce variety of facial frames and the focal point it creates changes the overall effect dramatically. In many men the front hairline recedes and this is often a sign of male pattern baldness. This influences the choice and positioning of perimeter fringe shapes. Always give this some thought before cutting the hair.

In men, the side hairlines, sideburns or sideboards bridge the hairstyle and beard shape. These need to fit, and care must be taken in shaping them. Lining the hair above the ears and along the sides of the nape is usually carried out with the scissor points or with inverted clippers.

Ears

Nature does not guarantee symmetry, and this is particularly true with faces. One side of the face is not exactly the same as the other and this applies to ears too. One may be larger than the other; they may be irregular in shape

---

REMEMBER ✔

Hair growth patterns – the movement and direction of hair is particularly problematic on shorter hair styles. Make sure that you take this into consideration during your consultation with your client.

ACTIVITY ←→

When you compile your men's style book, include notes on style design. Use pictures (rough sketches, detailed drawings or photographs), as appropriate. You may wish to use your book when consulting with clients, so consider the format carefully.

REMEMBER ✔

In order to create clean lines around the ears on shorter hairstyles, you will need to hold the tops of the ears down so you can see what you are doing and ensure that you are working safely.

REMEMBER: CHECKLIST ✔

Men's short hairstyles often benefit from washing again after cutting. This removes all the shorter clippings and makes them more comfortable.

REMEMBER: CHECKLIST ✔

Tapering and thinning encourage the hair to curl at the ends, while club cutting increases density and reduces that tendency.

Feathering and texturising can produce extra lift and bounce.

REMEMBER ✔

If your client has a build up of wax, gel or moulding crème on their hair you must insist that the hair is washed to get it out or off the hair before you attempt the hair cut.

KMS California

Rounded neckline

Tapered neckline

Square neckline

or at different heights. You need to make sure that you have considered this before you start. Unevenness on long hair doesn't matter, but when it's on short hair the imperfections will be made clear.

You need to find out how your client feels about his facial features. Sometimes these natural imperfections are not a concern, they are merely a characteristic of the client's personality. Don't forget to check on whether your client wears glasses or a hearing aid; take all of these factors into your assessment.

Finally you and your client will be able to agree exactly what look is required, and you will then have a basis on which to decide how the work is to be carried out.

Hair type

If your client's hair is very curly, do remember that it will coil back after stretching and cutting. Similarly, wavy hair, when cut too close to the wave crest, can be awkward to style as it tends to spring out from the head. Very fine straight hair will easily show cutting marks or can disclose unwanted lines from clippering if you take too large sections. Make sure that the sections you take are accurately divided and sectioned.

Wet and dry cutting additional notes

1   If the hair is dirty, then for hygienic reasons it must be washed before you cut it. Wet hair is a necessity for blow drying and finishing, but not necessarily a convenient arrangement for a quick trim before work or during lunch.

2   Clean, dry hair should not be cut with a razor because of the discomfort to your client due to the tearing and dragging action of the razor on the hair.

Remember the basic principles of cutting

● Accurate sectioning and **graduation** produces fine layering. This is partly determined by how much hair there is to cut. Longer lengths can be sectioned with the comb and taken between the fingers, while short lengths are best tackled either by clipper over comb or scissor over comb techniques. A section (that cannot be held between the fingers) is lifted with the comb and a guideline is created by cutting straight across. Subsequent lifting with the comb to the guideline length produces the next section to be cut.

● With short layered styles, clippers must be used to tidy the neckline, graduating from the natural line out from the head. How far up the head and how short the cut needs to be is determined by the style and shape agreed with your client. If longer lengths are required higher in the back hair, then the clippers need to graduate away from the head sharply.

- Crosschecking is an essential part of cutting. Its your way of including a quality control. As you progress through the cut, you obviously need to change your stance, holding position and holding angle. These factors can lead you to go wrong. Typically problems might be that the back section doesn't integrate with the sides properly or the top doesn't blend with the sides, or the fringe doesn't fit with the top. Whatever the potential problem the easiest way to compensate for this is to crosscheck to make sure that the cut works well in different planes.

KMS California

Crosschecking

If your holding angle has been in vertical plane like this.

Then you make your cross check in a horizontal plane like this

REMEMBER ✓

Wet hair stretches by anything from a third to half its length. Allow for this if you cut stretched hair, so that when it reverts back to the original length it is not too short.

STEP BY STEP: GENT'S CONTEMPORARY CUTTING

Suitable for any work or social event.

Step 1 Before

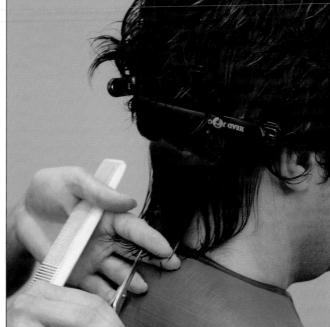

Step 2 Start the haircut by point cutting at the nape. This creates a shattered effect and adds texture to the hairstyle

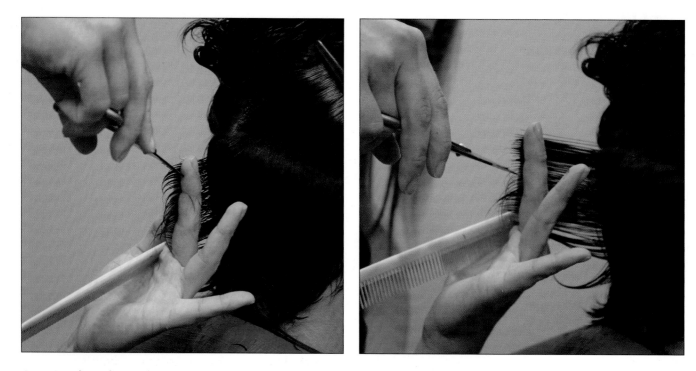

Step 3 When the outline is completed, cut the interior in a similar way, working up the back

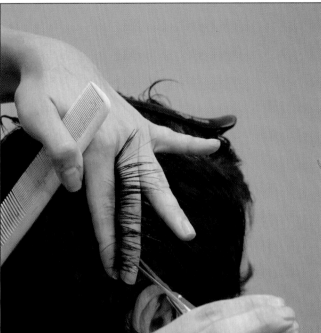

Step 4 Now introduce chipping to remove weight from the upper sections of the hair

Step 5 Continue texturising into the sides

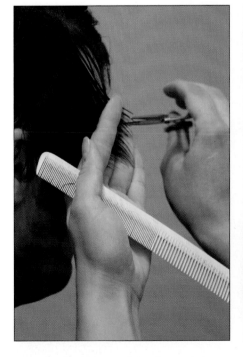

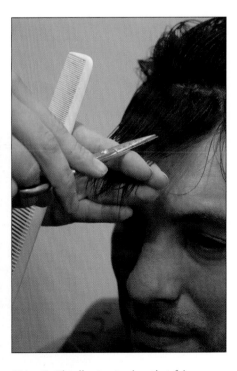

Step 6 Remove weight from the front profile on both sides

Step 7 Cut the top to retain some length, although the weight has been reduced

Step 8 Finally, texturise the fringe area to complete the effect

The finished effect

STEP BY STEP: GENT'S CONTEMPORARY RAZOR CUT

Step 1 Start the razor cut at the back of the head, securing the rest of the way

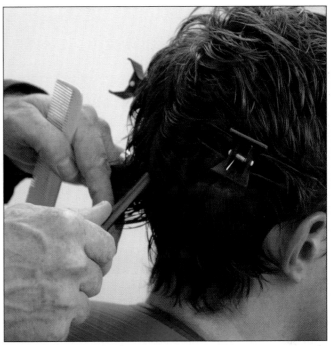

Step 2 Texture is introduced by razoring; this will both remove thickness and create a textured effect at the same time

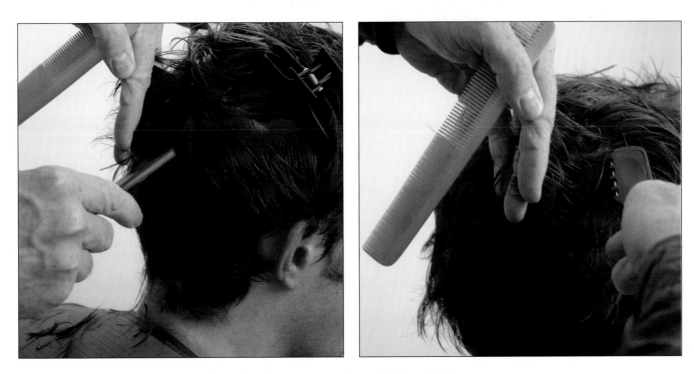

Step 3 Hold the razor at an angle so that it removes only small slices of hair

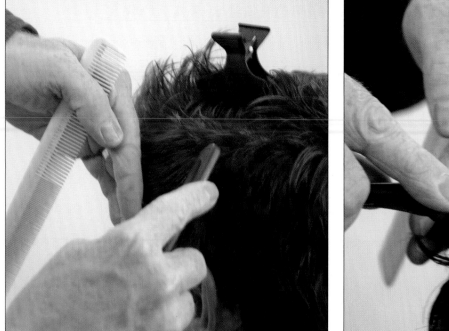

Step 4 Continue this technique around the sides . . .

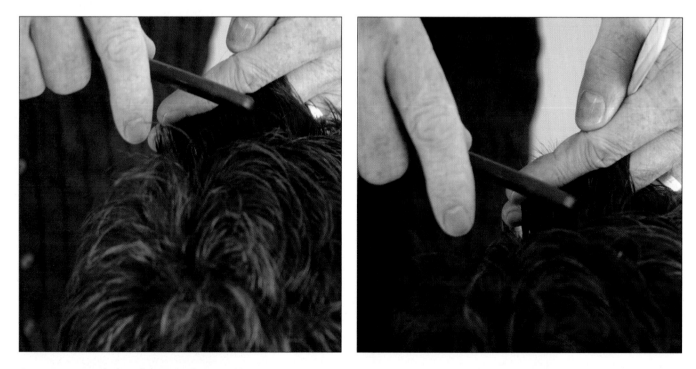

Step 5 . . . and also through the top

The final effect

Metal backed plastic attachment combs/grade to fit Wahl Professional Vibrator Clippers

Clipper attachment size	Length of cut hair
No attachment	Very close to skin, almost like shaving
1 = 3 mm ($\frac{1}{8}$ inch)	Very short, on darker hair it will leaves a shadowing effect over the scalp
2 = 6 mm ($\frac{1}{4}$ inch)	Close cut, will see some skin on finer hair
3 = 9 mm ($\frac{3}{8}$ inch)	Typically cuts to short scissor over comb lengths
4 = 13 mm ($\frac{1}{2}$ inch)	Longer scissor over comb type effects
8 = 25 mm (1 inch)	Not particularly popular for hair cutting, often used as a cutting guide for beard shaping

Note: There are no set standard sizes for clipper attachment combs/grades; you will need to adapt the hair length required by your client in light of the make and model clippers that you have/or your salon provides.

Clipper attachments   BaByliss

CLIPPERS

Clippers are and have been an essential item of equipment for men's styling. They have been invaluable for the popularity of short hairstyles but are equally important for the shaping and trimming of necklines and facial hair shapes.

The electric clippers cut hair by oscillation: the side-to-side movement of a upper metal blade passing over a lower rigid or fixed one. On each pass of the upper blade, the hair caught between the teeth of the lower blade is cut and falls away.

Regular cleaning and lubrication will prolong the blades' useful life and keep the cutting edges sharp. Without this care the constant friction of one blade passing over another will impair their ability to work effectively. In use, electric clippers generate quite a lot of heat and, if they have not been maintained, their ability to cut deteriorates. New blades are relatively expensive, as they can often cost half the price of a new pair of clippers. If the clipper blades are unable to cut keenly you will not be able to shape neck or facial hair accurately.

You should always take care not to drop them, as this can easily cause damage to the cutting teeth or even break! Any missing areas of teeth along the blades will be extremely dangerous and could easily cut the client if they were used. So when they are not in use, hang them up out of the way or replace them back in the charger unit.

Clipper blades should always be checked for alignment before each time they are used. The fixed lower blade is adjustable and this allows for small adjustments to be made backwards, forwards or even side to side.

Clipper and maintenance items
BaByliss

Loosening the small retaining screws underneath allows the blades to be adjusted. This also provides access to the upper blade, for removal, cleaning and essential oiling.

When the blades are replaced the retaining screws must be retightened properly, if this is not done, the vibration will dislodge the alignment and this could easily take a chunk out of your client's hair, or worse, even cut him!

Well-maintained clippers will cut both wet or dry hair with equal ease, although many stylists prefer to remove the hair first, then wash the hair after to remove any small fragments and make any final checks.

Disposal of waste and sharps

Much of the waste produced in a salon or barbers is harmless, and as long as it has been placed in a strong polythene bin liner and tied at the top, it can be disposed of as general commercial rubbish. However, some items should be cleared away promptly or handled and disposed of with care.

For example, simple hair clippings left on the salon floor are a potential hazard, although they would not be considered as hazardous waste. They become a risk to health and safety when they are left on the salon floor. There they could easily be slipped on if they are not swept away immediately.

Salons also use a lot of chemicals and many of these such as shampoos, conditioners and styling products, are not necessarily potential hazards. In fact much of the other chemical waste created by salons ends up being rinsed down the sinks too and unless this form of disposal is legislated against, then these chemicals shouldn't present a disposal hazard either.

But sharp items such as disposable razor blades do need to be handled with extreme care. Used sharps must be disposed of carefully to prevent any injury or cross-infection. They should be put in the sharps box and sealed properly before refuse collection.

SHAPING AND TRIMMING FACIAL HAIR

Beards and moustaches rely upon facial shapes just as much as hairstyles do. Their suitability is directly linked to proportions, distribution and balance. The size of the beard or moustache should be in relation to:

- head shape and size
- size of mouth
- bone structure and facial contours
- width and depth of chin and jaws.

Rechargeable clippers   BaByliss

Neck brush Cricket Co.

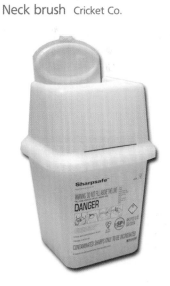

Sharps box SP Services

REMEMBER	✓
Always make sure that the clippers are cleaned before they are used. Any hair caught between the blades will limit their ability to work, and is unhygienic for the client.	

BaByliss

BaByliss

Facial hair shaping   BaByliss

And, as with hairstyles, there are classic and fashionable effects for beards.

There is nothing new in the shaping and lining of men's hair. Much of the current linear effects that can be seen etched over the scalps or around the faces of men today, have their *roots* in ancient tribal cultures. Many of the ancient civilisations used this as a form of body art to distinguish one unique culture from another.

This type of adornment, unlike jewellery or fine textiles, was achievable by many people because then, like now, its effects were short lived and easily changed or modified to create something new.

Aspects to consider

Some men have a heavy growth of facial hair and they find that they need to shave every day. This heavy growth can be obvious for a range of reasons.

1   The growth appears heavy because of the contrast against the skin due to natural colour.

2   The hair seems to grow particularly fast.

3   The density of hair distributed on the face is particularly thick.

4   Combinations of these factors put together.

So, bearing these aspects in mind – initially, the males that are most likely to choose to grow beards and/or moustaches will have ticked two or more of the above. But they are not the only ones who choose to do this, as many others with a poorer growth or definition will grow facial hair for fashion reasons.

Head shape and size

As a general guide the facial hair should not outweigh the proportions of hair on the head. This may be fine for people with plenty of hair, as this would allow them to grow their beards to a longer length. But many men with male pattern baldness also like to grow a beard or moustache too. In these situations, closer cut effects seem to suit the wearer better than thick bushy ones.

Mouth and width of upper lip to base of nose

The size and width of the mouth forms the basis for any moustache. The distance between the upper lip and the base of the nose creates a sort of canvas for the moustache. If the distance between the two areas is quite deep, it will provide more outline shape options for the wearer rather than if it were narrow.

Similarly, the width of the face at the cheeks will also determine the best, suited affect. Someone with a wide face, will be able to wear a fuller moustache, whereas someone with a narrow face could be *swamped* by this much hair.

Thin moustache   Thick narrow moustache   Wide thick moustache

BaByliss

Bone structure and facial contours

You should take particular care for clients who have a well-defined bone structure, i.e. cheekbones, jaws and facial contour. If they have a particularly linear aspect to their facial features then it would be wiser to retain that similar effect with the overall shapes and outlines. (That's unless they wanted to disguise themselves!)

Conversely, the client who has a rounder, fuller face can benefit, aesthetically, from a shape that augments the face with a more structured effect. Although these people can wear beards with fuller effects than those men with narrower facial features.

Width of chin and depth of jaw line

Facial hair growth forms a frame for the physical features of the face and it is the width of the chin and the depth down to the bottom of the jaw that become the focal point of any facial hair shaping. The outlines of the shapes created here are more noticeable than any others. Traditionally, beards were left relatively full; this meant that there was very little upkeep for the wearer, apart from keeping the beard from getting to bushy. Latterly, the fashions for wearing more chiselled effects has meant that not only thickness but an outline shape has to be maintained too.

Facial hair trimming

Every client is different; they all have differing needs, features and requirements. Therefore, they should always be handled with individual care and attention. Your consultation and analysis will need to reflect this and you will have to adapt to their requests. Normally, the process of trimming and shaping beards or moustaches will be the same in any event; that being:

● you remove the bulk from the interior of the feature first, then
● you tidy and shape the outline to finish the effect.

Facial hair is bristle; it is stiffer than hair on the head and this is due to the frequency that it is cut in relation to hairstyles. This makes the hair

BaByliss

REMEMBER ✔

Always look for any contra-indications before you start any facial hair shaping. Look carefully for any suspected infestations or viral or bacterial infections.

coarser and this creates its own problems, as it is more difficult to cut by 'scissor over comb' method. This leads stylists and barbers to choose 'clipper over comb,' as the mechanical advantage makes the job far easier. But as you need to use one hand to steady and position the comb, you can only have one other holding the clippers. This technique is more complex than using clippers held with two hands and clipper grade attachments.

Therefore the clipper over comb technique should work in a way that starts by combing and lifting away the ends, then skimming over these to remove wispier bits first. The benefit of this will allow you to:

- see if any areas show less density in growth than others
- make sure that you don't reduce these areas resulting in skin showing through in a patchy effect.

In doing this though one other negative aspect occurs. Bristles are strong and when they are cut into smaller fragments they can fly all over you and the client. This can be dangerous as bristles can stick in any areas of unprotected skin! Or worse, they can enter into the eye. To prevent this happening to the client, it would be safer get him to close his eyes while you trim away.

When the interior of the facial hair shape has been cut you can then concentrate on defining the shape by creating the outside perimeter line. Hair growth can often be uneven across the head, let alone the face. Even if the client is a regular visitor to the salon you will need to check for balance throughout the shaping, to make sure that the growth doesn't occur thicker and deeper on one side than the other.

Although comfort is always a major concern, for beard trimming it may be easier to start your outlining with the clippers, centrally up the neck, to the point below the chin to start the profile shape. By doing this, you can define the exact position where you stop and you will find that you can then work on either side of the client to create an even symmetrical finish. After this you can complete the shape behind or over the jaw and finally form the cheek area, down to the desired top profile of the beard.

On the other hand most moustaches are trimmed at or above the upper lip by scissors; this is easier to handle and stops the vibration of the clippers, tickling the client and causing them to pull back. The upper perimeter line can then be augmented by the clippers to give a clean, finished profile shape.

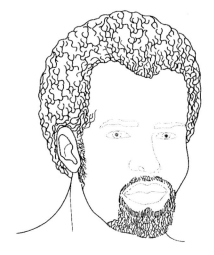

Examples of beard shapes

ADVICE AND HOME MAINTENANCE

No service is complete unless the client leaves in the knowledge that he can
achieve the same result as that done in the salon. If he can't achieve a
similar effect he is unlikely to return. You can make sure that he does. You
have gone through a lot of training and have worked hard to get this far.
The real sign of success is your client rebooking his next visit before he
leaves the salon. You can achieve this easily by making sure you tell him:

- how long the effect will last and when he needs to come back
- which products and equipment you have used and how they might
  benefit the client at home
- what he needs to do in order to achieve the same effect when he next
  washes his hair.

Skin care

Skin care for men is as important as it is for women; the only difference is the products available. Men who shave regularly will already know that blunt razors and shaving creams are a contributing factor for causing minor skin infections or blocking pores and follicles and starting inward growing hairs. When this occurs, a spot forms on the surface of the skin and the bacteria will have started a small infection. This, like ingrowing hairs, is uncomfortable and itchy and can easily be avoided if you give the client the correct advice.

Exfoliation is beneficial to the client; it removes dead skin cells from the epidermis and stimulates blood circulation, which will generally improve the skin's condition. There are many different products now available for men and these can be bought as grains that are mixed with water and applied as a paste or, alternatively, a wide range of ready-to-use products with a variety of bases such as fruit acids or herbal with essential oils.

I understand the reasons for and methods of sterilising barbering equipment ☐	I know and understand the principles of positive communication ☐	I know how to and why the client should be protected from loose hair clippings ☐	I always recognise the critical influencing factors when I carry out consultation ☐
I can utilise a range of barbering techniques and know when to use them in my work ☐	I know how the angle at which hair is held and cut is critical to the finished effect ☐	I always carry out working practices according to the salon's hygiene and safety policy ☐	I know why I should keep the work area hygienic, safe and clean avoiding cross-infection and infestation ☐
I always explain technical terms eliminating ambiguity and false beliefs ☐	I know how to achieve a variety of cutting effects by using scissors, razors and clippers ☐	I understand the necessity of personal, hygiene + presentation ☐	I know how to work with the natural lie and fall of the hair and why I should cross check the cut during and after the service ☐
I know that my posture and the client's seated position is important for accuracy and health and safety aspects ☐	I know the factors that affect the ways in which facial hair can be cut and shaped ☐	I know and respect the client's rights: data protection, equal opportunities, anti-discrimination and consumer legislation ☐	I know when and to whom to refer clients to, in situations where external assistance is required ☐

CHECKER BOARD ✔

Self-test section

Quick quiz: A selection of different types of questions to check your knowledge

Q1 Which 'T' is a cutting effect that is not used in men's styling _ _ _ _ _ _ _?   Fill in the blank

Q2 If a man normally has his hair clippered, you would refer to this as being clipped.   True or False

Q3 Select from the following list, the texturising techniques: Multi-selection

Club cutting	☐	1
Graduation	☐	2
Slice cutting	☐	3
Layering	☐	4
Point cutting	☐	5
Chipping	☐	6

Q4 Scissor over comb produces a similar effect to clipper over comb.   True or False

Q5 Which of the following techniques is not suitable for fine hair?   Multi-choice

Thinning	☐	a
Blunt cutting	☐	b
Clippering	☐	c
Layering	☐	d

Q6 A receding hairline is an indication of male pattern baldness.   True or False

Q7 Which of the following are typical outlines for men's hairline perimeters?   Multi-selection

C shape	☐	1
U shape	☐	2
T shape	☐	3
Rounded	☐	4
Square	☐	5
Oval	☐	6

Q8 A grade 1 attachment will cut hair _____ than a grade 2 attachment.   Fill in the blank

Q9 Which of the following techniques is not done with scissors?   Multi-choice

Layering	☐	a
Moustache shaping	☐	b
Beard trimming	☐	c
Neck shaving	☐	d

Q10 Men's hair grows faster than women's hair.   True or False

chapter 8

HAIR EXTENSIONS

Unit H23 Add hair extentions to create a variety of looks

H23.1   **Maintain effective and safe methods of working when adding hair extensions**

H23.2   **Plan and prepare to add hair extensions**

H23.3   **Add hair extensions**

H23.4   **Cut and finish hair extensions**

H23.5   **Remove hair extensions**

What do I need to learn?

You need to know and understand:

- The range of products and equipment used in hair extension work
- The techniques of safe application and removal of extension products
- The blending, handling and mixing of colours and fibres
- How to shape and finish styles incorporating hair extensions

What does it mean?

This chapter covers the technical aspects of consultation, planning, preparation, application, and removal of real and synthetic hair extensions.

What do I need to do?

- You need to make sure that you conduct a comprehensive client consultation so that a correct plan of action can safely take place
- You need to be able to prepare materials appropriately and according to service requirement
- You need to be able to safely apply, shape, style and remove both real and synthetic hair extensions

Other info

Related topics and other useful information:

- Client consultation
- Health and safety
- Health and safety legislation
- Client consultation

KEY WORDS

Contra-indication   Any factor or state (of the hair or skin) that will affect the planned service for a client

Synthetic fibre extensions   A range of alternative, fibrous materials (nylon, acrylic, kerkalon etc.) used for extending hair

Real hair extensions   Naturally occurring hair types derived from organic proteins found in humans and animals used for extending hair

Dome Cosmetics, exclusive suppliers of Monofibre hair extensions

CHECKERBOARD

At the end of this chapter the checkerboard will help to jog your memory on what you have learned and what still remains to be done. Cross them off with a pencil as you cover each of the topics. (See end of chapter p. 307.)

INTRODUCTION

This chapter covers the increasingly popular and exciting optional unit of hair extensions. At Level 3 this comprises the following five elements:

H23   Add hair extensions to create a variety of looks

    H23.1   Maintain effective and safe methods of working when adding hair extensions

    H23.2   Plan and prepare to add hair extensions

    H23.3   Add hair extensions

    H23.4   Cut and finish hair with extensions

    H23.5   Remove hair extensions

Hair extensions are now accepted as a routine hairdressing service. What was once a specialism for just a few has grown so much in popularity that it is now a core service for the comprehensive salon that endeavours to provide a host of service options for its clientele. This chapter provides the essential knowledge for the application, styling and maintenance of both real hair and synthetic fibre hair extensions.

HAIR EXTENSIONS CONSULTATION

Conducting a thorough **hair extension** consultation before a stylist or client embarks on a hair extension hairstyle is one of the most important parts of the hair extension service as there are many issues to cover and explain. Armed with this knowledge both parties can conclude the suitability of this service for each client. A consultation appointment should be booked for the minimum of 30 minutes.

An extension hair stylist should then thoroughly analyse the client's natural hair. The stylist is checking the client's hair condition as the natural hair should be strong and healthy enough to hold an attachment of extension hair in place for a three-month period of time.

The stylist is looking at the first 2–4 inches of the client's natural hair as this area is where an extension will be secured. The analysis includes establishing whether the client's hair is normal, fine, coarse, dry or greasy. If a client has a greasy hair condition that necessitates shampooing on a daily basis, then a hair extension service is not suitable. The sebum will either break down the bonds securing the extension in place or make the natural hair too slippery and the attached extensions will slip down the hair shaft and fall out.

> **REMEMBER** ✔
>
> The stylist has to satisfy himself that a client's fine hair will be strong enough to hold a secured extension in place for up to three months.

> **REMEMBER** ✔
>
> The porosity of the client's natural hair has to be analysed from root to point, checking whether the client's hair is normal, dry, chemically treated or bleached.

- The first question that should be asked is what hair extension hairstyle is to be achieved – length, thickness, volume, body, colour, decoration or texture?
- It is vital to establish what style is to be achieved before embarking upon this service as this will determine which hair extension application technique can be used and whether the client's natural hair length, condition and porosity is suitable for the required hairstyle.
- A client's natural hair should be a minimum of 3 inches long to apply a textured extension hairstyle.
- A client's natural hair should be a minimum of 4 inches long to apply hair additions that create decorative looks, e.g. crystal strands, highlights or flashes of colour.
- A client's natural hair should be a minimum of 5 inches long to create volume and thickening extension hairstyles.
- A client's natural hair should be a minimum of 6 inches long to create a natural-looking lengthened extension hairstyle. When applying a weave or weft extension to ethnic/African Caribbean hair types, the client's natural hair must be long enough to enable the stylist to create a continuous and firm tight corn braid or scalp plait.

The extension stylist has to establish whether the client's natural hair is strong enough to withstand extension hair attached at the root area and whether the mid-lengths and ends of the client's hair will withstand the friction and wear and tear of added extension hair for up to three months. If the client's natural hair is delicate or broken then it will not be strong enough to wear a hair extension hairstyle.

Contra-indications for hair extensions

The following are the contra-indications (issues that adversely affect a service being performed) of wearing a hair extension hairstyle that have to be taken into account during a hair extension consultation:

- clients suffering hair fall or who are having medication or treatment for hair fall
- clients who suffer from any form of alopecia
- clients with thin or thinning hair
- clients with breakage through the first 2–4 inches of their hair at the root area
- clients taking medication or treatment for cancer
- clients who are pregnant or during the first six months after giving birth
- clients suffering from psoriasis or eczema on the scalp
- clients who suffer skin allergies or excessive skin sensitivities
- clients who have excessively oily hair and scalp.

Extension hair choice

After establishing that the client's hair condition, porosity and length are suitable for the requested hair extension hairstyle, the stylist must then choose what extension hair is suitable for the client.

Real human hair, either Asian or European hair (real hair) or synthetic acrylic fibre hair (fibre) can be applied. The choice of extension hair to be used to create the extension hairstyle depends on the client's budget, suitability of the client's natural hair or the choice of application tools and attachment techniques.

Real hair is sold in different lengths from 10–24 inches. Synthetic fibre is sold in various lengths from 35–60 inches.

Establish the length of extension hair needed for the required style to be achieved. Real hair is supplied in several structures, straight, soft wave, deep wave, curly or spiral curled. Synthetic hair is supplied in several structures, straight, soft wave, deep wave. Pre-made dreadlocks, braids and crimped hair can be purchased. During the consultation establish the correct structure suitable for the client extension hairstyle. After establishing the extension hair that is to be used – either real hair or synthetic hair – the extension hair colour must be selected. Using a colour ring or colour shade chart select the base colour, major tone and minor tone required (see colour selecting, mixing and blending section p. 288).

During the consultation, the stylist should educate the client about the home aftercare products and procedures that need to be followed throughout the duration of the extension hairstyle (see advice and home care maintenance p. 303). There are two different product ranges and procedures to follow, depending on whether the client is wearing real extension hair or fibre extension hair.

Each hair extension hairstyle needs regular maintenance appointments at the salon. These appointments are every two, four or six weeks depending on the hairstyle, application technique and extension hair used to create the style. During the consultation each client should be informed about the maintenance appointments required for their hairstyle.

> **REMEMBER** ✔
>
> The price of the extension hair normally increases as the length of the hair increases.

> **REMEMBER** ✔
>
> Hair extension hairstyles can take from 30 minutes to 10 hours to apply. During the consultation clients should be informed about the length of time needed to apply their hairstyle.

> **REMEMBER** ✔
>
> On average a trained extension stylist should take one minute to apply one extension. A lengthened hairstyle needs approximately 150–250 single extensions. The time of each appointment will be dictated by the amount of extensions to be applied and the hairstyle required.

> **REMEMBER** ✔
>
> All hair extension hairstyles are to be removed from the client's natural hair after three months' wear. All removal should be conducted in the salon by a professional trained person as the removal of extensions, if poorly performed, will break and damage the hair.

GOOD PRACTICE/HEALTH & SAFETY ✚

Each person loses 80–100 hairs per day in natural hairfall. Whilst wearing extensions this hairfall cannot fall out and becomes trapped at the root area above the extension attachment. If the extension strand is left in the hair for more than three months, the trapped hair will begin to matt. When the matting occurs it becomes impossible to remove an extension hairstyle without damaging the natural hair.

REMEMBER: CONSULTATION ✔

- Analysis of the client's natural hair condition, porosity, strength, length and required style.
- Selection of the extension hair type, style, length, colour and structure.
- Advising the client about the correct after-care products, maintenance appointments and removal procedures.
- Quotation of the total price, including application, maintenance appointments, removal service and aftercare products.
- Booking the correct time for each appointment and ensuring you have the trained staff available to complete the service.
- Ordering the correct extension hair structure, length and colour for the client.

Price quote

The price of the extension hairstyle is quoted during the consultation. Finally an appointment date and time are booked. It is vital to record the consultation on a record card as this assists the salon reception when booking the appointment time, maintenance appointments and the removal appointment. Additionally the record card assists in ordering the extension hair required and selecting the correct aftercare products.

HAIR EXTENSION PRODUCTS AND EQUIPMENT

The products and equipment required to perform the hair extension service are many and varied, depending on which application technique you choose to work with. The following is a list of products and equipment needed when working with several extension systems.

Hair extension connector tools

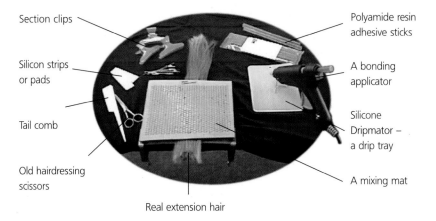

Section clips
Polyamide resin adhesive sticks
Silicon strips or pads
A bonding applicator
Tail comb
Silicone Dripmator – a drip tray
Old hairdressing scissors
A mixing mat
Real extension hair

Application of hot bonded real hair extensions Mane Connection Enhancement System

1 **Professional heat clamp**. Heat clamps are designed to attach and seal fibre extensions. They will not attach real hair extensions. This tool has two heated tips that melt fibre hair at a specific temperature. This tool heats from 140°C to 220°C. When the fibre has melted it creates a hard heat seal bond that holds a fibre extension in place at the root area or seals the end of a fibre extension when the stylist has created a braid or dreadlocks (see below).

2 **Professional bonding applicator**. This tool accommodates polymer resin adhesive sticks that are inserted into the tool. This tool heats to a temperature of 180°C. The resin is then dispensed from a nozzle of the applicator, enabling the stylist to deposit the resin on to real hair or fibre hair and then attach an extension in place by creating a polymer resin bond (see above).

Heat sealer or heat clamp
Hair Direct

3 **Heated pre-bonded extension applicator**. This tool has one or two heated tips that reach a temperature of 100°–140°C. This tool melts pre-bonded extensions, which are extension strands with a wax, protein or keratin polymer resin already applied to the end of a piece of extension hair. Pre-bonded applicators melt the resin on to the natural hair, creating a bond that attaches the extension in place. Pre-bonded applicators will attach pre-bonded fibre hair and pre-bonded real hair.

4 **Needle and thread**. A curved mattress needle can be used to sew weaves or wefts on to ethnic/African Caribbean hair. The weave is sewn on to a scalp plait or corn braid. The thread used is designed to sew weaves on to hair. It is a silk thread that can be purchased in a variety of colours.

Hair Direct

GOOD PRACTICE/HEALTH & SAFETY ✚

- Perform a skin test before using cold fusion liquids as some of these products can cause allergic reactions.
- Read the manufacturer's instructions contained with these tools and products before using them.

Hair extension connector products

1 **Liquid, cold fusion adhesives**. These products vary greatly from gum to rubber or latex-based liquids. They are applied from bottles that have brushes attached to the lids, similar to the application of a nail varnish. Cold fusion liquids will attach fibre hair and real hair in place by painting the liquids on to the real hair and extension hair, then placing the two hair types together. These products are not heated.

2 **Polymer resin adhesive sticks**. This is a resin stick inserted into a bonding applicator that is melted and then dispensed from the applicator. Designed to create extension bonds on individual fibre or real extension hair.

3 **Synthetic acrylic fibre hair**. This extension hair is made from acrylic and designed to be used for extension hairstyles. The fibre is manufactured in a variety of deniers (thickness or fineness). The deniers are designed to look and feel as similar to natural hair as possible with an acrylic. Fibre hair is manufactured in specific colours that once produced cannot be altered. The fibre comes in a variety of structures – straight soft wave, deep wave, braids and dreadlocks and crinkled structures that mimic straightened ethnic/African Caribbean hair textures. Fibre structure can be changed using heat from a hot hairdryer or heated rollers. Fibre hair will be damaged or melted when excessive heat is applied to it.

Fibre can be purchased in lengths from 35–160 inches, and comes in more than 100 colours ranging from natural colours to neon fantasy colours. Fibre is packaged in 100-gram bales or packets or it is sewn into weaves/wefts. The weaves/wefts are sold in 4 oz packets.

4 **Real human extension hair**.

- *Asian hair*
  Asian real hair comes mainly from China or India. This hair is cleansed in a caustic soda solution to remove infestation. It is then

Hair Direct

Hair Direct

REMEMBER ✓

Do not use heated electrical hairdressing tools on fibre hair, e.g. tongs or straighteners, as this will melt the fibre and cause irreparable damage.

REMEMBER ✓

Neon-coloured fibre hair will glow under ultra-violet lights.

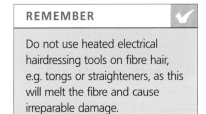
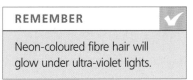

rinsed and dried, bleached and coloured to match manufacturer's colour shade charts. When wavy or curly structures are required, the Asian hair is permed. After the above chemical treatments have been performed the cuticle layer of the Asian hair is damaged and must be treated as chemically damaged hair when applied into natural hair. Asian hair is coarse in structure and very strong, which is why it is used for extensions, wigs, toupées and hair pieces. Asian hair comes in a variety of lengths from 10–24 inches. It is normally packaged in 4oz packets or sewn into weaves/wefts. The weaves/wefts are sold in 4oz packets.

- *European hair*
  This hair comes mainly from former Soviet states such as Russia. It is coloured to match extension colour shade charts. If a wave or curl structure is required it is permed. European hair is finer than Asian hair and should be treated as chemically damaged when applied into natural hair. It comes in a variety of natural colours and fantasy colours plus several lengths from 10 to 24 inches. It comes in 1oz packets and is sometimes sewn into weaves/wefts in 1oz packets. European virgin hair has had no chemical treatment. It comes in only natural colours and structures. This hair comes in lengths from 10 to 24 inches. It is very rare and very expensive. It comes in 1oz packets and is sometimes sewn into weaves/wefts in 1oz packets.

5 **Pre-bonded extensions**. These are strands of fibre or real hair with wax, protein or keratin resin applied at the root end of an extension at the manufacturers. These are applied using a heated pre-bonded tool. These extensions come in a range of structures and a variety of colours and lengths. Pre-bonded extensions come in packets of 5, 10, 20 or 25 strands.

6 **Silicone pads**. These are small pieces of heat-resistant silicone sheet measuring 2 cm by 4 cm. They are used during the application of bonded extensions. The silicone pads protect stylists' fingers from the intense heat of resin bonds and are used to roll resin into bonds at the root area of the natural hair attaching extensions in place.

7 **Scalp protectors or scalp shields**. These are circular plastic discs 4cm in diameter. They are placed at the root area of an extension. They are secured on to the natural hair before attaching an extension in place. Scalp protectors have a small hole in the centre where natural hair feeds through. This strand of natural hair will have the extension attached. Scalp protectors prevent loose strands of natural hair becoming trapped in an extension bond and keep the natural hair sections clean and neat.

8 **Soft bristle brush**. This is a brush that has a padded face and soft bristles which protrude from the padded base. Soft bristle brushes should be used when blending, mixing and brushing extension hair.

9 **Mixing mats**. Mixing mats are designed to hold real hair root point correctly and they assist in the blending of real hair colours. They are used to hold real hair safely whilst applying extensions. They are two square mats, 6 × 6 inches. Each mat has small wire teeth or pins protruding from one side. These teeth are slightly bent. They are bent backwards (away from you) on the bottom mat and forwards (towards you) on the top mat. The two mats are then placed together so that the teeth can interlock, trapping the real hair in between. The real hair is

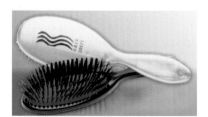

Hair Direct

then drawn out of the mats in small pieces the size of an extension. This hair then has a resin bond dispensed on the root end of the real hair ready to be attached to the natural hair as an extension.

10 **Removal tool**. This tool is similar to a small pair of pliers. It crushes and breaks extension seals and resin bonds during the removal of extension.

11 **Removal solutions**. These are acetone, alcohol, oil or spirit based solutions that are recommended by the extension product companies to break down the resins, acrylics, rubber, latex and wax bonds which attach extensions in place.

12 **Resin drip tray**. A metal dish or silicone mat the size of an ashtray is placed underneath the nozzle of a bonding applicator to catch dripping resin.

13 **Client aftercare products**

- *Clarifying shampoo* – shampoo designed to remove sebum, oil, wax, styling products and pollutants from the extension hair and natural hair. This shampoo must be oil and silicone free.

- *Light conditioner* – a conditioner specifically designed for fibre hair and natural hair. It is manufactured by extension product companies and designed to coat the fibre hair, forming a surface barrier and protecting the fibre from any heat or friction damage caused by brushing and styling. It is a light conditioner for the natural hair.

- *Daily maintenance spray* – a spray mist that is applied to the mid-lengths and ends of the fibre. It untangles the fibre and protects the fibre from heated appliances used for styling. The spray is manufactured by extension product companies. The daily maintenance spray must be used before brushing fibre and before any heated styling tools are used to style the fibre.

- *Reconstructive conditioner* – a conditioner that works within the hair shaft designed to strengthen and rebuild hair. Reconstructive conditioners are manufactured by extension product companies specifically for real hair.

- *pH balanced rinse* – an acid balanced rinse that has the same pH as hair and skin (4.5–5.5). This product is diluted in water: 1 part rinse to 10 parts water. It is used after shampooing and conditioning and applied through the mid-lengths and ends of the hair. The acid balanced rinse is designed to close the cuticle layers of the real hair, therefore reducing tangles and matting that can occur when the real hair is wet. A pH balanced rinse is manufactured by extension product companies specifically for real hair.

14 **Colour ring or swatch**.

15 **Cutting comb, pin tail or tail comb**.

16 **Hairdryer or air styler**.

17 **Flat sectioning clips**.

18 **Hairdressing scissors, pair of thinning scissors, razor and razor blades**.

19 **Selection of round brushes or blow drying brushes**.

20 **Flat stable work surface** on which to place heated bonded tools and a hairdressing trolley.

GOOD PRACTICE/ HEALTH & SAFETY

Stylists should wear protective rubber gloves when using removal solutions to protect their hands. Always use these products in well-ventilated areas. Do not smoke or have naked flames near these products as some of them are highly inflammable.

Hair Direct

REMEMBER

Do not use your best pair of hairdressing scissors as extension hair will blunt scissors.

SELECTING AND BLENDING EXTENSIONS AND COLOURS TOGETHER

Creating extension hairstyles requires learning new skills over and above the stylist's existing hairdressing knowledge. Selecting, mixing and blending fibre hair and real hair is an additional skill that requires a new understanding of selecting colours. When applying a natural-looking extension hairstyle it is important to create extension hair which is the same colour as the natural hair. If there is seen to be even a fractional difference in colour the extension hairstyle will look false. Therefore selecting, mixing and blending colours is a vital new skill for a stylist to learn with this service.

Handling and controlling extension hair can be awkward at first but with practice and proper practical training these new skills can be mastered. Find below the broad principles of selecting, blending and mixing extension hair to match a client's natural hair colour.

> **REMEMBER** ✓
>
> It is very rare to find extension hair that matches natural hair exactly. Often a second or third colour will have to be selected and mixed into the base colour to get an exact match of natural colour. Natural hair is not one colour but made up of several colours. Extension hair must mimic this natural phenomenon.

> **REMEMBER** ✓
>
> - Fibre extension hair is packaged in 100 g bales.
> - Real extension hair is packed in 4 oz bulk or weaves/wefts.

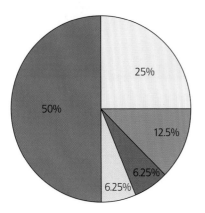

Selecting extension hair colours to match to the natural hair colour

Take a hair extension colour ring or shade chart. Place the colour ring swatches of hair colour against the client's natural hair. Select the extension hair colour that is the nearest colour to the client's own hair colour. This is the *base colour or first colour*. Use the colour ring to identify the second colour that is the nearest colour to the client's own hair colour. This is the major tone or second colour. Use the colour ring and look closely for the *third colour* that matches the hue (glint) of the client's natural hair colour. This is the minor tone or third colour.

You have now selected the base colour, major tone and minor tone of the natural hair. Blending the extension colours in their correct proportions to match natural is a very visual technique. However, find below a formula to follow that will assist you in calculating the correct proportions of colour to mix in order to make an exact colour match.

Colour formula for mixing extensions

Adding 25 per cent (25 g or 1 oz) of a second colour to the base colour will lighten or darken the base colour.

Adding 12.5 per cent (12.5 g) of a second colour to the base colour will give a strong tone.

Adding 6 per cent (6 g) of a second colour to the base colour will give a hue or glint of colour.

Adding equal amounts (25 g + 25 g) of two different extension hair colours together will change the base colour.

Blending extensions together

Remove the selected base colour of extension hair from its packaging, then divide 25 per cent, 12.5 per cent or 6.25 per cent of the second colour and third colour from the packing (using the formula above). After selecting the quantities of extension hair, place the colours together. Ensure the ends of the extension hair are together. When blending fibre hair colours together, hold the fibre hair in the centre. Lightly spray fibre with a daily conditioning spray. Use a soft bristle brush to blend the fibre hair colours together. Start brushing from the ends of the fibre, working towards the centre.

When blending real hair colours together, always place real hair in a mixing mat with the root ends together.

Place the first colour or base colour onto the mixing mat. Then place the second colour and third colour on top of the base colour. Place the lid of the mixing mat on top of the selected colours. As you draw the real hair out of the mixing mat during application the colours will mix together.

REMEMBER: SPECIAL NOTE ✔

Do not place the root of the human hair at the tip end of the human hair. It is vital that real hair is always placed root point correct – this means roots together and tips together. If the real hair is mixed with root and tips laying in opposite directions then the hair will severely matt, locking together as tightly as velcro. When real hair is in this state it is virtually impossible to separate or untangle.

Megamixing

Megamixing is the process of mixing a number of colours together until the fibres are totally blended.

1 Decide on the colour or colours to be achieved.

2 Select the appropriate fibres to be mixed. Carefully remove the required amounts of fibre from the packs.

3 Take the base colour – the greatest amount – and place the fibres in the palm of your hand, holding them near one end. Place any secondary colours – the lesser amounts – on top. Close your fingers and hold the fibres tightly in your hand.

4 With your thumb, fan out the fibre along your first finger.

5 Now, using a bristle brush, brush the fibre downwards. This will tend to mix the fibres.

6 Hold the opposite end of the fibres in your palm and repeat this process. This will mix the fibres further.

7 Continue brushing and changing ends until the colours have been totally blended and the final colour is uniform.

Block colour

Block colour gives a more defined colour or highlighting effect.

1 Take the base colour – the greater amount – and hold it centrally in the palm.

2 Lay the secondary colour – the lesser amount – on top, keeping the ends together.

3 Starting with your hands about 20 cm apart, bring your hands together. Divide the fibre into two equal amounts and separate your hands. Slight mixing will have occurred.

4 Again, place the fibre in one hand on top of the fibre in the other. The fibre is now all in one hand, partially mixed.

5 Bring your hands together and again divide the fibres into two. Further mixing will have occurred, but the fibres will still be in blocks of colour.

6 Repeat until the colour is sufficiently mixed.

7 Gently brush the fibre to remove any tangles, but not so as to mix the fibres further.

ADDING HAIR EXTENSIONS

There are a number of different methods of attaching extensions to natural hair. The method chosen by a stylist or client will vary depending on whether the stylist is attaching fibre or real-hair extensions.

In the following section of this book you will find a number of step-by-step guides to the process of adding hair extensions. They include a step by step guide to attaching synthetic hair, a step by step guide to attaching real hair and pre-bonded method, which can be used to attach either synthetic or real hair.

You will also find in this section descriptions of two extension hairstyles and diagrams that will demonstrate how to undertake the planning and placement of extensions to create hairstyles from synthetic fibre or real hair.

Step by step: Attaching synthetic fibre extensions

1 Prepare the fibre to be used.

2 Prepare the heat-sealing device – clean it, select the temperature setting, and plug into the power point.

3 Prepare other tools and materials: combs, clips, brushes, scissors, styling sprays, and bonding solution (if required).

4 For hair extensions over the whole head, section the head into five areas.

5 Leave a 7 mm section of natural hair out around the hairline.

6 Start at the nape area. Take a band of hair above the hairline; secure the remainder out of the way with clips.

7 Starting in the centre of this band, take a section of hair 5 mm by 5 mm and again clip the remainder out of the way.

8 Divide the section of natural hair into two.

Attaching Monofibre™ extensions Dome (www.domecosmetics.com)

9 Your assistant now takes a similar amount of fibre and lays it centrally in between, forming a cross.

10 Cross the two pieces of natural hair over, right over left, and hold the hair apart while your assistant crosses left over right.

11 Cross again, right over left.

12 Your assistant leaves the top weft of fibre out and subdivides the bottom weft into two, pulling these apart so that you can cross over between them.

13 You both continue crossing until you have 12 mm of braided 'hair'.

14 With your assistant holding the top of the plait between thumb and index finger, wrap the weft of fibre left out (step 12) around the braid.

15 With the heat sealer, close the tips over the bound braid approximately 20 mm down the braid. To close the tips, gently press them on to the fibre for 2 seconds. Lift the top tip and give a half turn, then close your tips again. Remove the heat after 2 seconds.

16 Pinch and roll the heated area between your fingers. Ensure that you have a smooth, round seal.

17 Repeat steps 1–16.

18 When the nape row is complete, continue up the head row by row.

19 After all the extensions have been applied, cut and dress the hair into the desired style.

Step by step: Attaching real hair

Step 1 Take a ½ cm square section of natural hair, approximately the size of a highlight. Place a section clip underneath this section to keep the area clean from travelling hairs

Step 2 Draw a small amount of real extension hair from the mixing mat. Select the same quantity of real extension hair to natural hair, approximately the size of a highlight

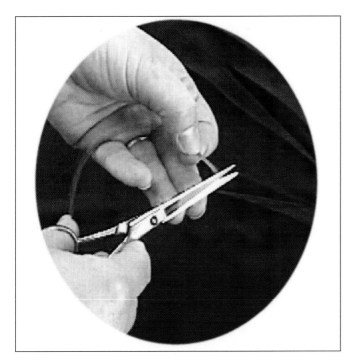

Step 3 Blunt cut and level off the root end of the real hair

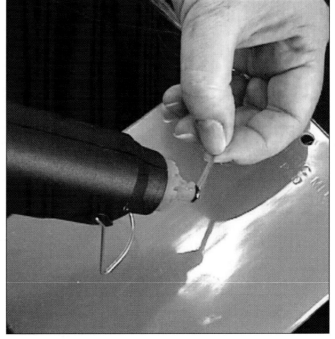

Step 4 Take the real hair to the nozzle end of the applicator and dispatch a small drop of resin onto the root area. Wipe excess resin off onto the nozzle of the applicator

Step 5 Take the real extension hair to the root area of the client's natural hair. Place the resin underneath the natural hair section. Place it 1cm away from the scalp. In one hand hold both pieces of hair together, leaving your other hand free to pick up a silicone pad and place this underneath the resin

Step 6 Gently press and push the resin through the natural hair. This ensures even coverage of resin through real and extension hair

Step 7 Use the silicone pad gently to mould and roll the resin into a bond that is the size of a small bead. The bond must be closed at the bottom

Step 8 The bond takes 30 seconds to cool down, creating a secure attachment holding real extension hair onto the client's hair for up to three months

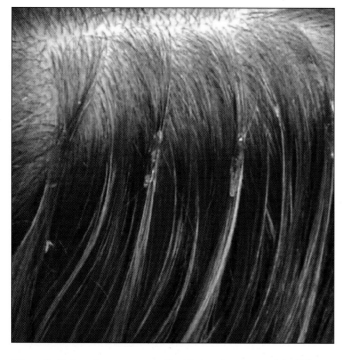

Step 9 Extensions are applied into the natural hair in rows that are 1–2 cm apart. A row of natural hair is left out in between a row of extension hair. Each extension attachment should lie flat to the head

Finished look

Attaching pre-bonded hair extensions

Natural hair extensions bought from the supplier arrive prepared by the manufacturer. They are available in a variety of strand colours, sizes and types – finer strands are for use around hairlines and partings, thicker strands are for use in other areas. You can also choose between straight, wavy and curly hair types. The wefts of hair are 'gummed' together with a polymer resin, so no colour blending is required. They are ready to attach to the hair.

Although the procedures for natural hair extensions may seem similar to those for synthetic hair extensions, in reality the processes are quite different. The polymer resin is activated by a device which emits ultra-high-frequency sound waves: once activated it moulds around the section of hair and creates a strong permanent bond.

Natural hair extensions can be styled by blow drying, tonging or using heated rollers. It is possible to use semi-permanent or temporary colours, but perming and colouring are not recommended.

Step by step: Attaching processed hair extensions

1 Prepare the high-frequency equipment according to the manufacturer's instructions.

2 Prepare the other tools – the plastic strand shield, brushes, combs, clips and whatever else you will need.

3 For hair extensions over the whole head, section the head into five working areas.

4 Leave a 7 mm section of hair out around the hairline.

5 Start at the nape area. Take a band of hair above the hairline. Secure the remainder out of the way with clips.

6 Starting in the centre of this band, take a section of hair 5mm × 5mm and again clip the remainder out of the way.

7 Slide on the plastic protection shield and push it near to the scalp area.

8 Place the polymer-bonded end of the extension into the centre of the hair section, approximately 12 mm from the scalp and forming a V-shaped wedge of hair around the bond. An even distribution of natural hair should surround the bonded end of the hair extension, to prevent uneven tension or breakage.

9 Place the grooved tip of the high-frequency device below the hair section.

10 Wait for the polymer to bubble before rolling it smoothly between your index finger and thumb. (Bubbling will occur in just a few seconds.)

11 Check that the bottom end of the bond is adequately sealed.

12 Continue the process, repeating steps 1–11 until the complete row is finished.

13 Continue working up the back of the head until the section is complete.

14 After all the extensions have been applied, cut and dress the hair into the desired style.

Great Lengths

PLANNING AND PLACEMENT

So many extension hairstyles can be created with this service using fibre hair and real hair. Once the principles of the planning and placement of the extensions are understood, virtually any style can be created.

Sectioning of client's natural hair

This diagram shows the sectioning of the client's natural hair and the areas where extensions can be placed. Hair extensions are applied in the interior of the natural hairstyle. They are placed 1–2 cm behind the hairline, parting and crown area. The natural hair is sectioned into six areas.

- **Area 1** is the nape section. Take a section using a tail comb from the top of the ear to the top of the ear across the occipital bone.
- **Area 2** is at the back section of the head above the occipital bone up to the crown. Take a section using a tail comb from the top of the ear to the top of the ear over the top of the head and through the crown area.

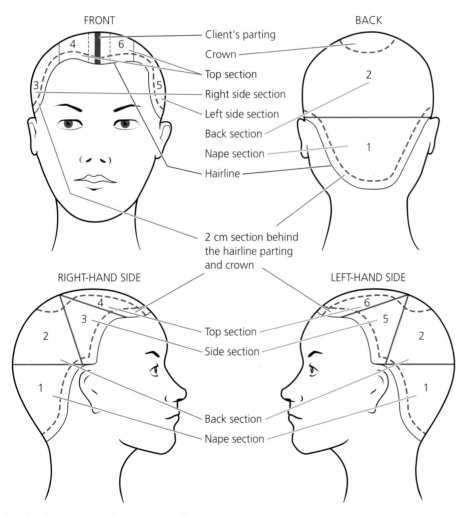

Sectioning of client's natural hair

- **Area 3** is at the right-hand side or temple area section of the head from the ear to the top of the recession area. Take a section from the top of the recession at the front hairline straight back to the crown area.
- **Area 4** is from the top of the right-hand recession to the client's parting and reaching back to the crown area.
- **Area 5** is the left-hand side or temple area section of the head from the ear to the top of the recession area. Take a section from the top of the recession at the front hairline straight back to the crown area.
- **Area 6** is from the top of the left-hand recession to the client's parting and reaching back to the crown area.

Extensions are placed in the interior of a hairstyle always placed 1–2 cm away from the hairline and placed 1–2 cm away from the parting and crown.

Planning and placement of extensions

This diagram shows a natural looking lengthened hairstyle using fibre. The extensions are placed 2 cm behind the hairline. The natural hair is divided into six sections. A heat clamp was used creating individual extensions held in place with fibre heat seals.

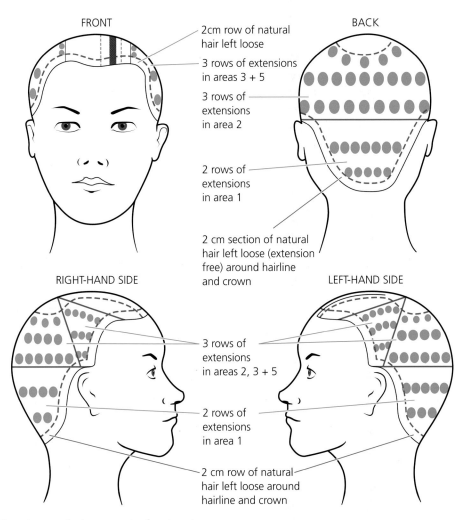

FRONT

2cm row of natural hair left loose

3 rows of extensions in areas 3 + 5

3 rows of extensions in area 2

2 rows of extensions in area 1

2 cm section of natural hair left loose (extension free) around hairline and crown

BACK

RIGHT-HAND SIDE

3 rows of extensions in areas 2, 3 + 5

2 rows of extensions in area 1

2 cm row of natural hair left loose around hairline and crown

LEFT-HAND SIDE

Planning and placement of extensions

Before Hair by Sharon Forrester   After Hair by Sharon Forrester

- **Area 1** has two rows of extensions applied. They are placed 2 cm away from the hairline. A 2 cm section of natural hair was left extension free across the occipital bone. This section is left extension free. If extensions are applied on this bone they will protrude and create a distorted shape.

- **Area 2** has three rows of extensions applied right up to the crown, placing the extensions 2 cm away from the crown area.

- **Areas 3 and 5** have three rows of hair extensions applied. A 1 cm section of hair is left extension free in Areas 3 and 5 above the second row. This area is the widest point of the head and is often left loose as extensions applied here will protrude and distort the hairstyle shape.

There are 100 extensions in this hairstyle. It takes three hours to apply these extensions, using 150g of fibre hair, which is one-and-a-half packets. The colours used are 50g or pale blonde, 50g of cool blonde/ash blonde, 25g of light brown, 25g of gold.

The fibre is blow dried using a warm hairdryer. The style was cut using scissors, point cutting the perimeter lines and slide cutting to create some layers at the front of the hairstyle. This hairstyle has to be completely removed after three months' wear.

Textured extension hairstyle

The diagram shows the planning and placement of extensions to create a large curly, **textured** extension hairstyle. This is a lengthened spiral curled look. The extensions are placed 1 cm behind the hairline. A heat clamp was used creating individual extensions held in place with fibre hot seals. Two stylists were required to work on this hairstyle (see attaching synthetic fibre extensions, p. 290). The natural hair is sectioned into six sections.

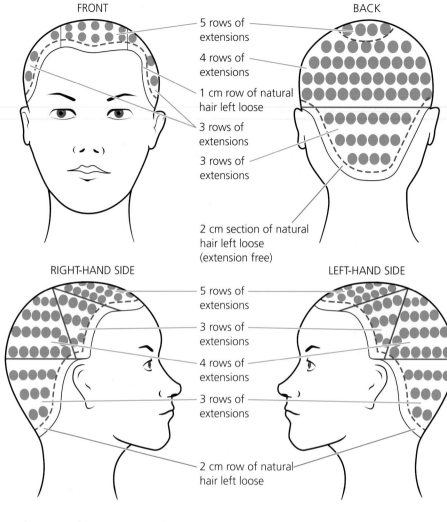

Application of hair extensions

- **Area 1** has three rows of extensions applied. They are placed 1cm away from the hairline. A 2 cm section of natural hair was left extension free across the occipital bone. This section is often left extension free. If extensions are applied on this bone they will protrude and create a distorted shape.

- **Area 2** has four rows of extensions applied right up to the top of the head.

- **Areas 3 and 5** have three rows of hair extensions applied. A 1cm section of hair is left extension free in Areas 3 and 5 above the second row. This area is the widest point of the head and often left loose as extensions applied here will protrude and distort the hairstyle shape.

- **Areas 4 and 6** have five rows of extensions applied covering the whole top area right back and over the crown.

There are 250 extensions in this hairstyle. It takes four hours to apply these extensions, using 300g of fibre hair, which is in three packets. The colours used are 50g of white, 50g of light blonds, 100g of cool/ash blonde, 50g of light brown, 25g of ginger and 25g of gold.

Hair by Jackie McShannon, photograph by Irvin Miskell-Reid

The fibre is curled on heated bendi rollers. The style was cut using scissors. The curled fibre was blunt cut and shaped visually. Gel is used to reduce fizzy ends and hold the curls in shape. The fibre has to be recurled every 4–6 weeks as the curl will drop. This hairstyle has to be completely removed after three months' wear.

CUTTING, STYLING AND FINISHING

Cutting extension hairstyles

The cutting tools that can be used on extension hair are: hairdressing scissors, a razor, clippers and thinning scissors. All extension hairstyle cutting is performed on dry extension hair as creating the styles are visual haircuts using soft blending techniques and not technical blunt haircuts. The principles of hairstyle balance and proportion must be retained in creating a finished result.

Use a razor or clipper on very straight extension hair as these tools will create soft lines in the hairstyle. If scissors are used on straight fibre it will exaggerate blunt or straight lines that are cut into them which can make the finished hairstyle look very false.

Use hairdressing scissors or clippers on wavy or curly extension hair as these tools will give a soft line in the wavy or curly hair without thinning the ends of the extension hair to such a degree that the ends will frizz, matt or tangle.

Most of the cutting techniques recommended for cutting extension hair can be used on natural hair styles. These cutting techniques are designed to create soft, thinned, tapered or graduated blending results that are most suitable for extension hair, ensuring that the finished hairstyle looks natural.

Cutting techniques for extension hairstyles

1 **Blunt or club cutting**. This is a technique that cuts a heavy straight line and is created using scissors.

2 **Soft tapering**. This is a technique that cuts a soft, thin layer into the mid-lengths and end of the extension hair and is created using a razor or thinning scissors.

3 **Spiral tapering**. This is a technique that cuts uneven lengths through the mid-lengths and ends of extension hair and is created using a razor or scissors.

4 **Layering**. This is a technique used to connect short hair into long hair by sliding a razor or scissors down the hair length creating a soft lightly layered profile line.

5 **Surface graduated layering**. This is a technique used to layer extension hair without removing weight and bulk from the extension hair and is created using scissors or clippers.

6 **Skim or surface clippering**. This is a technique used to break up surface layers of extension hair or reduce length and bulk at speed and is created using electric clippers.

7 **Point cutting**. This is a technique used to cut an even perimeter line into extension hair without cutting a false looking straight line, created using scissors or thinning scissors.

Styling hair extensions

The tools that can be used to style fibre extension hair are hairdryers or airstylers set at a medium temperature or heated rollers.

The tools that can be used on real extension hair are hairdryers or airstylers, heated rollers, curling tongs, crimpers, hot brushes and straightening irons. Always avoid using heated hairdressing tools onto the bonds that attach extensions in place as the heat will soften the bonds and the extensions will fall out. Whilst styling extensions incorporate the natural hair in with the styling, do not separate the extensions away from the natural hair as this will make blow drying and setting very difficult. It will also give variable structure to the finished hairstyle, making the result look unnatural.

Wavy or curly fibre extension hair will drop after a couple of weeks. The curl or wave will fall out as the fibre is softened from the heat of the client's body temperature. The fibre will need recurling regularly through out the hairstyle's life span of three months.

Styling products for use on extension hair

- mousse
- gel
- setting lotions
- hairspray
- pomade – use sparingly.

Apply styling products to the mid-lengths and ends of the extension hair. Avoid the root area as some styling products contain oil, wax, silicone and alcohol ingredients which can break the extension bonds down, making the extension fall out, or making the natural hair very slippery so the extensions slip out down the hair shaft.

Dome Cosmetics, exclusive suppliers of Monofibre™ hair extensions

ADVICE AND HOME-CARE MAINTENANCE

There are two types of extension hair that can be used to create hair extension hairstyles:

- synthetic, acrylic fibre extension hair
- real human extension hair that is either Asian or European hair.

The two hair types need different home-care products. The following client advice and home-care procedures should be given to clients who wear extension hairstyles.

Synthetic, acrylic fibre extension hair

The home care products required for fibres are:

1 **A clarifying shampoo**. This is a shampoo designed to remove sebum, oil, wax, styling products and pollutants from the extension hair and natural hair. This shampoo must be oil and silicone free.

2 **A light conditioner**. This is a conditioner specifically designed for fibre hair and natural hair. It is normally manufactured by extension product companies and designed to coat the fibre hair, forming a surface barrier and protecting the fibre from any heat or friction damage caused by brushing and styling the fibre. It is a light conditioner which sits on the surface of the natural hair.

3 **A daily maintenance spray**. This is a spray mist that is applied to the mid-lengths and ends of the fibre. It untangles the fibre and protects it from heated appliances used for styling. The spray is only manufactured by extension product companies. The daily maintenance spray must be used before brushing fibre and before any heated styling tools are used to style the fibre.

4 **A soft bristle brush**. This is a brush that has a padded face and soft bristles that protrude from the padded base. Soft bristle brushes should be used when blending, mixing and brushing hair.

> **REMEMBER** ✔
>
> Oil and silicone based shampoos can break down the bonds attaching extensions in place. They can also build up on the hair shaft, causing the extension to slip out of the hair.

> **REMEMBER** ✔
>
> Conditioner must not be applied to the root area of the client's hair or directly onto the bonds that attach the extensions in place. If applied to the roots or bonds it will leave a deposit on the natural hair causing the extension to fall out and it can break the bonds down.

REMEMBER ✓

Do not use brushes that have balls on the end of the bristle as this can rip and tear fibre and damage the bonds holding the extensions in place.

REMEMBER ✓

All home-care products and tools must be recommended to the client by the stylist who has created the extension hairstyle. Products used on extensions that are not recommended by a stylist could damage or make extensions fall out.

REMEMBER ✓

Do not allow natural oils to build up at the scalp area as this can break down the bonds and then the extensions slip out.

Real extension hair

The home-care products required for real hairs are:

1 **A clarifying shampoo**. This is a shampoo that is designed to remove sebum, oil, wax, styling products and pollutants from the extension hair and natural hair. This shampoo must be oil and silicone free.

2 **A reconstructive conditioner**. This is a conditioner that works within the hair shaft, designed to strengthen and rebuild hair. Reconstructive conditioners are manufactured by extension product companies specifically for real hair. Real hair has gone through several chemical processes before application, making it porous and chemically damaged. Reconstructive conditioners should be used to assist in maintaining the strength, shine and manageability. Light conditioners are not recommended for real hair as these products would build up on the real hair, making it dull, lifeless and heavy.

3 **A pH balanced rinse**. This is an acid balanced rinse that has the same pH as hair and skin (4.5–5.5). This product is diluted in water 1 part pH rinse to 10 parts water. This product is used after shampooing and conditioning and is applied through the mid-lengths and ends of the hair. The acid balanced rinse is designed to close the cuticle layers of the real hair, therefore reducing tangles and matting that can occur when the real hair is wet. This rinse can be used as a daily product contained in a water spray and applied to damp down real hair before restyling. A pH-balanced rinse is manufactured by extension product companies specifically for real hair.

4 **A soft bristle brush**. Soft bristle brushes should be used when brushing real hair extension hairstyles.

Home care advice for extension hairstyles

This is a step-by-step procedure to be followed consecutively by clients when cleansing conditioning and styling extension hairstyles.

1 Shampoo extension hairstyles at least twice a week, reducing natural oil build-up at the root area.

2 Before shampooing brush gently with a soft bristle brush. Begin brushing at the ends of the hair in downward strokes until you reach the root area. Then brush from the root through to the tips.

3 Using your fingers ensure all the extensions are separated at the root area.

4 Whilst shampooing real hair the head should be in an upright position. Standing in the shower is an ideal position. The hair and water should flow in a vertical downward direction. The water temperature should be warm.

5 Use a clarifying shampoo recommended by your stylist specifically for your hair extension hair. Using your fingertips, stroke the shampoo gently into the hair from the roots to the tips. Do not massage or rub the extensions when wet.

6 Apply a recommended conditioner to the mid-lengths and ends of the extension hair. Then rinse thoroughly.

7 After shampooing and conditioning, wrap a towel around the hair and pat gently to remove excess water. Wrap hair in a towel and leave for 20 minutes for the towel to absorb all the moisture from the extensions and natural hair.

8 Separate the extensions at the root area with your fingers before drying.

9 Dry the extensions with a warm hairdryer using a diffuser if required.

10 After drying the root area brush gently from the ends towards the root area in a downward direction. Always hold the hair extensions at the roots whilst brushing to avoid placing unnecessary tension on the bonds and root area.

11 Long or lengthened hair extensions must be plaited and secured with a covered band on the ends before going to bed at night. Do not go to bed with damp or wet extensions as matting and tangling will occur.

> **REMEMBER**
>
> Hair extension hairstyles must be dried immediately at the root and bonded area. Do not brush or comb extensions when they are still wet as the bonds can break down and fall out.

> **REMEMBER**
>
> Do not apply excess tension on the root area by tying tight ponytails.

Styling extension hairstyles dos and don'ts

- Always use brushes and styling products that are recommended by your stylist.

- Use hairdryers and heated rollers on the fibre hair. Heat will straighten or curl fibre extensions. Once heated and cooled down the fibre will retain this texture until more heat is applied to recurl or straighten. Water will not alter the movement of fibre extensions. Do not use curling tongs, curling brushes, straighteners or crimpers directly on the fibre.

- Use hairdryers and heated rollers on real hair. Electric curling tongs, straighteners and hot brushes may be used on Asian or European hair extensions.

- Always avoid the bonded areas with these heated tools as direct heat will soften the bonds.

- Do not backcomb the hair extensions as this will cause irreparable tangling.

- Do not use styling products that contain oils, wax, silicone or excessive alcohol as these will break down the extension bonds.

REMOVING HAIR EXTENSIONS

This is an example of one of the main techniques to remove hair extensions:

> **GOOD PRACTICE/HEALTH & SAFETY** +
>
> Some removal solutions can irritate the skin or dissolve nail polish and nail extensions – ensure you wear rubber gloves.

> **GOOD PRACTICE/HEALTH & SAFETY** +
>
> Some removal solutions are highly flammable so make sure you work in a well-ventilated area. Ensure there is no smoking and no naked flames while the solution is being used.

STEP BY STEP: REMOVING HAIR EXTENSIONS

Step 1 You need a removal tool, removal solution (if applicable), pad of cottonwool and rubber gloves. If you are removing real hair extensions have a mixing mat available

Step 2 Dip your removal tool in the removal solution, placing a pad of cottonwool underneath the resin bond. Then apply a drop of removal solution onto the resin bond that attaches the extension in place

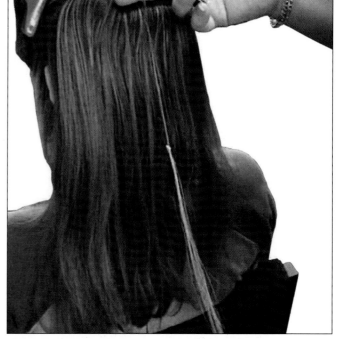

Step 3 Crush the resin bond with the removal tool and the bond will begin to crumble

Step 4 Holding the end of the extension slide the extension out of the natural hair

There may be some residue of resin left in the client's natural hair. Brushing the natural hair, and shampooing and conditioning will easily remove this.

Started it ☐	I know and understand the principles of a hair extension consultation ☐	I always recognise the contra-indications for hair extension services during consultation ☐	I recognise the differences between the different hair extension types ☐
I can identify the range of different tools and products required for this service ☐	I know how to select the correct proportions of extension hair colours to enable me to mix it to match the client's natural hair colour ☐	I recognise and understand that there are several different extension application techniques ☐	I understand the natural hair sectioning to take before applying extensions ☐
I understand the planning of a hair extension lifestyle ☐	I know where to place extensions in a client's hairstyle ☐	I can identify the range of cutting techniques used for cutting extension hairstyles ☐	I know how to advise a client to style a hair extension hairstyle ☐
I know what aftercare products to advise clients to use on their extension hairstyles ☐	I know how to apply and remove one of the hair extension applications ☐	Done it all! ☐	**CHECKER BOARD** ✓

Self-test section

Quick quiz: a selection of different types of questions to check your knowledge

Q1 The condition of the client's hair near the _ _ _ _ _ _ _ is particularly important when considering a hair extension service. — Fill in the blank

Q2 Clients who have to wash their hair on a daily basis are suited to hair extension services. — True or False

Q3 Which of the following are contra-indications for hair extensions? — Multi-selection

Psoriasis	☐	1
Dandruff	☐	2
Alopecia	☐	3
Excessive oily scalp	☐	4
Warts	☐	5
Gel, mousse or hair wax	☐	6

Q4 Synthetic fibre and acrylic fibre are the same thing. — True or False

Q5 A full head of extensions would on average amount to: — Multi-selection

75–125 single extensions	☐	1
150–250 single extensions	☐	2
300–500 single extensions	☐	3
500–1000 single extensions	☐	4

Q6 The cost of real hair extensions is proportional to the length. — True or False

Q7 Which of the following are not connector products for hair extensions? — Multi-selection

Heated pre-bonded extension applicator	☐	1
Cold fusion adhesive	☐	2
Polymer resin adhesive sticks	☐	3
Mixing mats	☐	4
Acetone	☐	5
Spirit based solutions	☐	6

Q8 In making colour choices the main or first colour is known as _ _ _ _ _ _ _ _ colour. — Fill in the blank

Q9 Which of the following is not recommended as home-care maintenance for real hair extensions? — Multi-choice

Washing the hair with a clarifying shampoo	☐	1
Refreshing the hair with a daily maintenance spray	☐	2
Applying conditioners to the root area	☐	3
Drying the hair with a warm drier	☐	4

Q10 You should always hold the hair extensions at the roots whilst brushing. — True or False

chapter 9

AFRICAN CARIBBEAN HAIRSTYLING

Unit H33 Style hair using thermal techniques

H33.1 Maintain effective and safe methods of working when using thermal styling techniques

H33.2 Prepare hair and equipment for thermal styling

H33.3 Straighten hair using pressing techniques

H33.4 Create a variety of fashion looks using thermal styling techniques

Unit H35 Create complex styles using African Caribbean styling techniques

H35.1 Maintain safe and effective methods of working when creating complex styles using twisting and plaiting techniques

H35.2 Create complex styles using twisting and plaiting techniques

Unit H31 Provide corrective relaxing services

H31.1 Maintain effective and safe methods of working when correcting relaxing problems

H31.2 Determine the problem

H31.3 Plan and agree a course of action

H31.4 Correct relaxing problems

What do I need to learn?

You need to know and understand:

- Your salon's policy in respect of clients preparation, services and safety

- How you should work safely and hygienically

- How and why you test the hair before chemical treatments

- The hair science relating to chemical and thermal services

- The products and equipment that relate to chemical, thermal and styling services

- The techniques that are used in corrective relaxing, thermal styling, plaiting and twisting hair

What does it mean?

- Thermal styling and pressing uses a variety of heated equipment to create different temporary hairstyle effects.

- A range of complex styles are created by plaiting and twisting hair.

- A corrective relaxing treatment is a process applied to previously treated hair in order to even out incorrect processing.

What do I need to do?

- You need to take adequate precautions in preparing yourself and the client before any relaxing treatment, thermal styling service or plaited or twisted hairdressing techniques

- You need to be able to use a variety of chemical products and thermal styling equipment.

- You need to conduct a variety of tests on the hair before and during chemical and thermal processing.

- You need to be able to create a variety of finished effects that meet the client's expectations and that involve non-routine, complex procedures.

- You need to be able to reduce movement from hair evenly, by using relaxing treatments.

Other info

There is a lot of information relating to this chapter that can be found elsewhere in this book. Please review the chapters on health and safety, consultation, cutting hair, perming hair and colouring hair, at the relevant points.

KEY WORDS

Thermal styling A range of techniques that use special combs or tongs to style hair by the direct application of heat

Thermal pressing A technique of smoothing curly tight hair with thermal combs

Curl rearranger A term that refers to changing the amount and position of natural curl by a chemical process

Lye and no-lye A term referring to the chemical composition of relaxing treatments, either; based on sodium hydroxide (**lye**) or other compounds (no-lye)

Disulphide bonds The bonds within the hair that are permanently rearranged during perming, relaxing and neutralising

CHECKERBOARD

At the end of this chapter the checkerboard will help to jog your memory on what you have learned and what still remains to be done. Cross them off with a pencil as you cover each of the topics. (See p. 339.)

GOOD PRACTICE/ HEALTH & SAFETY +

Make sure that you always follow the manufacturer's instructions when chemically processing hair

INTRODUCTION

This chapter is a compilation of work that covers a variety of special practices, techniques and skills that address three units from Hairdressing NVQ Level 3.

The first part of the chapter looks at the topic of thermal styling. We would normally consider blow drying, setting and general curling with tongs as part of a styling process that is created by heat. These techniques are covered in the styling hair chapter. Thermal styling for African Caribbean hair differs from this, as the equipment used is quite different to other electrical styling tools.

The second part of the chapter looks at the creative side of plaiting and twisting hair. These complex techniques take a lot of time but the outcomes are well worth it, as they can create a wide variety of durable, decorative and unique effects.

The last part of the chapter covers corrective relaxing procedures. As this is only a part of the wider subject of relaxing hair, we have recovered the whole relaxing process so that no essential information is missed out.

Kathryn Longmuir @ Ishoka, Aberdeen

THERMAL STYLING

Thermal styling is a very effective way of initially straightening tight, curly hair and then curling or shaping the hair to finish off the effect. During the process the heat transferred from the styling tools modifies the structure of the hair, providing a groomed or more controlled effect that will last until the hair is wetted or absorbs moisture in other ways. (For more information on how temporary setting works see the section in Chapter 4 on physical changes during setting.)

SCIENCE BIT! DID YOU KNOW: CURL PATTERNS – WHY IS IT TIGHT AND CURLY? ?

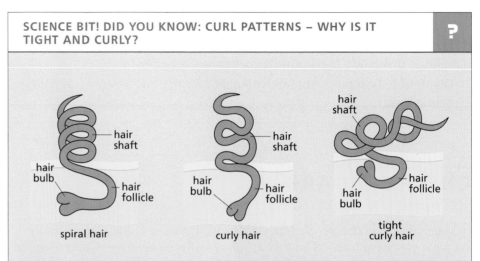

There are a variety of different curl patterns and in some situations they can all be seen on the same head.

The degree of hair curl is determined by the direction that the hair bulb lies within the skin and the route taken by the follicle to the surface of the scalp. Putting this in another way: the degree of contortion of the hair protruding from the scalp results from the angle or position of the hair bulb in relation to the surface of the epidermis.

Where the hair bulb is almost pointing away from the scalp, the follicle finds a route that circles around to the surface and will always produce a tight, curly hair. When the hair bulb is parallel to the scalp surface the follicle doesn't have so far to bend, so the resultant curl shape is not so pronounced.

Preparing the client

As with any service, a thorough consultation must precede any other activity. Thermal styling uses very hot equipment and it is because of this that the major and most obvious concern to the client's health and safety is burns, or the damage caused to their hair by burning or excess heat.

So bearing this in mind, you must assess the client's hair to make sure that the thermal styling technique that you need to use to achieve the desired effect is suitable for her hair and its condition.

Make sure that the client is adequately protected with a clean, fresh gown and a towel around the shoulders. This will stop any spillages of products getting through and onto the client's clothes.

After the consultation has taken place, you will need to shampoo and condition the hair, making sure that all previous styling products or grease are removed from the hair. If the hair isn't clean before you the start, the residue will either smoke as the heat is applied or give off an unpleasant smell.

Look for contra-indications

Hair length	• Is the hair length suitable for the styling technique?
Porosity	• Is the hair condition suitable for thermal styling?
Breakage	• Are there any signs of previous damage that will be made worse by adding heat to the hair? (The repeated application of heat on the hair will weaken or lessen the hair's natural condition and could even cause further damage.)
Infection/infestation	• Are there any signs of infection or infestation?
Cuts or abrasions	• Is the scalp damaged or sore?
Previous processing	• Have there been any previous thermal or chemical processes that will be affect or prevent further services? If the hair has been relaxed and it is growing out, is there enough regrowth to work with?

EQUIPMENT

Thermal pressing combs

Thermal pressing combs come in a range of different shapes and sizes. The styling end of the comb is made from a metal and is heated by electricity (like tongs, crimpers and straighteners) or by gas in a small stove. The profiles of thermal combs vary, depending on how they are to be used in styling the hair.

As the comb is drawn through the divided sections of hair, different parts of the comb are used in different ways to produce the desired effect.

- The shape of the back of the comb can vary in width and roundness; the wider the comb, the gentler the curvature is. This helps to smooth down the hair, straightening the styling effect or be used to add movement to other parts of the hair.
- The teeth of the combs can be set together quite closely or wider apart. This caters for different hair tendencies, textures and densities. As with a normal cutting comb, this difference in the tooth pattern can provide better control on very tightly curled hair. On coarser, smoother hair types a wider-toothed comb would be used.

Non-electrical pressing combs will get hotter than electrically heated ones and this is because of the way in which they are heated. These types of comb are heated up by putting them into a small gas powered oven. As there isn't any heat regulation for this type of equipment, the combs just get hotter and hotter.

Because of this, the temperature must be checked before the combs are introduced to the hair and, if necessary, they should be allowed to cool before they are used. See p. 314 – Hair pressing.)

Electrical pressing combs operate at a cooler temperature than gas heated ones and have the benefit of an inbuilt thermostat. From a safety point of

Pressing combs Golden Supreme

Electric or gas type stove
Golden Supreme

Smoothing irons Golden Supreme

view, this regulates the temperature like that of tongs or straightening irons, ensuring that they are never too hot for most hair types and conditions. The only drawback with these is that sometimes they may not be hot enough to straighten the hair.

REMEMBER: HAIR DENSITY ✔

The amount of hair that the client has will influence the size of the sections you take. The thicker the hair, the finer the sections, otherwise the heat will not be able to penetrate deep enough to straighten all of the hair.

Products for thermal styling	
Pre-thermal styling sprays	These are protecting sprays which are used before styling. They coat the hair, helping it to resist the damaging effects of very hot equipment and to repel moisture making the finished, styled effect last longer.
Post-thermal styling sprays	These are fixative sprays, which coat the hair. They help to make the effect last longer, like hairspray, but resist the absorption of moisture from the atmosphere again making the finished style last longer.

Method for safe use of thermal pressing combs

First of all collect together all the products and equipment that you will need:

- pressing combs
- gas heated stove (if non-electrical equipment is used)
- de-tangling comb
- sectioning comb/tail comb
- sectioning clips
- water (misting) spray
- thermal cooling pad (to help control the temperature of the styling tools)
- tissue paper.

Then, after protecting the client, wash and condition the hair. Then blow dry the hair into shape keeping it smoother and reducing the body or lift. Remove the tangles as you work through the sections with a wide-toothed comb. Then…

Hair pressing

1 Select the pressing comb suitable for the thickness of the hair.
2 Check the temperature of the pressing comb by placing it onto a plain white tissue. If the tissue scorches or burns the comb is too hot.
3 If the pressing comb is too hot, reduce the temperature by placing it on the cooling pad and if it is a stove heated comb, spray it with water, otherwise, if it is electrical, leave it to cool.

4   When the tools are ready to use, divide the hair centrally down the back of the head and secure each side with sectioning clips away, leaving the first section at the nape ready for straightening.

5   Place the heated pressing comb about 1.5 cm away from the scalp on a section of hair held out, but downwards, away from the head at 45° degree angle.

6   Introduce the pressing comb into the hair section, holding it at an angle so that the back of the comb comes into contact with the section of hair.

7   Draw the thermal comb through the mid-lengths of the hair smoothly and slowly towards the ends. (For a better straightening effect on thicker or coarser hair) do this on the underneath of the section first, before doing the upper part of the section.)

8   Repeat the process working up the head on each subsequent section in the same way.

Note. Natural hair may need two passes with the pressing comb whereas previously relaxed hair should only be done once.

Kathryn Longmuir @ Ishoka, Aberdeen

Thermal curling tongs

Like thermal combs, thermal tongs are available in a range of different shapes and sizes. The size and shape that you use and the way that the comb is applied to the hair can create a variety of different effects.

The following curl shapes can be achieved by thermal tonging:

- waves
- spiral curls
- barrel curls
- root curls.

Stove heated curling irons

These are available in sizes ranging from the width of a finger to a large roller. They get much hotter than electrically heated irons and this makes them more appropriate to African Caribbean hair types. Again, like thermal pressing combs, these items of equipment get extra hot, so they could easily burn if misused or handled with undue care and attention. The temperature of the tongs can be roughly gauged when they are removed from the stove by testing on plain white tissue. If they scorch or mark they are too hot and will need to be cooled before they can be used.

Kathryn Longmuir @ Ishoka, Aberdeen

Electrically heated curling irons

Unlike the stove heated irons, electrically heated ones are thermostatically controlled. This added safety feature ensures that the irons can only heat to a preset temperature, preventing them from getting too hot. Gauging the heat required to smooth or curl different hair textures of hair comes with practice and experience, but, as a rule, coarser hair needs more heat than finer heat for a similar result to be achieved. But as with any client this totally depends upon individual needs and thorough client consultation.

> **REMEMBER** ✓
>
> Always keep an even pressure and tension when pressing the hair. This will provide a better, more even result with the finished style.

Thermal tongs Golden Supreme

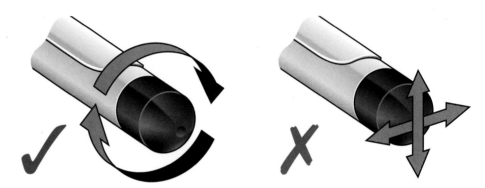

Holding position for curling irons Sandra Gittens

The correct way to hold curling irons/tongs

Both types of thermal tongs (electrically heated or stove) are based on the principle, that the hair moulding part of the tool is kept still while the hair securing part opens and closes. This closing movement traps the hair against the body of the moulding part and the heat is passed through to the hair, fixing it into style, resembling the curvature and shape of the body of the irons. The action of the tongs is similar to that of scissors, i.e. a central fulcrum or pivot provides a hinge system enabling them to be operated.

This can be easily mastered with a little practice.

1 Hold the irons with curl body former at the bottom and the securing clasp at the top.
2 Place the first three fingers on the outside of the handle, and your thumb on the inside and nearest to you.
3 The little finger should straddle the lower handle and be on the opposite side to the first three fingers.
4 Open and close the irons controlling the smoothness of the action with the thumb and little finger.

When you are used to the open and closing technique you can practise turning them without the curl body moving up or down or side to side.

Turn curling tongs without moving up and down or side to side

Method for safe use of thermal (non-electric) curling irons/tongs

First of all collect together all the products and equipment that you will need:

- thermal irons/tongs
- gas heated stove (if non-electrical equipment is used)
- de-tangling comb
- sectioning comb/tail comb
- sectioning clips
- water (misting) spray
- thermal cooling pad (to help control the temperature of the styling tools)
- tissue paper.

1 Select the size of tongs to be used according to the length of the hair and the effect you want to achieve.

2 Check the temperature of the tongs/irons by placing them onto a plain white tissue. If the tissue scorches or burns the styling tool is too hot.

3 Start by sectioning off the hair so that you can work on the underneath section first. If you have previously straightened the hair, be careful not to kink or spoil the effect by poor or cramped sectioning.

4 Place the tongs at the position required, clamp around and turn to achieve the desired degree of movement.

5 If the curl body is required to give lift near the scalp use a comb between the tongs and the scalp to stop them burning the client

Curl types

Caroline Owensby at Salon, Atlanta; photograph: Michele Jorsling @ Bronner Brothers

Barrel curls

These work best on short to medium-length hair creating lift and directional movement. The curling technique can be started at the ends or on coarser more resistant hair, nearer the scalp, turning and tucking hair in as the tongs are rotated. Each section can be lightly sprayed and left to cool in position.

Desmond Murray

Spiral curls

This style is suited to longer hair, allowing the lengths to cascade down vertically in uniform ringlets. The hair should be started underneath first, then take oblong vertical sections about 1.5–2 cms wide and 4 cms in depth. Place the irons close to the root end of the section, then with a small opening and closing movement turn the irons through as many revolutions as it takes for the irons to work through and consume all of the hair down to the points. Each section can be lightly sprayed and left to cool in position.

Desmond Murray

Off-base tonging

Suited to most lengths of hair, this technique adds no lift or body but is used to style and shape the ends.

PLAITING AND TWISTING HAIR

This section covers the aspects of creating complex effects by plaiting and twisting hair. You are required to create these effects for both full- and part-head applications and cover a range of techniques that produce:

● scalp plaits and twists

● loose, hanging, single plaits and other twisted effects

● plaited or twisted effects, dressed as knotted designs.

You may already know many of the terms or names of styles used in this aspect of hairdressing. Some of these may seem confusing or relate to regional or tribal names, but they may have simpler, popular names too. For example:

● cane or **corn rows**

● Senegalese twists

● Zulu plaits.

Preparation for the service

A thorough consultation for this type of work is essential. All of these intricately designed effects take a lot of time and you need to have a clear idea of what you are trying to achieve before you start. Plaiting and twisting involves some additional tension on the hair and this can put the hair roots under excess stress. Our clients want their hair designs to be neat, controlled, easy to manage and to last for as long as possible, and, because of this, it is very easy to cause traction alopecia.

Traction alopecia is caused by the excessive and continuous strain put on the roots by hairstyled effects such as plaits and twists. You need to make sure that you ask the client throughout the service, that the work that you are doing is comfortable and not pulling at different areas across the scalp.

You need to be able to recognise during consultation any previous signs of traction alopecia. The first indications of traction alopecia can be seen around the front hairline, often around the temples. This shows as an area of thinned or missing hair and if the condition is recent, it will be sore and tender.

Before any plaiting, twisting or weaved effects can be applied to the hair, you need to assess the suitability of this form of styling for the client.

Other factors affecting the choice of style

● Style terminology.

● Style suitability.

● Hair condition.

● Hair length.

● Removal of previous plaits or braids.

REMEMBER ✔

Traction alopecia is also a problem caused by hair extensions.

Hair is capable of sustaining its own weight and, within reason, a certain amount of mechanical wear and tear, such as brushing, combing and detangling knots. Any added hair is an extra weight or mass upon the hair roots and where extensions have been bonded to small areas of the hair, thinning or baldness can occur!

Style terminology This is an important aspect for client consultation. It is all too easy for the client to understand a technical term as meaning one thing, while you know it to mean something completely different. This communication aspect may seem rather basic, but it is still the single main reason why clients end up being dissatisfied with a service. It is always better to get down to basics; try to refrain from using clever technical terms. It might be appropriate with your colleagues as you speak the same language. But often the terms used by clients (wrongly) are words picked up from magazines, TV and other people, such as friends or work colleagues. Different people have different ways of saying things; a braid to one person could mean a Senegalese twist to another.

These complex ways of styling hair involve a lot of work and take a lot of time. In most cases they would take considerable time to unravel and redress. So make sure that you both have a clear idea of what you are trying to achieve. Use visual examples; pictures communicate effects that often cannot be put easily into words.

Style suitability This is an important aspect of consultation. Any work that you are planning to do should be really thought through beforehand. If you were to do a full head of scalp plaits, would they suit the client's head and face shape? It may look elaborate when it's finished, it may impress other people, but you do need to ask yourself whether the style enhances the client and is an improvement on what she looked like before. All of this type of work takes a lot of time and when it's done well, the final effects are long lasting too.

For more information on style suitability see Chapter 2 on client consultation.

Hair condition Look for poor elasticity, damage or over-porous hair. Hair that is weakened for any reason is a contra-indication for plaiting or twisting. If the client is definitely intent on having some form of braid or twisted hair design work, think about recommending a course of restructurants or hair strengtheners beforehand.

The hair texture is also a major consideration: if the hair is curly it will need smoothing or straightening first, so that the hair is easier to handle and to improve the final look of the designed work. Remember, hair curl patterns can vary across the scalp; some areas such as the lower nape may be tighter than other areas, so make sure that you check the hair and scalp all over.

Hair length This is an obvious consideration, make sure that the hair is long enough to produce the effect that you want to achieve. If not, would the hair benefit from added hair extensions?

Removal of previous plaiting

If the client needs her previous design work removed you should dissuade her from having a new set of plaits or twists put in straight after. However, if she is used to this as a regular service you may want to re-consider, depending on the consultation.

ACTIVITY

When you see examples of different or complex effects, make sure that you keep them for use in the future.

What will take you five minutes to cut and paste into a style book could save you ages in a consultation situation.

S/NVQ3 H31/33/35 CORRECTIVE RELAXING, THERMAL TECHNIQUES AND COMPLEX STYLES

REMEMBER ✔

Previous plaiting is difficult to remove. Make sure that you are careful and patient when you disentangle the hair.

Extra care should always be taken when removing the old plaits, as the scalp may be quite tender, sensitive or even sore. Over time, products can build up around the scalp and this can bond the hair together making de-tangling quite difficult. In any event you will need patience and care to disentangle or unravel the hair, so that it is not weakened, broken or damaged any further.

When plaits are removed you may also find that the scalp sheds a lot of dead skin cells. This is quite normal and shouldn't be mistaken for something more sinister. Scalp plaits can be washed, but the wearer seldom rubs them too much as they don't want to spoil the effects. This means that dead cells are locked in and cannot be shed in the normal way, over time. This is easily remedied when you cleanse and condition the hair thoroughly.

Shampoo and condition the hair

The hair must be shampooed and conditioned thoroughly before any plaiting or twisting service is done. You need to make sure that any traces of product – moisturisers, gels, sheens and oils are removed from the hair first. Dryness and brittleness tend to prevail as a natural condition for black hair and the clients often tend to remedy this by applying a wide range of products (rightly or wrongly) to their hair. These products can often leave the hair with a sticky or oily residue and this can be made worse if they are applying it to previously plaited hair, as they will not necessarily be removing the build-up each time.

Drying into shape

Both plaiting and twisting techniques tend to make the hair appear shorter, as with braids, much of this length is used laterally as decoration. So you would need to blow dry the hair first, to make the most of its overall length. This is necessary anyway, as the hair needs to be dried and made smoother before any other work can take place. After blow drying, the hair and scalp can be prepared with hair oils or dressings. Any moisturising will be beneficial to the hair, making it more elastic, improving its brittleness and making it more pliable.

Like any other thoroughly executed task, the success starts with the planning and part of the planning is knowing what you want to achieve.

The design that you create is based on a sort of graphical layout. Regardless of whether you are doing scalp plaits, singles or twists, the direction in which they flow is related to their starting position on the scalp and accurate sectioning creates this.

Cane rows

Cane rows are a type of scalp plait that creates linear designs across the head. They will last anything from one week to a couple of months, although with washing and general wear and tear they tend to look a little untidy after a couple of weeks. Cane rows create design patterns across the scalp by working along pre-defined channels of hair. These channels are secured to the scalp by interlocking each of the subdivided stems as the plaiting technique progresses.

Short or even layered hair can be made to look longer still by adding hair extensions to the client's hair during the process. The added hair is plaited into the style along each of the sections that create the braided effect.

Advice should be given on handling and maintaining the hair although regular shampooing can still be carefully achieved. This type of work is ideal for natural hair as it can be worn with or without added hair extensions, even making short hair look long. They are easily removed although the smaller the plait stems and sections the more difficult and fiddly it becomes.

Method of cane rowing

1 Wash, condition and pre-dry the hair smooth.

2 Section out a channel of hair with a tail comb to create the direction of the design required.

3 Use a sectioning clip to secure the other parts of the remainder hair out of the way.

4 For cane rows without added hair, subdivide the client's hair from the front of the channelled section into three stems.

5 Holding the front, first section between the middle and third finger of the left hand and the next, middle section between the index finger and thumb. Now take the last or third section, between the middle and third finger of the right hand.

6 Pass the middle section with the index finger of the left hand under the last outer section of the right hand and pass the new middle section under the outer section of the left hand.

7 Pick up a little hair along the channel with the fourth finger and incorporate into the outer third stem.

8 Repeat 6 and 7 until you have worked along the complete channel of hair until the point where the plait leaves the scalp to hang freely.

9 Then continue plaiting the single, three stems until all of the hair is plaited.

10 Secure the ends with a covered professional band and start steps 2–10 again on the next cane row.

Method for adding hair into the cane row

The method for adding or extending the hair is similar to the above except that narrow strands of hair extensions are taken and added to take the place of the two outer sections i.e. it is looped across the client's natural hair to create the first and third stem of the braid. Then as each time the outer braid introduces part of the client's hair, the added hair is secured down to the scalp.

Added hair or extension hair can be made from a variety of materials that can be natural or synthetic. They come in a variety of different textures, types and colours and can be added to the client's natural hair for a variety of different styling reasons. Subtle, harmonising tones and textures can be added to make the client's own hair appear longer than it is. Conversely, bright fashion colour extensions can be added to create dramatic, contrasting effects.

Single plaits

Single plaits are a popular method of styling for men or women. They can be done on natural or chemically processed hair although the effects are more dramatic on longer hair. This doesn't mean that people with shorter hair can't have plaits; they are obvious candidates for extensions and added hair. Single plaits are quite durable and typically they will last for up to three months, but, like cane rows, their appearance deteriorates after a few weeks. The ends of the plaits can be secured with professional rubber bands; extensions can be sealed with heat.

Method for single plaits

1   Wash, condition and pre-dry the hair straight.

2   Starting at the nape section the hair horizontally and secure the remainder.

3   Subdivide the horizontal section into small 1 cm × 1 cm square sections and separate into three equal stems.

4   Hold the first section between the middle and third finger of the left hand and the next, middle section between the index finger and thumb. Now take the last or third section between the middle and third finger of the right hand.

5   Continue to cross the outer stem on the left, over the centre stem, and then pass the outer stem on the right over what is now the centre stem.

6   Repeat this down to the ends of the hair and secure with a professional band.

7   Move to the next square section of hair and repeat steps 4–6.

8   Continue this by working up the back of the head, then to the lower sides and again up to the top of the head.

If added hair extensions are required, do the above steps 1 and 2 then at:

3   Subdivide the horizontal section into smaller square sections, then attach extension hair to each of the stems of the client's hair and plait as normal as a three-stem plait above.

Twisting techniques

Twists are an alternative to braided styles, they will last for up to a month before they become untidy. Unlike braids they don't involve any interlocking of hair, so they require an application of pomade or gel to bond the hair while the twists are being formed. Twisting is achieved by using the fingers or a comb to twist the hair into strands. This can be done in linear patterns along the scalp such as flat twists, or off the scalp as with single twists or two stem twists.

Method for creating single twists

1   Wash, condition and towel dry the hair.

2   Divide the hair into four quadrants and secure with sectioning clips.

3   Section off a horizontally at the nape and secure the remainder out of the way.

4   Subdivide the horizontal sections into smaller areas of just a few millimetres across. (The smaller the sections the tidier the twist will look.)

5 Apply the gel or pomade throughout the length of the twist stem.
6 Place a tailcomb into the stem close to the root and start to turn in either a continuous clockwise (or anti-clockwise) movement. Work down the section of hair to the end.
7 Continue on to the next twist in the horizontal section and repeat steps 5 and 6.
8 Continue working up the head.
9 When all of the twists have been completed, arrange them neatly in the direction of the desired style and place under a dryer for 20–30 minutes
10 When completely dry, apply product; either a spray fixative or sheen to complete the look

Note: If the client would like to grow her locks over a longer term, you will need to ask her to return on a six-weekly basis so that the regrown hair can be twisted, until locks are formed.

Method for creating two-stem twists

1 Wash, condition and towel dry the hair.
2 Divide the hair into four quadrants and secure with sectioning clips.
3 Section off a horizontally at the nape and secure the remainder out of the way.
4 Subdivide the horizontal sections into smaller areas of just a few millimetres across. (The smaller the sections the tidier the twist will look.)
5 Apply the gel or pomade throughout the length of the twist stem.
6 Subdivide the single stem, making two stems and start twisting left over right (or vice versa) and continue through the length of the hair.
7 Continue on to the next twist in the horizontal section and repeat steps 5 and 6.
8 Continue working up the head.
9 When all of the twists have been completed, arrange them neatly in the direction of the desired style and place under a dryer for 20–30 minutes.
10 When completely dry, apply product – either a spray fixative or sheen – to complete the look.

Senegalese twists

Senegalese twists are a scalp twist effect; they consist of stems of hair that are always twisted in the same direction with hair crossing over and creating a rope effect.

1 Wash, condition and pre-dry the hair smooth.
2 Section out a channel of hair with a tail comb to create the direction and the design required.
3 Using the fingers, start close to the root, take a small section of hair and twist it in a clockwise movement.
4 As you work along the channel pick up and work in more sections of hair to create the scalp twist effect.
5 When the channel of twisted hair is finished, secure until all of the others are finished.
6 The free ends of the twists can be interlocked together, and then after they have been dried under a dryer the effect can be thermally styled to complete the total effect.

REMEMBER

If hair is left in a plaited or twisted style for too long the quality and condition of the hair can deteriorate. Here is a list of the potential effects:

- dryness and brittleness – the hair lacks moisture
- hair damage or breakage
- traction alopecia from constant root tension
- hair knotting or matted and impossible to remove without cutting
- scalp dryness and flaking.

STEP BY STEP: HAIR UP INCORPORATING CONTRASTING ADDED HAIR

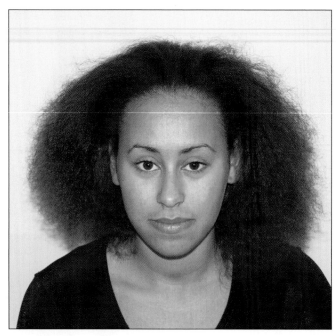

J & E Training

Step 1 Before

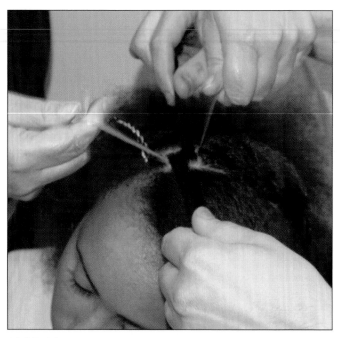

J & E Training

Step 2 After deciding the positioning of the contrasting detail, neatly divide the hair into two stems and place the weft of added hair against the scalp, firmly locking it into position by crossing them over. Then continue down the length of the hair, interweaving the added hair as you go

J & E Training

Step 3 Create several single plaits in the same way. Then, using ceramic straighteners, smoothe out the remainder of the hair to improve the sleekness of the effect

J & E Training

Step 4 Take a triangular section and twist the hair down

J & E Training

Step 5 Fix the twist into place and continue by taking the next section of hair down and twisting it in the same way

J & E Training

Step 6 As you get near the lower nape, take the next section of hair across without twisting it, to cover the previously fixed ends. Secure the free ends underneath

J & E Training

Step 7 Position the single plaits flat against the head and secure into place with the added hair decorating the effect

J & E Training

Finished effect

RELAXING HAIR

Relaxing processes have always, in one form or another, been applied to hair. Throughout hairdressing history, people with very tightly curled hair have wanted less curly or smoother looks. Most early relaxing processes were physically based and temporary in their effects, but today's chemical techniques can produce effective and permanent results.

In this section we will look at the application of permanent methods currently used in salons to reduce or remove curl from the hair.

Relaxing hair is a process of removing curl or wave, wholly or in part. Clients with naturally very curly, kinky or frizzy hair may want it looser, softly curled or straight. After a total-head treatment the regrowth will need redoing from time to time.

Kathryn Longmuir @ Ishoka, Aberdeen

SCIENCE BIT!
DID YOU KNOW: THE PRINCIPLES OF RELAXING HAIR   ?

Two-step process

The chemistry of hair relaxing with a thioglycollate derivative is a two-step process, similar to permanent waving. The disulphide bridges in the cystine links between the keratin chains of the hair are reduced (broken) by the action of the ammonium thioglycollate in the relaxing cream/gel/lotion. This softens the hair, which can then be moulded into its new, relaxed shape. This is followed by neutralisation, which is an oxidation process (reaction with oxygen). Cysteine groups pair up again to form cystines, and the disulphide bridges re-form in new positions. (See the section on neutralising in Chapter 6.)

One-step process

Other chemicals, such as sodium hydroxide, can also be used. Sodium hydroxide breaks down the disulphide bonds in hair by hydrolysis – that is, the breakdown of a substance by, and with, water. Cystine groups are separated into cysteines, and sulphuric acid is also formed; continued processing produces lanthionine – another amino acid – and other single sulphur links. The hair softens and relaxes, tight curls are loosened, and the hair can be moulded into a more relaxed shape. When a sufficient degree of relaxation is reached the hair is shampooed with an acid-balancing neutralising shampoo, which returns to its normal acid state. No oxidising neutraliser is used.

This one-step chemical process differs from the relaxing and perming processes using ammonium thioglycollate reduction followed by oxidation. It is very important to vet closely the subsequent use of other chemical processes on the chemically relaxed hair because the basic nature of the hair has been changed. Fewer disulphide bridges are now present, so further reduction processes should not be used.

Namasté Salon Systems

Splinters Academy for Namasté Salon Systems

REMEMBER: CHECKLIST   ✔

Once the hair has been relaxed with sodium or non-sodium compounds the structure of hair is permanently changed. With just one sulphur bond the hair can never be permed.

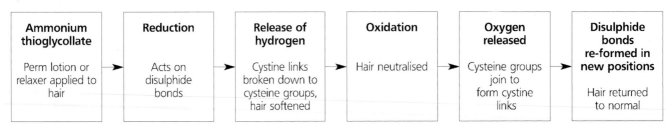

Ammonium thioglycollate	Reduction	Release of hydrogen	Oxidation	Oxygen released	Disulphide bonds re-formed in new positions
Perm lotion or relaxer applied to hair	Acts on disulphide bonds	Cystine links broken down to cysteine groups, hair softened	Hair neutralised	Cysteine groups join to form cystine links	Hair returned to normal

Relaxing hair: Two-stage reduction and oxidation

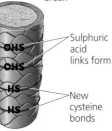

Cystine

Before relaxing

Sodium hydroxide applied – bonds break

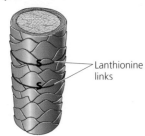

Sulphuric acid links form

New cysteine bonds

Sulphuric acid and cysteine links form

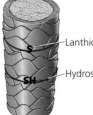

Lanthionine links

Further reaction produces lanthionine, a single sulphur amino acid link

Lanthionine

Hydrosulphide

Other sulphur combines with water to form hydrosulphide

After relaxing, mostly single sulphur lanthionine left, and hydrogen and salt links reformed

Relaxing hair: a continuous one-stage process (simplified)

REMEMBER: CHECKLIST ✔

Relaxing is a chemical process which will affect the hair structure. Some styling options may not be possible once the process has taken place.

GOOD PRACTICE/HEALTH & SAFETY: DISPOSABLE GLOVES (PPE) ✚

Your salon will provide disposable gloves for your personal safety when handling any chemicals in the workplace. It is recommended that these are vinyl and only used once and should then be discarded. If your gloves tear or stretch during use change them immediately as their protection will be impaired.

GOOD PRACTICE/HEALTH & SAFETY ✚

The Control of Substances Hazardous to Health Regulations (COSHH) 2003 lays out the potential risks that hairdressing chemicals can have. You need to make yourself aware of the information provided by the manufacturers about their handling, storage and safe disposal.

Contra-indications for chemical relaxing

The following list indicates situations when relaxing should *not* be undertaken:

- When the hair is particularly porous (possibly over-bleached).
- When the scalp has abrasions or sensitive areas.
- When the hair is weakened, broken or damaged.
- When the hair is in-elastic (does not have any ability to stretch and return to same length).
- When incompatibles have been used on the hair (Just for Men, Grecian 2000, compound henna etc.).
- When the hair has varying levels of porosity throughout the lengths (a result of being poorly coloured or bleached).
- When there is any evidence of physical or chemical changes on the hair or scalp and the client is unable to provide you with a full, satisfactory account of what actions have been taken.

Consultation for relaxing hair

Find out your client's requirements – what is expected from the service – and determine whether this is the best solution bearing in mind the added maintenance, care and attention needed to achieve the desired effect.

- Consider the style and cut, together with your client's age and lifestyle.

- Examine the hair and scalp closely. If there are signs of inflammation, diseases, or cut or grazed skin, do *not* carry out the service. If there is excessive grease or a coating of chemicals or lacquer you will need to remove these by washing with a deep cleansing shampoo first. Previously treated hair will need special consideration.

- Analyse the hair texture.

- Always read manufacturers' instructions carefully.

- If this is a regular client, refer to the records for details of previous work done on her hair.

- Advise your client of the time and costs involved. Summarise what has been decided; to be sure there aren't any misunderstandings.

- Minimise combing and brushing to avoid scratching the scalp before the relaxing treatment.

Analysis/examination

It is important to make sure you choose the most suitable relaxer solution, the correct processing time and the right type of curl for the chosen style. Consider the following factors.

- **Hair texture** – for hair of medium texture, use a lotion of normal strength. Fine hair may require a weaker lotion.

- **Hair porosity** – the porosity of the hair determines how quickly the lotion is absorbed. Porous hair in poor condition is likely to process more quickly than would hair with a resistant, smooth cuticle.

- **Previous treatment history** – look at the previous records to see what has been used and any special information relating to tests or individual needs.

- **Style** – how smooth a result do you want? Is it feasible, taking on board the other factors?

- **Incompatibility** – relaxing lotions and other chemicals used on the hair may react with chemicals that have already been used – for example, in home-use products. Hair that looks dull may have been treated with such chemicals. Ask your client what products are used at home, and test for incompatibility.

M. Balfre

M. Balfre

REMEMBER ✔

Always record the details of the consultation/service for future reference.

REMEMBER ✔

Temperature has a major impact on relaxing. The general salon temperature has an impact upon development; processing times will be *reduced* considerably.

REMEMBER ✔

A protective base should always be applied around the hairline to stop the action of the chemicals upon the skin.

GOOD PRACTICE/HEALTH & SAFETY ➕

PPE vinyl gloves provide you with a guaranteed barrier against the action of harsh chemicals upon the skin.

REMEMBER ✔

Underlying hair is often more resistant to relaxing so start the process at the nape first.

REMEMBER ✔

Read labels and check contents of boxes – before use.

ACTIVITY ↩

Collect a variety of hair clippings from the salon, then process athem with one type of relaxer on each of the different hair samples. Neutralise and record the differences that you find between them.

GOOD PRACTICE/ HEALTH & SAFETY ✚

In all relaxing processes you must take great care to prevent damage to your client's hair or skin. You must ensure that the client is adequately protected throughout.

GOOD PRACTICE/HEALTH & SAFETY ✚

Always read the manufacturer's instructions carefully before applying any chemical products.

GOOD PRACTICE/HEALTH & SAFETY ✚

Take care not to splash your client's face while rinsing. Even diluted chemicals can irritate the skin.

If any chemicals enter the client's eye, flush out immediately with cold running water. Ensure the water drains downwards away from the face. Seek help from a qualified first aider.

M. Balfre

Alamy

Relaxing products (lye and no-lye)

One step relaxing products contain sodium hydroxide, which is also referred to as *lye.* These products are strong alkalis, they are likely to cause irritation and some discomfort. As an alternative to lye-based products, *No-Lye* products are also available. These are just as strong and tend to be caustic potassium or calcium based compounds.

In two-step treatments where ammonium thioglycollate based products are used to modify the hair structure, the neutralisers are similar to those used in perming. The oxidising agents can be either hydrogen peroxide based, or, for kinder, gentler use on African Caribbean hair, derived from sodium bromate (although this does tend to lead to longer processing times).

Test the hair

Always make tests on your client's hair to ensure that it is in a suitable state for relaxing, particularly when dryness, brittleness or breakage of the hair are evident. The following tests are recommended:

- Elasticity check, to determine the hair condition.
- Porosity check, to determine the rate of absorption.
- Testing a strand, to check on process development.
- Incompatibility test, to detect the presence of metallic compounds.
- A test cutting, to check the likely result of the intended process.

Hair tests relevant for relaxing hair

Elasticity test: This tests the tensile strength of the hair. Hair in good condition has the ability to stretch and return to its original length, whereas hair in poor or damaged condition will stretch and not return to original length. This lack of elasticity will make the hair difficult to manage and maintain. To get a clear indication for this ask the client how long her style lasts after it has been done. When the styling drops or can't be sustained in the hair, the hair has probably lost this vital attribute. Take a single **hair strand** and hold firmly at either end, then stretch it between your fingers. If it breaks easily the cortex may be damaged and relaxing could be harmful.

Porosity test: The purpose of this test is to find out how well protected the inner cortex is by the cuticle layers. Porous hair has a damaged cuticle layer and readily absorbs moisture; this presents a problem when drying, as this hair takes longer to dry and often lacks the ability to hold a style well. You can do this best by taking a small section of hair and sliding from the root, through to the points, between your fingertips. From this you can feel how rough or smooth it is. Rougher hair (as opposed to coarse hair) is likely to be more porous, and will therefore process more quickly.

Incompatibility test: Hairdressing products are based upon organic chemistry formulations. These are incompatible with inorganic chemistry compositions and will cause damage to the client's hair. This test will identify whether metallic salts are present within the hair, which is a clear contra-indication to the service being carried out. Protect your hands by wearing gloves. Place a small cutting of hair in a mixture of hydrogen peroxide and ammonium hydroxide. Watch for signs of bubbling, heating or discolouration: these indicate that the hair already contains incompatible chemicals. The hair should not be processed, nor should it be coloured or bleached. A relaxing treatment might discolour or break the hair, and might burn the skin.

Test cutting: If you are unsure about how your client's hair will react under processing you could always take a test cutting. Cut a small section of hair from the lower back of the head and apply the chemicals. Check the development and record the details.

GOOD PRACTICE/ HEALTH & SAFETY

Always remember to wear protective gloves when handling chemicals

Pre-relaxer treatments

If the hair is dry or porous you should apply a pre-relaxer before you apply the relaxing cream. This will put a protective coating on the hair that prevents the relaxer from:

- taking unevenly at different points along the hair
- taking too quickly; it controls the processing time of the relaxer.

Basing creams or gels

The skin can be protected from the action of lye-based relaxers too. **Basing** products tend to have a petroleum formulation; they are easy to apply and will spread evenly on the skin providing a barrier against harsh chemicals. Be careful not to overlap onto the hair otherwise this could affect the processing of the relaxer.

Factors affecting product choice and application

Product knowledge is essential. Whatever you decide to use, you must be familiar with it. You must study the manufacturer's instructions for use before your client arrives or before you attempt to apply the product. (This also applies to your tools and equipment.) You should only decide on the most suitable strength of chemical product after:

- the consultation with your client, and making sure you know exactly what your client requires
- checking to determine whether your client is taking any prescribed medication, and if she has any allergies
- examining the hair and scalp condition
- the results of the relevant tests are known
- checking with a salon senior or specialist (proceed only after agreement is reached)
- ensuring products are in stock, to avoid disappointing your client
- deciding whether the hair is fine, medium, coarse, thick, thin, porous or resistant (coarse hair requires the longest processing time, and fine hair the shortest; grease or heavy chemical build-up on hair can block the relaxer product; hair that has been previously bleached, permed, straightened or relaxed can be very receptive and may process very fast)
- noting any other helpful information.

You can begin the relaxation process once you have considered the following factors:

- Whether the hair is in a suitable condition for processing (for instance, a rough cuticle could indicate uneven porosity, which would be likely to affect the result).
- The salon temperature: a hot salon could speed processing, a cold one could delay it.

- The hairstyle required after the hair has been relaxed, your client's head and face shape, and her hair growth patterns. If the client's hair is to change from very curly to very straight, she may need guidance from you about managing it afterwards and about home maintenance products.

Relaxing methods and procedures

The permanent methods are chemical ones. These involve the use of strong chemicals, which must be used with care. The types of chemical relaxers currently available include:

- creams or gels based on sodium hydroxide, called lye (caustic soda)
- creams or gels based on potassium/calcium hydroxide, called non-lye products, made for tightly curled hair and a wide range of hair textures creams based on ammonium and sodium bisulphites.

Important differences between these products are:

- the strengths – how much of the active chemical is present:
- the pH – the degree of alkalinity: the higher the alkalinity the stronger the product
- the contact time (length of processing) required.

In general, do not apply any heat that that would accelerate the chemical process, causing damage to the hair and irritation to the skin. Some newer products, however, specifically recommend a certain amount of applied heat.

Alamy

> **REMEMBER** ✓
>
> New products are being launched all the time. Always check with the manufacturer's instructions, particularly for processing times suitable for the different hair textures and types.

> **REMEMBER** ✓
>
> Most of the methods of curling hair can be used to relax hair. Relaxing is the term given to describe curl and wave reduction. As with curling, relaxing hair may be temporary or permanent.

> **REMEMBER** ✓
>
> Protective gels or creams should always be applied to the skin and around the hairline and ears before the relaxing process commences. Relaxing products tend to swell whilst the hair is processing and if the application has been made quite close to the skin it will prevent these chemicals making contact with it and causing any irritation or discomfort.

STEP BY STEP: REGROWTH RELAXER

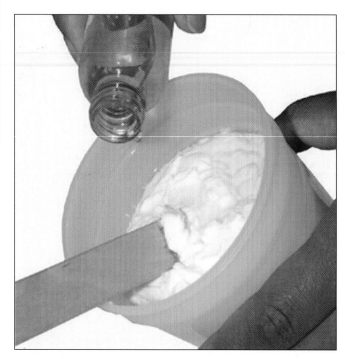

Namasté Salon System

Namasté Salon System

Step 1 Please read the instructions carefully before beginning your application. If using a Calcium Hydroxide No Lye Relaxer, mix the crème and liquid activator for a minimum of 1 minute. If using a Sodium Hydroxide Relaxer, use straight from the tub

Step 2 Section the hair and apply Scalp Protector to the scalp, hairline, top of ears and nape of neck. Apply Cuticle Protector to hair shaft of previously relaxed hair

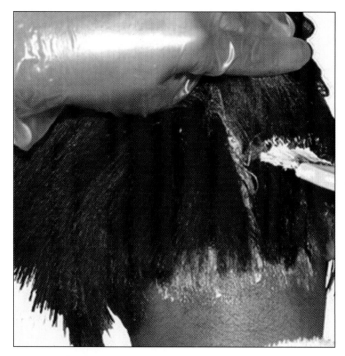

Namasté Salon System

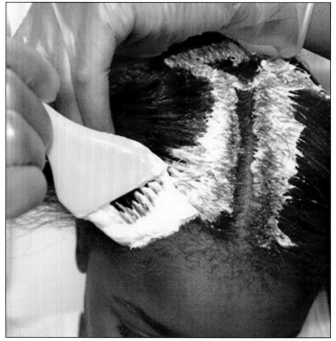

Namasté Salon System

Step 3 Apply relaxer to most resistant area of hair first, and then work through to all sections ensuring all regrowth areas are covered while smoothing the hair. Avoid putting relaxer over previously relaxed hair

Namasté Salon System

Namasté Salon System

Step 4 Complete the smoothing process for designated processing time according to Timing Chart: e.g. Fine hair 10-12 minutes; Normal hair 12-15 minutes; Coarse hair 12-18 minutes; Resistant 15-20 minutes. After the desired straightness is achieved, thoroughly rinse the relaxer from the hair using warm water, starting where you first applied the relaxer and then through to all areas, particularly around the ears, nape and hairline. This step is important as it prevents damage to and over-processing of the hair

Step 5 Apply Neutralising shampoo 2-3 times, leaving last application on the hair for 2-3 minutes. Rinse, lathering thoroughly each time, ensuring all traces of relaxer are removed. Towel-blot the hair and apply Conditioner as per instructions

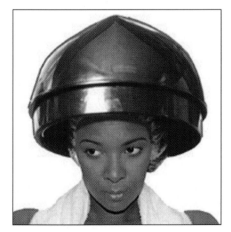

Namasté Salon System

Namasté Salon System

Namasté Salon System

Step 6 Once conditioned, rinse, towel-blot and apply either a pea sized amount of Thermal Lotion if Blow-Drying and Thermal Curling the Hair, or Styling Lotion if using other styling method. Style as desired

A relaxing method for African Caribbean type hair

The following is an outline of a suggested application method for a virgin head, using sodium or non-sodium based relaxer, but this should not be used in place of the manufacturer's instructions.

1 Apply a pre-relaxer treatment if the hair condition is dry or porous.

2 Apply a protective barrier cream to protect the skin.

3 Divide the hair into four: centrally from forehead to nape and laterally from ear to ear

4 Apply the relaxer cream to the mid-lengths and ends first. Start from the nape area or the most resistant part of the head towards the crown; leave the front hairline until last as this is usually the weakest area. Use small subsections of hair, smoothing and combing the hair as you work.

5 Once you have applied the relaxer to the mid-lengths and ends go back and apply to the roots.

6 Comb the hair from roots to ends and smoothe the hair with your fingers until the required degree of straightness has been achieved. To check if the hair has been relaxed enough, take a strand of hair and remove the product with cotton wool. If the strand of hair stays straight and does not revert to its original curl then you can remove the relaxer.

7 Rinse the hair thoroughly, using tepid water as the scalp will be sensitive. The force of the water and gentle finger movements will remove the product from the hair. Check to make sure all traces of the relaxer have been removed from the hair and scalp.

8 Apply a neutralising shampoo to the hair. Shampoo gently and rinse thoroughly. Re-apply the neutralising shampoo at least once more to ensure that all the relaxer has been removed.

9 Post-processing treatments can be used after a relaxer. These are acidic and will help to bring the hair back to its natural pH level of 4.5–5.5 close the cuticle and to a stable condition.

10 Gently towel dry the hair and comb through. You can now apply styling products and style the hair.

Dealing with regrowth

As hair grows approximately 12 mm ($\frac{1}{2}$ inch) each month, within a few weeks after relaxing very curly hair will begin to show itself above the scalp. This will need to be processed if the client wishes to continue with relaxed hair. When applying a process to the regrowth – called retouching – you must take care to avoid the scalp; make sure it is based well where required.

Applying a regrowth application

1 Apply a pre-relaxer treatment to the hair that has already been relaxed.

2 Apply a protective barrier to protect the skin.

3 Always use the same product type that has been used previously, either sodium or non-sodium based, as the two different types are not compatible.

4 Section the hair in the same way as a virgin application. When applying the relaxer it is best to work across two sections to keep the application even instead of applying the relaxer and completing one section first before moving onto another

5 Use small subsections and starting in the nape area or most resistant area first apply the relaxer to the roots of the hair about 6 mm away from the scalp using the back of a comb. This will allow the relaxer to expand and creep up the hair to the scalp without it actually touching the scalp. Do not apply to the hair that has previously been relaxed as it will damage the hair or cause the hair to break.

6 Once you have applied the relaxer to the whole head go back to the beginning and start combing the product through the hair and smoothing it with your fingers. Make sure that you do not comb beyond the regrowth area and that you do not scrape the scalp. It is kinder on the scalp to smooth with your fingers.

7 Take a strand test to make sure the hair has been relaxed enough before rinsing and neutralising. This is done in the same way as in the virgin application described above.

Regrowth treatments

It is necessary to carry out the service again once the new root hair has grown. It is better to keep to the same straightening products previously applied to the lengths of the hair for matched results. Always make a note of the materials and the processes applied.

Applying a corrective relaxer treatment

A corrective relaxer treatment is carried out when a previous relaxing treatment hasn't processed evenly or adequately. A relaxer can be re-applied, as a corrective measure, but only where there are no contra-indications to this.

If the ends, mid-lengths or root area of the hair are still curly, it is probably due to underdevelopment.

As caution is always the main concern, it is quite easy to remove the product before it has had long enough on the hair to do its job. This can be readdressed in the following way.

Method for corrective relaxing treatment

1 Check the elasticity, porosity and general condition of the hair.
2 Apply a protective barrier gel around the hairline to protect the skin.
3 Then apply pre-relaxer protective treatment to all areas of the hair.
4 Apply the relaxer cream only to the areas requiring correction (be careful not to overlap on to other areas).
5 Process until the desired result is achieved.
6 Shampoo the hair with the correct neutralising shampoo and apply a post-relaxer conditioner.

REMEMBER ✔
If relaxers are allowed too much contact with the hair they will have a depilatory action! They may remove the hair completely, so use a timer to carefully monitor the chemical processes.

REMEMBER ✔
Never mix different chemical relaxers when retouching.

REMEMBER ✔
Avoid overlapping previously chemically treated areas. This could cause breakage or permanent damage.

Namasté conditioning sensitive scalp no-lye relaxer
Namasté Salon Systems

Aftercare advice

You want the client to continue looking after their hair when they get home. This can only happen if you provide the right advice. The right advice is the starting point for a complete care regimen which you need to recommend as the best way for them to maintain this look themselves at home.

Using the right products is a major part of this care routine; you need to be able to suggest a variety of options for products that will maintain the look between salon visits.

Relaxing faults and what to do about them

Problems	Possible cause	What to do
Hair breakage before relaxing	Poor dressing or results of previous relaxing methods; poor condition	Do not relax hair; wait until it is improved; refer to your senior/trainer
Hair breakage after relaxing	Over-processing or relaxers too strong or poor neutralising	Condition and restructure if possible
Bald areas	Traction baldness due to poor relaxing or over-processing	Do not relax hair. Avoid tension and treat gently
Sore scalp	Harsh treatment (e.g. combing) or sign of disease, or relaxers too strong or left too long	Do not relax hair. Wait till improved. Refer to your senior/trainer
Discolouration or pink colour	Metals present or wrong relaxer used or over-processing	Test and check. Recondition. Colour rinse. Avoid using further chemicals
Hair too curly (see corrective relaxer treatment)	Not relaxed enough or wrong method chosen or not neutralising sufficiently	Condition the hair. Choose the correct method and relax again after two weeks if the condition permits

Relaxing products Namasté Salon Systems

I know and understand the principles of relaxing and neutralising hair ☐	I know and understand the health and safety aspects that must be considered before carrying out any chemical process ☐	I know why, when and how I conduct tests on the hair for relaxing ☐	I always recognise contra-indications when I analyse the client's hair ☐
I am familiar with a range of thermal styling equipment and the techniques used to create a variety of effects ☐	I know the basic science of how thermal styling, relaxing and neutralising chemicals affect the hair during processing ☐	I always carry out working practices according to the salon's policy ☐	I know the effects of lye and no-lye products upon the hair during relaxing ☐
I know and understand the ways of plaiting and twisting hair ☐	I know when to use complex styling techniques and the methods for producing different effects ☐	I understand the necessity of personal hygiene and presentation ☐	I know how and when to provide advice for home maintenance for a range of styling and relaxing services ☐
I know and respect the clients rights: data protection, equal opportunities, anti-discrimination and consumer legislation ☐	I know the reasons for always following manufacturers' instructions ☐	I know how to advise, promote and sell other services and products to clients ☐	I know why pre- and post-relaxer treatments are used upon the hair as protective measures ☐

CHECKER BOARD ✓

Self-test section

Quick quiz: a selection of different types of questions to check your knowledge

Q1 Corn rows are the same as _ _ _ _ _ rows.   Fill in the blank

Q2 A client with short hair is easier to plait than a client with longer hair.   True or False

Q3 Which of the following are types of single scalp plaits?   Multi-selection

French plait	☐	1
Corn row	☐	2
Senegalese twists	☐	3
Dreadlocks	☐	4
Zulu knots	☐	5
Cane row	☐	6

Q4 Scissor over comb produces a similar effect to clipper over comb.   True or False

Q5 Which of these tends to stay tidier as scalp plaits?   Multi-selection

Natural, curly hair	☐	1
Natural, frizzy hair	☐	2
Synthetic fibre hair	☐	3
Synthetic sewn wefts	☐	4

Q6 Over-plaiting is the same as under-plaiting.   True or False

Q7 Which of the following are not plaiting or braiding techniques?   Multi-selection

French plait	☐	1
Corn row	☐	2
Senegalese twists	☐	3
Dreadlocks	☐	4
Zulu knots	☐	5
Cane row	☐	6

Q8 What 'E' is hair added into a plait to make it longer?   Fill in the blank

Q9 When applying twists to hair, which of the following can be used to create the twists?   Multi-choice

A razor	☐	1
Perm curlers	☐	2
A comb	☐	3
A brush	☐	4

Q10 Senegalese root twists are a scalp plaiting technique.   True or False

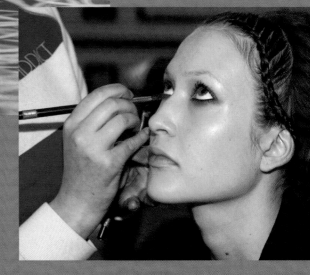

TONI & GUY AT THE 50TH ANNIVERSARY
L'ORÉAL COLOUR TROPHY, LONDON, MAY 2006.

ANTOINETTE BEENDERS AT THE 50TH ANNIVERSARY
L'ORÉAL COLOUR TROPHY, LONDON, MAY 2005.

TREVOR SORBIE AT THE 50TH ANNIVERSARY
L'ORÉAL COLOUR TROPHY, LONDON, MAY 2005.

CHARLES WORTHINGTON AT THE 50TH ANNIVERSARY
L'ORÉAL COLOUR TROPHY, LONDON, MAY 2005.

M. BALFRE AT THE ALTERNATIVE HAIR SHOW, 2005.

part three

chapter 10

FINANCE AND RESOURCES

Unit G10 Support customer service improvements

G10.1   Use feedback to identify potential customer service improvements

G10.2   Contribute to the implementation of changes in customer service

G10.3   Assist with the evaluation of changes in customer service

Unit G11 Contribute to financial effectiveness of the business

G11.1   Contribute to the effective use and monitoring of resources

G11.2   Meet productivity and development targets

What do I need to learn?

You need to know and understand:

- How legislation affects the way that business operations are conducted with clients
- The importance of good communication techniques
- The principles of effective stock control
- Effective and efficient ways to handle salon resources

What does it mean?

This chapter will explain how you can help your manager/employer to maximise the salon's resources and how customer service operations and personal output can be improved.

What do I need to do?

- You need to ensure that your input at work makes the best use of the salon's stock, equipment and time available.
- You can also support the salon by helping to improve customer services and achieve personal targets.

Other info

Related topics and other useful information:

- **Health and safety legislation (see p. 18)**
- **Consumer and retail legislation**
- **Data Protection Act**
- **Working time directives**
- **Equal opportunities**
- **Disability discrimination**

Productivity The levels of output achieved in a work setting

Effectiveness The quality of output achieved in a work setting

Resources   The variety of means available that can be utilised or employed within any given task or project: time, money, people etc.

CHECKERBOARD

At the end of this chapter the checkerboard will help to jog your memory on what you have learned and what still remains to be done. Cross them off with a pencil as you cover each of its topics. (See p. 376.)

INTRODUCTION

This chapter combines two optional units and covers the following five main outcomes:

G10 Support customer service improvements

    G10.1 Use feedback to identify potential customer service improvements

    G10.2 Contribute to the implementation of changes in customer service

    G10.3 Assist with the evaluation of changes in customer service

G11 Contribute to the financial effectiveness of the business

    G11.1 Contribute to the effective use and monitoring of resources

    G11.2 Meet productivity and development targets

This chapter looks at the monitoring and effective use of salon **resources**, meeting targets and customer service issues. You can be effective at work in a number of ways. It's not just about selling; it's more to do with how you work by minimising waste, working together as a team and taking particular note of customers' requests and expectations. Collectively, this will help the business operate more smoothly, running like a machine.

We could describe business as operating a bit like a car. If it is left alone, switched off, it will generate nothing. It may have all the component parts, but collectively they will not be able to create any output and therefore will not go anywhere. However, when the engine is started, the vehicle can move off, gather speed and a journey begins: that is providing the driver knows how to drive and where he is going. In this analogy we could look at the aspects that relate to the car and to business. The essential parts are:

Engine – this is the hub of the vehicle that generates power by converting the input of petrol, diesel or gas into an energy which will ultimately provide momentum. This complex machine is made up of many components and these can be likened to the working team: a group of people that only collectively, by working together in harmony, can generate the business output.

Radiator/cooling system – the engine may be fine when it is first started. However, disaster is only around the corner unless the engine cooling system is working. The engine generates a lot of energy that converts into heat. If the cooling system isn't working or there isn't any water in it the engine seizes up. This is similar to the systems that control and harness the business. How would a salon operate if there wasn't a telephone, an appointment system, electricity and water?

Gauges and speedometer – the bigger the car, the more sophisticated are the gauges. Without being told the temperature of the engine, how much fuel we have and how fast we are going, we would soon be in trouble. This information provides a way of monitoring all of the essential systems, giving us up-to-the-minute details, ensuring that we can keep up progress and stay on the right side of the law.

Bodywork and styling – this is what catches people's eye. The shiny, unblemished, body of the car is the image that the salon portrays. It can shout quality, luxury, prestige and status without even being tried out. Conversely, a dirty, dented and slightly battered exterior conveys something else.

Interior – the car's upholstery and fitted interior are like the salon's interior. The quality of fittings, colour scheme and materials used are all what the clients get to see and experience when or if they come in.

Driver – the *qualified* person in control that manages to harness the power, enabling the vehicle to be taken from A to B, steering carefully to avoid obstacles, controlling the speed and observing the conditions outside at all times.

Therefore in this chapter we consider the factors that contribute to the effectiveness of the business and the way we provide customer care. Being effective in our work is essential. The way in which we use salon resources and maintain productivity has a direct impact on the viability of the business. We can look at these two aspects in closer detail:

- resources
- productivity.

The resources are the key aspects that are available to the business. The way they are utilised and controlled enables the business to function properly and refers to the salon staff, salon materials, equipment and time.

ACTIVITY

As a group activity, discuss the various methods of communication that your salon uses and find out what advantages and/or disadvantages each method presents. Record the details of your findings.

Key skills: Communication

2.1 Take part in discussions
2.2 Produce written materials

HUMAN RESOURCES

Hairdressing is a *labour intensive* service industry. It relies solely on the profits generated from the sales of services and treatments to clients. The people that work within a hairdressing salon are therefore an essential part of the business. Many people are involved in the process. The receptionist meets and greets the clients. She handles bookings over the telephone, operates the till and assists in the selling of retail products. The stylists tend to their clients, providing them with services and treatments. The junior staff are in training and adding to the skill base of the salon. They also tend to the clients by providing customer services. The manager delegates the tasks, collects information and makes decisions in order for the business to function. The cleaners ensure that all areas are fit for their purpose and hygienically safe. They are all part of one team and work together collectively in order to make the business work.

The way that the team is orchestrated, i.e. managed, really counts. Each and every member of staff has a duty to perform and personal targets to achieve. So, in order for a business to succeed, it has to make best use of its human resources, engaging people in their work and applying their different skills to achieve one common aim. Assuming that the business has a sufficient and available work force, the manager would be planning staff cover, setting individual goals and monitoring their achievements.

Changing patterns in our working and leisure time now require hairdressing businesses to be more flexible. This will ensure that both the needs of clients and the salon dovetail together. This flexibility will mean that:

- a mix of both full-time and part-time staff could be used
- more staff will generally be required towards the end of the week
- there needs to be a rota for days off when salons open six or seven days a week
- there needs to be a balance of junior and senior staff
- salons could be open at times other than just 9 am to 5.30 pm.

ACTIVITY: CUSTOMER SERVICE

With the help of your receptionist you can conduct a simple survey to find out when salon customers want to come in. Create a simple graph displaying the days of the month along the bottom axis and a range of times (say 8.00 am–8.00 pm) along the vertical axis. When customers call the salon, mark each point on the graph to show when they want to come in as opposed to what is available. Each plotting point could be colour coded to refer to different staff members. Run the exercise over a complete calendar month to see what happens.

- Are there any specific days that people would like?
- Are there any specific times that people would like?
- Do the findings of the survey highlight any discrepancies with the present work system?

Key skills: Application of number

2.1 Collect and record data

2.2 Tackle problems

Maintaining productivity

Low productivity is the result of poor service, lack of training and ineffective use of materials and time. The guaranteed outcome of this is easy to forecast. It also signifies a failure of management. If people are not given the time, skills and materials in the first place, they can not achieve anyway.

Good productivity is the result of achievement, so it is easy to see that in order to achieve there must be clear objectives. Targets should be clearly understood and attainable. Virtually all salons work on the basis that stylists earn a basic salary with commission incentive scheme. Commission is payable as a bonus on top of wages when individual or group targets have been achieved.

Targets

We may not like the thought of targets, but we all need them. We all like the benefits that come with achievement: credit and praise, higher self-esteem, increased confidence, an ability to please others and, last but not least, rewards. All these are positive outcomes for doing what is expected of us. They are the food on which we all thrive. Collectively, well-defined targets forge a unity within a working team that acts as a motivator for everyone involved.

Targets should be an incentive though. In order for people to respond to the challenge, the targets should be realistic, achievable and tailored to the individual. Unrealistic targets, which from the outset are perceived as unrealistic and unachievable, will have a very negative impact. The result will be a reduction in the bond of the working team and demotivation in the struggling individual.

Targets are not just about selling though. The targets that you will encounter at work can also be relevant to personal learning.

SMART productivity

For a hairdressing business to be successful, the salon owner has to take an overall view of productivity. As we have established the business to be mainly labour intensive, there needs to be a continuous analysis of *personal performance* which can only be measured against a *target* figure.

First, the salon owner has to set an overall salon target. This figure can then be divided between departments of stylists, technical and retail. Each person in each department then has a personal target which they understand and agree with. The personal target can be worked out as follows:

target = service price × number of clients

For example, if stylist Kerry charges £30 for a cut and blow dry and can take ten clients a day, her daily takings for this service would be £300 and her weekly takings would be £1,500 (based upon a five-day week). This may be adjusted to allow for different daily performances. We cannot ensure consistent bookings, although through analysis we can establish high and low points. In addition to the styling takings we would also expect some retail sales, so the overall personal target would include this. Target setting should follow the SMART principle and should be:

- **Specific** – clearly defined
- **Measurable** – quantifiable in some way
- **Agreed** – between both parties
- **Realistic** – able to be achieved
- **Timed** – for the duration of a fixed time period

Targets may be **confidential** between the manager and employee, in which case salon procedures relating to confidentiality must be observed. Personal reviews or appraisals provide an opportunity for management to establish an employee's performance level, to compare it against her target and to discuss ways of improving productivity. Most hairdressing businesses work on an incentive payment scheme. This can have a major impact on the overall salary rates. The salon owner needs to establish fixed costs and variable costs and the wage percentage needs to be established in order for the necessary profit margins to be maintained. From the overall wage portion of income, an individual target is set for each stylist.

REMEMBER: STAFF INCENTIVES #1 ✔

Cars, cash, hot air balloon flights, holidays abroad, time out – all of these have been used to spur staff towards new peaks of achievement and some still are, alongside ever more popular perks like private healthcare, childcare, life assurance and pensions.

All incentives closely follow the economy. Cars may rate tops for young employees, but performance-related pay, medical insurance and share options are by far the preferred choice of older staff.

Within hairdressing, as elsewhere, incentives are developed by trial and error and depend largely on what's affordable.

What do you offer?

Image Setters, Gloucestershire: 'We really concentrate on incentives. One which worked a treat was a holiday cruise to Spain, or £100 cash. Most took the holiday. It gave them something to work for and takings went up in all four of our salons.'

Jane Roberts, Northamptonshire: 'We concentrate on quality employment, but do operate incentives spasmodically, including membership of a live music club and bar, percentages off treatments and retail, the occasional skiing holiday or weekend in Paris and vouchers for M&S and Selfridges. Most of the staff have been with us now for more than ten years.'

HQ, Surrey: 'Our schemes include a £100 cash bonus for anyone who hits their sales target six times during a 12-week period, paid for courses with Vidal Sassoon in London and also the opportunity to work on photographic shoots.'

The Cut Club, Yorkshire: 'We've given stylists one free product for every five sold, plus a pair of scissors and a hairdryer for the one who achieved the most sales. It's worked quite well.'

Hairaware, Hampshire: 'We give 10 per cent commission on retail sales, commission on client treatments and let staff have products at cost.'

So why bother?

Money is the greatest motivator, according to American business beliefs, so why not use it as the prime 'carrot'? The best reason is that cash just doesn't guarantee results.

Confederation of British Industry surveys show that more and more personnel think their performance should determine their pay rise. As far as the company owners are concerned, well-implemented incentives have a positive impact on key areas – turnover, profitability, client service, staff recruitment and retention. Proven results include higher earnings, improved loyalty and commitment, more efficient teamwork, personal development, increased skill levels and less absenteeism and sickness.

It's really about developing people's confidence and creating an environment of encouragement, but this has to be translated in the right way. Individuals should not only be allowed to make mistakes, but also given praise and recognition. There should be both financial targets and learning targets. Training is a major incentive – with relevant rewards. People need to be competitive in a healthy, non-destructive way. It's important that everybody understands each other's roles and is willing to help. This takes time to develop. Much of it is about communication. Regular meetings act as incentives because people *feel* involved.

Evaluating results

The benefits must suit individuals and prove worthwhile. Typical amounts spent vary from 3 to 5 per cent of turnover on training budgets, to 30 per cent salary equivalent on total packages. Measuring the return is notoriously difficult since incentives can have a ripple effect. But healthcare benefits (check-ups, dental treatments, counselling) are also tangibly cost effective.

Working together

Always remember that your work colleagues also need your help to meet their targets. Sharing the workload is working as a team and can be achieved by:

- providing support
- anticipating the needs of others
- maintaining harmony
- communicating effectively.

In some salons, you might see some staff busy attending to their clients while others hang about around reception, flicking through magazines or disappearing off to the staffroom for a coffee. Teamwork is about making an active contribution, seeking to assist others even if only by passing up rollers. It is good for staff morale and presents a good image to the clients. In short, make yourself useful and contribute to the team effort by assisting your fellow workers.

Anticipating the needs of others follows on from providing support. Clean and prepare the work areas ready for use, locate and prepare products as and when they are required. This will help the smooth operation of the salon. Co-operate with your colleagues. Make a positive contribution to your team by assisting them to provide a well-managed and co-ordinated quality service. Be self-motivated and keep yourself busy. Don't wait to be asked to do things. Maintain harmony and try to minimise possible conflicts. Most good working relationships develop easily. However, others may need to be worked at. Whatever your personal feelings about your fellow work associates, the clients must never sense a bad atmosphere within the salon caused by a friction between staff. You will spend a lot of time in the company of people you work with, but you will not always like everyone you meet. At work, in order to maintain teamwork, a mutual respect for others is more important than close friendships. So remember, treat others with respect and be sensitive and responsive to other's feelings. Show concern and care for others.

Personal development

Managers of people use *performance appraisal* or *progress reviews* to evaluate the effectiveness of the work team. An appraisal is a system whereby you and your manager, in an interview situation, review and evaluate your personal contribution and/or progress over a predetermined period of time, as measured against expected targets or standards.

A similar process would take place at suitable points within a personal programme of training in order to review progress and training effectiveness, measured against specific training objectives.

Measuring effectiveness

To measure progress towards overall work contributions as well as training targets, there need to be clear stated expectations of the performance required. These standards should show:

- what tasks need to be performed
- what training activities will take place
- what standards are expected to be reached
- when assessment should be expected
- when a review of progress towards the agreed targets is to take place.

In normal, ongoing work situations, performance appraisal will be based on the following factors:

- results achieved against targets and job requirements

- additional accomplishments and contribution
- contribution made by the individual compared with those of other staff members.

The job requirements are outlined in the employee's job description. A job description is a written specification of the main purposes and functions expected within a given job. Good job descriptions will include the following:

- job title
- work locations
- responsibility (to whom and for what)
- the job purpose
- main functions (listed)
- standards expected
- any special conditions.

Standards expected from the job holder will often include behaviour and appearance. If these have been stated from the outset, the job holder will know what is expected of her.

Job description – Stylist	
Location:	Based at salon as advised
Main purpose of job:	To ensure customer care is provided at all times To maintain a good standard of technical and client care, ensuring that up-to-date methods and techniques are used following the salon training practices and procedures
Responsible to:	Salon manager
Requirements:	To maintain the company's standards in respect of hairdressing/beauty services
	To ensure that all clients receive service of the best possible quality
	To advise clients on services and treatments
	To advise clients on products and aftercare
	To achieve designated performance targets
	To participate in self-development or to assist with the development of others
	To maintain company policy in respect of:
	● personal standards of health/hygiene ● personal standards of appearance/conduct ● operating safety whilst at work ● public promotion ● corporate image
	as laid out in employee handbook
	To carry out client consultation in accordance with company policy
	To maintain company security practices and procedures
	To assist your manager in the provision of salon resources
	To undertake additional tasks and duties required by your manager from time to time

The appraisal process

At the beginning of the appraisal period, the manager and employee discuss jointly, develop, and mutually agree the objectives and performance measures for that period. An *action plan* will then be drafted, outlining the expected outcomes.

During the appraisal period, should there be any significant changes in factors such as objectives or performance measures, these will be discussed between the manager and employee and any amendments will be appended to the action plan.

At the end of the appraisal period, the results are discussed by the employee and the manager, and both manager and employee sign the appraisal. A copy is prepared for the employee and the original is kept on file.

An appraisal of performance will contain the following information:

- employee's name
- appraisal period
- appraiser's name and title
- performance objectives
- job title
- work location
- results achieved
- identified areas of strength and weakness
- ongoing action plan
- overall performance grading (optional).

Self-appraisal

In order for you to manage yourself within the job role, you need to identify the areas where you meet the expectations of your job and also the areas where there is room for improvement. Measuring your own strengths and weaknesses against laid-down performance criteria (as found in the NVQ Level 3 standards of competence) is one way of monitoring your own progress. Simply use the performance criteria set out within the standards as a checklist. This will help you to:

- identify areas where further training is required
- identify areas where further practice is needed
- identify areas where competence can be achieved.

TIME RESOURCES

Time is a resource that, although not tangible, is of importance to the financial effectiveness of the business. It affects issues such as pricing structure and staff training. As the financial income of the salon is largely based on client service, the price structure will reflect on the length of time a service takes. For example, a cut and blow dry may have a time allowance of 45 minutes, while a highlighting service may have an allowance of two hours and will therefore be correspondingly more expensive, irrespective of other resources that have been used, i.e. light and heat, laundered items, equipment and products.

This analysis of the efficiency in usage of a time is measured during a *time and motion study*. This involves the observation of staff members over a specific period of time, while keeping detailed records of how many times they carry out each procedure and how long it takes.

Ineffective use of time comes from not doing the *right* job at the *right* time. Wasted or what we can now call lost time cannot be made back up in the normal allocation of work. So therefore by having to spend extra time clawing back to where we were before, we expend more efforts and usually more money in the process. This ineffective work method is directly linked to inefficiency and is a burden on all those other people pulling together to try to work as a team.

ACTIVITY: WORK STUDY

Ask a fellow work colleague if they mind taking part in a work survey.
Over a period of six observations, see how long it takes them to complete the following services:

- Cut and blow dry (short hair including shampoo/conditioning, etc.)
- Cut and blow dry (shoulder length hair including shampoo/conditioning, etc.)
- Blow dry (short hair including shampoo/conditioning, etc.)
- Blow dry (shoulder length hair including shampoo/conditioning, etc.)

You can also choose your own specific services. Then at the end of the period review your records to average out the amount of time spent on each activity. How does this fit in with the salon's expected timescales?

Key skills: Application of number

2.1 Collect and record data

2.2 Tackle problems

Time management

We could probably think that as hairdressers we are good managers of time, particularly when our total working life insists that we work and keep to time. We may never keep clients waiting, not even five minutes, but it doesn't end there. It's not just how we manage our time in our work that counts. It's a lot more to do with how much impact does our work have on other's time. Do we shine purely by eroding other people's time? Quite simply, putting it another way, do we achieve our goals at someone else's expense? If you are busy in constant turmoil, other staff will be affected in the same way and in turn this will affect someone's clients, if not your own.

Get organised

If you don't take control and organise your time, you'll never have time for anything. After people, time is the most important asset to the business so it must be used constructively. You have to take control of the time at your disposal and decide how you want to spend it.

Prioritising things to do

Tasks need to be graded in order of priority. For example, it may be your job to check the stock levels on a weekly basis. If this is not done at the right time, what happens? Don't waste time dealing with non-urgent tasks. Make a list of things to do. Once you have a complete list of everything to do, you can set about prioritising the content. (This list could be tabulated, see below.) Lists are very useful time management tools, but they only work if you stick to them rigidly. Find a system that works for you and a way of keeping your list to hand so that you can work with it, add to it and finally cross things off when completed.

Write things down

People are neither computers nor infallible. If you don't write things down you may forget some of them, only remembering at the last minute or too late. Build list writing into a daily routine and set aside time to review the items on the list on a regular basis. There is a saying: 'Never handle a piece of paper more than once.' Attend to the important issues as soon as possible. We could all spend our lives putting them off until tomorrow so if we get those annoying little things done straight away we could save so much time.

People who are really in control of their time plan their activities, remembering that social and leisure time are just as important as their working life.

REMEMBER: THINGS TO DO LIST		✔
Things to do today	Things to do this week	Things to do this month

Key skills: Communication

2.2 Produce written materials

2.3 Use images

OTHER SALON RESOURCES

The other resources of a salon include:

- stock
- fixtures and fittings
- utilities (electricity, water and telephones)
- tools and equipment
- space.

Salons cannot function without these resources and it is your job to ensure that they are used in the correct manner.

Stock control

This involves the monitoring of all stock movements: i.e. *consumables*, the items used within the salon on clients; *retail stock* purchased for resale to clients for home use.

The systems that your salon use will provide management with up-to-date information for controlling stock. You can support your salon by helping to maintain stock control. These systems will deal with:

- reordering stock
- movements of stock
- usage of stock
- shortages of stock
- the safety and security of stock.

Consumables may be used in the salon or sold to clients for home use. Either way the salon must have enough stock or it won't be able to function. Products are purchased by the salon in varying quantities, for short-term or long-term availability. To ensure that the products remain usable or saleable, the stock controller must monitor them and will therefore need to be aware of:

- shelf life
- handling
- losses
- damage.

Stock held in store is a valuable asset to the company. The stock controller is responsible for its safe storage between delivery and use or sale.

Stocktaking

Items for use such as tools, small pieces of equipment and potentially hazardous chemicals should be kept in a locked store, the size of which will depend on the salon and its needs. Individual items are accounted for by stocktaking.

Stocktaking at regular intervals provides management with up-to-date information of stock movement. Without regular stocktaking, individual items and product lines could run out, creating a situation in which services and treatments normally offered were not available. This would mean lost profit to the salon, both at the time and later through a damaged reputation. Every business requires accurate, reliable accounting systems which:

REMEMBER: STOCK ROTATION ✓

When new stock is placed on shelves for sale or use, ensure that old products are brought forward so that they may be sold first.

- categorise products
- monitor usage
- identify shortages
- report damages or defects
- update records.

These guidelines provide the basis for a simple yet effective stock management system.

Product coding

Many salons now use the technology of personal computers to produce management information. Stock control is one of the facilities available in software systems for salon management. Salons turning over large quantities of stock find it helpful to devise coding systems for the products they use and sell. The product's manufacturer, its category, name and size can all be stored as a single alpha numerical code, the *product code*. These codes can streamline the processes of stock control, monitoring, pricing and tax calculation.

Products received into storage are individually itemised and allocated the relevant product code. The information is then fed into the computer, as is the information that a product has been used or sold. The computer continually recalculates the stock levels, providing management with automated stock control information and printouts for use in manual stocktaking checks. This coded system is one form of *point-of-sale* (POS) *management*. Another form uses *bar coding*. The principle here is exactly the same, but the product information is converted into a series of stripes printed on labels or directly on to the product. The bar codes can be read directly by the computer via a scanning bar code reader, which recognises the product and makes the necessary stock control adjustments.

Ordering stock and taking delivery

Products are purchased either directly from the manufacturer or via a wholesaler, on a credit or cash-based agreement. *Credit account* terms are arranged with the supplier, usually on a monthly payment system.

A bar code

REMEMBER: STOCK RECORDING ✔

The example shown in the figure provides a simple format for a paper-based stock recording system. We can see that in the first column there is a range of product types: e.g. L'Oréal Kerastase. Each family of products – shampoos, conditioners, etc. – is grouped together. In the next column the product's unit size is identified.

The next two columns are each repeated several times. These contain space to enter the date, product minimum holding levels, amount in stock and quantities for order. Stock is then ordered when the amounts fall below the minimum holding levels. When repeated over several columns it is easy to identify faster moving products and trends or patterns.

Key skills: Application of number

2.1 Collect and record data

2.3 Interpret and present data

Stock Master			Date	12/Sept 00		Date			Date		
L'Oréal Retail Products	Size		Minimum Holding Level	In Stock	Order	Minimum Holding Level	In Stock	Order	Minimum Holding Level	In Stock	Order
KERASTASE											
Neutrative Hair Baths											
Satin	250ml		4	(3)	1 box						
Enriching	250ml		4	4	0						
Revitalising	250ml		3	7	0						
Neutrative Treatments											
Protein cond	250ml		4	(2)	1 box						
Elixir Vital	250ml		4	(2)	1 box						
Masqu. Thick	400ml		2	4	0						
Masqu. Fine	400ml		2	4	0						

Manual stock recording system

Placing an order

A salon's order may be placed with a company representative, who completes a *purchase order* on the salon's behalf. The purchase order is a paper system documenting all the manufacturer's product listings and categories. This is returned to the company so that the order can be processed and despatched.

Taking delivery

When the stock order arrives at the salon it will be accompanied by a *delivery note* that will list the items so far despatched and any that are to follow, such as items temporarily out of stock. The delivery note must be checked against the contents of the consignment and discrepancies or damages in transit identified before countersigning the order and confirming the delivery. Any discrepancies between the documents should be referred to the management for later adjustment.

The incoming stock should be moved immediately from reception to a secure location away from the working area of the salon. At a convenient time the salon stock systems can be updated and stock put into storage.

After a period of time the supplier will send an *invoice*, a request for payment. Details of the invoice must be checked against the delivery note and the stock actually received.

Choice of stock supplier

Wholesalers carry stock from a wide range of manufacturers, providing the salon owner with a choice of products and differing prices to suit various budgets. When orders are placed through a manufacturer's representative, the salon is restricted to buying the products available from that manufacturer.

You may be able to visit a nearby wholesale cash-and-carry warehouse. Such warehouses provide an alternative service to the salon, holding stocks ranging from consumable product lines to sundry items such as towels, gowns and hair ornaments, and even coffee and washing powders. Wholesalers like this provide the salon with a one-stop shopping facility.

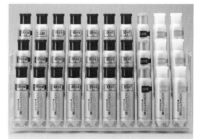

Goldwell

Stock handling

Most products used by salons are packaged and many are chemicals. Movements of stock into or within the salon may involve lifting, stacking, dispensing, displaying or pricing, all of which are subject to stringent legislation (see Manual Handling Regulations 1992, in Chapter 1, p. 26).

The Health and Safety at Work Act 1974 relates to all workplace health and safety, although the Act has specific requirements for the employer. *Employees* have a duty under the law not to endanger their own health or safety, or that of other people who may be affected by their actions. The responsibilities of the *employer* are summarised below:

- Ensure that the building and the people within it are as safe as possible.
- Train staff in safe working practices and the use of equipment.
- Maintain an accident book and provide first-aid facilities.
- Maintain all equipment and tools.
- Provide safe systems for the handling, transit and storage of all materials.
- Implement immediate action when any hazard is reported.
- If the salon employs more than five staff, provide a written health and safety policy describing arrangements for employees.

All cosmetic products come under strict legislation (Cosmetic Products (Safety) Regulations 1989) and a specific guide to health and safety in the salon relating to the control of substances hazardous to health (the COSHH regulations) has been written by the Cosmetic, Toiletry and Perfumery Association (CTPA) with the co-operation of the Hairdressing and Beauty Suppliers' Association (HBSA). This guide assesses substances potentially hazardous to health and provides information to employers about exercising adequate controls.

Apart from basic rules for hairdressers relating to hair product and salon safety, substances are categorised as 'potential' or 'unlikely' hazards. Each type of product identified is specified by:

- name – including ingredients and a general description
- health hazard – from inhalation, ingestion, absorption, contact or injection
- precautions – during work activity, storage, and disposal or spillage
- first aid – in relation to eyes, skin or ingestion
- fire risk – if applicable.

Copies of this guide are available from the HBSA (for further information, see Chapter 1 on health and safety).

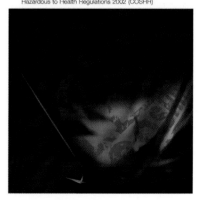

COSSH regulations HMSO

Security

Stock in storage is a valuable asset to the company. Thieves are often opportunist, not always planning their activities. They will seize opportunities as they arise – money left around, products on display, unlocked doors and open windows. You should take all necessary precautions to maintain a secure working environment.

GOOD PRACTICE/HEALTH & SAFETY ✚

Don't:

● leave keys in locks or lying around

● leave products or valuables unattended

● allow unauthorised entry, even by friends or family, to staff only areas

Do:

● report to management any items that appear to be missing

● ensure that materials and equipment are returned to safe areas

● make available company policy with regard to theft, loss, or damages

---

Avoiding waste and damage

Regular checks on goods through careful stock control will assist in minimising shortages, but shortages can still occur if items are neglectfully wasted, such as preparing a colour using a whole tube of colour where half would have been enough. Applications should be carefully measured. Manufacturers' recommendations can be found on all products. Other physical resources can also be misused:

Utilities Staff should be given clear guidelines about the efficient use of utilities as wastage will increase costs for the salon. For example, taps should not be left on between shampoos. Hood dryers should not be left running after the client has finished. Personal calls should not be made from the salon telephones.

Tools and equipment Regular checks on tools and equipment will help minimise problems. These may still occur, however, if items are misused. Using tools for purposes other than those intended could be negligent, if not dangerous. Think of the risks involved in changing a plug using a pair of scissors instead of a screwdriver. Staff must know how to use and maintain tools and equipment in the proper manner and should be given relevant health and safety training.

Space Effective use of space should also be monitored. Turnover can be measured against the square metre to gauge the productivity of a given area, for example, retail sales.

REMEMBER ✔

If your salon uses tubes of permanent colour, encourage staff to replace part-tubes in marked original packaging.

FINANCIAL RESOURCES

In order to make informed decisions about the direction of the business, the owner must have a clear picture of the financial situation. Efficient systems must be put in place to deal with daily financial transactions. Records must be kept so that basic information is available to the salon owner and, as legally required, to Customs and Excise and the Inland Revenue at the end of the financial year.

Financial systems

Company policy will determine the systems and procedures relating to the cashpoint and the format for recording information. These will reflect the line of responsibility. If the salon is a **franchise** or concession within a **host company**, the overall organisation may dictate specific information and presentation requirements, and the salon's manager may be committed to certain obligations built into the business agreement. If the salon stands alone, however, company policy should be established by the owner or manager. It should concern itself with the following:

- personnel responsible for cash handling
- operation of the till (manual, automatic or **computerised**), including unders, overs, **voids** and refunds, changing of the till roll
- till reconciliation, banking
- recording of information on the daily sheet, in the day book and petty cash book.

The policy should take account of special circumstances that may occur very seldom, if ever:

Systems breakdown – what are the procedures in the event of a systems breakdown or power failure? Suppose, for example, you were using an automatic till and it *crashed*, what would you do? How would you continue to offer service to the client whose transaction you were dealing with?

Security – what are the security procedures in the event of fire evacuation? What happens to the takings? Do you lock the till? Who has the key?

Company policy should also determine who is responsible for each function:

Line management – what are the set down financial procedures for cash transactions? Who is authorised to take money, to process bills, to go to the bank, and to cash up at the end of the day?

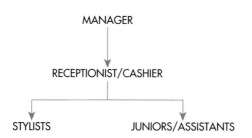

Line management for cash transactions

Training – who is responsible for the delivery and format of training in relation to taking cash and to processing sales? Remember that the training programme needs to be updated to allow for the introduction of new facilities and systems. When a new facility such as an automatic till is introduced into the salon, the company from which it is leased or purchased will usually provide a session of staff training without further charge, but how will ongoing training be delivered for new members of staff?

The cashpoint

The systems required at the cashpoint need to be created to match the technical resources. The procedures will therefore differ for manual tills, automatic tills and computerised cash desks.

Manual tills

When operating a manual system, a lockable cashbox or drawer is used to store the cash safely. As the name suggests, a manual system relies upon each transaction being recorded by hand. A daily record (a minimum requirement) should itemise each client, with the bill total alongside in the relevant column. This kind of system can be time consuming and is the most likely to incur human error.

Client	Stylist 1	Stylist 2	Sales
Reynolds	£10.00		
Walker	£12.50		
Davies		£10.00	£5.00

Automatic tills

Automatic tills can be programmed for a number of functions. Each person may be given a *department key* which identifies her takings; this code can be used to calculate commission payments. On an automatic till, a *turn key* system can display X and Z totals. When printed out these readings are used to check the amounts registered against the actual amount in the till.

X readings may be used to provide subtotals throughout the day. This is particularly useful in larger companies where it may be helpful to check takings when the cashier or receptionist leaves the till, remove cash, etc. from the till, or for breaks and for lunch. The Z reading is a figure taken at the close of business at the end of day.

Computerised cash desks

Computerised cash desks provide the same facilities as an automatic till but offer many other functions as well. The most important of these functions are the storing and recording of data and the preparation of management reports.

A computerised till   Sharp

Cashpoint functions

Whichever system is in operation, fundamental procedures are needed to maintain accuracy and efficiency. At all times the person acting as **cashier** must ensure the client's goodwill.

Float

At the beginning of each working day the cashpoint must be primed with a float – an amount of money which is surplus to the income from daily **transactions**. The float amount should be determined from experience, according to the average daily cash flow. It should be made up of the small denominations likely to be required for change.

Methods of payment

Payments for sales and services may be made in a number of ways. The salon's house policy will determine what is acceptable.

Cash – in the UK cash payments will be in pounds sterling and your salon will probably decline payment in any other currency. Be prepared for unfamiliar coins or notes from other parts of Britain and euros from the EU.

Cheques – your salon should not accept a cheque unless backed by a *cheque guarantee card*; this will have a limit such as £50, £100 or £250. Company policy may require additional information such as the address of the client and a telephone number. Some salons may choose to waive this requirement with regular clients as a measure of goodwill.

Switch/Connect, Solo cards – these cards act as automatic cheques. The transaction process is the same as for a cheque or credit card, but once processed the account is debited immediately from the client's bank account.

Cash

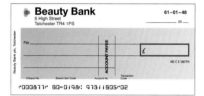

A cheque

A credit card
Courtesy Barclaycard plc

Accounts – your salon may provide an account facility for regular clients and a formal arrangement whereby all bills for an individual or family are paid at agreed intervals. It is advisable to ask the client to sign the bill at the time of service. It should be clear to the stylist when the commission will be paid – either at the time of service or at the time of the account payment.

Traveller's cheques – are these acceptable to your company? If so, in which currencies? Usually traveller's cheques are taken only if they are in sterling. They should be checked against the bearer's passport for proof of identity.

Gift vouchers – vouchers may be sold by the salon for payment against hairdressing and beauty services or retail sales. When the salon is operating as a concession, gift vouchers may be available for purchase from the host company. You in turn will require reimbursement from the source of the voucher. Company policy should outline procedures for issuing and receiving gift vouchers.

Hair Studio

31 High Street
Great Perming   **Tel: Perming 4242**

This voucher entitles

_____

to purchase services and treatments
to the value of £_____

Signed: Date:

Valid for six months from date of purchase

A gift voucher

Credit cards – these cards (such as Mastercard and Visa) may be tendered for payment. Upon authorisation from the issuer or their servicing agents, the amount specified is charged to the cardholder. The salon is charged a percentage on all transactions processed.

Charge cards – these cards (such as American Express) may be tendered for payment in the same way as credit cards. Again, the salon is charged a percentage on all transactions processed.

Card payments

Registered companies may apply to a credit card company to become a *credit card authority*. Upon acceptance of the application, the credit company will issue a transaction machine and the stationery required to make purchase transactions and follow set banking procedures. Credit cards are accepted as a method of payment at the discretion of the salon. When a card has been accepted as the method of payment, a charge will be imposed by the credit company for the use of this facility.

A list of cards that are accepted by the salon for payment should be clearly displayed. Clients usually presume that payment by card will be acceptable; failure to inform them to the contrary can cause an embarrassing situation to arise. Card payments are given a 'ceiling' limit by the card company. Payment will be honoured up to a specific amount but for large amounts prior authorisation by telephone is required. Thorough training needs to be given if staff are to understand these procedures.

Financial records

In order to maintain and analyse the finances of the business, daily records must be completed which will provide weekly, monthly and yearly information. This information can form the basis of development and expansion. The main purpose of these records is to display two things:

1 **Cash receipts** and the proportional amount of value-added tax (VAT).
2 **Varying expenses** paid out – these are usually paid through a petty cash system.

Company policy will determine the layout and systems of records of all daily financial transactions.

Value-added tax (VAT)

VAT is money taken by the business as part of the cost of services and sales and paid to Customs and Excise. VAT is a percentage added to the total, the percentage being set by the government and changed from time to time. VAT registration is required only for companies whose annual turnover exceeds some current threshold imposed by government.

ACTIVITY: DEDUCTING VAT

When the amount taken is the gross figure, we need to deduct the VAT to find the net figure. This calculation is more complicated. In this case we know that the gross amount includes VAT at the current rate. If VAT is charged at 17.5 per cent the gross amount is 117.5 per cent of the net amount.

Gross amount	£11.75
Deduct VAT: divide by 117.5 and multiply by 17.5	−£1.75
Net amount	£10.00

(This is the same as dividing by 47 and multiplying by 7, which you may find simpler.)

Key skills: Application of number

2.2 Tackle problems

ACTIVITY: ADDING VAT

Stylist Graham charges £10 (the net amount) for a cut and blow dry. Assuming VAT is charged at 17.5 per cent:

Net amount	£10.00
Add VAT @ 17.5%	£ 1.75
Gross amount	£11.75

Key skills: Application of number

2.2 Tackle problems

Day sheets

Cash receipts are recorded in the first instance on a day sheet. This breaks down the total amount of *gross* takings into components, services and sales. The VAT is then calculated from the gross amount and deducted to give the *net* amount. (A gross amount is an amount including VAT.) The purpose of the VAT calculation is to know what proportion of the total takings is usable income.

The day book

The analysis of each day sheet is transferred into a day book. The day book may include other information as well as records of financial transactions. The basic layout of the book should display the gross amounts taken by each sales and service department, the VAT, and the net takings. This can be totalled weekly, monthly, quarterly, and six-monthly to provide details for precise analysis.

A day sheet

Day			Date			
STYLIST	SALES	BILL NO.	AMOUNT		TOTAL	
				Gross	VAT	Net
		TOTAL				
		EXPENSES				
		TOTAL LESS EXPENSES				
		AMOUNT BANKED				
		PAYING-IN NO.				
		UNDER				
		OVER				

SIGNED ....

CUSTOMER SERVICE OPERATIONS

Hairdressers do exceptionally well in providing good customer service. Their focused work practices have always been directed to the core of a good business strategy, that being customer centred. The reason why this particular occupational sector is not troubled by the 'disease' that most others find hard to implement and ultimately satisfy is because of the way that the industry provides a personal service. Following is a list of factors supporting a strong customer focus within hairdressing, assuming the industry comprises of 34,500 salons of which +90 per cent are small, privately owned 'micro' businesses employing five or fewer staff:

- Stylists deliver services on a one-to-one basis with their clients.
- Competition keeps technical standards to 'better than average' levels.
- Clients expect a high level of accountability from their hairdresser.
- Experienced staff develop excellent communication skills with clients.
- Clients are able to develop relationships directly with the people from whom they choose to buy.
- From the numbers of clients that stylists come into contact with, they are able to remember individual likes and dislikes, as well as personal information.

So, good news for hairdressers, but this doesn't mean that you can relax, there's plenty to do. Good customer services are continually developed and improved and it is the rate at which these improvements are made that will give salons a competitive edge in winning new clients.

Improving customer services

The drivers for improvements to services will occur from these three possible sources:

- trade and industry bodies
- information from clients
- competitor information.

The first provides an 'around and about' rough idea to what is happening on a countrywide or national basis. The second option is the most obvious pointer for collecting useful data. The last must be considered too and could be the most important of all.

Trade and industry bodies

Large industry organisations and lead manufacturers play a pivotal role in shaping your salon's customer services. They do not necessarily have any direct link with the day-to-day operations within the salon, but they do have an impact for a number of reasons.

Employer groups, i.e. trade associations, training organisations and sector skills councils, play a strategic role within the industry. They exist by providing a range of beneficial, diverse services to the occupational sector.

> **REMEMBER** ✔
>
> Your salon's new clients are somebody's old ones!

> **REMEMBER** ✔
>
> On average, it costs 20 times more to find a *new* customer that it does to *retain* an existing one!

These services contribute overall to the way in which we work. Their resources in relation to knowledge and collected data about the sector have been sampled, analysed and shaped into policy long before it reaches the salon's doorstep. The training lead body, HABIA, has access to a national network of experts who collectively help to take the industry forward. They do this by shaping the qualification structure and specific training objectives in advance of any demographic, economic and consumer-led expectations: e.g. this book is a new edition that reflects these changes, which is then used by candidates in preparation for meeting new challenges.

Product manufacturers, e.g. L'Oréal, Procter & Gamble, Wella, also play a major role in shaping the services that we do in the salon. Their immense marketing powers influence the consumer's buying habits, which in turn cascade down to individual salons. An example of this would be in the home colouring market. In the 1990s manufacturers recognised that demographically a large section of the female market within this country were reaching a certain age bracket. This group or market segment had a number of factors that targeted them for a major push in home colour.

Taking all these influencing factors into consideration, it was obvious that if the salons would not buy sufficient levels of colouring product then it could be marketed and sold direct. Home colour products are now one of the biggest retail ranges, by sales volumes, in the home-care market.

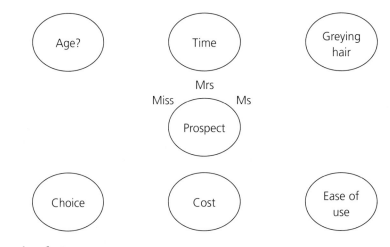

Influencing factors

So how does this affect hairdressing services to clients? Because of the external competition created by the manufacturers, salons changed their practices to maximise their position. Salons moved into highlighting, lowlights and partial colour effects in a big way. The salons created new, attractive services by modifying colouring techniques and upshifting the levels of expertise. This boom in colouring techniques is still going on.

The manufacturers have helped the sector in other ways too. National advertising campaigns influence consumers by what they see on TV in magazines and the press. Quite simply, they either sell or create fashion. By employing A-list celebrities in their commercials, they send a strong message to 'wannabes'. This in turn is reflected by the number of clients asking 'Have you seen x on the Elvive advert?' or producing cut-out pictures and saying 'I would like it cut like this'.

Customer feedback

We learn a lot about our services from those people receiving them, or at least we should do. Customer feedback is extremely important. Their likes and dislikes are the first indicators of what works for them and we respond. However, customers expect more. They want to be able to replicate what we do and this has led to the continuing growth in salon retailing. Salons sell a vast number of different items ranging from hair ornaments, silk scarfs, beach bags, towels and equipment, as well as home-care follow-up and treatments.

It doesn't end there. The feedback that we get from our clients should shape what we do in the future. Nothing remains the same. We cannot allow the existing service provision to stay as it is. Continuing business is about improvement, and improvement is born out of continuing development. Unless we accept this fact we will be unable to satisfy our clientbase in the future. 'You can satisfy *some* of the people *most* of the time. You can satisfy *most* of the people *some* of the time. But you can't satisfy *all* of the people *all* of the time!' This saying is a little overused, but serves a purpose. Salons lose customers all the time and this can happen for a number of reasons:

- moving home
- job moves
- friend's influence
- poor service
- boredom.

Home moves and job moves are unfortunate for business, but obviously necessary for the clients and their families. This loss of client is a form of *natural wastage* and part of the acceptable percentage that the business has to be prepared for. It is also satisfying when they keep in touch. Most salons will have a few clients who have moved away but can't bear to think of forging new associations with another salon. We love to talk about it too, particularly when others can't understand why they want to travel so far to have their hair styled.

Friends' influence has a powerful yet negative impact on the business. Social groupings have their leaders and followers and this is no good for anyone. When friends pressurise your clients to try their own hairdresser you have a three to one odds of retaining the custom, which is fine if you like gambling:

1 The client likes the new experience and you lose.
2 The client doesn't like the new experience but is too ashamed to return and drifts off. You lose again.
3 The client doesn't like the new experience and can't wait to get back to your safety. You win.

Then again your clients are out there busily recommending your great talents. In this situation you can win again. The power of personal recommendation is immense and should be encouraged. Many salons run *introduce a friend* campaigns. This is a strong business builder so use it.

Poor service – there isn't much too say about this as it is self-explanatory and totally unacceptable (see client complaints p. 78).

Boredom is unfortunately the main reason why salons lose clients. It's very hard to predict when boredom will set in, but if you have a strong rapport with your client you should be able to spot the signs. Typically, it will occur when you fall into the trap of regularly doing the same style over and over again. This may not be your fault either. It is human nature to stick to what you know and it is very damaging. There are only a handful of styles that *truly* suit the client. Shocked? This is based on a number of significant factors and mainly physical proportions, client competence/ability and client lifestyle routines. Embarking on other styling routes is an interesting journey, but you will find that the client will gravitate back to the safe home ground of 'tried and tested' at some point in the future. So when a returning client undergoes the same service as the last time or returns back to the style she has had before, you can 'hammer another nail into the coffin of boredom'. You can combat boredom though in the way in which you handle your client's styling preferences.

Product manufacturers do exactly the same in marketing. *'New and improved!'* means we have modified what you have been happy with before and given it a new slant, in either formulation, packaging or both. In marketing terms this is called 'extended product life'. We can invent a new strategy and call it *'extended client life'*.

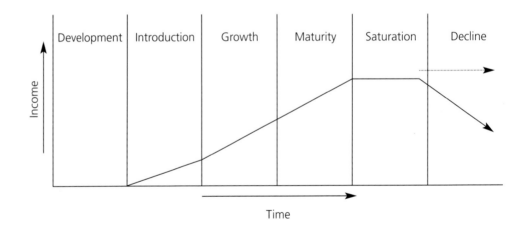

Extending product service/life

From the diagram we can see the typical graph for a newly introduced product. Taking it through the development phase (this can be similar to planning new services or treatments), we move into the introduction phase where sales start to increase following advertising and promotion. Moving forwards, further sales bring steady growth, which leads to the maturity phase. If continued interest is not stimulated, it is soon followed by a fall-off in sales during saturation. It is at this *boredom* point that the marketers reinvent the product with 'new and improved' in order to achieve an extended life of the sales.

This drop-off in business can be staved off either by introducing new services to your clients or by revival, i.e. reviewing where they are with their present image and ensuring that they are happy with it.

Collecting information from the client

You have a unique opportunity to sample the service that you provide to clients by collecting the information and putting it to good use. This can be done openly or discreetly and is purely a matter of choice. However, if you do keep the collected information on computer etc. you will need to ensure that you do not contravene any personal rights, e.g. the **Data Protection Act**.

The most popular open form of collecting data would be through a client suggestion box or alternatively via client questionnaire. These are very useful systems but they do need a lot of preparation and planning. If not carefully focused they can create too much information. Suggestion boxes can collect so many diverse comments that these may be difficult to address through the range of available or potential customer services. However, they do point to *real* client feelings and give clear indications and directions towards clients' expectations.

Questionnaires are very useful tools for collecting customer feedback. They do pinpoint customer feelings and provide sufficient data for analysis. This is because well-drafted consumer surveys are designed to 'steer' responses into clear, specific, quantifiable areas. They need a lot of thought in their construction and will often use the multiple choice type of question as a way of channelling the answers. The favoured style of question for eliciting the strength of people's feelings about a specific issue is shown in the figure.

Shampooing and conditioning

Q. The newly introduced, complementary head massage has been a useful addition to the backwash service.

☐ Strongly agree

☐ Agree

☐ No opinion

☐ Disagree

☐ Strongly disagree

Multiple choice using the Likert scale

There are many ways of sampling consumer opinion. In the salon it is often easier to talk to the clients as part of the routine conversation that takes place during visits. If it becomes part of the salon's policy for getting this feedback, a system for collectively discussing and providing this feedback to management needs to be devised. This system should be able to:

- provide fair, unbiased feedback from a wide sample of clients
- welcome contributions from all staff members
- record and 'formalise' the findings of the sampled client feedback
- provide sufficient quantifiable data for future analysis.

Competitor information

Knowing your business well is fundamentally crucial to its ongoing success. When a business is started its whole operation and the way in which it is planned to engage with its market are mapped out within a business plan. The climate in which the business operates is constantly changing though. Therefore the originally drafted business plan also needs to change. There are many reasons that necessitate the change, but the main one is competition.

Your salon's market position is constantly being undermined by the increased pressures that your competitors bring to bear. *Your competition wants your customers.* The success of your business is dependent upon increasing:

- service quality and value
- market share
- prices for services and treatments
- levels of staff competence and ability.

Therefore, in order to achieve these goals, better understanding and knowledge about your competition are essential. Competitor analysis is big business. There are a growing number of specialist companies offering a wide range of 'undercover' services designed to infiltrate and make comparisons between service quality levels. The types of information that competitors want varies, but the most pointed attacks will elicit your pricing policy and service standards.

You will have seen this at work already. How often does a *bogus client* contact the salon to find out the current costs for particular services or stylist availability? Even if you are sure that another salon is trying you out for size, it would be difficult to decline the information. Pricing policy depends on many things though, so in isolation the information is meaningless. Only when other aspects of service are brought into play can a far more useful customer comparison be made. The pricing of salon services is linked to:

- labour costs
- business fixed costs, i.e. rent, rates, light, heating, insurances
- costs of materials
- expected margins
- target market.

So if these factors relate to the total viability of the business, what would happen if the information fell into the wrong hands? The only additional costs that they will incur are those involved in trying to attract your clients through marketing, promotion and advertising. The management guru Michael Porter indicates that there are five forces which act upon any business:

- power of competitors
- power of buyers in the market
- power of suppliers to the business
- threats posed by potential entrants
- threats posed by substitute products.

REMEMBER: COMPETITOR COMPARISON ✔

If your competitors know part of this formula, then your salon is vulnerable. The shocking thing is they do!

1 Other businesses know what they should be paying staff.

2 Business costs in relation to salon location are public domain information. Local authorities keep a rateable value listing for all commercial properties. The rates payable for any premises are set at 42 per cent of the market rental. Other costs, e.g. electricity, are common to all.

3 If your competitor knows what products you use, then he knows what he would have to pay for them.

4 From the tariffs you charge, your competitors know which *socio-economic category* you are trying to attract.

The one thing that they have to calculate is the profitability of the service and whether it is something they can match or even beat on price.

You need to put your services and products to the test, which will mean making like-for-like comparisons between your salon and the competition. The table shows the types of information that you should address.

Much of this information is available through your clients from their feedback and general discussion, but beware the difference between useful data and idle gossip.

The other popular method is mystery shopper, or in this case *mystery client*. This favoured option is an ideal way of making comparisons between you and the competition. If they are using a system on you similar to the one above, then the business is going to be easy to assess. Other useful information includes:

- consumer legislation
- retail legislation
- Data Protection Act 1998
- Working Time Directive 1998
- equal opportunities.

Consumer Protection Act 1987

This Act follows European directives to protect the buyer from unsafe products. The Act is designed to help safeguard the consumer from products that do not reach reasonable levels of safety.

Consumer Safety Act 1978

There is a requirement to reduce the possible risk to consumers from any product that may be potentially dangerous.

Prices Act 1974

The price of products has to be displayed in order to prevent a false impression to the buyer.

Service attributes	Worse (−3, −2, −1)	Same	Better (+1, +2, +3)	How vital is this attribute (essential, preferred, other)?
Service availability				
Range of services/treatments				
Ranges of products				
Communication standards				
Presentation/appearance				
Quality of work output				
After-care and advice				
Consultation				
Time allowed				
Refreshments + costs				
Payment options				
Salon image and location				

Trades Descriptions Act 1968 and 1972

Products must not be falsely or misleadingly described in relation to their quality, fitness, price or purpose, by advertisements, orally, displays or descriptions. Since 1972 it is also a requirement to label a product clearly, so that the buyer can see where the product was made.

Resale Prices Act 1964 and 1976

The manufacturers can supply a recommended price (MRRP), but the seller is not obliged to sell at the recommended price.

Sale and Supply of Goods Act 1994

The vendor must ensure that the goods they sell are of *satisfactory quality*, i.e. defined as the standard which would be regarded by a reasonable person as satisfactory having taken into account the description of the goods, the price and other relevant circumstances and *reasonably fit*, i.e. ensuring that as a vendor the goods can meet the purpose they are claimed to do.

Data Protection Act 1998

The Data Protection Act 1998 exists to ensure that personal information held on record is not mishandled, mismanaged or used inappropriately. It requires every data controller who is processing personal data to make notification unless they are exempt. *Notification* is the process by which a data controller informs the Commissioner of certain details about the processing of personal data carried out by that data controller. Those details are used by the Commissioner to make an entry describing the processing in a register which is available to the public for inspection. (For more information online go to www.dpr.gov.uk.)

Consumer Protection (Distance Selling) Regulations 2000

These are derived from a European Directive and cover the supply of goods and/or services made between suppliers acting in a commercial capacity and consumers, i.e. an individual acting outside a trade business or profession. The Regulations should be of concern to any individual purchasing goods or services by telephone, using the internet, digital TV or mail order catalogues and conversely be of concern to any suppliers dealing with consumers through these media.

Working Time Directive (1998)

The Working Time Directive (WTR) came into force on 1 October 1998. The Regulations implement the European Working Time Directive and parts of the Young Workers Directive which relate to the working time of adolescent workers (workers above the minimum school leaving age but below 18). The basic rights and protections that the Regulations provide are:

- a limit of an average of 48 hours a week which a worker can be required to work (though workers can choose to work more if they want to)
- a limit of an average of 8 hours work in 24 which nightworkers can be required to work
- a right for night workers to receive free health assessments
- a right to 11 hours' rest a day
- a right to a day off each week
- a right to an in-work rest break if the working day is longer than six hours
- a right to four weeks' paid leave per year.

Equal opportunities (EO)

There are five main Acts of Parliament aiming to eliminate discrimination at work. The main purpose of the legislation is to ensure that people are not discriminated against on the basis of their sex, racial origin or disability, either in terms of pay or by any other means:

- **Sex Discrimination Acts 1975 and 1986 (SDA)** and the **Equal Pay Act 1970 (EPA)** aim to eliminate discrimination on the basis of gender. These Acts receive additional support from European law in the form of the Equal Treatment Directive and Treaty of Rome
- **Race Relations Act 1976 (RRA)** aims to eradicate racial discrimination
- **Disability Discrimination Act 1995 (DDA)** aims to eliminate discrimination against disabled people
- **Trade Union and Labour Relations (Consolidation) Act 1992** makes it unlawful for an employer to treat trade union members less favourably than non-members, and vice versa.

Started it	I know and understand the principles of positive communication	I can communicate positively and professionally with the clients	I always use stock items effectively, minimising wastage
☐	☐	☐	☐
I am knowledgeable in the services, treatments and products that the salon offers	I know how to monitor the salon's resources	I always carry out working practices according to the salon's policy	I've covered most of it!
☐	☐	☐	☐
I always explain technical terms eliminating ambiguity and false beliefs	I know when and to whom to refer clients in situations where external assistance is required	I can achieve personal targets in line with salon expectation	I know how to advise, promote and sell other services and products to clients
☐	☐	☐	☐
I know and respect the client's rights: data protection, equal opportunities, anti-discrimination and consumer legislation	Done it all!		CHECKER BOARD ✔
☐	☐		

Self-test section

Quick quiz: a selection of different types of questions to check your knowledge.

Q1 Visa and mastercard are both forms of .... card. — Fill in the blank

Q2 A charge card is the same as a debit card. — True or False

Q3 Which of the following card types are debit cards? — Multi-selection

Loyalty card	☐	1
Switch card	☐	2
American Express card	☐	3
Mastercard	☐	4
Solo card	☐	5
Affinity card	☐	6

Q4 The VAT within a selling price is calculated by deducting 17.5%. — True or False

Q5 The inclusive VAT figure for an item selling for £10 is? — Multi-choice

0.175	☐	a
1.75	☐	b
1.49	☐	c
8.51	☐	d

Q6 You should always take a contact number when making appointments. — True or False

Q7 Which of the following are examples of ineffective use of resources? — Multi-selection

Explaining services and costs to clients on the telephone	☐	1
Discarding excess product after application	☐	2
Overrunning on appointments	☐	3
Turning the lights off in corridors and staff areas	☐	4
Washing up in the dispensary	☐	5
Ordering stock over the telephone	☐	6

Q8 .... retail products are for maintaining hair between visits. — Fill in the blank

Q9 Which of the following stock procedures is the least important within salons? — Multi-choice

Stock control	☐	a
Monitoring wastage	☐	b
Retail product and display cleaning	☐	c
Stock rotation	☐	d

Q10 A job description is a document containing the employee's terms and conditions of employment. — True or False

chapter 11

CREATIVE BUSINESS PROMOTION

Unit H32 Contribute to the planning and implementation of promotional activities

H32.1   Contribute to the planning and preparation of promotional activities

H32.2   Implement promotional activities

H32.3   Participate in the evaluation of promotional activities

Unit H24 Develop and enhance your creative skills

H24.1   Plan and design a range of images

H24.2   Produce a range of creative effects

H24.3   Evaluate your results against the design plan objectives

What do I need to learn?

You need to know and understand:

- the aspects of art and design which can be applied to hairdressing
- how visual effects can be used in promotional activities

What does it mean?

This chapter explains the creative aspects of hairdressing in reference to design concepts and then shows how these can be utilised for commercial applications, e.g. demonstrations, promotions photography and competition.

What do I need to do?

- You need to be able to adapt a range of design concepts into physical applications and develop your presentation skills.

Other info

Related topics and other useful information:

- SMART objectives, selling and sales techniques
- advertising, photography and professional PR

KEY WORDS

Features The functions of what a product or service does
Benefits The results of those functions, i.e. how the product or service will benefit the client

CHECKERBOARD

At the end of this chapter the checkerboard will help to jog your memory on what you have learned and what still remains to be done. Cross them off with a pencil as you cover each of its topics. (See p. 404.)

INTRODUCTION

This chapter combines two optional units and covers the following five main outcomes:

H32   Contribute to the planning and implementation of promotional activities

   H32.1   Contribute to planning and preparation of promotional activities

   H32.2   Implement promotional activities

H24   Develop and enhance your creative skills

   H24.1   Plan and design a range of images

   H24.2   Produce a range of creative images

   H24.3   Evaluate your results against the design plan objectives

The content in this chapter covers the 'fun' aspects of the business: external displays, stage demonstrations, competitions and photo shoots. These events are what a lot of people consider to be the 'glitzy' side of hairdressing. They are also hard work. The immense scale of planning, preparation, honing down on the final effects and stress are draining. But this is your chance to shine and, what's more, it is also good for business.

HAIR CREATIVITY

'Hair creativity' is a term associated with artistic interpretation, geometric understanding and design. It involves a variety of specialist skills:

- appreciation of shape, dimension, image, colour and textures
- understanding balance, imbalance, suitability and application
- expressing creativity by designing, moulding, shaping and forming the hair
- explaining visual interpretations to clients during consultation
- analysing what can be seen and touched
- manipulating and manoeuvring the hair into position.

Francesco Group

Hairstyling can be artistic, practical and scientific. A hairdresser who can bring together the skills of artistic perception, practical ability and sound knowledge will always be in demand by clients. This chapter sets out to capture these essential components, helping you to build a picture from a jigsaw puzzle. Bit by bit, piece by piece, you will discover the *aesthetic building blocks* of style artistry: a pattern of thinking.

How is an image created?

Image is understood by different people in different ways. If we look up the word in a reference book, its meaning is given as: 'representation, likeness, semblance, form, appearance, configuration and structure'. In general terms, an image is examined by our senses:

- sight
- hearing
- touch
- taste
- smell.

These senses enable us to form an overall impression. Let's take a look at one particular image: the salon in which you work. What sort of image does it portray to the public? What do your clients sense?

1 **What do they see?** Is the salon in a basement or upstairs? Is it on the main high street or in a housing estate? What colour schemes have been used inside? Is this carried through in printed information, for instance cards, price lists and service information?

2 **What do they hear?** How are they spoken to on the telephone? How are they greeted when they enter the salon? How are they received, directed and consulted afterwards? What background noise can they hear?

3 **What do they feel?** Can they feel the quality of fresh towels and gowns? Can they feel the level of professional contact in the ways that services and treatments are carried out?

4 **What can they smell?** What is the salon atmosphere like? What do the products used smell like? Do the staff smell clean and hygienic?

5 **What can they taste?** Are they provided with any drink or food while they are in the salon?

The client will judge the levels of quality and professionalism within these individual aspects and form an overall impression. This book does not set out to define a total image for salons, but it should help you in creating total image concepts for your clients.

CREATIVE STYLE DESIGN

Creative style design is a process of logical analysis which sets out to achieve a 'personalised' overall appearance or image. This is rather like following a recipe. We use, mix, add and blend various essential ingredients, which together combine to take on a new form that is completely different from what we started with. If the recipe is followed carefully, the result can be guaranteed. If it is not, a disaster may occur.

A creative stylist can imagine the final effect and then work out the components needed to create that particular look. This increased level of expertise is what separates the creative and artistic stylist, who may be a specialist in certain hairdressing fields, from the average 'all-round' technician. Salons do not need to employ specialists and in many cases larger salon groups prefer to employ staff with all-round abilities. However, in progressive salons, where style directors are employed, we might expect them to pass their skills to others through training and developmental activities.

Analysing the essential components

If you look at the style components in isolation, as building blocks, you will be able to approach the task of style artistry in a logical and systematic way:

- shape and form
- lines and angles
- applied techniques
- apparent texture
- movement and direction
- dimensions, distribution abundance
- colour depth and tone
- condition
- hair type
- work method
- specialised techniques
- moulding, forming and shaping
- application of product.

Shape and form

Gemis

- Does the client have a photograph of the image she wants?
- Will the overall effect be right for the client's type of hair?

The overall effect is created by the structure of the underlying parts of the hair. This image is carefully composed of shape, form, direction and dimension. As hairdressers, you must mentally interpret what you see. Often clients have specific styles in mind and may show you pictures to describe what they want. You must imagine a three-dimensional effect from a two-dimensional illustration. Getting this right, and relaying the information back to the client in a way that is easy to understand, is half the battle. This is an essential part of style composition and professional consultation.

Use your skills to fill in the missing information relating to contour, length, distribution of weight and proportions which will ultimately affect style suitability. Certain styles may be 'right' in that they enhance or accentuate the client's features. Others may be 'wrong' in that unsuitable effects spoil and undermine professional hairdressing disciplines. Having analysed these overall impressions, you can dissect the style further into its component parts.

Lines and angles

- How does the line, the direction in which the hair is positioned, flow?

Hair by Sean Hanna, colour by
Fiona Connolly

Maurice Medcalf

Echoes

The perimeter of the hairstyle is formed by the outside line of the hair. The distance of this line from the scalp forms the depth of the shape. The lines and angles of the hair inside the perimeter affect the finished shape of the style. The hair outline forms semicircles which may be seen from the front, sides and back. The lines within this may be vertical, horizontal or crossing diagonally. These features help to create the visual effect.

Applied techniques

- How will you achieve the finished hairstyle?
- How will this affect the style you create?

Hair can be styled and finished with a variety of techniques. Each has its own specific principles, allowing hair to be crafted and positioned in different ways. You can create a range of different effects by using any one or a combination of **blow drying**, scrunch drying, finger or hand drying, **stretching** or straightening, backbrushing, backcombing, teasing, wet or dry setting, and tonging. These techniques can be used to lift, smooth, bend or flatten hair. Individually or collectively, they contribute to the inner and outer style structure and directions in which the hair moves.

Apparent texture

- What is the texture of the hair?
- What impact will this have on the final effect?

Texture is the term given to the way an object feels: rough or smooth, fine or coarse. In hairdressing, we can see the visual textural effects and we can also feel the textural aspects. At NVQ Level 2 you were required to analyse individual hair textures, but at the higher levels of understanding you need to look holistically at the impact that texture has within and on the whole hairstyle.

Movement and direction

- What movement and direction will the final effect have?
- Are the final effects a flowing shape or disjointed random texture?

The direction that the hairs take, individually and collectively, affects the overall style. The position and line of the hair gives direction to the style. The variation of this line produces direction within the style: the more varied the line direction, the more movement will be seen, showing as texture, wave or curl. A fluid or flowing line gives a softer effect, whereas broken lines of movement create a harder visual impact. The more breaks within the style continuity, the greater the contrasts produced.

Dimension, distribution and abundance

- What are the style dimensions height, depth, etc.?
- What is the natural distribution of the hair?

The dimensions of a style are formed by the height at which the hair is positioned, the width of the bulk of the hair and the depth of the style. The length of the hair gives the visual effects of perimeter line and internal style structure.

The hair's natural abundance and distribution pattern are also important. Height can make round faces look longer; width can broaden a thin face; hair can be angled away from or towards extreme features to make them look bigger or smaller. However, it is essential to remember that there is a limit to what can be done.

The number of actively growing hairs on a client's head is a basic element in deciding on style and shape, as well as taking into consideration texture, length, hair type and patterns of growth. You should consider hair whorls or distinctive growth patterns before attempting to cut or style. This can reduce the chance of error in style planning. There may be places where the hair grows abundantly, or not at all. Alternatively, you may see whole heads of sparse or thickly growing hair. All these eventualities need careful consideration.

Martine Finnegan

Colour depth and tone

- How light or dark is the hair?
- How light or dark can you take it?
- What tonal quality does the hair have?
- Can it be changed to another tonal range?

Lightness and darkness, shade and shadow, harmonious and discordant colour, tints and hues create a varied range of effects which highlight or encompass the hair shape.

Roberta Kneller at Bobs Hair Company
Photograph by John Rawson

Condition

- What is the condition of the hair?
- Can it be improved before styling?

The condition of the hair – its state of health – affects most of the other style components. It directly affects all aspects of style choice and also the durability and manageability of the hairstyle to be created. Poor hair health should be discussed with the client and stabilised or adjusted before any other procedures are carried out.

Roberta Kneller at Bobs Hair Company
Photograph by John Rawson

Hair type

- What type of hair are you working with?
- Imagine the limitations that Oriental hair poses as opposed to European hair.

Hair types fall into three main categories: Caucasian, Mongoloid and African Caribbean.

Caucasian (European) hair is usually loosely waved or straight and can range in colour from light to dark brown. It has a medium, soft texture.

Mongoloid (Asian) hair tends to be straight. Its colour ranges from darkest black to mid-brown. The texture is predominantly coarse so chemical treatments are usually more complex on this type of hair.

African-Caribbean hair is usually tightly kinked or curly. Again, darker hair colouring is more predominant, requiring careful chemical treatment.

Roberta Kneller at Bobs Hair Company
Photograph by John Rawson

Clive Boon at Boons. Photograph by John Rawson

Clive Boon at Boons. Photograph by John Rawson

Anne McGuigan. Photograph by John Rawson

Work method

- Plan the sequence of events which achieve the desired result.
- Always consider safety first.
- Follow manufacturer's instructions.

Methods of creating different style effects vary and there is usually more than one route to achieving the required effect. If you apply your chosen method systematically, it can be repeated if and when required again. You will not be successful if you attempt to achieve style and shape without prior thought and consideration. This kind of haphazard and confused work will usually result in failure. Different and new ways of application can be tried when experimenting on models.

You should ensure that you are comfortable while you work. Minimise stress and strain, keep your hand positions relaxed and make sure your tools are comfortable to hold. Select those that enable you to achieve the specific effect you require.

Methods of application of chemical products are recommended by the manufacturers and these must be followed. They will have tried and tested the best methods before the products are released for sale and public use.

Specialised techniques

- Decide which effects you want to create before you start.
- Is there any special equipment needed to achieve the desired effect?

Hair moulding, shaping, **finger waving**, curling, plaiting, pleating, twisting and weaving can all be used to create special styling effects. Rollers, velcro-rollers, flexible foam-covered rollers, spiral rollers, pins and clips are the tools of hair shaping. You must decide which effects are required before you apply these tools. These are the mechanical aids to hair styling and are additional to the chemical tools and techniques now available.

Moulding, forming and shaping

- Shaping and forming – cutting and moulding.
- Hair symmetry/asymmetry should balance the final effect.

Some types of hair can now be styled in ways which were previously impossible. Unruly hair can now be tamed and difficult hair can achieve realistic shapes. To shape and form hair is to cut and mould – to create. This involves the distribution of portions of hair into fitting outlines and positions. Proportioning the hair means arranging and fitting it to the underlying head and face foundation. The outline shape or silhouette can be viewed from different directions and the balanced symmetry of the hair shape should generally be pleasing and harmonious.

Application of product

- Select the styling product to achieve the desired effect.
- Select the finishing product to achieve the desired effect.

Goldwell

Roberta Kneller at Bobs Hair Company
Photograph by John Rawson

Special and careful consideration needs to be given to hair products. Their contribution to styling makes them an additional hair-crafting tool. As well as the vast range of shampoos and washes, internal and external conditioners, dressings and moisturisers available, you can now create texture, volume and movement by using a variety of gels, sculpting creams, moulding mousses, fixing waves, hair thickeners and other hair controllers. To gain the maximum benefit from these products, it is vital to know how they should be used and applied. Always study the manufacturer's instructions.

Style design

In day-to-day salon work, i.e. commercial hairdressing, hair stylists seldom have the opportunity to let creativity have free rein. (At this point I can hear several people take a sharp intake of breath.) Commercial hairdressing is when your clients believe that you are being creative. The truth is that most of the day-to-day salon work is very routine, dare I say mundane. It is only when creating effects for promotional activities or special events that the creative juices start to flow. So why is that?

Cheynes Training

Have you ever looked closely and studied great fashion hair images? (I now use the term images instead of photographs.) What is it about images that gives *impact* and appeal? Conversely, what is it about commercial work that seems routine? You could say that it is make-up or clothes. Is it the lighting, the ambience or location? All these factors contribute to the final effect, but as yet we haven't been looking at the hair!

Balance or imbalance?

- Does balance relate to symmetry?
- Does imbalance relate to asymmetry?
- If balance and symmetry convey harmony, do imbalance and asymmetry convey discord?

The vast majority of commercial work undertaken in salons today leads us, as hairdressers, to ensure that both sides of the haircut are of an even length, that weight is proportionally distributed, that degrees of curl or straightness are maintained throughout the hairstyle. What we are required to do by the majority of clients is to produce a finished effect that may have originated from a picture; that is modified to suit the client and become the perfect example of symmetry. This may be a *nice* style, but does it still have the same impact as the original picture? Why not? (Well, we had to take the fringe shorter so the client could see out, or we needed to calm down the volume so that it would be suitable for work, etc.)

What is often happening with the best fashion images is that we automatically convert an impactive, dynamic, asymmetrical image into a recessive, passive, symmetrical style. If you have never considered this before, start analysing your favourite style images. Going back to the questions *Does balance relate to symmetry?* and *Does imbalance relate to asymmetry?* the truth is that the best images, which are often asymmetrical in appearance, contain a visually excellent artistic balance. The diagrams try to explain further this unlikely concept. In the first figure we have a 'seesaw' with equal masses on each of the opposing ends. As these masses are of equal weight we arrive at an equilibrium, an apparent balance which is symmetrical and harmonised. In the second figure we have a seesaw which has a weight on one end and another heavier weight counterbalanced across the pivotal point. We now arrive at another form of equilibrium or balance that is asymmetrical and discordant. Looking at the two figures in turn, which one catches your eye more readily? This is the attention span afforded by your clients when looking through magazines and that brief opportunity that both PR and marketing have in which to sell.

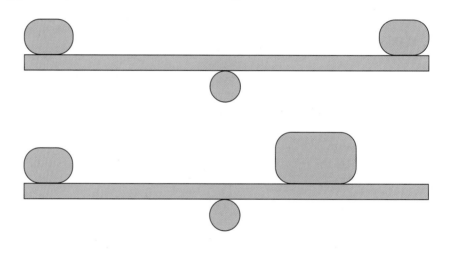

PROMOTING THE SALON

Your salon may already organise some form of promotion, for example, a colour or perm incentive. During quiet times, when the salon takings are expected to be at their lowest, offering a discounted price for colouring or a perm may attract new clients to the salon, thereby increasing revenue. However, there are also other forms of promotion that your salon might want to consider, including demonstrations and advertising. In order to promote your services, you need to recognise how they are perceived by prospective clients. To do this you need to consider each service in terms of its features and its benefits:

- **features** are the functions – what the service does
- **benefits** are the results of the functions – what the service achieves.

For example, suppose you hope to persuade a client to spend £30 on a cut and blow dry. Why should she do so? What are the benefits of the service?

- The feature is a precision cut.
- The benefits are keeping shape and easier home styling – the client must decide whether the payment of £30 is justified by these benefits.

Consider a second example: application of a semi-permanent colour. In this case the *feature* is that the colour is not permanent and is applied in a conditioning base. The *benefit* is that it will wash out after six to eight shampoos and meanwhile it will create shine. Knowledge of service and product features enables you to sell your clients the benefits. You thereby create a need and once the client has accepted the need you are in a good position to make the sale.

The first step is therefore to gain a thorough knowledge of each service and product available in the salon and to convert this knowledge into a recognition of the features and benefits in each case. The next step is to inform the potential market by means of promotion. Successful promotion requires careful planning. Time and thought need to be given to each aspect.

Identify the objectives

What do you want the promotion to achieve? Is it to attract new clients, for example, to increase colours or perms, or to increase retail sales? Whatever the objectives, it is most effective always to concentrate the promotion on a *single aim*.

Decide on the type of promotion

There are many possibilities and here are a few:

- offering an introductory discount to new clients
- offering a service with another service, for example, a complementary conditioning treatment with colouring
- introducing a retail product, for example, offering a free retail conditioner for permed hair with each perm treatment
- implementing an incentive scheme for staff who reach sales targets in product sales and treatments
- demonstrating your services through a 'hair show', either at the salon or at a venue chosen to suit the target group.

Prepare promotional activities

It is best to write an outline or plan of your promotion. From that you will be able to identify each area requiring preparation.

Order stock and promotional materials

You may need to have leaflets printed or place an advertisement to inform potential clients. You may need additional materials: for instance, for a perm

Wella/James Kimber Salon, Birmingham

ACTIVITY: FEATURES AND BENEFITS

With your colleagues, select six of the services provided by your salon and jointly consider what the features and benefits to the client are in each case. Make a record of the collective opinions and keep this within your portfolio for future reference.

Key skills: Communication

2.1 Take part in discussions
2.2 Produce written materials

REMEMBER

When running a salon promotion, everyone needs to be informed about the campaign. Make sure before the promotion is rolled out that there are sufficient staff meetings to make everyone aware of the event.

promotion you will need to order additional perms. Most product houses will provide advice and merchandising support.

Inform staff

Ensure that all staff are fully aware of the promotion. This may require refresher training, for example, in product knowledge. Your presentation to the staff needs to make them enthusiastic. They will then be able to sell the idea to clients.

ACTIVITY: PROMOTIONAL EVENTS

With your colleagues, identify three promotional activities that could be introduced into your salon.

1 Work out the costs involved in respect of people's time, resources and materials.

2 Schedule the event campaign.

3 Present the information to the management.

Key skills: Application of number

2.1 Collect and record data

2.2 Tackle problems

2.3 Interpret and present data

Inform your target group

Select the best medium of communication. You may inform clients verbally. You may try a mail shot, distribute leaflets, display posters or notices, or advertise in local papers or selected magazines. In any written literature, remember to highlight the features and benefits of the service.

Evaluate the outcome

After the promotion, evaluate its success by monitoring your business. If you have been successful, sales will have increased. You may find that promoting a specific service – perming, for example – will generate an increase in salon revenue overall. This is obviously good in itself, but to obtain the true result of the promotion, the increased business should be set against the initial objective. Thus, if the aim of the promotion were to increase the number of perms during February, you would need to know exactly how many clients had perms in that month and how many you would have expected without the promotion.

Record the results

To make full use of the promotion result, you need to keep a permanent record of the facts. This record can then be referred to later. Gradually you will identify strengths and weaknesses and be able to repeat or amend the promotion, depending upon the results.

Date: ....

Promotional Outline: ....

Date .... Leaflets Mailshot (No.).......................................
.... Posters (No.)..
.... Advertisement (Type/Place): ....

Leaflets Returned: Week ending: .... No.: ....
Week ending: .... No.: ....
Week ending: .... No.: ....
Week ending: .... No.: ....

New Clients Recorded:

Revenue Increases: Cutting:...%
Colour: ....%
Perm: ....%
Sales: ....%
Beauty: ....%

Comments: ....
....

Overall Success Rating: ....

Hairdressing demonstration

Hairdressing demonstrations form a very important part in training and promotion. Displays, both of the skill of the hairdresser's technique and the finished style that she produces, provide opportunities for increasing sales. Informally, of course, every person working in the salon is continually demonstrating their skills from shampooing through to technical services, but there is also a place for the formal demonstration. To organise a demonstration, you again need to keep to a structure in your planning:

● **Identify the objectives**. What is the *purpose* of the demonstration? Is it, for example, staff training or salon promotion?

● **Prepare the resources**. What resources do you need? How many people do you expect to attend?

Select the venue

Is the demonstration going to be carried out in the salon, or at a local hall or hotel?

● Will the audience be able to see the demonstration area? Are lighting and sound provided? Can you make use of a raised platform or stage, panoramic mirrors, or revolving hydraulic chairs?

● Are shampooing and dressing facilities available?

● Do you need to arrange transport to the venue for your models and equipment?

A hair show and demonstration
Best of British

- Is the venue easily accessible to your audience by public transport? Are there parking facilities?
- Will you offer refreshments?

Set the budget

You may have a budget available within salon expenditure. If not, you can charge for tickets to pay for your expenses. To calculate the ticket price, you need to divide your total expenses by the number of people you *expect* to attend (not the number you *hope* will attend!). For example, if your expenses total £500 for an expected audience of 50, the ticket price will be £10. You will need to sell 50 tickets to cover your costs – if you sell more, of course, you will make a small profit. Your costs need to include:

- fee for your guest artist, where applicable, and payments to models
- payments to a make-up artist or clothes stylist, where applicable
- hire of the venue
- hire of lighting, sound and equipment, transport costs
- cost of refreshments for demonstrators, models and audience
- marketing costs, including advertising and printing of tickets and programmes
- staff costs, either in salary or cost to the salon of giving time in lieu.

Plan the demonstration

Consider the model, the content, the method and the explanation. Depending on the scale of the demonstration, you may need to build in opportunities for the audience to participate and ask questions. This is not possible when demonstrating to a very large number of people, but good communication skills are always essential in creating a rapport with your audience.

Expect the unexpected

To maintain control of the event, your preparation needs to include contingency plans in the event of things going wrong. For example, what would you do:

- if your model did not arrive on time?
- if your guest artist was delayed?
- if there was a power failure?
- if there was a security evacuation?
- if you did not achieve your desired result?

Give thought to each component of the event and be mentally prepared for any eventuality. You will then feel confident and your demonstration will be a success.

Make a time schedule

Once you have planned the event, it is advisable to make a checklist with a time schedule. To do this, start with the event time and work backwards, for example:

REMEMBER: STORYBOARDING ✔

Be professional. Always create a storyboard of the event processes and actions, starting with the listings of equipment and resources, people, contact information and other external factors, right through to the expected running pattern of the event.

During the planning of the promotion, always remember to update your storyboard in line with any changes.

6.00 pm	The event. Guest artist will demonstrate the latest long hair fashion.
5.30 pm	Facility open to the audience.
5.00 pm	Final check: platform, demonstration chair, lighting, microphone/sound. Feed models and platform artist.
4.30 pm	Check platform tools and equipment. Prepare tray: this should contain everything that the artist will use during her demonstration. Check that all sprays work. (For a cutting demonstration it is a good idea to include a plaster – even the best hairdressers cut their fingers occasionally.)
3.30 pm	Model to be made up.
3.00 pm	Arrival of make-up artist.
2.00 pm	Arrival of model and guest artist.
12.00 noon	Organiser to arrive at venue. Arrange eating, erect display material. Check preparation area.

Alongside this schedule, make a checklist of each item needed or the event. Remember, planning ahead ensures smooth running.

Advertising

Advertising is always a useful way of promoting your salon's services. It is important to define the purpose of the advertisement so that you can choose the most appropriate form of advertising:

- Do you want to attract new customers?
- Do you want to advertise a new service?
- Do you want to increase the salon's profile?
- Do you want to increase retail sales?
- Do you want to maintain loyalty with regular customers?
- Do you want to draw customers' attention to other services on offer?

There are many different forms of advertising, including:

- magazines
- newspapers
- directories
- leaflets/posters
- local radio
- calendars.

Advertising can be very expensive. Therefore, the form of advertising you choose will also depend on the budget available. If you decide to advertise your business through printed media, careful consideration must be given to the content of the message you wish to convey. As this is a very special and important form of promotion you do need to consider whether the content as well origination are handled by the professionals. For many salons the *printed* image is the only one that the potential client gets to see. Therefore the graphics, images and text all need to harmonise with the image of the salon. The idea is that the reader of the advert will have

ACTIVITY:
LOCAL RESEARCH

Make a list of all the venues that can accommodate a seated audience of over 100 people in your local area. What additional facilities do they have to offer?

Key skills: Communication
2.1 Take part in discussions
2.2 Produce written materials

received enough information to conjure up a *feeling* of the business without even knowing anything else about it.

Local newspapers and business directories provide comprehensive advertising services, hence combining all of the individual considerations listed below. However, their ability to get to know the needs of your particular business are poor. Here is a simplified overview of the different processes involved:

- *Commercial artist* – responsible for creating graphical illustrations through image manipulation and typography.
- *PR consultant/agency* – responsible for content and media management.
- *Reprographics* – the intermediaries, between the originators and printer, who create the film or digital output.
- *Printer* – the company employed to produce the finished material.

Public relations

Public relations (PR) is an effective tool with which to promote the business or product. It targets the media best suited to the company image or product profile, hence bringing the finished package to the eye of the consumer and thus increasing your business potential. Salons can opt to handle their own PR or employ the services of a PR constancy.

DIY PR

With the right contacts and more importantly the time, it is possible to promote the business effectively as a team. However, be aware that dealing with the press is not necessarily a simple case of a phone call and then a letter. It is a question of knowing whom to contact, working on them and then how to get your message across. E-mail is particularly useful medium for putting information on to the right desk and in front of the right eyes. However, it is also a question of degree: How much promotion do you want? Is it for one specific project or is it ongoing? If the latter, then be prepared for PR to take up a lot of your time.

> **REMEMBER** ✔
>
> If you make contact with any representative of the local press, remember to get their direct e-mail address for swift access to the 'right' pair of eyes!

The press

Trade and consumer press are completely different so it is therefore essential that they are each approached in the appropriate manner.

Trade press Aimed at other businesses within the same industry, the trade press is interested in news items within the trade (e.g. new salons, trends, techniques, etc., plus charity events and product launches). It is also very warm to launching new photographic collections, showcasing salon interiors and conducting business profiles. On the whole, trade journalists tend to be easier to deal with and more accessible. After all, they are already sympathetic to your salon's product and require your salon's help to fill their pages.

Consumer press Aimed at the general public, consumer magazines reach a great number of people who may never have heard of you or your product, but are about to do so through effective PR. Public relations is about editorial endorsement. This is quite different from advertising. It means the journalist is giving your salon magazine space without expecting any

Press Information

For Release: Saturday 26th October, 1996

Patrick Cameron at "Salon Live"

Patrick Cameron will be showing his only preview to his 1997 hair collection at "Salon Live" in Wembley's Grand Hall Theatre.

Patrick will use the dramatic visual frame of the "tango" to take his show back to the basics of the art of dressing hair. "This show will be different from anything I have done before" says Patrick. "I will be exploring the different aspects of femininity". Deep finger waves and skilfully placed braids will create a new texture in Patrick's work. The shapes and the balance presented will demonstrate a new theatrical image of timeless elegance.

The costumes will reflect the same theme of texture provided by intricate beadwork and rich colours to compliment the strong shapes of the hair cuts.

The show will take inspiration from the Hispanic and Latin cultures. The "tango" theme will provide a sumptuous costume drama with all the glamour of a Paris couture show.   Ends.

A press release Patrick Cameron

payment for it. Such editorial endorsement can be much harder to secure, but the benefits can be huge. The consumer press is not interested in new staff appointments, but it does want to know about innovative techniques, upcoming seasonal trends, latest product advancements and new salons. Happily, more and more consumer magazines are coming round to the idea that the consumer is interested in her hair, and, through increased hairdressing standards and higher stylist profiles, are becoming increasingly confident in our industry. Magazines now have hair supplements banded to their issues and these have to be filled.

Hair salons and product companies with effective PR are the ones who are helping to fill these supplements and hair features, supplying press releases to the appropriate journalists outlining new techniques and products, photographic material, seasonal trends and quotes.

Employing a PR

Communication on an ongoing basis with the relevant journalist is the secret to grabbing column inches. Employing a professional PR consultant can do this and has many advantages, with just one disadvantage: involving your company in an additional monthly salary. However, this disadvantage can build your business, lift its profile, bring new clients through the salon door, sell more products and make you more money. So will management see this additional monthly salary worth the burden? They might – so long as the right PR is employed for the business. The secret is to approach the right, potential sources. Ask journalists whom they would recommend. Start with the trade press or, if it's consumer coverage you're after, speak to one or two beauty editors on the magazines you think the business would be right for. The journalist will feel flattered that you have asked for her opinion. Remember, journalists are dealing with professional PRs on a regular basis and will know which ones are on the ball.

When the PR is interviewed they will give samples of their work, i.e. press cuttings of editorial secured with other clients. This provides management with an idea of the type of editorial they are able to achieve – that is providing there is sufficient material for them to work with. A PR will provide the salon with a tailor-made proposal that outlines what can be achieved for the company and a rough time scale. Also ascertain approximately how much time will be spent per month on your account.

The salon must know which other clients the PR is working for. This ensures that there is no conflict of interests. While it is not necessarily a disadvantage for a PR to handle clients in the same area of business (e.g. hair salons), it certainly could be if those clients included some of your direct competition. The business will need to know exactly what the fee includes so there are no hidden surprises. For example, most PR fees are quoted exclusive of expenses. However, exactly what these expenses consist of and approximately how much they will be each month needs to be known.

A PR should be asked how often management reports are provided. A good PR will draw up a report every four to six weeks – unless mutually agreed otherwise. The PR should have a clear brief in terms of what is expected out of the relationship. This is normally in writing and will ensure a complete understanding on both sides. A contract should be agreed on and signed by both parties. This provides for one month's notice to be given on either side. Remember, while the impossible can be achieved, miracles take a little longer. In other words, ensure you have enough material for a PR to work with: inspired ideas, photographic work, etc. Is the PR on the same wavelength as you? Does she seem to speak your language? No matter how good the PR is, if there are personality clashes then the relationship will be a difficult one.

How much will PR cost?

Fees vary and are governed by a number of factors: the amount of time spent on the business; the level of press required e.g. trade press, consumer press, local press or overseas press; how active the PR will be on other aspects of the business, e.g. staff recruitment, advertising, staff training, size of the business.

A fee of £700 a month will buy basic PR consumer and trade press for a hair salon. A fee of £2500 per month is a starting point for a product company, depending on its size. But remember that, besides time, the company will also be buying the PR's invaluable knowledge of the industry and her magazine contacts. Just as clients buy your expertise, the firm is purchasing that of another experienced and trained professional. Public relations can be the making of a business. So long as management keep an open mind to it, you could help secure the services of the right PR consultant and you could be working together with that consultant to help achieve both your own and the salon's goals.

HAIR INSPIRATION

1-7 These choppy cuts feature lots of disconnection, razored sections and Eighties pop star credentials in the form of rockabilly quiffs and textured fringes. A fringe is one of the easiest and least traumatic ways to transform a hairstyle you're bored with. Heavy block fringes can be severe so choose a lighter, feathered version if you're a first-time fringer. You should also steer clear of heavy fringes if you have a round or square shaped face. Long faces can be shortened to more balanced proportions with a fringe.

8 Naturally straight hair can be transformed into full bodied curls and waves, providing you have the right tools and a bit of know-how. Prior to blowdrying with a diffuser use a curl activating product through the lengths and ends of the hair. Gently blowdry using your fingertips to tease curls into place. For extra definition use curling tongs on two-inch sections of hair picked at random.

Hair: Nick Malenko, Midlands Hairdresser of the Year, Royston Blythe, Wolverhampton
Make-up: Jackie Barnard
Photography: Anthony Mascolo

Bend Me, Shape Me

Forget poker straight locks – texture is back with a vengeance and curls are no longer under wraps…

A magazine spread Hair Flair

Photography and photo sessions

Why do it?

The power of a good photograph is undeniable. It instantly says more about your work and the image you want to project than any free editorial or paid for advertising. However, while fun, photo sessions are not easy. They can be time consuming, expensive and sometimes disappointing if not properly co-ordinated. So how do you go about things? First, ask yourself why the salon would want to invest in an expensive photo session:

- to attract more clients into the salon through coverage in the consumer press?
- to raise your industry profile via the trade press?
- for salon advertising?

Next, study the magazines and newspapers in which you hope to have your salon's work published and check the sort of photographs they use. Individual titles will have a distinctive house style: the type of work published in *Vogue* and *Elle* is very different from that in teenage magazines, and a world apart from local newspapers.

A model portfolio spread Alistair Hughes

REMEMBER: ART DIRECTION ✓

Define your look. Questions to consider are:

- Will the look be classic, fashionable, avant-garde or themed?
- Will the finished effect be the result of a process, say a colouring, cutting or other technique, or created by specific products?
- Will the look have more impact in black and white or colour?
- What clothes and accessories are best suited to the look?
- What image effect are you trying to create – natural, classic, dramatic or romantic?
- Should the photographer have free rein in the creative aspects of lighting, props, camera angles, backdrops and effects?

Putting it together

Once you've decided on the look you're going to go for, start to create your photographic team.

The model Picking a suitable model can be a tricky task. A common mistake is to choose a pretty girl with unsuitable hair or vice versa; ideally she should have a combination of both. Remember that a conventionally pretty face isn't always photogenic, so study each model's photographic portfolio carefully:

- Look for regular features and bright, clear eyes. Avoid prominent chins and noses, over-full lips or dark circles under the eyes. The skin should be clear (even the most skilful of make-up artists won't be able to disguise completely obvious blemishes), and she should have a long, slim, unlined neck and a good profile to give the photographer maximum scope.

- Ensure the hair suits the type of work you plan to do. Most professional models won't allow you to cut, colour or perm their hair, so your choice needs to be the right length, shade, texture and style. The model must also have the right features to fit your look – a sweet face is no good if you want an aggressive punk image.
- Always use professional models.
- Call a casting and take polaroids of all the girls you like and make notes to refresh your memory later.
- Don't book more than four models for a one-day session – rushed results won't work.
- *Never* cut, colour or perm a professional model's hair (even if she agrees) without checking with her agency first.

The photographer Always opt for someone who specialises in hair, beauty or fashion photography. See as many as you can, with portfolios, to check their ideas are in tune with yours. Confirm the booking in writing and brief him/her in detail on the image and 'feeling' you are aiming for.

A photographic studio Mahogany

Saks Premier Collection

The make-up artist A good make-up artist is vital. Bad make-up will ruin a shot. If you can afford it, always use a professional, but don't ask for the impossible. A make-up artist, however good, can't completely change a model's face. Research and brief a make-up artist as you would a photographer.

Clothes and accessories Decide on the time of year you hope to have the photographs published and bear in mind that most monthly magazines work three months ahead. What type of clothes work best? Obviously this depends on the image you want to achieve and whether you are working with a professional stylist. If you don't want your shots to date too quickly then go for neutral fashions that don't scream out a particular season. Necklines should be simple and jewellery effective, but don't overload – if in doubt, leave out.

Plan of action

Think about the designs and put together a storyboard by cutting out images you like from magazines. Once you've decided on the styles, work out how you are going to achieve them. By creating a theme for your collection you'll have more chance of greater coverage.

Teamwork is the key to a successful photographic session, so let those involved know exactly what they will be doing. Remember, studio time is valuable. Do any major hair preparation work before the shoot.

Draw up a list of the equipment and products you'll need, and check them off when packing your session tool kit. The general rule is to take everything – and then add anything else that might come in handy.

On the day

Have a clear idea of the looks you want to create but have in mind several alternatives as back-up. Pay attention to detail and make sure you see a polaroid of every style before the photographer starts snapping in earnest. Picking up on faults not obvious to the naked eye isn't always easy. Those to look out for include gaps in the style, stray hairs on clothes/face, rumpled clothes, pins showing or too much product/make-up.

Be decisive and don't settle for second best. If you're not completely happy with a shot, say so nicely. Always check through the camera; you'll be surprised how different something looks through the lens.

Keep backgrounds simple so as not to distract from the hair. The golden rule is slightly darker for blondes and lighter for darker hair so the shape shows up more clearly. Make sure hair is well lit and the photographer isn't indulging in some fancy lighting effects that show off his artistry rather than yours.

What's the price?

Cost is a four-letter word – so take a deep breath here. If using a top professional photographer and shooting in London, the minimum rates will be £1500 (and the price rises according to the photographer's fame). Then you've got the cost of the studio, models, make-up artist and travel expenses on top. As with most things, it's cheaper outside London. Keep a tight control on budget as costs can easily escalate. Often photographers' quotes only cover their time on the day, so check if heating, lighting and food are on top. Check also film, developing and reprint costs and remember to be clear about how you intend to use your shots. Prices can change depending on whether you use the photographs for one-off editorial, general PR or advertising.

Get the agreed charges in writing beforehand, and don't try to pull a fast one. If you say the shots are for one-off editorial, but use them for PR instead and get found out, you could be in breach of copyright and be sued – and that's expensive.

Getting the size right

Size matters. Individual publications will specify how they prefer to receive photographic material, but those most widely accepted are:

prints – shot on black-and-white or colour film, the best size is 10 in × 8 in (though 7 in × 5 in is acceptable)

colour transparencies – medium format 2.25 inches square or large format 5 in × 4 in transparencies, particularly if you're hoping for a cover (these films are more expensive). Regular 35 mm is also well accepted but these images can sometimes become grainy if blown up fairly big.

Magazines always prefer original transparencies as they reproduce better. However, these can get lost or misplaced, so it's best to get good duplicates to send out and hang on to your originals. The exception here is if your photograph is to be used on a cover. Never send glass-mounted slides. Journalists hate them as the glass always breaks (no matter how carefully packed) and scratches the transparencies, so making the image unpublishable.

Examples of different photo formats

35 mm transparency

60 × 70 mm transparency

Hairdressing competitions

Entering hairdressing competitions can be great fun and a great motivator for staff. It is however, very challenging and requires a lot of personal discipline, dedication and thorough practice in order to achieve the right look that will catch the eye of the adjudicators. Competitions vary enormously between local, regional and national and will also vary in the way that entrants partake. For example, the L'Oréal Colour trophy is a national competition. It is initially shortlisted at regional level by a photographic entry dossier. Entry dossiers are sent out to participating salons early in the new year. The closing date for finished dossiers is early March. After a preliminary judging, selected styling teams are invited to take part in the regional finals, where entrants have to demonstrate their work 'live' in front of a large audience and against the clock. Winners from each of the regions are then invited to take part in the *grand* final in a top London hotel in late spring.

Conversely, NHF competitions at regional levels allow all comers to participate on the competition floor. Finalists from individual regions are then invited to take part at national level. The British Hairdressing Awards (owned and presented by *Hairdressers Journal*) are again a national competition that is shortlisted by photographic entry. In this competition entrants take part in a variety of categories ranging from Regional, Avant Garde, Artistic Team, London and British Hairdresser.

REMEMBER

The Hairdressing and Beauty Industry Authority (Habia) have issued the following tips to help you get started before you step on to the competition floor.

- Watch the trade press for news about when and where competitions are taking place.
- Go along to competitions and watch what happens. See what type of work is successful in competitions and keep an eye on emerging trends and fashions.
- Ask trainers and tutors for advice. Also take advice from people who have entered or know about competitions.
- Read the rules carefully and know exactly what is required.
- Take time to find exactly the right model, one with the right type of hair, the right age and with looks that fit into the competition rules. A beautiful girl with good deportment helps considerably, but if her hairline is not up to scratch she may put you out of the competition.
- Understand that competition work is very different from salon work. Colouring in particular can often be a lot stronger on a competition floor than the salon floor.
- Regular competitors stress the importance of preparation.
- Check and prepare your equipment.
- Take time to find the right model particularly if you are trying to express a specific image or theme.
- Product knowledge and application is imperative. Never attempt to style a model's hair without testing the product's effects on her hair beforehand.
- Practise, practise and practise.

Many hairdressing organisations, colleges and major manufacturers run or sponsor competitions. If this is something that you would like your salon to be involved in, encourage your salon to run an in-house competition first. This is a good way of 'acclimatising' your staff to the pressures of competing.

Regular entry to competition keeps you up to date. You get a feel for the emerging undercurrents, fashions and trends, which is vitally important. The motivation gained by attending competitions is infectious and then passed on to younger members of staff. Competitions give you the opportunity to see what your competitors are doing. There is always something to be learnt by watching other salon teams and stylists at work.

Live competition (on the day)

You have prepared your model and you have practised the look for hours. Now the day of the competition has arrived. Stage fright has struck. Keep calm, there is nothing to worry about. Everyone, including the 'great names', suffers from nerves at this time – not just the stylists but the models too.

The style you do must conform to the competition rules: for example, if a day style is required, don't go over the top with elaborate hair up or hair ornaments. If it's free style, a wider choice is allowed. Once you and your fellow competitors have finished your models, you'll be asked to leave the floor so the judges can take over. These people are normally qualified hairdressers, hair and beauty journalists and, occasionally, previous winners. They proceed to choose the most competently designed and dressed head of hair. Depending on the type of competition, the judges will award points covering all aspects of style ranging from technical detail, shape, movement, use of colour and artistic adaptation.

The British Hairdressing Awards

The British Hairdressing Awards were created in 1985 and have become hairdressing's most prestigious and high-profile competition. Almost every top salon in the nation enters the Awards. For the winners it can be the highlight of – or indeed the launch pad for – a long and glittering career. In fact the Awards have been the making of many of our top stylists, as well as raising the standard of hairdressing photographic work overall in this country. Since 1990 the British Hairdressing Awards have been owned and presented by *Hairdressers Journal* (previously the event belonged to its sister publication *Hair And Beauty* magazine). Schwarzkopf UK, however, has been the exclusive sponsor since the Awards' inception.

How do they work?

There are 16 Awards categories: eight regional categories; six specialist categories (Newcomer and Artistic Team of the Year, plus Men's, Afro, Avant-Garde and Session Hairdresser of the Year); the more recent British Film Hairdresser of the Year; and the ultimate Award, British Hairdresser of the Year. Entrants are judged primarily on photographic work – they are required to supply four prints for an initial judging session, then another

Brendan O'Sullivan, Creative Director
Regis. Pure Collection 2003

four if they make it through to the finals – and on a resumé of the past year's show and seminar work they have conducted, plus trade and consumer press coverage they have obtained.

You can enter any category you like (so long as you meet the relevant requirements), except the British Film, Session and British categories. The winner of British Film is determined by experts within that particular field. Finalists in Session and British are nominated by a panel of trade and consumer hair and beauty experts. Session stylists are judged on their professional portfolio. British finalists are judged on their **portfolio** of eight photographic prints and, separately, on a resumé of their contribution to raising the profile of the British hairdressing industry over the past 12 months. On occasions, it has been the latter that has decided the overall winner.

There are two judging stages. First-round entries are judged by members of the British Hairdressing Awards Hall of Fame – hairdressers who have won an Award three times, plus honorary members, including Vidal Sassoon and Robert Lobetta. They have the invariably difficult task of whittling down each category to six finalists, examining each portfolio for technical expertise and commercial flair.

The second round judging takes place when finalists have submitted their additional four prints, and when nominees in the Session and British categories have submitted their portfolios and resumés. At this stage, the jury consists of around 30 prominent hair and beauty expert editors of consumer and trade magazines; for example, dignitaries from hairdressing associations and leading salon owners who have not participated in the Awards themselves. Their scores determine the overall winner in each category.

Finally, bringing months of nail-biting tension to an end, the results are announced at the British Hairdressing Awards presentation ceremony at the end of November in a top West End hotel. This is the time when the hairdressing industry turns out in its most sumptuous and glittering force – national press and TV cameras now cover the event as a matter of course. For some of the finalists the evening will inevitably end in disappointment. For 16 others, however, it will mark the beginning of a year of celebration and widespread recognition.

How can I win?

Ultimately, there is no recipe for guaranteed Awards success – who can predict what will catch the eye of the judges? However, experience shows that following certain photographic guidelines could possibly increase your chances of winning.

Be professional with your portfolio
Using a professional photographer, make-up artist and, above all, professional models is a must. Gone are the days when you could get away with taking four snapshots of your best friend with your back garden as a location. (Admittedly, some salons still do – but they never make the finals.) The more successful Awards entrants have long since wised up to the fact that an initial investment in people who will reflect their own hairdressing work to best effect usually reaps dividends later on down the

line. 'It would never occur to me not to use a professional model,' says Trevor Sorbie, 'even though they can cost me an arm and a leg.' Has the principle paid off? Well, Trevor has won British Hairdresser of the Year no less than four times so far.

Work to a theme

There is a theory (and recent results would seem to bear it out) that a portfolio of pictures shot specifically for the Awards stands a better chance of success than a random collection of prints culled from various shoots throughout the year. Certainly, judges seem to respond better to a set of pictures where there is an overall theme – all hair up, for example, or all black-and-white shots, as they tend to be easier on the eye and 'work' as a collection. Also, it shows you've really thought about your entry and how best to show off your talent.

Don't go overboard

With the exception of the Avant-Garde category, it's a pretty safe bet that the judges will be looking not only for technical excellence but also commercial relevance. In other words, fantasy hairstyles will not win you marks. Instead, try to have your pictures reflect current hair trends, or at least display images that your clients could actually respond to. That means wearable styles, great colour, beautiful perms and good all-round suitability to current tastes and fashions.

Started it ☐	I know and understand the principles of positive communication ☐	I can recognise buying signals and have good selling skills ☐	I understand the SMART objectives principles ☐
I can identify the features and benefits of services and products ☐	I know how to negotiate, reaching a mutually beneficial conclusion ☐	I have good presentation and demonstration skills ☐	I've covered most of it! ☐
I know how to evaluate promotional activities ☐	I can present information in a variety of applicable formats ☐	I understand principles of hair art and design ☐	I know how to work within budgetary constraints ☐
I know how legislation can have an impact on external business activities ☐	I prepare design plans for presentation / promotional activities ☐	Done it all! ☐	CHECKER BOARD ✔

Self-test section

Quick quiz: a selection of different types of questions to check your knowledge

Q1 Selling opportunities will occur when the features and _ _ _ _ _ _ _ of products are explained to the client.

Fill in the blank

Q2 Business will normally develop without promotion or advertising.

True or False

Q3 Which of the following are types of external, public promotion?

Multi-selection

Radio advertising	☐	1
Hairdressing competitions	☐	2
Hairdressing demonstrations	☐	3
Point-of-sale material	☐	4
Reception displays	☐	5
Merchandising	☐	6

Q4 PR is a term which refers to professional media handling.

True or False

Q5 What is the most cost-effective way of selling services to clients?

Multi-selection

External demonstrations	☐	1
Internal promotions	☐	2
Client consultation	☐	3
Point-of-sale material	☐	4

Q6 Merchandising is a retailing strategy.

True or False

Q7 Which of the following are effective methods of merchandising?

Multi-selection

'Shelf talkers'	☐	1
Electronic point of sale	☐	2
Backwash products	☐	3
'Take ones'	☐	4
Trial samples	☐	5
'Minimalistic' retail product displays	☐	6

Q8 The maximum 'hot spot' selling position is found at _ _ _ _ _ _ _ _ level.

Fill in the blank

Q9 Why do 'in-salon' displays have limited effectiveness in retailing?

Multi-choice

They don't stimulate interest or enquiries	☐	1
They must always be professionally designed and built	☐	2
They stop the customer from picking and handling the products	☐	3
They tend to blend in with the background	☐	4

Q10 The 'one-stop shop' strategy is designed to encourage people to buy all their household needs from under one roof.

True or False

self-test answers

Chapter 1

Answers

Q1   Hazard
Q2   True
Q3   1 3 6
Q4   False
Q5   C
Q6   False
Q7   2 4
Q8   First aid
Q9   D
Q10   True

Chapter 2

Answers

Q1   Catagen
Q2   False
Q3   1 2 4
Q4   True
Q5   D
Q6   True
Q7   2 3
Q8   Dermis
Q9   C
Q10   True

Chapter 3

Answers

Q1   Holding
Q2   True
Q3   1 2 4
Q4   True
Q5   D
Q6   True
Q7   3 5
Q8   Baseline
Q9   C
Q10   True

Chapter 4

Answers

Q1   Velcros
Q2   False
Q3   2 4 6
Q4   True
Q5   B
Q6   False
Q7   1 5
Q8   Pleat
Q9   B
Q10   False

Chapter 5

Answers

Q1   Skin
Q2   True
Q3   4 5
Q4   False
Q5   D
Q6   False
Q7   2 4 5
Q8   Red
Q9   B
Q10   True

Chapter 6

Answers

Q1   Curl
Q2   True
Q3   1 4 5
Q4   True
Q5   C
Q6   True
Q7   1 3
Q8   Cortex
Q9   C
Q10   True

Chapter 7

Answers

Q1   Tapering
Q2   False
Q3   3 5 6
Q4   True
Q5   A
Q6   True
Q7   2 4 5
Q8   Shorter
Q9   D
Q10 False

Chapter 8

Answers

Q1   Root
Q2   False
Q3   3 4
Q4   True
Q5   B
Q6   True
Q7   5 6
Q8   First
Q9   C
Q10 True

Chapter 9

Answers

Q1   Cane
Q2   False
Q3   2 6
Q4   True
Q5   C
Q6   False
Q7   3 4 5
Q8   Extensions
Q9   C
Q10 False

Chapter 10

Answers

Q1   Credit
Q2   False
Q3   2 5
Q4   False
Q5   C
Q6   True
Q7   2 3
Q8   Home care
Q9   D
Q10 False

Chapter 11

Answers

Q1   Benefits
Q2   False
Q3   1 3
Q4   True
Q5   C
Q6   True
Q7   1 4 5
Q8   Eye
Q9   C
Q10 True

useful addresses and websites

Arbitration, Conciliation and Advisory Service (ACAS)

Head Office
Brandon House
180 Borough High Street
London SE1 1LW
Tel: 020 7210 3613
www.acas.org.uk

Black Beauty and Hair

Culvert House
Culvert Road
London SW11
Tel: 020 7720 2108
www.blackbeauty.co.uk

Caribbean and Afro Society of Hairdressers (CASH)

7 Hinckley Road
London SE15 4HZ
Tel: 020 8299 2859

City and Guilds (C+G)

1 Giltspur Street
London EC1A 9DD
Tel: 020 7294 2800
www.city-and-guilds.co.uk

Commission for Racial Equality

Elliot House
10–12 Allington Street
London SW1E 5EH
Tel: 020 7828 7022
www.cre.gov.uk

Cosmetic, Toiletry and Perfumery Association (CTPA)

Josaron House
5–7 John Princes
Street
London W1M 9HD
Tel: 020 7491 8891
www.ctpa.org.uk

Department for Education & skills

www.dfes.gov.uk

Equal Opportunities Commission

Arndale House
Arndale Centre
Manchester M4 3EQ
Tel: 0161 833 9244
www.eoc.org.uk

Fellowship for British Hairdressing

Peel House
High Street
Tisbury
Wilts. SP3 6PS
Tel: 01747 870310
www.britishhair.org

Freelance Hair and Beauty Federation

8 Willenhall Close
Luton
Bedfordshire LU3 1PY
Tel: 01582 593593
www.fhbf.org.uk

Guild of Hairdressers (GUILD)

Unit 1E
Redbrook Business Park
Wilthorpe Road
Barnsley S75 1JN

Tel: 01226 786 555

www.hairguild.org

Hairdressers Journal International

Quadrant House
The Quadrant
Sutton, Surrey SM2 5AS

Tel: 020 8652 3500

www.reedbusiness.com

Hairdressing and Beauty Industry Authority (Habia)

2nd floor, Fraser House
Nether Hall Road
Doncaster DN1 2PH

Tel: 01302 380000

www.habia.org.uk

Hairdressing and Beauty Suppliers' Association (HBSA)

Bedford Chambers
The Piazza
Covent Garden
London WC2E 8HA

Tel: 020 7836 4008

www.martex.co.uk/hairdressing_and_beauty

Hairdressing Council (HC)

12 David House
45 High Street
South Norwood
London SE25 6HJ

Tel: 020 8771 6205

www.haircouncil.org.uk

Hairdressing Employers' Association (HEA)

2nd Floor, Fraser House
Nether Hall Road
Doncaster DN1 2PH

Tel: 01302 380000

Health & Safety Executive

HSE infoline
Tel: 0870 545500

hseinformationservices@natbrit.com

www.hse.gov.uk

Institute of Trichologists

2nd Floor, Fraser House
Nether Hall Road
Doncaster DN1 2PH

Tel: 01302 380000

www.trichologists.org.uk

Lifelong Learning

www.lifelonglearning.co.uk

National Hairdressers' Federation (NHF)

1 Abbey Court
Fraser Road
Priory Business Park
Bedford MK44 3WH

Tel: 01234 360332

www.the-nhf.org

Qualifications and Curriculum Authority

83 Piccadilly
London W1J 8QA

Tel: 020 7509 3097

www.qca.org.uk

Union of Shop, Distributive and Allied Workers (USDAW)

188 Wilmslow Road
Fallowfield
Manchester M14 6LJ

Tel: 0161 224 2804

www.usdaw.org.uk

World Federation of Hairdressing and Beauty Schools

PO Box 367
Coulsdon, Surrey CR5 2TP

Tel: 01737 551355

glossary

accelerator A machine that produces radiant heat (infra-red radiation); can speed up chemical hair processes such as colouring or condition.

access and egress The ways in and out of the building.

acid A substance that gives hydrogen ions in water and produces a solution with a pH below 7.

activator A chemical used in bleaches or some perm lotions to start or boost its action.

albino hair Hair that contains little or no pigment. Albino hair is nearly white or very pale yellow; the condition is usually present at birth.

alkali A substance that gives hydroxide ions in water and produces a solution with a pH above 7.

alopecia Baldness.

anagen The stage of hair growth during which the hair is actively growing.

anterior Towards the front.

antioxidant A substance that prevents or slows down deterioration due to oxidation.

appointment A time and place arranged for a meeting.

apocrine gland A gland whose secretions include a part of the secreting cells themselves (e.g. some sweat glands).

arrector pili The muscles that raise the hair (in humans they are very feeble).

assessment Judging the worth of something or the results of a task; evaluation, appraisal.

assignment A task or a practical activity.

asymmetrical Unevenly balanced, without an equal distribution of hair on either side.

autoclave A device for sterilising items in high temperature steam.

backcombing/backbrushing Pushing hair back to bind or lift the hair using a comb or brush.

backdressing Backcombing or backbrushing.

balance The effect of hair shape on the features of the face and head; even proportions.

baldness traction Hair loss due to harsh physical and chemical treatments, e.g. tight braids and heavy ponytails.

barbering The art of cutting and shaping men's hair.

baseline An initial cutting line from which later cutting lines are established.

basing cream A form of skin protection used when perming or straightening hair.

bleach A substance that removes natural colour; acts first on black pigments, then on brown, red and yellow.

bleaching Removing colour from hair.

block colouring Colouring areas of hair in a way that is intended to enhance the cut style.

blow drying Drying and shaping hair using a handheld dryer.

blow-stretching Temporary straightening of the hair by smoothing the hair while blow-drying.

blow-waving Waving the hair while blow-drying.

bob cut A hairstyle in which the hair is cut to a level length around the head.

body language Communicating by means of body actions and/or posture rather than words.

brighteners Lightening (bleaching) shampoos or rinses.

canities Hair that is without pigment and therefore grey or white.

case study Examination of a topic as exemplified by a particular event or occasion.

cashier The person responsible for transactions at the point of payment.

castle serrations Reducing areas of a hair section with special serrated scissors.

catagen The stage of hair growth during which the hair stops growing, but the hair papilla is still active.

chemical hair treatment A term that includes perming, colouring or tinting, bleaching, streaking, highlighting or lowlighting, frosting, lightening, permanent straightening.

club cutting Cutting a hair section straight across, producing blunt ends.

cold permanent waving A perming process that does not rely on heat for its activation.

collodion A protective covering used in skin testing.

colour depth Lightness or darkness of hair colour.

colourant Any type of colouring substance used on hair.

colour filling Applying a preliminary colouring of red to hair so that new colour will adhere.

communication The exchange of information and establishment of understanding between two people as, for example, between the stylist and client.

compensation Providing money or services to offset a deficiency and make amends.

complainant Someone who expresses dissatisfaction or a grievance.

compound colourings Mixtures of vegetable and mineral dyes.

computerised Operated automatically using electronic apparatus.

concave Sloping inwards.

concept An idea, impression or thought.

conditioner A product used to correct or improve the state of the hair.

confidential Private information, not for general use.

consultation A process of communication in which the client expresses her wishes and the hairdresser gives advice.

contra-indication A reason why a proposed course of action or treatment should not be pursued because it may be inadvisable or harmful.

convex Sloping outwards.

corn row Fine plaits running continuously across the scalp.

creative Individual ability to make a form, shape or style which ideally enhances.

crew cut Short, spiky style with hair standing straight up.

croquignole winding Winding a curl from point to root.

cutting angle The angle at which hair is held and cut.

cutting line The direction in which cutting is made to follow the contours of the head.

cutting method A considered sequence of cutting techniques.

Data Protection Act 1984 Legislation designed to protect the client's right to privacy and confidentiality.

databank A manual or computerised store of data or records.

decolouring Removing synthetic colour from hair.

demonstration A display and explanation of a physical instruction.

depilatory Designed to remove hair.

designer Creator of images.

development time The 'taking time' of a chemical action such as tinting.

diagnose Determine the condition of the hair and scalp.

disclaim To renounce or reject legal responsibility.

discolouration Unwanted colour produced by a chemical.

dreadlocks Long thin plaits.

dressing The forming and blending of hair into a finished shape or style.

emollient A substance used (e.g. in conditioners) to soften and enhance the appearance of hair.

end paper A tissue or wrap used during winding to secure a hair point.

endorsement A signature in confirmation of some statement, affirming that it is true.

eumelanin Black and brown pigment in the skin and hair.

feathering Tapering action using scissor points.

finger waving Forming waves in wet hair using the hands as a comb.

fish hook A point of hair that has been bent back during rollering or winding.

folliculitis Inflammation of the hair follicles; may be caused by bacterial infection.

formative assessment A tool for the regular monitoring and review of students' progress and a means of regular diaglogue between trainee and tutor.

fragilitas crinium Splitting of the hairs at their ends.

franchise Authorisation to sell company goods or services in a specified area.

freehand cutting Cutting without forcing the hair out of its natural position.

French roll A vertical fold of hair, usually on the back of the head.

graduation A sloping variation from long hair to short, or from short to long, produced by cutting the hair ends at a particular angle.

hair extension Real or synthetic fibre added to existing hair.

hair strand A section of hair; a mesh, tress or piece.

HASAWA Health and Safety at Work Act 1974.

heat moulding Shaping the hair while it is softened by heat (e.g. with heated tongs).

historical evidence Evidence resulting from activities that have been undertaken in the past.

host company A company that authorises others to operate, similar to a franchising company but with more direct involvement in daily procedure.

image Likeness, what is seen or portrayed, overall appearance.

incentives Rewards for effort.

incompatible Causing a chemical reaction on mixing; as between a chemical being added to the hair and another chemical already on the hair.

induction The familiarisation process that staff undergo when they first join an organisation (this may include a health and safety requirement).

keratin The principal protein of hair, nails and skin.

lightening Removing colour from hair.

line The line of a style is determined by the directions in which the hair is positioned.

lye The common name for sodium hydroxide.

manually By hand.

melanins The pigments that give colour to skin and hair.

merchandise Goods for sale.

mis-en-pli Putting hair into set.

monilethrix Beaded hair.

movement Variation of the line of a style, such as waves.

negotiation The process of reaching agreement by discussion.

neutraliser A chemical formulation used to return hair to its normal condition after cold perming.

non-verbal communication Means of communication other than words – gestures, facial expressions, stance, and so on.

occipital bone Bone forming the back of the head.

originality New, created for the first time, the ability to be original or inventive.

ornamentation Flowers, ribbons, jewellery and the like worn to enhance the hairstyle.

oxidation Reaction with oxygen, as in the neutralising of a perm.

parietal Bones forming the upper sides of the head.

perimeter The outside line of the hair.

personalising A term which refers to a variety of cutting techniques applied to a style dependent on the client's specific needs.

personality The mannerisms, habits, ways and characteristics of a person – individual identity.

pheomelanin A natural hair pigment.

physiognomy The general appearance of the head and face.

pincurling Forming hair into curl shapes which are held with pins or slips until dried.

porosity The ability to hold moisture.

portfolio A file or folder containing evidence that supports practical activities which have been carried out previously.

postiche A dressed hairpiece.

pre-pigmenting Applying a preliminary colouring of red to hair so that new colour will adhere.

promotion Advertising by way of a publicity campaign.

quality assurance The process by which a desired outcome is guaranteed by means of monitoring and verification.

quality management The establishment and implementation of systems and procedures relating to each function and task.

quality standard Required criteria for a function or part of a function.

recolouring Adding further colouring to hair.

relaxing Reducing the curl or wave in hair.

resources Means of supplying needs (people, stock or facilities).

retouching Colouring regrowth.

reverse graduation A cut in which the top layers are longer than those beneath.

senses The means by which we see, hear, touch, smell and taste.

serrations The saw-like edges of some scissors.

shingling Cutting a short layered style graduating from the nape of the neck.

stabiliser A chemical added to hydrogen peroxide to maintain its strength, for example, phosphoric or sulphuric acid.

straightening Reducing the curl or wave in hair.

summative assessment A means of final evaluation of a trainee's competence against the standards indicated by the stated performance criteria.

symmetrical Balanced by means of an even and equal distribution of hair on either side.

synthetic Artificially made, not natural.

systems Procedures, ways in which things are carried out.

systems manual A book, file or folder displaying the complete system for each aspect of procedure.

tapered Thinner towards the hair points.

tapering Cutting a hair section to a tapered point (i.e. a point like that of a sharpened pencil).

tariff A displayed list of fixed charges.

telogen The period during which a hair ceases to grow before it is shed.

temporal Bones forming the lower sides of the head.

tension The stress or stretch experienced by hair.

texture The feel or appearance of the hair – rough, smooth, coarse or fine.

textured Shaped to take account of the fineness or coarseness of hair, giving lift and fullness.

texturising A term which refers to a variety of cutting techniques.

toning Adding colour to bleached hair.

traction Stress or pull applied to hair.

traction baldness An area of baldness resulting from the stress or pull applied to hair.

training techniques Approaches to training – demonstration, observation, private study, and so on.

transaction The execution of a specific task, together with payment for this task.

trichologist An expert specialising in the treatment of diseases affecting the hair.

void To make invalid.

whorls Hair growth patterns.

index

accelerator 410
access and egress 410
accidents 14
   burns 16
   eye injuries 16
   first-aid box 14
   general guidance on first aid 15
   minor injuries 15
   recording 14–15
   special hazards 16
   suspected broken bones 16
   wounds and bleeding 15
acid 230, 410
acne 64
activator 410
advertising 391–2
African-Caribbean hair 383
   client preparation 35
   contrasting added hair 327–9
   equipment 316–20
   plaiting 321–5
   relaxing 330–41
   thermal styling 314–16
   twisting 325–6
aftercare
   advice, relaxing hair 341
   products
      clarifying shampoo 287, 303, 304
      daily maintenance spray 287, 303
      light conditioner 287, 303
      pH balanced rinse 287, 304
      reconstructive conditioner 287, 304
      soft bristle brush 303, 304
albino hair 410
alkaline 229–30, 410
alopecia 65, 410
anagen 410
animal (parasitic) infestations 62
anterior 410
antioxidant 410
appointment 410
aprocine 410
arrector pili 410
Asian (Mongoloid) hair 285–6, 383
assessment 410
   evidence requirements xiii –xiv

guidance xiv
   requirements xiii
assignment 410
asymmetrical 95, 100, 410
   contemporary style 108–12
autoclave 410

backcombing/backbrushing 135, 410
backdressing 410
bacterial diseases 61
balance 95, 410
baldness traction 410
banding 162, 199–200
barbering 410
barrel curls 145–7, 320
baseline 100, 410
basing cream 335, 410
bleaching and lightening 183, 410
   activating the bleach 183–4
   chemistry 183
   choice of bleach 185–7
   colour correction 194–203
   colour variants 188
   full head 185–6
   highlights 186–7
   methods 188–94
   over-bleaching 185
   root application 186
   slices, blocks and slab 187
block colouring 290, 410
blow drying 126, 410
   blow stretching 410
   blow waving 126, 410
   natural drying 126
   scrunch drying 126
bob cut 117–21, 410
body language 35–6, 79, 410
body position and gestures 36–7
breakages 5
brick cutting 89
brighteners 410
British Hairdressing Awards 401
   how they work 401–2
   how to win 402
      don't go overboard 403
      professional portfolio 402–3
      work to a theme 403

brushing 134–5
business effectiveness 345–6

cane rows 323–4
   adding hair 324
   method 324
canities 410
case study 410
cashier 410
castle serration 410
catagen 410
Caucasian (European) hair 286, 383
chemical hair treatment 410
chemical properties
   amino acids 53
   disulphide bridges 53
   hydrogen bonds 53
   keratin 53
   polypeptides 53
   salt bonds 53
chemical sterilisation 8
chignon 151–5
client 42–3
   age of 98
   care 103
   features 67
      body shape 70–1
      ears, nose and mouth 69, 261–2
      expression 67
      eyes 70
      face and head shape 68–9, 92–3
      hair and hair growth patterns 67–8
      lifestyle, personality and age 71
      make-up 70
      neck and shoulders 70
   lifestyle 203
   male 248–9, 254–5
      facial features 252
      physical features 252
   perm preparation and planning 225–7
   positioning 128
   preparation 89, 127–9, 315
   protection 128
clipper over comb 247
clippers 270–1
   electric 259

clockspring curl 130
club cut (clubbing, blunt cutting) 247, 410
Code of Hygiene for Hairdressers and Barbers (HABIA) 26–9
cold permanent waving 228, 410
collodion 410
colour
    charts 73
    choice 168
        client requirements 169
        measuring flasks and mixing bowls 169–70
        relevant factors 169
    co-ordination 47–50
    correction 162, 194–5
        banded hair colour 199–200
        diagnosing 217
        discoloured highlights/lowlights 200–3
        partial applications 200–3
        planning 217
        reapplying to natural depth 197, 199
        reintroducing colour into bleached hair 195–6
        removal of permanent/synthetic hair dyes 198
        removal of synthetic hair dye 196–7, 198
    depth 410
    filling 410
    grab 199
    gradated 199
    principles
        depth and tone 164–6
        mixing colours 164
        pigmentation 164
        seeing colour 163–4
    problems 218
    selection
        choice, state and condition 170–1
        current condition 173–4
        grey hair 171–2
        grey/white hair 172
        harmonising and contrasting effects 174–7
        pre-softening white hair 172–3
        principles 170–7
        temperature 174
        timing 173–4
    stability 201
    suitability 47–9
        autumn client 50–1
        spring client 50
        summer client 49–50
        winter client 49
colour-related tests 177
    elasticity 178
    incompatibility 178
    porosity 178

skin or patch test 177
    strand 179
colourant 410
communication 35–7, 410
    male clients 249–50
    understanding/being understanding 89–91
compensation 410
competitions 400–1
    awards 401–3
    live/on the day 401
competitor information 372–3
complaints
    complainant 410
    handling 78–80
    if in doubt leave it out 80
    prevention is better than cure 80
    summary 80
compound colourings 410
computer-generated images 73
concave 100, 410
concept 410
conditioner 287, 303, 304, 410
confidential 411
connexions cut 113–16
consultation 33, 43, 128–9, 411
    after the consultation 74
    age 98
    balance 95
    communication 89–91
    fashion trends 91
    hair positioning, type, growth and tendency 95
    hard and soft effects 97–8
    head and facial shape 92–3
    male clients 249–55
    movement 97
    objective analysis 51–66
    partings 96–7
    quality, quantity and distribution of hair 94
    reason or purpose for hairstyle 93–4
    style line 96
    style or service selection 74
    style suitability 95
    subjective analysis 44–6
    visual aids 72–3
Consumer Protection Act (1987) 373
Consumer Protection (Distance Selling) Regulations (2000) 375
Consumer Safety Act (1978) 373
contra-indication 252–4, 282, 411
Control of Substances Hazardous to Health Regulations (COSHH) (1999) 22–3
convex 100, 411
cornrowing 411
creative 411
crew cut 411
critical influencing factor 32
croquignole winding 411

curl rearranger 314
curling and winding techniques 129–31, 134–5
customer service 39–40, 367
    collecting information from client 371
    customer feedback 369–70
    improving 367
    trade and industry bodies 367–8
cuticle damage 66
cutting
    after 102–3
    angle 411
    basic principles 262–3
    before 102
    connexions cut 113–16
    contemporary asymetric 108–12
    dry 256
    during 102
    freehand 411
    gent's 255–71
    inverted bob 117–21
    line 411
    method 411
    point cutting 89
    restyle long hair/graduated layers 104–7
    safe practice 255–9
    techniques 258–60
    tools 98–9, 258–9
        clippers 99–100
        razors 99
        scissors 99
    wet and dry 256, 262

dandruff 64
Data Protection Act (1984 & 1998) 374, 411
databank 411
decolouring 162, 196, 411
    process preparation 196
demonstration 389–90, 411
depilatory 411
designer 411
development time 411
diagnose 411
Disability Discrimination Act (DDA) (1995) 375
disclaim 411
discolouration 162, 411
discoloured highlights/lowlights 200
    lifestyle 203
    longer highlighted hair 201
    newly introduced colours 201–2
    over-porous hair 202
    poorly executed application 202
diseases 61
    infectious 61–3
    non-infectious 64–6
disinfectants 8, 27–8
disposal of sharps 6, 271

disposal of waste 5–6, 271
disulphide bonds 314
double brushing 134
double processed hair 197, 201
dreadlocks 411
dressing 134, 411

effectiveness *see* business effectiveness
Electricity at Work Regulations (1999) 23
emollient 411
empathy 39
end paper 411
endorsement 411
environmental safety 4
equal opportunities 375
Equal Pay Act (EPA) (1970) 375
equipment 7–8, 284, 360
  African-Caribbean hair 316–20
  hair extensions 284–7
  heated 135–7
  perming 241–2
eumelanin 164, 411
European (Caucasian) hair 286, 383
experience 88–9
extensions 156–8
  advice/home-care maintenance 303,
    304–5
    do's and don'ts 305
    real hair 304
    synthetic, acrylic fibre 303
  attachment techniques
    pre-bonded 295
    processed hair 295–7
    real hair 292–4
    synthetic fibre 290–2
  choice 282–3
  consultation 281–4
  contra-indications 282
  cutting 301–2
    blunt/club 302
    layering 302
    point 302
    skim/surface clippering 302
    soft tapering 302
    spiral tapering 302
    surface graduated layering 302
  planning/placement 297, 298–9
    sectioning natural hair 297–8
    textured hairstyle 299–302
  price quote 284
  products and equipment 284
    aftercare products 287
    bonding applicator 284
    connector products 285–7
    connector tools 284–5
    heat clamp 284
    heated pre-bonded applicator 285
    liquid, cold fusion adhesives 285
    mixing mats 286–7
    needle and thread 285
    polymer resin adhesive sticks 285

  pre-bonded 286
  real hair 285–6
  removal solutions 287
  removal tool 287
  resin drip tray 287
  scalp protectors/shields 286
  silicone pads 286
  soft bristle brush 286
  synthetic acrylic fibre hair 285
  removing 305–6
  selecting/blending colours 288–90
    block colour 290
    colour formula 288
    megamixing 289
  styling 302
    products 303

facial hair 271–2
  aspects to consider 272
  bone structure and facial contours 273
  head shape and size 272
  mouth and width of upper lip to base
    of nose 272
  trimming 273–4
  width of chin and depth of jaw line
    273
fashion industry 38
feathering 180–2, 411
film and media industry 38
financial resources 361
  cashpoint 362
    automatic tills 362
    computerised cash desks 362
    float 363
    function 363–5
    manual tills 362
  financial systems 361
    breakdown 361
    line management 361
    security 361
    training 362
  records 365
    day book 366
    day sheets 366
    value-added tax (VAT) 365
finger waving 130–1, 411
fire safety 11–12
  fire escape 13
  fire extinguisher 13
  firefighting 12
  raising the alarm 12
  training 14
fish hook 411
folliculitis 61, 411
formative assessment 411
fragilitas crinium 411
franchise 411
French roll 140, 141, 411
fringe 261
fungal diseases 63
furunculosis 61

graduation 411

hair
  colour types
    longer-lasting 168
    permanent 168
    quasi-permanent 168
    semi-permanent 167–8
    temporary 167
  damage
    chemical 58
    physical 58
    weathering 58
  growth 56, 95
    cowlick 68, 253
    double crown 68, 253
    male patterns 253
    nape whorl 68
    nape whorls 253
    stages 56–7
    thinning/baldness 253
    widow's peak 68, 253
  manageability 72
  moisture of 222
  porosity 225
  straight 100
  strand 58, 179, 411
  tests 58
    colour 58
    curl check or test 60
    elasticity 60, 178
    incompatibility 60, 178
    peroxide 60
    porosity 61
    strand 58, 179
    test curl 60
    test cutting 59
  texture 57, 225, 231
    indicators of good condition 57
    indicators of poor condition
      57–8
  type
    difficult 94
    dry and frizzy 94
    good condition 94
    straight hair 94
    tight curly hair 94
    wavy hair 94
  up 148–50
    added hair 156–8
    chignon 151–5
    classic effect 151–8
hair creativity 379
  image creation 380
  style design 380–1
    apparent texture 382
    application of product 384–5
    applied techniques 382
    balance or imbalance 385–6
    colour depth and tone 383
    condition 383

dimension, distribution and abundance 382–3
essential components 381–5
hair type 383
lines and angles 381–2
moulding, forming and shaping 384
movement and direction 382
shape and form 381
specialised techniques 384
work method 384
hair extension see extensions
hairdressing demonstration 389
expect the unexpected 390
make a time schedule 390–1
plan 390
select venue 389–90
set budget 390
hairdressing level 3 xiv–xv
hairstyling
classic or traditional 91
current fashion trends 91
emerging fashions 91
general principles 126–9
hard and soft effects 97–8
partings 96–7
reason or purpose 93–4
style line 96
suitability 95
see also men's hairstyling
HASAWA see Health and Safety at Work Act
hazard 3, 4, 16
head lice 62
Health and Safety at Work Act (1974) 3–4, 18
Health and Safety at Work Regulations (1999) 19
Health and Safety (Display Screen Equipment) Regulations (1992) 25
Health and Safety (Information for Employees) Regulations (1989) 25
heat moulding 411
heated styling equipment 135–7
ceramic straighteners 136
crimping irons 136
straightening irons 136
tongs 136
henna 59
herpes simplex 62
highlights
colour corection 204–6
discoloured 200–3
feather and flare 180–2
full head 189–91
gents dappled colour techniques 192–3
longer hair 201
techniques and products 186–7

historical evidence 411
home care advice
extensions 304–5
men 275
host company 411
how to use this book xvi–xxi
human resources 347
appraisal process 353
evaluating results 350
maintaining productivity 348
measuring effectiveness 351–2
motivation 350
personal development 351
self-appraisal 353
SMART productivity 348–9
targets 348
working together 350–1

illness 14–15, 16
image/personality types 44, 411
classic 46
dramatic 45
natural 45
romantic 46
impetigo 61
incentives 411
incompatible 32, 226, 411
incurling 412
individuals 41–2
induction 411
infection prevention 8
International Colour Chart (ICC) System 165

keratin 53, 411

learning 38–9
legislation 18–28
lightening see bleaching and lightening
line 411
long hair 104–7
agree effect before you start 138–9
assessing suitability 138
building structure and support 138
classic effect with barrel curls 145–7
clear ideas on 137–8
contemporary effect with twist 142–4
creative 137–41
hair up 148–58
incorporating added hair 156–8
styles 140–1
lowlights, discoloured 200–3
lye and no-lye 314, 333, 411

Manual Handling Operations Regulations (1992) 26
manually 411
medical referral 32
melanin 164, 411
memory 41
men's hairstyling 247–8

advice and home maintenance 275
basic cutting principles 262–3
client preparation 248–9
communication 249–50
consultation 249–55
contemporary cutting 264–6
contra-indications 252–4
ears 261–2
examination of hair and scalp 254
facial shapes 252
finding out what client wants 254–5
genres of hairstyling 251
hair growth patterns 253
hair type 262
outline shapes 261–3
physical features 252
protecting the client 256
razor cut 267–9
safe practices 255–9
scissors, clippers, combs and brushes 258–9, 270–1
seat positioning 256
shaping and trimming facial hair 271–4
skin are 276
wet and dry cutting 262
work position 257
see also hairstyling
merchandise 411
mis-en-pli 411
Mongoloid (Asian) hair 285–6, 383
monilethrix 66, 411
movement 97, 126, 411
music industry 38

negotiation 411
neutralising 232, 411
applying 233–4
first rinsing 233
how it works 233
preparation 233
second rinsing 234
successful 234
non-verbal communication 411

objective analysis 51–66
control 51
responsibility 51
occipital bone 411
off-base tonging 320
ornamentation 411
oxidation 411

parietal 411
payment methods
accounts 364
card payments 364–5
cash 363
charge cards 364
cheque 363
credit cards 364

gift vouchers 364
switch/Connect, Solo cards 363
traveller's cheques 364
perimeter 411
perming
  analysis/examination
    hair porosity 225
    hair texture 225
    incompatibility 226
    length and density of hair 226
    previous treatment history 226
    size of rod, curler, other former 226
    style 226
  equipment
    chopsticks 241
    foam rollers and formers 241
    u-stick rods 242
  pre-perming/post-perming treatments 226–7
  preparing and planning 225–7
  principles 223–4
  problems and solutions 242–3
  technique
    acid and alkaline solutions 229–31
    after perming 235
    applying lotion 231
    body perms 240
    cold perm sectioning 228
    curlers 232
    directional 243
    general preparation 227
    general sectioning 228
    hair texture and condition 231
    pin, roller, semi- or demi-perms 240, 243
    processing and development 231–2
    rinsing and neutralising 232–4
    root perms 240, 243
    spiral 243
    temperature 232
    testing curls during processing 232
    weaving 243
    winding techniques 228–9, 232
    zigzag 243
  tests
    elasticity 226
    incompatibility 226
    porosity 226
    processing 226
    test curl 226
personal
  appearance 9
    clothes 10
    hair 10
    jewellery 10
    posture 10–11
    shoes 10
  attributes 34
  confidence 40
  experience and interests 42

eye contact 36
hygiene 8, 27
  body 9
  hands and nails 9
  mouth 9
interest in people 37–8
posture 10–11, 36–7
relationships 34–5
Personal Protective Equipment at Work Regulations (PPE) (1992) 21
personalising 247, 411
personality 411
pheomelanin 164, 411
photography/photo sessions
  putting it together 396
    clothes and accessories 398
    cost 398–9
    on the day 398
    getting size right 399
    make-up artist 398
    model 396–7
    photographer 397
    plan of action 398
    reasons for doing 395
physical properties
  capillary action 53–4
  hygroscopic 53
  porous 53
physiognomy 412
pincurling 130
  barrel curl 130
  clockspring curl 130
  common faults 130
plaiting 321
  cane rows 323–4
  drying into shape 323
  preparation 321
  shampoo and condition 323
  single 325
  style
    choice 321
    hair condition 322
    removal of previous plaiting 322–3
    suitability 322
    terminology 322
plaits 140
  three-stem French plaited style 141
  three-stem plain 140–1
polymerisation 168
porosity 53, 225, 226, 412
  test 178
portfolio 402–3, 412
postiche 412
pre-pigmenting 162, 210–14, 412
Prices Act (1974) 373
productivity 345
products
  dressing cream 132
  hairspray 133
  heat protection 133
  mousse 131

serum 132
setting lotion 131
styling gel/glaze 132
wax 133
promotion 412
  business 74–5
  salon 386–7
    advertising 391–2
    decide on type of promotion 387
    evaluate outcome 388
    hairdressing competitions amd awards 400–3
    hairdressing demonstration 389–91
    identify objectives 387
    inform staff 388
    inform target group 388
    order stock and materials 387
    photography and photo sessions 395–9
    prepare activities 387–8
    public relations 392–4
  selling ourselves 75
Provision and Use of Work Equipment Regulations (PUWER) (1998) 26
public relations 392
  consumer press 392–3
  cost 394
  DIY PR 392
  employing a PR 393–4
  trade press 392

quality
  assurance 412
  management 412
  standard 412

Race Relations Act (RRA) (1976) 375
razors 99, 259
recolouring 412
relaxing hair 330, 412
  after care advice 341
  analysis/examination
    hair porosity 332
    hair texture 332
    incompatibility 332
    previous treatment history 332
    style 332
  base creams or gels 335
  chemical 337–8
  consultation 332
  contra-indications for chemical relaxing 331
  corrective treatment 340
  dealing with regrowth 339–40
  methods and procedures 336
  one-step process 330
  pre-relaxer treatments 335
  product choice and application 335–6
  products (lye and no-lye) 333
  tests 334
    elasticity 334

incompatibility 334
porosity 334
test cutting 334
two-step process 330
for virgin head 339
Reporting of Injuries, Diseases and
Dangerous Occurrences
Regulations (RIDDOR) (1995)
24–5
Resale Prices Act (1964 & 1976) 374
resources 345, 346, 412
financial 361–6
human 347–53
salon 355–60
time 353–5
retail 76–7
retouching 412
reverse graduation 412
risk 3
young workers 19
risk assessment
further guidance for COSHH risk
assessment 22–3
procedure for conducting 19–20
rollering 129
common problems 129–30

Sale and Supply of Goods Act (1994)
374
salon
hygiene 6
equipment 7–8
floors and seating 6
mirrors 7
preventing infection 8
styling tools 7–8
towels and gowns 7
working surfaces 7
image 77–8
handling complaints 78–80
promotion 386–403
resources 355–6
stock control 356–60
safety 5–6
security 17
external provisions 17
internal provisions 17–18
scabies 62
scissor over comb 247
scissors 99, 258–9
Japanese style 259
thinning 259
seat positioning 256
sebaceous cyst 66
seborrhea 64
sectioning 228
security 17–18
self-motivation 40
senses 412
serrations 412
services 75

setting 126–7
decreasing volume 126
increasing volume 126
movement 126
physical changes 127
Sex Discrimination Act (SDA) (1975 &
1986) 375
shaping and texturising
accuracy and checks 101
achieving lift and volume 101
enhancing movement 101
producing non-uniform effects 101
removing bulk without affecting
length 100–1
shingling 412
skin
care for men 276
sensitivity tests 58, 59, 177
slicing 89
slider cutting 89
spillages 5
spiral (vertical) curls 320
hair of different lengths 238
monitoring perm process 237
normalising 237
problems 238
securing the wind 236
selecting size/position of curls 236
starting the wind 236
split ends 66
sponged texturising 215–16
stabiliser 412
sterilisation procedures 27–8
stock control
avoiding waste and damage 360
space 360
tools and equipment 360
utilities 360
choice of supplier 359
ordering stock/taking delivery 357–8
product coding 357
security 360
stock handling 359
stocktaking 356–7
straightening 136, 412
structure of hair
chemical properties 53
cortex 52
cuticle 52
elasticity 52
medulla 53
physical properties 53–4
structure of skin 54
dermis 55
epidermis 54
hair follicle 55
hair muscle 56
oil glands 55
subcutaneous fat 55
sweat glands 55–6
subjective analysis 44–6

colour co-ordination 47–51
image/personality 44–6
summative assessment 412
sycosis 61
symmetrical 95, 100, 412
synthetic 412
systems 412
systems manual 412

tapered 412
tapering 412
tariff 412
telogen 412
tension 412
texture 57, 225, 231, 382, 412
textured 299–302, 412
texturising 89, 247, 412
theft 17
missing items of stock 18
money missing from till 17–18
personal possessions 18
thermal curling tongs 318
electrically heated 318
holding 319
safe use of 319–20
stove heated 318
thermal pressing 314
thermal pressing combs 316
electrical 316–17
non-electrical 316
safe use of 317–18
thermal styling 314–15
time resources 353–4
time management 354
get organised 355
prioritising 355
write things down 355
tinea capitis 63
tinting back 162, 195–6
no step process 210–14
single step process 207–9
toning 194, 412
traction 412
traction baldness 412
Trade Union and Labour Relations
(Consoloditation) Act (1992)
375
Trades Description Act (1968 & 1972)
374
training 362
techniques 412
transaction 412
treatment 75
chemical 410
corrective 340
history 226, 332
perming 226–7
relaxing hair 335
trichologist 32, 412
twisting techniques 325
Senegalese 326

single 325–6
two-stem 326

ultraviolet radiation 8
units and main outcomes xi
    knowledge and understanding xiii
    performance criteria xii
    range xii
    unit structure xi

Value Added Tax (VAT) 365
vertical roll (French pleat) 140
viral diseases 62
visual aids

colour charts 73
computer-generated images 73
pictures 72–3
void 412

warts 62
water waving 130
weaving 141, 240, 243
whorls 68, 412
winding techniques 228–9, 232, 236
    directional 238, 243
    movement 238–40
    piggyback (double wind) 240, 243
    spiral (vertical) curl movement

236–8, 243
    stack 240, 243
    staggered 240
    weave 240, 243
working safely
    disposal of waste 5–6
    environmental hazards 4
    obstructions 5
    spillages 5
Working Time Directive (1998) 375
Workplace (Health, Safety and Welfare)
    Regulations (1992) 20–1

young workers at risk 19